PROCESSED MEATS

some other AVI books

Food Science and Technology

BASIC FOOD CHEMISTRY   Cloth and Soft Cover   *Lee*
COMMERCIAL FRUIT PROCESSING   *Woodroof and Luh*
COMMERCIAL VEGETABLE PROCESSING   *Luh and Woodroof*
ENCYCLOPEDIA OF FOOD ENGINEERING   *Hall, Farrall and Rippen*
ENCYCLOPEDIA OF FOOD TECHNOLOGY   *Johnson and Peterson*
FABRICATED FOODS   *Inglett*
FOOD COLORIMETRY: THEORY AND APPLICATIONS   *Francis and Clydesdale*
FOOD PROCESS ENGINEERING   Cloth and Soft Cover   *Heldman*
FOOD PRODUCTS FORMULARY, VOL. 1   *Komarik, Tressler and Long*   VOL. 2   *Tressler and Sultan*
FOOD SCIENCE, 2ND EDITION   *Potter*
MEAT   *Cole and Lawrie*
MEAT HANDBOOK, 3RD EDITION   *Levie*
MICROWAVE HEATING, 2ND EDITION   *Copson*
NUTRITIONAL EVALUATION OF FOOD PROCESSING, 2ND EDITION   Cloth and Soft Cover   *Harris and Karmas*
POTATO PROCESSING, 3RD EDITION   *Talburt and Smith*
POULTRY: FEEDS AND NUTRITION   *Schaible*
POULTRY PRODUCTS TECHNOLOGY   *Mountney*
PRACTICAL MEAT CUTTING AND MERCHANDISING, VOLS. 1 AND 2   *Fabbricante and Sultan*
PRINCIPLES OF PACKAGE DEVELOPMENT   *Griffin and Sacharow*
PROGRESS IN REFRIGERATION SCIENCE AND TECHNOLOGY, VOLS. 1, 2, 3, AND 4   *Pentzer*
PROTEINS AND THEIR REACTIONS   *Schultz and Anglemier*
PROTEINS AS HUMAN FOOD   *Lawrie*
QUALITY CONTROL FOR THE FOOD INDUSTRY, 3RD EDITION, VOLS. 1 AND 2   *Kramer and Twigg*
SOYBEANS: CHEMISTRY AND TECHNOLOGY, VOL. 1 PROTEINS   *Smith and Circle*
TECHNOLOGY OF WINE MAKING, 3RD EDITION   *Amerine, Berg and Cruess*
THE FREEZING PRESERVATION OF FOODS, 4TH EDITION, VOLS. 1, 2, 3, AND 4   *Tressler, Van Arsdel and Copley*
THE TECHNOLOGY OF FOOD PRESERVATION, 3RD EDITION   *Desrosier*
TOMATO PRODUCTION, PROCESSING AND QUALITY EVALUATION   *Gould*
WHEAT: PRODUCTION AND UTILIZATION   *Inglett*

Agriculture

AN INTRODUCTION TO ANIMAL PHYSIOLOGY   *Svendsen*
COMMERCIAL CHICKEN PRODUCTION MANUAL   *North*
LIVESTOCK AND MEAT MARKETING   *McCoy*
PRINCIPLES OF ANIMAL ENVIRONMENT   *Esmay*
SEVENTH NUTRITION CONFERENCE FOR FEED MANUFACTURERS   *Swan and Lewis*
SYMPOSIUM: VERTICAL COORDINATION IN THE PORK INDUSTRY   *Schneidau and Duewer*

PROCESSED MEATS

by   **W. E. KRAMLICH**

Research and Development Department,
John Morrell and Company,
Chicago, Illinois

A. M. PEARSON

Department of Food Science and Human Nutrition,
Michigan State University,
East Lansing, Michigan

F. W. TAUBER

Marketing Department,
Films-Packaging Division,
Union Carbide Corporation,
Chicago, Illinois

WESTPORT, CONNECTICUT

THE AVI PUBLISHING COMPANY, INC.

1973

ST. PHILIPS COLLEGE LIBRARY

Preface

This book was written to serve as a text and reference for advanced undergraduate and graduate students enrolled in meat-processing courses. The emphasis of the book is on sausages, smoked meats, and meat canning. In recent years, there has been increased emphasis placed on teaching principles of meat processing at the university level. This has been brought about by the increased needs of industry and government for personnel having knowledge of processed meats technology. In addition to serving students and teachers, it is hoped the book will prove valuable as a reference for industrial and government personnel concerned with the processing of meat.

W. E. KRAMLICH
A. M. PEARSON
F. W. TAUBER

Contents

CHAPTER 1

Introduction to Meat Processing

Meat processing as discussed in this text includes all processes utilized in altering fresh meat except for simple grinding, cutting, and mixing. In the broadest sense, this includes curing, smoking, canning, cooking, freezing, dehydration, production of intermediate-moisture products, and the use of certain additives such as chemicals and enzymes. However, the definition excludes cutting, grinding, and packaging of fresh meats in retail stores and in homes. In this way, the definition differentiates between (1) those processes that enter into the preservation and manufacturing of meat products, and (2) those that alter the form of fresh meat in preparation for consumption.

HISTORICAL

The origin of meat processing is lost in antiquity but probably began when primitive man first learned that salt is an effective preservative, and that cooking prolongs the keeping quality of fresh meat. In any case, meat processing had its origin before the dawn of civilization. The ancient Egyptians recorded the preservation of meat products by salting and sun-drying. The early Romans are credited with being the first to use ice and snow as a means of preserving food. Modern food processing traces its origin to the development of canning for which Nicholas Appert, a chef, received an official commendation from the French government in 1809. Since that time, advances in technology have continued to change processing methods.

Newer methods of meat preservation include (1) chemical additives, (2) development of intermediate-moisture foods, (3) freeze dehydration, (4) enzyme treatments, and (5) irradiation. Increased scientific information and technological advances have greatly changed many processing methods. Among examples of this are the developments that have led to commercial freezing and new techniques of curing and smoking.

Many of the revolutionary new developments came as a consequence of war. The early American Indians probably developed jerky (thin dried strips of meat) and pemmican (a mixture of dry and semidry meat pounded together with dried fruits and vegetables covered with melted fat) as sources of high-energy, light-weight foods for use while on the warpath. Although the origins of jerky and pemmican are not well documented, the development of canning can be traced definitely to the need for stable foods during the Napoleonic War in France. Freezing of meat on a large scale also was accelerated by World War

1

I, while irradiation, freeze dehydration, and antibiotic preservation were outgrowths of World War II. Although many of these developments might have occurred anyway, the impetus for usage was the need to meet the requirements of a well-fed, well-clothed army. Meat, being a morale builder, has played a central role in almost all military-oriented food research. Intermediate-moisture foods are presently being developed to meet current military needs for a safe, stable, and acceptable product that does not require refrigeration.

PURPOSES OF MEAT PROCESSING

The original basis for meat processing was preservation by inhibiting or deterring microbial decomposition. Early meat-processing developments were based on this concept. In addition to preventing spoilage, preservation also resulted in flavorful and nutritious products. With the advent and almost universal availability of refrigeration, meat processing has now taken on the additional aspects of providing both convenience and variety. Today, processed meats are regarded highly because of these two characteristics. Thus, processed meats are frequently purchased because of convenience and the variety imparted to the meat portion of the diet.

Meat processing has resulted in major changes in the demand for certain cuts of meat. At the turn of the century, pork was the only meat processed in quantity. Today, beef and mutton are also used in large amounts in a variety of processed products. Recent advances indicate that quantities of boneless poultry meat will be incorporated into processed meat products. Boneless turkey and chicken rolls are commonly found in the market, but the use of boneless comminuted poultry meat derived from low-priced cuts (backs, necks, and wings) in sausages has just started. Usage will probably increase as long as prices remain attractive.

Increased prices for lean meats have also altered processing practices and encouraged the incorporation of increased percentages of less expensive fat. Similarly, high meat prices and technological advances in manufacturing vegetable proteins, such as spun soy protein, have resulted in the development of meat substitutes. It seems likely that lower-cost vegetable proteins will be used as meat extenders in combination products containing meat and vegetable proteins. Development of synthetic meat flavors may result in entirely new kinds of meat substitutes which could alter the conventional meat industry.

The processed meat industry now accounts for approximately 35%

of the total volume of the meat industry. Long-term trends indicate that meat processing will maintain its importance and encompass a large portion of total meat production. The profitability and new technological advances will probably affect the rate and ultimate extent to which meat is processed.

In 1971, meat packers processed a record volume of 36.9 billion pounds of meat (dressed weight). Total sales were estimated at $22,775 million, while net earnings reached an all-time high of $330 million. This amounted to an overall net return on sales of 1.5%. For purposes of comparison, 15 individual United States corporations each had net earnings that exceeded the $330 million of the entire meat-packing industry. The return on sales of these 15 companies averaged 7.9%. Thus, the earnings-to-sale ratio for meat packing is lower than that of any other major manufacturing group. However, the earnings of the meat-packing industry as percentage of total assets were high, amounting to 7.10% as compared to 5.08% for the manufacturing industry as a whole. Earnings as percentage of net worth were also high for meat packing, reaching 12.94% in 1971.

Table 1.1 shows the breakdown of the sales dollar by different categories of expenses. It also shows the costs of livestock, meat, and other raw materials, and the gross margin. Although the classification of companies does not differentiate between companies that are strictly processors and those that are strictly slaughtering livestock and selling fresh meat, the data show a trend of higher gross margins, a larger proportion of operating expenses for wages and salaries, and slightly higher earnings for the processing companies. Closer segregation of the companies into processors and slaughterers would unquestionably increase these differences, since processors are marketing more labor and service.

Table 1.2 shows the percentage breakdown of source and disposition of income by types of companies. It also shows that selling and administrative expenses are higher for meat processors than for meat packers. This is not surprising, however, when one notes the difference in size. Also processors tend to have higher costs of distribution by nature of the store-to-store servicing that is necessary.

The meat-processing industry tends to be localized near centers of consumption, whereas slaughterers and large packers tend to be located close to livestock-producing areas. Location, however, may be dictated by other factors, such as transportation and zoning ordinances. Convenience to transportation centers and the availability of raw materials may determine the location of meat-processing plants to a considerable extent.

Table 1.1

BREAKDOWN OF SALES DOLLAR BY VARIOUS TYPES OF MEAT COMPANIES

Item	Meat Packing Companies					Meat Processing Companies		
	National (a)	Regional (b)	Sectional (c)	Local (d)	All	Sausage (e)	Other (f)	All
Cost of meat, livestock, and raw materials	69.7	82.3	76.3	71.3	73.7	67.7	68.4	68.1
Gross margin	30.3	17.7	23.7	28.7	26.3	32.3	31.6	31.9
Total sales (%)	100.0	100.0	100.0	100.0	100.0	100.0	100.0	100.0
Operating Expenses (cents)								
Wages and salaries	11.2	7.2	9.8	12.8	10.0	13.8	13.4	13.6
Employee benefits	2.9	1.3	1.6	2.0	2.4	2.5	2.7	2.6
Interest	0.3	0.3	0.3	0.4	0.3	0.4	0.2	0.3
Depreciation	0.8	0.6	1.0	1.2	0.7	1.2	1.0	1.1
Rents	0.5	0.2	0.3	0.3	0.4	0.5	0.6	0.5
Taxes (g)	0.3	0.2	0.2	0.3	0.3	0.4	0.3	0.4
Supplies and containers	4.3	2.4	3.0	3.7	3.7	2.7	4.3	3.6
All other operating costs	7.1	3.5	4.0	5.1	5.9	7.2	6.9	7.0
TOTAL	27.4	15.7	20.2	25.8	23.7	28.7	29.4	29.1
Earnings before taxes	2.9	2.0	3.5	2.9	2.6	3.6	2.2	2.8
Income taxes	1.3	0.9	1.6	1.2	1.2	1.7	1.0	1.3
Net earnings	1.6	1.1	1.9	1.7	1.4	1.9	1.2	1.5

(a) National packers include meat companies with national sales and distribution for several years with annual sales over $250 million. Includes 10 companies.
(b) Regional packers include 34 companies who do not distribute product nationally with sales from $25 million to $250 million.
(c) Sectional packers include 29 companies with product distribution usually extending to areas beyond the community where the principal plant is located with annual sales from $5 million to $25 million.
(d) Local packers include 19 companies whose market is limited to the immediate area of the community where the principal plant is located and with annual sales less than $5 million.
(e) Sausage manufacturers include 18 companies that are primarily manufacturers of sausage products but may also produce other processed meats.
(f) Other meat processors include 23 companies that perform various processing operations such as boning, curing, and canning of purchased meat.
(g) Taxes other than social security and income taxes.
Source: American Meat Institute 1971

Table 1.2

PERCENTAGE BREAKDOWN OF SOURCE AND DISPOSITION OF INCOME
BY DIFFERENT TYPES OF COMPANIES

Company Classification (a)	Income			Disposition of Income		
	Operating	Other	Total	Non-Operating Charges	Dividends Paid	Earnings Retained
Meat-packing companies						
National packers	89.6	10.4	100.0	0	66.3	33.7
Regional packers	92.4	7.6	100.0	4.6	22.5	72.9
Sectional packers	89.2	10.8	100.0	0.9	12.3	86.8
Local packers	84.6	15.4	100.0	11.0	9.2	79.8
All packers, average	90.2	9.8	100.0	1.1	54.3	44.6
Meat-processing companies						
Sausage manufacturers	78.5	21.5	100.0	3.7	14.5	81.8
Other meat processors	77.4	22.6	100.0	5.4	12.9	81.7
All processors, average	78.0	22.0	100.0	4.5	13.8	81.7

(a) For numbers and distribution of plants, see Table 1.1 footnotes.

Source: American Meat Institute 1971

MAGNITUDE AND RELATIVE VALUE

There are two sources of information relating to the quantity and value of processed-meat shipments: (1) the meat-inspection program conducted by the U. S. Department of Agriculture, and (2) the Census of Manufactures, Bureau of the Census, U. S. Department of Commerce. The Federal meat-inspection program collects volume data in pounds on a weekly basis from manufacturing plants under Federal inspection. It has been estimated that in 1971 about 72% of total shipments were included in Federal inspection reports. The American Meat Institute reports are based on the data collected by the U. S. Department of Agriculture. The Census of Manufactures collects production volume and value data at 5-year intervals from all manufacturing plants. The most recent census year was 1967.

The organization and structure of the meat-packing industry, as noted in Table 1.3, are based on classifying establishments according to function. These are (1) slaughtering and processing, (2) processing, and (3) warehousing. The majority of plants engage in processing because it is usually quite profitable. Some processors maintain slaughtering operations, however, in order to have a ready supply of raw materials. Thus the combination of processing and slaughtering adds flexibility to an operation and permits better control of raw materials. Note that the information in Table 1.3 is for State and Federally inspected meat-packing plants.

Table 1.3

OPERATIONS IN MEAT-PACKING ESTABLISHMENTS: STATE AND FEDERAL INSPECTION

Type	Number of Establishments		
	Federal Inspection	State Inspection	Total
Meat slaughterers that process	475	2,000	2,475
Meat processors	2,225	4,050	6,275
Meat warehouses*	200	50	250
Total	2,900	6,100	9,000

* Includes packer branch houses and retailer warehouses that process meats.
Source: American Meat Institute 1971

The data in Table 1.4, which include the number of establishments engaged in slaughtering and processing fresh meats and poultry, are from the Census of Manufactures. Information about poultry-processing plants is included for comparison, and to present some perspective of the value of poultry processing. Also included in Table 1.4 are data reflecting value of shipments from establishments in 1967. The 2,697 meat-packing plants accounted for 72% of shipments, valued at $15.6 billion. It is estimated that 20% or $3 billion of processed meat shipments are from meat-packing plants. The 1,374 meat-processing plants accounted for 14% of shipments, valued at $3 billion.

Table 1.4
GENERAL STATISTICS FOR MEAT PRODUCTS

Item	Meat Packing Plants	Meat Process-ing Plants	Poultry Dressing Plants	Total
Total establishments	2,697	1,374	843	4,914
Cost of materials (million dollars)	13,384.3	2,261.0	2,358.5	18,003.8
Value of shipments (including resales) (million dollars)	15,576.3	3,007.7	2,936.1	21,520.1
Percent of shipments	72	14	14	100
Value added by manu-facture (million dollars)	2,220.5	742.5	588.0	3,551.0

Source: Census of Manufactures 1967

The 843 poultry-processing plants accounted for 14% of shipments, valued at almost $3 billion. The value added by manufacture is highest in meat-processing operations. This reflects the investment in time, labor, and equipment used in producing processed meats and the increased value that results.

The quantity and value of shipments from meat-packing and meat-processing plants are noted in Table 1.5. Shipments of beef, not including that canned or made into sausage, accounted for 43% of total shipments. The average value per pound of meat-packing plant shipments ranges from $0.099 for lard to $4.731 for hides, skins, and pelts. The most important products in the processed-meats classification are sausages, 13% of the total, and processed pork products, almost 12% of the total. The average value per pound of processed-meat shipments ranges from $0.504 for canned meats to $0.537 for sausage.

Table 1.5

INDUSTRY—PRODUCT ANALYSIS: SHIPMENTS BY PRODUCT CLASS

| Product Class | Total Shipments | | | Average Value/lb $ |
| | Quantity Million lb | Value | | |
		Million $	% of Total	
Beef*	17,866.5	7,398.5	42.9	0.414
Pork, fresh & frozen	7,950.1	2,791.0	16.2	0.351
Lamb and mutton*	689.5	312.7	1.8	0.454
Veal*	634.8	307.7	1.8	0.485
Hides, skins, and pelts	58.4	276.3	1.6	4.731
Lard	1,848.9	182.2	1.1	0.099
Miscellaneous meat-packing plant by-products	†	561.7	3.3	†
Sausage and similar products	4,254.6	2,286.6	13.3	0.537
Pork, processed or cured	3,963.1	2,008.0	11.6	0.507
Canned meat (except dog & cat food) containing 20% or more meat	1,700.8	856.4	5.0	0.504
Natural sausage casings	†	83.4	0.5	†
Miscellaneous meat processing plant by-products	†	183.8	1.1	†

* not canned or made into sausage
† not available
Source: Census of Manufactures 1967

RELATIVE IMPORTANCE OF PROCESSED MEATS

Processed meats account for 35% of the meat shipments from Federally inspected plants. In 1969, the value of these shipments was $19 billion. Based on these data, meat comprises the largest single class of food products, contributing approximately 25% of the total food dollar. Processed meats accounted for 8% of the total food dollar, with a value of $7 billion in 1969. Processed-meat production has been increasing substantially each year. For example, Federally inspected sausage production has increased for 13 consecutive years. During 1971, sausage production totaled 3.8 billion lb, an increase of 9% over 1970. Sausage processors consume over 10% of total red-meat production and convert over three billion lb of beef, pork, and mutton into processed-meat products. Federally inspected smoked or cured pork production totaled 3.4 billion lb in 1971, an increase of 8% over 1970. The development of new processing techniques has also contributed to the increased production of processed meats. For example, production of freeze-dried foods reached 250 million lb in 1969. Meat is a major portion of this production.

Quantity and value of shipments of sausage, processed pork products, and canned meats are included in Tables 1.6, 1.7, and 1.8.

Sausages accounted for 44% of the value of processed meat shipments in 1967. Smoked and cooked sausages accounted for 40% of total sausage shipments, frankfurters for 25%, and fresh pork sausage for 16%. The average value per lb ranged from $0.496 for frankfurters to $0.746 for dry and semidry sausages. The high value for dry sausages reflects the investment in time and technology required in their manufacture.

Processed-pork products amounted to 40% of the value of total processed-meat shipments in 1967. The most important pork products are (1) bacon, (2) hams, and (3) picnics, accounting for almost 75% of processed pork shipments. The average value per lb of ham is $0.523, while sliced bacon is $0.529. Note that the average value of slab bacon by comparison is $0.450.

Canned meats, excluding pet foods, comprise about 16% of all processed meats by both weight and value. Canned hams are the largest single item, although sausages and certain types of luncheon meats are also canned in large quantities.

Natural sausage casings are also made by some processors, and comprise 0.5% of the total value of all processed products. This operation is confined to large livestock slaughterers where considerable quantities of raw materials are available. Although these plants usually utilize a portion of the casings, they generally produce more than they use, and serve as suppliers for other sausage manufacturers.

Table 1.6

QUANTITY AND VALUE OF SAUSAGE SHIPMENTS (NOT CANNED) BY ALL PRODUCERS

Sausage	Total Shipments				Average Value/lb $
	Quantity		Value		
	Million lb	% of Total	Million $	% of Total	
Smoked and cooked sausages (bologna, liverwurst, Polish sausage, luncheon meats, etc.)	1,649.8	38.8	913.3	39.9	0.554
Frankfurters	1,158.8	27.2	574.6	25.1	0.496
Fresh sausage, pork sausage, breakfast links, etc.	720.5	17.0	359.2	15.7	0.499
Dry and semi-dry sausages (salami, cervelat, pepperoni, summer sausage, pork roll, etc.)	254.6	6.0	189.8	8.3	0.746
Jellied goods and similar products (head cheese, meat loaves, scrapple, puddings, chili con carne, etc.)	227.1	5.3	118.8	5.2	0.523
Sausages (not specified as to kind)	243.8	5.7	130.9	5.7	0.537
Total	4,254.6	100.0	2,286.6	100.0	0.537
—Made in meat-packing plants	2,078.8	48.9	1,020.7	44.6	0.491
—Made in meat-processing plants	2,175.8	51.1	1,265.9	55.4	0.582

Source: Census of Manufactures 1967

TRENDS IN PRODUCTION

Increased demand for convenience foods has resulted in expansion of the processed-meat industry. This has been accelerated by the relatively large number of women employed outside the home and the consequent lack of time available for preparation of meals. Since meat has always required the longest period for preparation, it has benefited most from development of convenience items. This is best illustrated by the growth of heat-and-eat meals, such as TV dinners, where meat as the entree is the major contributor to the meal. Luncheon meats,

Table 1.7

QUANTITY AND VALUE OF PROCESSED PORK PRODUCT: SHIPMENTS BY ALL PRODUCERS

| Product | Total Shipments | | | | Average Value/lb $ |
| | Quantity | | Value | | |
	Million lb	% of Total	Million $	% of Total	
Smoked hams and picnics	1,349.7	34.1	705.2	35.1	0.523
Sliced bacon	1,163.1	29.4	615.1	30.6	0.529
Slab bacon	373.9	9.4	168.4	8.4	0.450
Sweet pickled or dry-cured pork (not smoked or cooked)	337.9	8.5	142.4	7.1	0.421
Other smoked pork	283.3	7.2	134.1	6.7	0.473
Boiled ham, barbecue pork	158.7	4.0	137.6	6.9	0.867
Dry salt pork	155.9	4.0	33.9	1.7	0.218
Cured or processed (not specified as to kind)	140.6	3.6	71.3	3.5	0.507
	—	—	—	—	—
TOTAL	3,963.1	100.0	2,008.0	100.0	0.507
—Made in meat-packing plants	2,668.2	67.0	1,324.0	66.0	0.496
—Made in meat-processing plants	1,294.9	33.0	684.0	34.0	0.528

Source: Census of Manufactures 1967

Table 1.8

QUANTITY AND VALUE OF CANNED MEAT: SHIPMENTS BY ALL PRODUCERS

| Product | Total Shipments | | | | Average Value/lb $ |
| | Quantity | | Value | | |
	Million lb	% of Total	Million $	% of Total	
Total canned meats (except dog and cat food) containing 20% or more meat	1,700.8	100.0	856.4	100.0	0.504
—Made in meat-packing plants	869.5	51.1	490.4	57.3	0.564
—Made in meat-processing plants	831.3	48.9	366.0	42.7	0.440

Source: Census of Manufactures 1967

such as frankfurters, bologna, and meat loaves, have also been major beneficiaries of the increased use of convenience foods.

It seems that the trend toward complete processing for consumer convenience and development of new products will continue. It is likely that the emphasis on convenience meat products will continue and that more processing and cooking will be demanded by consumers, resulting in more prepared and precooked items. The ingenuity of meat processors in anticipating and even in creating such demands may well determine the future of the processed-meat industry.

FUTURE OF MEAT PROCESSING

Speculation as to what the future holds is always dangerous; however, it is reasonably safe to prognosticate that the meat-processing industry will undergo changes during the next few years. Past developments and trends offer some clues to future changes. Government regulations on food safety and inspection offer some insight. Such measures promise to lead to more carefully controlled sanitation and quality control practices, which might be self-policed by processors. If they accept the challenge, processors must set up specific quality control standards. This means that they must develop quality control groups with the necessary personnel and laboratories for enforcement of standards. Thus, processors will need to be better informed, and to have a capable quality control department with direct responsibility to management.

Development of quality control procedures will necessarily increase costs and indirectly result in a need for greater efficiency. This might result in efforts to consolidate smaller companies and force small independent operators out of business or into a rapid expansion. Consolidation and diversification have already influenced the meat business and promise to continue in the future. Emphasis will be upon growth and expansion as long as efficiency can be improved. It seems likely that small operators will have to emphasize quality production. Quality can be a basis for competing effectively, since small operators have been successful in the past, either because they were exempt from government regulations or because they produced high-quality products. With strict enforcement of meat inspection regulations, exemptions cannot be expected, and it seems that profitable operations will require manufacturing and marketing of quality products. The trend has been toward concentration in the meat-packing industry, and this is likely to continue.

The diversity of operations in plants may also change. The trends point toward an increase in the amount of processing within plants.

Expansion of convenience products appears inevitable, with more trimming, shaping, cooking, and packaging represented in the finished products. More production of complete heat-and-serve products is probable.

Another innovation still in early developmental stages is production of mixed foods such as processed meats containing proteins from other sources, such as soy beans and sunflowers. These might be tailored to satisfy nutritional requirements, with a reduction in fat or a change in the content of unsaturated fatty acids. The rate at which this development occurs depends on the availability and costs of raw products of both animal and plant origin. Another aspect of this development could be the availability of artificial meat flavors and emphasis upon nutritional adequacy and balanced diets.

BIBLIOGRAPHY

American Meat Institute. 1971. Financial Facts About the Meat Packing Industry. American Meat Institute, Chicago, Ill.

BORGSTROM, G. 1968. Principles of Food Science, Vol. 1. Macmillan Co., New York.

National Live Stock and Meat Board. 1969A. Meat Board Reports 2, No. 13, 2. National Live Stock and Meat Board, Chicago, Ill.

National Live Stock and Meat Board. 1969B. Meat Board Reports 2, No. 23, 3. National Live Stock and Meat Board, Chicago, Ill.

U. S. Dept. of Agr. 1971. The Livestock and Meat Situation. U. S. Department of Agriculture, Washington, D. C.

U. S. Bureau of the Census, Census of Manufactures. 1967. Industry Statistics, Part 1, Major Groups 2, 20. U. S. Government Printing Office, Washington, D. C.

WESTERHOFF, J. 1969. Processing meat is a big, big business. Natl. Provisioner 161, No. 16, 88.

CHAPTER 2

Composition and Nutritive Value of Raw Materials and Processed Meats

Although meat is recognized as a highly nutritious food, being an excellent source of high-quality protein, rich in most B-complex vitamins, and a good source of certain minerals, especially iron, its composition can greatly alter its nutritive value. Therefore, composition and nutritional value will be discussed together. Since information on processed meat is fragmentary and incomplete, emphasis will be placed upon the raw products, including their composition and nutritional qualities. Thus, the present discussion will first cover the composition and nutritive value of fresh meat as a raw material. It will center upon some of the functional properties of the various nutrients. Data will also be presented to show some of the available information on the nutritive value of various processed-meat items.

EMPHASIS ON NUTRITION

The nutritive value of all foods, including meat and meat products, is being seriously considered in view of consumer interest and demand. Nutritional labeling has been proposed by interested groups, and it is quite likely that some listing of the content of nutrients will be required on all processed foods within the next few years. The Food and Drug Administration is already considering guidelines and procedures to be followed in listing essential nutrients and their contribution to daily nutritional requirements. This development is being accelerated by the production of combination foods or meals, in which the consumer can no longer recognize the traditional food groups and utilize such information in properly balancing his own diet. Since many processed-meat items are also manufactured foods, they also may be required to have labels specifying their nutritive content.

COMPOSITION AND NUTRITIVE VALUE OF MEAT

The composition of meat cannot be described simply in terms of the different components and their percentages, since meat includes the entire carcass along with the muscles, fatty tissues, bones, tendons, edible organs, and glands. This obviously gives a wide range of components, and thus, of composition and nutritive value. Consequently, when speaking about meat, it is necessary to specify the tissue or cuts and whether or not it includes the bone and tendon, as well as the amount of external fat covering and the quantity of marbling. This is clearly shown in Fig. 2.1, where the relative changes in fatty tissues, muscle, bone, and tendon are plotted relative to the percentage fat in the carcass. The percentage of separable lean varies widely and is inversely related to the fat content. It is also interesting to note that the percentage of bone and tendon declines directly with the amount of muscle.

Variation in composition results in differences in nutritive value. This is further complicated by the fact that variation in composition also occurs from species to species. It is impossible to cover the different causes of variation adequately, so the reader is referred to the bibliography of this chapter for more complete details.

Composition of Meat

Water and Fat.—Grossly speaking, meat is composed of water, fat, protein, mineral (ash), and a small proportion of carbohydrate. Table 2.1 presents data for these components in some carcasses and cuts that are commonly used for the manufacture of processed-meat items. As can be seen from the data, water is the most variable of these components, but is closely and inversely related to the fat content and to a lesser extent to the ash and carbohydrate content. In general terms, if the fat content is held relatively constant, the percent of water declines until the animal body reaches chemical maturity, regardless of the species. However, as animals mature, they also usually increase in fatness, which causes an even greater decline in the percent

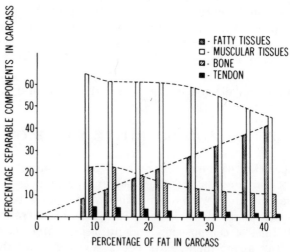

FIG. 2.1 CHANGES IN THE PROPORTIONS OF MUSCLE, FATTY TISSUES, BONE, AND TENDON AS THE CARCASS CHANGES IN FATNESS

of water. This is illustrated by the fact that a baby pig at birth contains approximately 77 to 80% water, 12 to 13% protein, and 3 to 4% ash, whereas 24 pigs weighing 181 to 220 lb averaged 49% water, 33% fat, 13.5% protein, and 2.7% ash. These above figures are for the entire body, including bone. On a carcass basis, the same pigs referred to above averaged approximately 46% water, 38% fat, 13% protein, and 2.7% ash. This shows that the fat content of the carcass is higher and the water content is lower than that of the intact animal. However, the bone content as reflected by percentage ash remained essentially unchanged.

These data bear out the inverse relationship between fat and water and the influence of fatness upon composition. This is not only true for chemically determined fat but also for fatty tissues, which have

Table 2.1

SOME SELECTED VALUES FOR THE CALORIE, WATER, PROTEIN, FAT, AND ASH
CONTENT OF VARIOUS GRADES AND CUTS OF MEAT ON A RAW
AND COOKED BASIS PER 100 GRAMS OF EDIBLE PORTION

Product and Grade	Calories	Water	Protein	Fat	Ash
Beef Carcass—Total edible, including Kidney and Kidney Fat					
Good grade—(66% lean, 34% fat) raw	323	54.7	16.5	28.0	0.8
Standard grade (73% lean, 27% fat) raw	266	60.1	18.0	21.0	0.9
Commercial grade (64% lean, 36% fat) raw	347	52.4	15.8	31.0	0.8
Utility grade (76% lean, 24% fat) raw	242	62.5	18.6	18.0	0.9
Beef round—Choice grade—separable lean-raw	135	72.7	21.6	4.7	1.0
Beef round—Choice grade—separable lean-cooked	189	61.2	31.3	6.1	1.4
Beef chuck—Choice grade—separable lean-raw	158	70.3	21.3	7.4	1.0
Beef chuck—Choice grade—separable lean-cooked	214	59.7	30.0	9.5	0.8
Lamb, composite of cuts (leg, loin, rib, and shoulder) trimmed—Good grade (79% lean, 21% fat) raw	247	62.5	16.8	19.4	1.3
Lamb leg—Good grade—separable lean-raw	127	73.8	19.9	4.7	1.6
Lamb leg—Good grade—separable lean-cooked	183	62.4	28.7	6.7	2.1
Lamb shoulder—Good grade—separable lean-raw	145	72.8	18.5	7.3	1.4
Lamb Shoulder—Good grade—separable lean-cooked	201	61.8	26.8	9.6	1.9
Pork, carcass—thin (53% lean, 47% fat) raw	472	41.1	11.2	47.0	0.6
Pork, carcass—thin separable lean-raw	156	70.7	18.3	8.6	2.4
Pork, shoulder—thin (75% lean, 25% fat) raw	368	51.7	13.6	34.4	0.7
Pork, ham trimmed thin (77% lean, 23% fat) raw	281	59.2	16.7	23.2	0.8
Pork, ham trimmed thin (77% lean, 23% fat) cooked	346	47.8	24.2	26.9	1.0
Pork ham, thin separable lean-raw	147	72.0	20.4	6.6	1.1
Pork ham, thin separable lean-cooked	210	59.3	30.2	9.0	1.5
Veal, carcass—thin (86% lean, 14% fat) raw	173	70.0	19.4	10.0	1.0
Veal, chuck—thin (90% lean, 10% fat) raw	139	73.0	19.9	6.0	1.1
Veal, round and rump—thin (91% lean, 9% fat) raw	139	73.0	19.9	6.0	1.1

Source: USDA Handbook No. 8

a relatively low water content. Values as low as 4.5% water and as
high as 64.5% water have been reported for beef fat from the kidney
knob and over the rib, respectively. These values are obviously
extremes, normal values being much less. Variations in the water
content of composite fatty tissues from pork carcasses fall within a
range of 8 to 15%, which still represents approximately 100% var-
iability. Thus, not only the amount of fatty tissue, but also its composition is required to accurately estimate its influence on the composition
and nutritive value of any processed meat product in which it is incorporated.

The fat content of the carcass, as already indicated, is highly variable
and inversely related to the moisture level. Figure 2.1 shows that
fatty tissues vary from a few percent to over 40% in the beef carcass.
Considerably higher values have been reported in the literature, some
beef carcasses containing as much as 50% separable fat and some sheep
(old ewes) over 60%. Similarly, high proportions of fat have also been
found in pig carcasses.

Animal fats are composed chiefly of neutral fats and phospholipids.
The neutral fats are principally glycerol esters of straight-chain carboxylic acids or triglycerides. The triglyceride may be simple or mixed,
depending upon whether the 3 fatty acids esterified to the glycerol
molecule are the same or different. This is shown by the following
structural formula in which all three R-groups (representing the fatty
acid radical) may be the same (simple) or different (mixed):

$$
\begin{array}{c}
\text{H} \\
| \\
\text{H-C} - \text{O} - \overset{\overset{\text{O}}{\|}}{\text{C}} - \text{R} \\
| \\
\text{H-C} - \text{O} - \overset{\overset{\text{O}}{\|}}{\text{C}} - \text{R} \\
| \\
\text{H-C} - \text{O} - \overset{\overset{\text{O}}{\|}}{\text{C}} - \text{R} \\
| \\
\text{H}
\end{array}
$$

Phospholipids are found in animal fats in small percentages; they
play a key role as structural and functional components of cells and
membranes. Phospholipids normally occur in meat as phospho-
glycerides. They normally comprise about 0.5 to 1.0% of lean muscle.
As the total lipid in a muscle decreases from 5% to 1%, the percentage
of phospholipid to total lipid increases from less than 10% to nearly
70%. Since phospholipids are more readily oxidized than triglycerides,

they play an important part in development of off-flavors and undesirable odors in meat products.

The major contribution of fat to the diet is energy or calories. This is true because fat has 2.25 times as much energy as an equal quantity of carbohydrate or protein. However, energy is not normally the limiting factor in most American diets; rather, too many calories is the more likely problem. On the other hand, limiting the intake of fat is a common method of weight control. This creates a demand for lean meat products with a low fat content, such as boiled ham, Canadian-style bacon, Lebanon bologna, and similar products.

Fat also supplies the essential fatty acids, which must be present in the diet to meet the needs of the body. Three fatty acids are considered essential for man—linolenic, linoleic, and arachidonic. However, if linoleic acid is present in excess of dietary needs, it can be converted to arachidonic and thereby meet the requirements for the latter. Nutritional deficiencies of the essential fatty acids are seldom encountered in man; thus typical mixed diets appear to supply adequate quantities. Pork and organ meats are good sources of linoleic and linolenic acids, but they also occur in lesser concentrations in other meats. Table 2.2 presents data showing essential and nonessential fatty acid distribution in bêef, pork, and lamb.

The controversy concerning animal fat in the diet and its relationship to heart disease and related circulatory disorders is worthy of mention, although the story is far from clear. Cholesterol came into prominence because it was found in high levels in the plaques obstructing the arteries of patients with heart disease. Subsequently, it was reported that high dietary levels of unsaturated fatty acids in the form of vegetable oils were effective in reducing circulating cholesterol in the blood stream of high-risk heart patients. Several recent studies have shown that there is no clear-cut relationship between the incidence of heart

Table 2.2

TYPICAL FATTY ACID DISTRIBUTION IN BEEF, PORK, AND LAMB FAT
GIVEN AS PERCENTAGE OF THE TOTAL

Fatty Acid	Beef	Pork	Lamb
Palmitic	29	28	25
Stearic	20	13	25
Palmitoleic	2	3	—
Oleic	42	46	39
Linoleic	2	10	4
Linolenic	0.5	0.7	0.5
Arachidonic	0.1	2	1.5

disease and the level of animal fats in the diet, thus tending to discount the role of cholesterol in heart disease. This is supported by the fact that cholesterol is formed in the body, even when completely absent from the diet. A great many other factors have also been implicated as contributors to coronary disease, including heredity, obesity, smoking, sugar intake, and lack of exercise. The causes of heart disease and the role of cholesterol and animal fats, if any, are difficult to assess. Nevertheless, awareness of the possible relationship is essential. If the relationship should be proved real, steps to correct the situation by reducing fat levels would be essential.

To briefly summarize, cholesterol is a minor but important component of animal tissues. It occurs either free (unesterified) or combined with a fatty acid (esterified). Lean beef, pork, and lamb contain 70 to 75 mg cholesterol per 100 g, 90% being in the free form. Fatty tissues contain about the same percentage, so that reduction of fat intake will effectively lower dietary cholesterol levels. Veal contains slightly more cholesterol than beef, pork, or lamb, whereas, liver and brain contain 300 and 2,000 mg per 100 g, respectively.

Minerals or Ash.—Ash content accurately reflects the mineral content but does not differentiate between minerals. Aside from bone or minerals added as curing salts or for seasoning, the mineral content of muscle is relatively constant. Due to the relatively low content of minerals in fatty tissues, the fat level also indirectly influences the mineral or ash content of meat and meat products.

As already indicated, bone, which is reflected in the amount of ash, is a major component of the intact carcass. High ash content alone, however, cannot be taken as indicative of high bone content, since the addition of curing salts increases the ash content, as already mentioned. Dry sausages may also have a high ash content, due to concentration of the natural minerals, as well as of the curing salts, during the drying process. Since curing salts are commonly used in most dried sausages or meat products, the added salts are also concentrated, and thus contribute to the total mineral content. The effects of curing salts and drying on the ash content are shown by the data for sausages and cured meats as summarized in Table 2.3.

Separable bone in the beef carcass varies from a low of 8 or 9% to a high of 23 or 24%. This is shown in Fig. 2.1, which also illustrates the inverse relationship of bone to fatness and a direct relation to leanness. Since most processed meat is boneless, one can estimate the yields of muscle that can be expected from beef carcasses of different fat contents.

Studies of the mineral content of meat have been largely confined to calcium, phosphorus, sodium, potassium, and iron. In addition to

Table 2.3

CALORIE, WATER, PROTEIN, FAT, CARBOHYDRATE, AND ASH CONTENT
OF SOME SAUSAGES AND CANNED MEAT ITEMS

Product Description	Calories	Water	Protein	Fat	Carbo-hydrate	Ash
Blood sausage or blood pudding	394	46	14.1	36.9	0.3	2.3
Bockwurst	264	61.9	11.3	23.7	0.6	2.5
Bologna, all samples	304	56.2	12.1	27.5	1.1	3.1
Bologna, all meat	277	57.4	13.3	22.8	3.7	2.8
Bologna with nonfat dry milk	—	57.1	13.4	—	—	—
Braunschweiger	319	52.6	14.8	27.4	2.3	2.9
Brown-and-Serve sausage, before browning	393	45.3	13.5	36.0	2.7	2.5
Brown-and-Serve sausage, after browning	422	39.9	16.5	37.8	2.8	3.0
Capicola	499	26.2	20.2	45.8	0	7.9
Cervelat, dry	451	29.4	24.6	37.6	1.7	6.7
Country style sausage (pork sausage—smoked)	345	49.9	15.1	31.1	0	3.9
Deviled ham, canned	351	50.5	13.9	32.3	0	3.3
Frankfurters, all samples, unheated	309	55.6	12.5	27.6	1.8	2.5
Frankfurters, all meat, unheated	296	56.5	13.1	25.5	2.5	2.4
Frankfurters with nonfat dry milk, unheated	300	54.2	13.1	25.5	3.4	3.7
Frankfurters, heated or cooked	304	57.3	12.4	27.2	1.6	1.5
Frankfurters, canned	221	66.0	13.4	18.1	0.2	2.3
Headcheese	268	58.8	15.5	22.0	1.0	2.7
Knockwurst	278	57.6	14.1	23.2	2.2	2.9
Liverwurst, fresh	307	53.9	16.2	25.6	1.8	2.5
Liverwurst, smoked	319	52.6	14.8	27.4	2.3	2.9
Luncheon meat, boiled ham	234	59.1	19.1	17.1	0	4.9
Luncheon meat, chopped, spiced pork	294	54.9	15.0	24.9	1.3	3.9
Meat loaf	200	64.1	15.9	13.2	3.3	3.5
Meat potted (beef, chicken, or turkey)	248	60.7	17.5	19.2	0	2.8
Minced ham	228	61.7	13.7	16.9	4.4	3.3
Mortadella	315	48.9	20.4	25.0	0.6	5.1
Polish style sausage	304	53.7	15.7	25.8	1.2	3.6
Pork sausage, link or bulk, raw	498	38.1	9.4	50.8	Trace	1.7
Pork sausage, link or bulk, cooked	476	34.8	18.1	44.2	Trace	2.9
Salami, dry	450	29.8	23.8	38.1	1.2	7.1
Salami, cooked	311	51.0	17.5	25.6	1.4	4.5
Scrapple	215	61.3	8.8	13.6	14.6	1.7
Souse	181	70.3	13.0	13.4	1.2	2.1
Thuringer	307	48.5	18.6	24.5	1.6	6.8
Vienna Sausage, canned	240	63.0	14.0	19.8	0.3	2.9
Turkey, meat only, canned	202	64.9	20.9	12.5	0	1.7

Source: USDA Handbook No. 8

these 5 minerals, recent studies have reported on the content of magnesium, copper, and zinc in baby foods and several other processed items. Meat is a good source of dietary phosphorus and iron, but is low in calcium. Recent data from Swift's Research Laboratory showing the nutritional value of several processed-meat products and baby foods containing meat provides up-to-date information on the mineral and vitamin content of these foods (Table 2.4).

It is interesting to compare the analysis in Table 2.4 with that found in Table 2.5 since both give values for baby foods containing meat. However, Table 2.4 gives data for analyses in 1972, whereas, Table 2.5 was published in 1963. Note that sodium levels are considerably lower in the present analysis (Table 2.4). Salt was added to these products until recent years, when it was voluntarily removed by the industry; thus the present levels are considerably reduced. Although there are other minor differences in the mineral content of the same products shown in Tables 2.4 and 2.5, they are of less importance. Note, however, that Table 2.4 (the 1972 data) also includes information on magnesium, zinc, and copper content, which reflects interest in more complete nutritional information. Table 2.4 also presents data showing the percentage of the recommended daily allowance supplied by a serving of each of the items for which recommended daily allowances have been established.

Protein.—From the standpoint of nutrition, the nitrogenous components of meat are probably the most important. These compounds can be divided into protein and nonprotein nitrogen (NPN). Nonprotein nitrogen exists chiefly as free amino acids and amides. The principal amides include urea, hippuric acid, guanidine, creatine, and glutathione. The free amino acids may include any of those found in the tissues. The nonprotein nitrogen fraction comprises only a small proportion of the total nitrogen in meat, and for practical purposes is not normally separated in the analysis.

Proteins are polypeptides or combinations of amino acids linked together into chains by the reaction of amino and carboxyl groups of adjoining amino acids by means of peptide linkages, as shown in the following formula:

$$R^1-CH_2-C = O \vdots H-N-CH-C = O \vdots H-N-CH_2-R^2$$
$$|$$
$$CH_3$$

Each dotted vertical line is at the point of the peptide linkage of adjacent amino acids, while the symbols R^1 and R^2 represent further chains of amino acids linked together by means of peptide linkages to form complete proteins. Various amino acids are, of course, included in the proteins.

In common with fats and carbohydrates, proteins contain carbon, hydrogen, and oxygen. However, they also contain a large and fairly constant proportion of nitrogen, normally in a range of 15.5 to 18%. Meat proteins also frequently contain sulfur, and a few contain phosphorus and iron. The nitrogen content of meat proteins is about 16%, which means the protein content of meat is 6.25 times the nitrogen content.

Muscle or meat proteins can be divided into three different fractions on the basis of function and solubility: (1) sarcoplasmic or water-soluble, (2) myofibrillar or salt-soluble, and (3) connective tissue or insoluble fraction. Actually, the solubility classification is only a simple guide, to which there are a number of exceptions, yet this classification is sufficiently accurate for the present discussion.

Sarcoplasmic Proteins.—The sarcoplasmic fraction consists of those proteins found in the sarcoplasm, or the fluid surrounding and bathing the myofibrils. Sarcoplasmic proteins are often referred to as water-soluble proteins, because they are commonly extracted with water or low ionic strength (0.06) salt solutions. This fraction contains the oxidative enzymes, including the cytochromes, the flavin nucleotides, the various heme pigments, and the mitochondrial oxidative enzymes. The sarcoplasmic fraction also contains the glycolytic enzymes, which control both aerobic and anaerobic glycolysis, thereby functioning in conversion of glycogen to lactic acid and the aerobic oxidation of pyruvate. In addition, the sarcoplasmic classification also contains lysosomal enzymes and nucleo-proteins, which function in hydrolytic degradation of waste material and regulate protein synthesis and deposition, respectively. It can be readily seen that the sarcoplasmic fraction covers a widely divergent group of proteins that control a widely differing group of tissue functions.

Sarcoplasmic proteins are effective emulsifiers of fat in model sausage systems, being equal or superior to the myofibrillar fraction. Emulsions formed by the sarcoplasmic fraction are not as stable as those formed by the myofibrillar proteins, but are more stable than emulsions in which the connective tissue fraction composes the protein matrix. Thus sarcoplasmic proteins make a contribution to sausage emulsions.

Myofibrillar Proteins.—Myofibrillar proteins are also known as contractile proteins by virtue of the key role they play in muscle contraction and locomotion in the living animal. After death, these proteins function in the development of rigor mortis, which is essentially an irreversible reaction limited by the unavailability of substrate. The principal proteins in the myofibrillar fraction include myosin, actin, and the

Table 2.4

NUTRITIONAL ANALYSIS OF SOME MEAT PRODUCTS

Nutrient—Amount	Brown N'Serve Bacon and N'Serve Sausage Heated	Brown N'Serve Sausage Heated	Mild Cured Nonsmoked Brown N' Serve Sausage Heated	Veal with Vegetables Strained Canned	Ham with Vegetables Strained Canned	Turkey with Vegetables Strained Canned	Beef with Vegetables Strained Canned	Chicken with Vegetables Strained Canned	Turkey with Vegetables Junior Canned	Beef with Vegetables Junior Canned	Veal with Vegetables Junior Canned	Chicken with Vegetables Junior Canned	Ham Fully Cooked Canned
Moisture—g/100 g.	47.2	45.0	41.7	84.7	79.9	84.7	81.2	84.7	81.2	78.4	78.6	81.7	62.2
Energy—Kcal/100 g.	361	388	431	68	109	67	99	68	83	112	109	83	223
Kcal or % RDA/serving	216	232	258	10.0	15.0	9.0	14.0	10.0	12.0	16.0	15.0	12.0	221
Protein—g/100 g.	16.5	14.6	13.0	6.3	6.3	5.4	5.7	5.3	5.8	6.6	6.6	5.4	18.1
% RDA/serving	15.0	13.0	12.0	50.0	50.0	43.0	45.0	42.0	46.0	52.0	52.0	43.0	28.0
Fat—g/100 g.	31.4	35.0	41.0	1.7	6.0	1.5	5.2	1.7	2.0	5.5	5.2	2.4	15.8
g/serving	18.8	21.0	24.6	2.1	7.6	1.9	6.6	2.1	2.5	7.0	6.6	3.0	15.6
Carbohydrate—g/100 g.	2.0	2.6	1.5	6.7	7.2	7.8	7.3	7.7	10.3	8.8	8.8	9.8	0.9
g/serving	1.2	1.5	0.9	8.5	9.1	9.9	9.3	9.8	13.1	11.2	11.2	12.5	0.8
Ash—g/100 g.	2.9	2.8	2.8	0.6	0.6	0.6	0.6	0.6	0.7	0.7	0.8	0.7	3.0
g/serving	1.7	1.6	1.6	0.7	0.7	0.7	0.7	0.7	0.8	0.8	1.0	0.8	2.9
Calcium mg/100 g.	Tr	Tr	Tr	Tr	Tr	64	Tr	19	80	Tr	Tr	24	Tr
% RDA	Tr	Tr	Tr	Tr	Tr	14	Tr	4	17	Tr	Tr	5.0	Tr
Phosphorus—mg/100 g.	130	110	100	55	63	63	49	57	83	74	76	67	190
% RDA	8.0	7.0	6.0	14.0	16.0	16.0	13.0	15.0	21.0	19.0	19.0	17.0	19.0
Iron—mg/100 g.	1.2	1.2	0.8	1.4	0.3	0.7	1.2	0.4	0.8	0.8	1.8	0.7	1.0
% RDA	4.0	4.0	3.0	12.0	3.0	6.0	10.0	3.0	7.0	7.0	15.0	6.0	6.0
Sodium mg/100 g.	870	850	860	130	140	150	150	160	140	160	170	150	850
mg/serving	522	510	516	165	178	191	191	204	178	204	216	191	844

Potassium mg/100 g.	210	180	160	110	100	64	88	54	100	170	220	110	240
mg/serving	126	108	96	140	127	81	112	68	127	216	280	140	238
Magnesium mg/100 g.	15	12	10	8	9	6	8	6	15	12	15	8	17
% RDA	2.0	2.0	2.0	15.0	16.0	11.0	15.0	11.0	27.0	22.0	27.0	15.0	4.0
Zinc—mg/100 g.	2.2	1.8	1.7	1.9	1.2	1.7	1.3	0.8	1.5	1.5	2.3	0.7	1.9
mg or % RDA/serving	9.0	7.0	7.0	2.4	1.5	2.1	1.6	0.8	1.9	1.9	2.9	0.8	13.0
Copper—mg/100 g.	0.07	0.04	0.03	0.18	0.07	0.09	0.07	0.02	0.14	0.14	0.10	0.07	0.06
mg or % RDA/serving	2.0	1.0	1.0	0.22	0.08	0.11	0.08	0.02	0.17	0.17	0.12	0.08	3.0
Vit. A—IU/100 g.	NA	NA	NA	624	559	841	888	442	1024	3105	3745	2610	NA
% RDA	NA	NA	NA	53.0	48.0	72.0	76.0	38.0	87.0	264.0	319.0	222.0	NA
Thiamine—mg/100 g.	0.44	0.34	0.35	0.09	0.08	0.01	0.01	0.01	0.01	0.01	0.01	0.01	0.92
% RDA	18.0	14.0	14.0	23.0	20.0	3.0	3.0	3.0	3.0	3.0	3.0	3.0	61.0
Riboflavin—mg/100 g.	0.17	0.15	0.14	0.06	0.06	0.04	0.07	0.04	0.07	0.05	0.07	0.06	0.20
% RDA	6.0	5.0	5.0	13.0	13.0	9.0	15.0	9.0	15.0	11.0	15.0	13.0	12.0
Niacin—mg/100 g.	3.66	3.47	3.41	1.29	0.95	0.40	1.16	0.62	1.36	0.53	1.53	0.81	3.17
% RDA	11.0	10.0	10.0	21.0	15.0	6.0	19.0	10.0	22.0	8.0	24.0	13.0	16.0
Pantothenic Acid—mg/100 g.	0.446	0.300	0.530	0.127	0.167	0.138	0.087	0.212	0.190	0.077	0.199	0.115	0.140
mg/serving	0.279	0.180	0.318	0.162	0.213	0.176	0.111	0.270	0.242	0.098	0.253	0.146	1.0
Vit. B6—mg/100 g.	0.045	0.042	0.038	0.019	0.025	0.120	0.019	0.019	0.23	0.016	0.021	0.023	0.198
% RDA	1.0	1.0	1.0	6.0	8.0	38.0	6.0	6.0	7.0	5.0	7.0	7.0	10.0
Vit. B12—mcg/100 g.	0.47	0.367	0.70	0.30	0.28	0.16	0.29	0.17	0.20	0.20	0.35	0.12	0.21
% RDA	5.0	4.0	7.0	19.0	18.0	10.0	19.0	11.0	13.0	13.0	22.0	8.0	3.0
Folacin—mg/100 g.	0.002	0.002	0.001	0.001	0.000	0.001	0.003	0.002	0.001	0.001	0.002	0.001	0.004
% RDA	Tr	Tr	Tr	1.0	Tr	2.0	4.0	3.0	2.0	2.0	3.0	2.0	1.0
Ascorbic Acid—mg/100 g.	NA	NA	NA	NA	NA	NA	NA	NA	NA	NA	NA	NA	NA
% RDA	NA	NA	NA	NA	NA	NA	NA	NA	NA	NA	NA	NA	NA

NA—not available

Tr—Trace

Source: Swift and Company's Nutritional Data Bank

Table 2.5

MINERAL AND VITAMIN CONTENT OF SOME CANNED BABY FOODS
CONTAINING MEAT, EXPRESSED AS AMOUNT PER 100 GM EDIBLE PORTION

Product Description	Calcium mg	Phosphorus mg	Iron mg	Sodium mg	Potassium mg	Vit. A I.U.	Thiamine mg	Riboflavin mg	Niacin mg	Ascorbic Acid mg
Beef noodle dinner	12	29	0.5	269	159	620	0.02	0.05	0.5	2
Cereal, egg yolk and bacon	29	60	0.8	301	36	520	0.05	0.06	0.4	—
Macaroni, tomatoes, meat and cereal	21	35	0.5	381	77	500	0.14	0.12	1.0	1
Split peas, vegetables and ham or bacon	29	79	0.7	295	112	600	0.08	0.05	0.5	1
Vegetables and bacon with cereal	17	28	0.6	282	130	2,200	0.07	0.05	0.6	1
Vegetables and beef with cereal	17	39	0.8	307	143	2,800	0.03	0.04	0.9	1
Vegetables and chicken with cereal	33	33	0.4	307	55	1,000	0.03	0.04	0.5	Trace
Vegetables and ham with cereal	25	42	0.3	360	90	1,000	0.08	0.05	0.5	3
Vegetables and lamb with cereal	23	37	0.7	269	148	2,700	0.03	0.05	0.7	1
Vegetables and liver with cereal	17	57	2.7	236	162	4,700	0.04	0.37	1.6	3
Vegetables and liver with bacon and cereal	11	42	2.6	284	131	4,600	0.03	0.33	1.3	2
Vegetables and turkey with cereal	22	26	0.3	307	46	400	0.01	0.03	0.4	1
Beef with vegetables	13	84	1.2	304	113	1,100	0.07	0.17	1.6	2
Chicken with vegetables	22	85	0.9	265	71	1,000	0.09	0.15	1.6	2
Turkey with vegetables	38	63	0.6	348	122	1.000	0.13	0.13	1.8	2
Veal with vegetables	11	71	0.8	323	95	800	0.08	0.15	2.0	2
Beef, Strained	8	127	2.0	228	183	—	0.01	0.16	3.5	0
Beef, Junior	8	163	2.5	283	242	—	0.02	0.20	4.3	0
Beef Heart	5	155	3.7	208	—	—	0.06	0.62	3.6	0
Chicken	—	129	1.9	263	96	—	0.02	0.16	3.5	0
Egg yolks with ham or bacon	71	185	2.8	313	82	1,900	0.10	0.23	0.5	—
Lamb, Strained	9	124	2.1	241	181	—	0.02	0.17	3.3	—
Lamb, Junior	13	156	2.7	294	228	—	0.02	0.21	4.1	—
Liver, Strained	6	182	5.6	253	202	24,000	0.05	2.00	7.6	10
Liver and bacon, strained	6	157	4.2	302	192	22,000	0.05	1.99	7.8	7
Pork, Strained	8	130	1.5	223	178	—	0.19	0.20	2.7	—
Pork, Junior	8	144	1.2	237	210	—	0.23	0.23	2.8	—
Veal, Strained	10	145	1.7	226	214	—	0.03	0.20	4.3	—
Veal, Junior	8	157	1.6	276	206	—	0.03	0.22	6.0	—

0 indicates no detectable amounts
— indicates no reliable data: the amount is believed to be negligible
Source: USDA Handbook No. 8

combination form of actomyosin, which results from contraction of muscle, or in the case of meat, during development of rigor mortis. In addition, the myofibrillar fraction includes tropomyosin, troponin, the actinins (α-and β-forms) and perhaps other minor regulatory proteins, which play major roles in muscle and meat, although present in lower percentages than actin and myosin.

The myofibrillar or so-called salt-soluble proteins are commonly extracted with potassium chloride, usually at an ionic strength of 0.3. The salt solubility of this fraction is normally taken advantage of in sausage manufacture by adding 2 to 3% salt before or during chopping or emulsification in order to extract and make a salt solution of the protein. The salt-soluble extract then coats the fat during formation of the emulsion. As already indicated, the myofibrillar protein-fat emulsion is not only efficient per unit of protein but also is very stable.

Connective Tissue Proteins.—Connective tissue proteins function as a supporting framework for the living body, and thus serve in numerous and variable functions. This fraction includes two distinctly different proteins, (1) collagen and (2) elastin, and also probably another (3) reticulin, which is less well-defined than the former two.

Collagen is the principal component of the connective-tissue fraction. It is found widely distributed in the body and comprises 20 to 25% of the total protein. It is the principal protein in bone, tendon, and skin. It also comprises the protein matrix for deposition of depot fat, and supports and contains the individual muscle fibers, the bundles of fibers, and the muscles themselves. Collagen fibers are not dissolved by dilute acid or alkali solutions or by concentrated solutions of certain neutral salts and nonelectrolytes unless they have been previously denatured by heat or urea. The fibers are readily digested by pepsin and collagenase, but are resistant to trypsin and chymotrypsin digestion. Collagen is characterized by undergoing a sharply defined thermal shrinkage at a given temperature, which is characteristic of the species at a given age. Prolonged heat treatment above the thermal shrinkage temperature converts collagen to soluble gelatin. The latter property is responsible for fat accumulation in sausage emulsions prepared from collagen and will be discussed in greater detail later in this section.

Collagen is characterized by an unusual amino-acid composition. Glycine represents nearly one-third of the total amino acid residues, while hydroxyproline comprises about 10%, alanine approximately 11% of the total, and proline 12%. Hydroxylysine, which is characteristically confined to collagen in nature, makes up a small (less than 1%) but consistent percentage of collagen. Tyrosine, histidine, and the sulfur-containing amino acids are present in amounts less than 1%, which is unusually low. Thus, the polar residues compose about 18% and amides 5% of the total amino acid residues. Collagen is characterized by inter- and intramolecular cross-links, the extent of cross-linking increasing with the animal's age. Collagen from older animals has more cross-linking, and is consequently more difficult to extract.

Elastin belongs to a unique class of proteins, being extremely unreactive. It is a minor component of most tissues but is found in appreciable amounts in the ligaments of the vertebrae and in the walls of large arteries. It has a yellow appearance and fluoresces as bluish white fibers under ultraviolet light. Elastin has a low content of polar groups and stains poorly with acidic or basic dyes, but does stain with orcein and some other phenolic dyes. Elastin contains 1 to 2% hydroxyproline. The content of tryptophan, tyrosine, and the sulfur-containing amino acids is low, similar to collagen. It does not contain any measurable hydroxylysine, but does contain two characteristic amino acids, desmosine and isodesmosine. Like collagen, glycine comprises about one-third of the amino acid residues.

The third recognized protein component of connective tissues is reticulin. It is chemically very similar to collagen and many researchers believe it to be merely another form of collagen. Reticulin fibers are fine and wavy and show some branching. Reticulin shows distinctly different morphological and histological characteristics from collagen. However, upon hydrolysis it yields gelatin. Reticulin fibers appear as black shining threads upon staining with ammoniacal silver solutions, whereas mature collagen stains brown. In view of its transformation to gelatin upon prolonged heating, reticulin probably behaves like collagen in sausage emulsions.

Collagen and apparently reticulin are extracted by the salt added to sausage, and coat the fat particles during emulsification. Their ability to emulsify fat is quite low in view of the instability of the finished emulsion. Upon heating the emulsion, collagen and reticulin are gelatinized and fat is released. This can be an important factor in the accumulation of fat during heat-processing of emulsion-type sausages. As elastin is relatively unreactive, it is not extracted and apparently has little effect upon sausage, but would likewise not contribute to the emulsifying capacity.

Unlike sarcoplasmic and myofibrillar proteins, which are high-quality proteins and contribute a good balance of essential amino acids, connective-tissue proteins are low in the sulfur-containing amino acids and tryptophan. Thus, connective-tissue proteins would require special dietary supplementation with trytophan and histidine to improve their nutritional value. Meat by-products that are high in bone or in hides are of relatively poor biological value. Fortunately, lean meat is largely composed of myofibrillar and sarcoplasmic proteins, and so is of excellent quality. The biological value of lean-meat proteins used for sausage emulsions and other meat products is excellent.

Carbohydrates

Immediately post-mortem muscle normally contains a small amount (about 1%) of glycogen, most of which disappears before completion of rigor. It serves an important function in controlling muscle pH, which is the net effect of the extent of glycolysis. Both the rate and amount of glycogen breakdown control the physical properties of meat, such as water-holding capacity, color, and tenderness. Rapid glycolysis, while the muscle temperature is still high, has been shown to be a causative factor in development of PSE (pale, soft, and exudative) muscle in the pig. Similarly, early freezing before completion of glycolysis has been found to cause excessive muscle shortening, thus contributing to toughness in meat. This has been well established in New Zealand, where excessive toughness in lamb has been encountered as a result of freezing immediately after slaughter. The closely related phenomenon of thaw rigor, which occurs on thawing of prerigor frozen meat and results in excessive drip losses upon thawing, can also be prevented by allowing meat to pass through rigor before freezing.

After completion of rigor mortis, the amount of glycogen is usually greatly reduced or in many cases completely absent. If the glycogen and creatine phosphate are all used up before the pH reaches the normal level of 5.3 to 5.6, the pH remains high. The resulting high-pH meat is commonly called "dark cutting" because of its dark appearance and low oxygen uptake. "Dark-cutting" meat has a high water-holding capacity, but bacterial spoilage is more likely to occur as a result of the favorable pH conditions for microbial growth. High-pH meat is not only objectionable from the standpoint of appearance and flavor, sometimes being "soapy" in taste, but also is subject to spoilage due to the favorable pH for bacterial growth. Bacterial growth on high-pH Wiltshire bacon has long been known to produce spoilage, which is recognized by the tainted flavor. Recent evidence has suggested that PSE pork and DFD (dark, firm, and dry) muscle in the pig are both associated with upsets in glycolysis and apparently are due to the same basic cause. The PSE condition is apparently due to immediate post-mortem stimulation of glycolysis in the presence of adequate glycogen supplies, and results in abnormally low pH values. The DFD condition, on the other hand, is the result of long-standing stimulation resulting in complete disappearance of muscle glycogen while pH is still high. PSE muscle is objectionable because of its excessive shrinkage and pale color. DFD muscle is objectionable because of the dark color, and can also result in meat spoilage; thus it is even more serious than the PSE condition.

As already indicated, the amount of remaining glycogen in post-mortem meat is quite low or even completely absent, so it has little effect on the nutritive value of meat and meat products. Some values for carbohydrate (chiefly glycogen) in various processed-meat items are shown in Tables 2.6 and 2.7. It is interesting to note that canned baby foods (Table 2.6), to which vegetables and/or cereal is/are added, have appreciable proportions of carbohydrate, although canned meats alone contain little or none. Similarly, Table 2.7 gives values for various processed-meat products, and also shows that considerable carbohydrate content is present in some mixed items containing other foods. It is also interesting to observe the values for cured meat products, such as bacon and dried beef, in which sugar added during curing is reflected. For some unexplained reason, no carbohydrate was found in cured ham (Table 2.7), but appreciable amounts were found in canned ham (Table 2.4).

To summarize, the carbohydrate content of meat and meat products is usually negligible unless it is added during processing either

Table 2.6

CALORIE, WATER, PROTEIN, FAT, CARBOHYDRATE AND ASH CONTENT OF
SOME CANNED BABY FOODS CONTAINING MEAT, EXPRESSED AS AMOUNT PER 100
GM EDIBLE PORTION

Product—Description	Calories	Water	Protein	Fat	Carbohydrate	Ash
Beef noodle dinner	48	88.2	2.8	1.1	6.8	1.1
Cereal, egg yolk and bacon	82	84.7	2.9	4.9	6.6	0.9
Macaroni, tomatoes, meat and cereal	67	84.5	2.6	2.0	9.6	1.3
Split peas, vegetables and ham or bacon	80	81.5	4.0	2.1	11.2	1.2
Vegetables and bacon with cereal	68	85.7	1.7	2.9	8.7	1.0
Vegetables and beef with cereal	56	87.0	2.7	1.6	7.6	1.1
Vegetables and chicken with cereal	52	87.8	2.1	1.4	7.7	1.0
Vegetables and ham with cereal	64	85.6	2.8	2.2	8.3	1.1
Vegetables and lamb with cereal	58	87.0	2.2	2.0	7.7	1.1
Vegetables and liver with cereal	47	87.8	3.1	0.4	7.8	0.9
Vegetables and liver with bacon and cereal	57	87.2	2.4	1.9	7.5	1.0
Vegetables and turkey with cereal	44	88.9	2.1	0.8	7.2	1.0
Beef with vegetables	87	81.6	7.4	3.7	6.0	1.3
Chicken with vegetables	100	79.6	7.4	4.6	7.2	1.2
Turkey with vegetables	86	81.3	6.7	3.2	7.6	1.2
Veal with vegetables	63	85.0	7.1	1.6	5.1	1.2
Beef—Strained	99	80.3	14.7	4.0	(0)	1.0
Beef—Junior	118	75.6	19.3	3.9	(0)	1.4
Beef Heart	93	81.1	13.5	3.8	(0)	1.2
Chicken	127	77.2	13.7	7.6	(0)	1.5
Egg yolks with ham or bacon	208	70.3	10.0	18.1	(0)	1.3
Lamb, Strained	107	79.3	14.6	4.9	(0)	1.2
Lamb, Junior	121	76.0	17.5	5.1	(0)	1.4
Liver, Strained	97	79.7	14.1	3.4	1.5	1.3
Liver and bacon, Strained	123	77.0	13.7	6.6	1.3	1.4
Pork, Strained	118	77.7	15.4	5.8	(0)	1.1
Pork, Junior	134	74.3	18.6	6.0	(0)	1.3
Veal, Strained	91	80.7	15.5	2.7	(0)	1.1
Veal, Junior	107	76.9	18.8	3.0	(0)	1.4

(0) indicates amount too small to measure
Source: USDA Handbook No. 8

as sugar or as other carbohydrate material. Nevertheless, the glycogen present at the time of slaughter, although it comprises only about 1%, plays a major role in determining the physical properties of meat.

Vitamins

Although the vitamins perform essential functions in man, serving as coenzymes in important life processes and in a variety of other body functions, lack of space precludes a detailed discussion. The reader is referred to the bibliography for more complete information. The material presented here will center on the levels present, their contribution to total dietary intake by man, and some effects of processing on the level in different meats and meat products.

The vitamins can be classified as fat-soluble and water-soluble. The fat-soluble group includes vitamins A, D, E, and K; the water-soluble group contains the B-complex vitamins and vitamin C. Generally speaking, meat is an excellent source of the B-complex vitamins and is poor in the fat-soluble group and vitamin C (ascorbic acid). However, the variety meats, especially liver and kidney, generally contain appreciable percentages of vitamins A, C, D, E, and K. Muscle is a poor source of A, C, D, E, and K, the small quantities present in fresh meat being largely destroyed during cooking and/or processing.

The vitamin content of meat is quite variable, being dependent upon the species and age of the animal, the degree of fatness, and the type of feed furnished to the animal. The species difference is most notable when comparing the thiamine content of pork with that of beef or lamb, since pork contains 5 to 10 times more of this B-complex vitamin. The effect of diet can also be shown best by differences in the thiamine content of pork in which the diet is high in thiamine. Such supplementation may increase thiamine content several-fold. Since the water-soluble vitamins are localized in lean tissues and the fat-soluble vitamins in fatty tissues, the effect of the amount of fat per unit of meat is obvious. The greatest variation takes place in the B-complex vitamins, since neither the fat-soluble vitamins nor vitamin C are present in appreciable quantities per unit fat or lean, respectively. The effects of age will depend upon the species and the particular vitamin in question. For example, veal is higher in thiamine, riboflavin, and niacin than beef. However, the young calf requires dietary B-complex vitamins during the early stages of growth, so veal could under certain circumstances be lower than beef.

The B-complex vitamins—thiamine, riboflavin, niacin, pantothenic acid, vitamin B_6, folic acid, biotin, and vitamin B_{12}—are all found in meats or variety meats. Meat and meat products contribute substantial amounts of B-vitamins toward meeting the dietary requirements of man. Generally, liver is higher than lean meats. This is shown by examining the vitamin content for products containing liver, as illustrated in Tables 2.4 and 2.5.

Most of the vitamins in meat are relatively stable during cooking or processing, although substantial amounts may be leached out in the drippings or broth. The drip exuding from the cut surface of frozen meat on thawing also contains an appreciable portion of B-vitamins (also of amino acids). This indicates the importance of conserving these fractions by making use of them in some way. Thiamine and, to a lesser extent, vitamin B_6 are heat-labile. These vitamins are partially destroyed during curing, smoking, cooking, canning, heat dehydration, and irradiation. Ionizing radiation causes losses as high as 60% for thiamine. Even mild curing and smoking results in destruction of about 15% of the thiamine. Typically, average losses of thiamine during cook-

Table 2.7

THE CALORIE, WATER, PROTEIN, FAT, CARBOHYDRATE AND ASH CONTENT OF
SOME CURED, CANNED OR PROCESSED FOOD ITEMS CONTAINING MEAT,
CHICKEN OR FISH

Product—Description	Calories	Water	Protein	Fat	Carbohydrate	Ash
Bacon—slab or sliced, cured—raw	665	19.3	8.4	69.3	1.0	2.0
Bacon—slab or sliced, cured—cooked and drained	611	8.1	30.4	52.0	3.2	6.3
Bacon—cured and canned—unheated	685	16.7	8.5	71.5	1.0	2.3
Bacon—Canadian, cured—unheated	216	61.7	20.0	14.4	0.3	3.6
Bacon—Canadian, cured—cooked	277	49.9	27.6	17.5	0.3	4.7
Beef and vegetable stew, home cooked with lean beef chuck	89	82.4	6.4	4.3	6.2	0.7
Beef and vegetable stew—canned	79	82.5	5.8	3.1	7.1	1.5
Beef—Roast—canned	224	60.0	25.0	13.0	0	2.0
Beef—Corned—boneless—medium fat—uncooked	293	54.2	15.8	25.0	0	5.0
Beef—Corned—boneless—medium fat—cooked	372	43.9	22.9	30.4	0	2.9
Beef—Corned—boneless—medium fat—canned	216	59.3	25.3	12.0	0	3.4
Beef—Corned Beef Hash with potato—canned	181	67.4	8.8	11.3	10.7	1.8
Beef—Dried and chipped—uncooked	203	47.7	34.3	6.3	0	11.6
Beef—Dried and chipped—creamed—cooked	154	72.0	8.2	10.3	7.1	2.4
Beef—Potpie—home prepared—cooked	246	55.1	10.1	14.5	18.8	1.5
Beef—Potpie—frozen—commercial—unheated	192	63.3	7.3	9.9	18.0	1.5

Chicken—boneless meat—canned	198	65.2	21.7	11.7	0	1.4
Chicken a la King—home recipe—cooked	191	68.2	11.2	14.0	5.0	1.6
Chicken fricassee—home recipe—cooked	161	71.3	15.3	9.3	3.2	0.9
Chicken—Potpie—home prepared—cooked	235	56.6	10.1	13.5	18.3	1.5
Chicken—Potpie—frozen—commercial—unheated	219	57.8	6.7	11.5	22.2	1.8
Chicken and Noodles, home recipe—cooked	153	71.1	9.3	7.7	10.7	1.2
Chili Con Carne with beans—canned	133	72.4	7.5	6.1	12.2	1.8
Chili Con Carne without beans (60% meat)—canned	200	66.9	10.3	14.8	5.8	2.2
Chop Suey with meat—canned	62	85.5	4.4	3.2	4.2	2.7
Chow Mein—chicken without noodles—canned	38	88.8	2.6	0.1	7.1	1.4
Haddock—smoked—canned	103	72.6	23.2	0.4	0	3.1
Halibut—smoked	224	49.4	20.8	15.0	0	15.0
Ham—Country style—dry cured—lean	310	49.0	19.5	25.0	0.3	5.8
Ham—commercially cured—medium fat—total edible—raw	282	56.5	17.5	23.0	0	3.0
Ham—commercially cured—medium fat—total edible—cooked	289	53.6	20.9	22.1	0	3.4
Picnic—commercially cured—medium fat—total edible—raw	285	56.7	16.8	23.6	0	2.9
Picnic—commercially cured—medium fat—total edible—cooked	323	48.8	22.4	25.2	0	3.6
Ham—canned—total contents of can	193	65.0	18.3	12.3	0.9	3.5
Pork and Gravy—(90% pork, 10% gravy)—canned	256	56.9	16.4	17.8	6.3	2.6

Source: USDA Handbook No. 8

Table 2.8

SOME SELECTED VALUES SHOWING THE MINERAL AND VITAMIN CONTENTS OF VARIOUS GRADES AND CUTS OF MEAT ON A RAW AND COOKED BASIS, EXPRESSED AS AMOUNT PER 100 GM EDIBLE PORTION

Product and Grade	Calcium mg	Phosphorus mg	Iron mg	Sodium[a] mg	Potassium[b] mg	Vit. A I.U.	Thiamine mg	Riboflavin mg	Niacin mg	Ascorbic Acid mg
Beef carcass, total edible including kidney fat and kidney										
Good grade, (66% lean, 34% fat) raw	10	152	2.5	65	355	60	0.07	0.15	4.0	—
Standard grade (73% lean, 27% fat) raw	10	166	2.7	65	355	40	0.08	0.16	4.3	—
Commercial grade (64% lean, 36% fat) raw	9	145	2.4	65	355	60	0.07	0.14	3.8	—
Utility grade (76% lean, 24% fat) raw	11	172	2.8	65	355	40	0.08	0.17	4.5	—
Beef round, Choice grade, separable lean, raw	13	217	3.2	65	355	10	0.09	0.19	5.2	—
Beef round, Choice grade, separable lean, cooked	13	268	3.7	60	370	10	0.08	0.24	6.0	—
Beef chuck, Choice grade, separable lean, raw	12	214	3.2	65	355	10	0.09	0.19	5.1	—
Beef chuck, Choice grade, separable lean, cooked	13	160	3.8	60	370	20	0.05	0.23	4.6	—
Lamb, composite of cuts (leg, loin, rib, and shoulder) trimmed, Good grade (79% lean, 21% fat) raw	10	151	1.3	75	295	—	0.15	0.21	4.9	—
Lamb leg, Good grade, separable lean, raw	12	185	1.8	75	295	—	0.18	0.25	5.8	—
Lamb leg, Good grade, separable lean, cooked	12	238	2.2	70	290	—	0.16	0.30	6.2	—
Lamb shoulder, Good grade, separable lean, raw	11	170	1.6	75	295	—	0.16	0.23	5.3	—
Lamb shoulder, Good grade, separable lean, cooked	11	219	1.9	70	290	—	0.15	0.28	5.7	—
Pork carcass, thin (53% lean, 47% fat) raw	6	116	1.7	70	285	(0)	0.54	0.13	2.9	—
Pork carcass, thin, separable lean, raw	11	210	2.7	70	285	(0)	0.89	0.21	4.8	—
Pork shoulder, thin (75% lean, 25% fat) raw	8	148	2.0	70	285	(0)	0.66	0.16	3.5	—
Pork ham, trimmed, thin (77% lean, 23% fat) raw	10	190	2.5	70	285	(0)	0.82	0.20	4.4	—
Pork ham, trimmed, thin (77% lean, 23% fat) cooked	11	252	3.2	65	390	(0)	0.54	0.25	4.8	—
Pork ham, thin, separable lean, raw	12	238	3.1	70	285	(0)	0.99	0.24	5.3	—
Pork ham, thin, separable lean, cooked	13	315	3.8	65	390	(0)	0.66	0.30	5.8	—
Veal carcass, thin (86% lean, 14% fat) raw	11	199	2.9	90	320	—	0.14	0.26	6.5	—
Veal chuck, thin (90% lean, 10% fat) raw	12	206	3.0	90	320	—	0.15	0.26	6.7	—
Veal round and rump, thin (91% lean, 9% fat) raw	12	206	3.0	90	320	—	0.15	0.26	6.7	—

a—Average values are given for the respective type meat, raw or cooked as the case may be.
b—Average values are given for respective type meat, raw or cooked as the case may be.
(0) indicates too small amount to be measured.
— indicates no reliable data
Source: USDA Handbook No. 8

ing and processing of meat and meat products amounts to about 25%.

Vitamin B$_6$ is more stable than thiamine, and heating results in losses normally equivalent to only about half the amount of thiamine. The high temperatures and time required in processing of canned meats results in less retention of these vitamins. Meat cut in thin pieces and cooked quickly retains a greater proportion of thiamine and B$_6$ than large roasts, where longer cooking times are required. Riboflavin and niacin are quite stable to conventional cooking and heat-processing. Some of these vitamins are lost in the drippings unless an effort is made to use them. Ionizing radiation may destroy most of the vitamin K, 25% of the riboflavin, and 10% of the niacin. Except for drip losses, freezing and frozen storage have little effect upon the vitamin levels. However, knowledge about the effects of cooking and processing upon pantothenic acid, biotin, folic acid, and vitamin B$_{12}$ is limited. Some loss does appear to occur during cooking.

The concentration of vitamins in cooked meat and meat products is often higher than in raw meat. This can be seen by comparing the same product before and after cooking, as shown in Table 2.8. The higher values for the cooked products do not indicate that no losses occur during cooking, but rather that cooking drives off moisture and renders out fat. The net result is that the concentration of most of the B-complex vitamins per unit weight increases during cooking and processing.

NUTRITIONAL VALUES OF SOME PROCESSED MEATS

Although the nutritional value of some fresh meats used for processing (Tables 2.1 and 2.8) and of some meat products (Tables 2.4 and 2.5) has already been presented, additional values for other products should be useful. Table 2.9 gives data on some cured, canned, or processed meat items. The same data are presented for some sausages and other canned products in Table 2.10. Such data should be useful for estimating the contribution of meat toward meeting the dietary requirements of man. Although much more information is needed on the nutritive value of meat and meat products, the information included in Tables 2.9 and 2.10 provides a beginning for some meat items that are not well understood as to their nutritive value.

SUMMARY

Meat and meat products are generally excellent sources of protein, containing a good balance of the essential amino acids and having a high biological value. The connective-tissue proteins are exceptions

Table 2.9

MINERAL AND VITAMIN CONTENT OF SOME CURED, CANNED OR
PROCESSED FOOD PRODUCTS CONTAINING MEAT, CHICKEN AND FISH

Product—Description	Calcium mg	Phosphorus mg	Iron mg	Sodium mg	Potassium mg	Vit. A I.U.	Thiamine mg	Riboflavin mg	Niacin mg	Ascorbic Acid mg
Bacon, slab or sliced, cured, raw	13	108	1.2	680	130	(0)	0.36	0.11	1.8	—
Bacon, slab or sliced, cured, cooked and drained	14	224	3.3	1,021	236	(0)	0.51	0.34	5.2	—
Bacon, cured and canned, unheated	15	92	1.4	—	—	(0)	0.23	0.10	1.5	—
Bacon, Canadian, cured, unheated	12	180	3.0	1,891	392	(0)	0.83	0.22	4.7	—
Bacon, Canadian, cured, cooked	19	218	4.1	2,555	432	(0)	0.92	0.17	5.0	7
Beef & vegetable stew, home-cooked with lean beef chuck	12	75	1.2	37	250	980	0.06	0.07	1.9	3
Beef and vegetable stew, canned	12	45	0.9	411	174	970	0.03	0.05	1.0	0
Beef roast, canned	16	116	2.4	—	259	—	0.02	0.23	4.2	0
Beef, corned, boneless, medium fat, uncooked	9	125	2.4	1,300	60	—	0.03	0.15	1.7	0
Beef, corned, boneless, medium fat, cooked	9	93	2.9	1,740	150	—	0.02	0.18	1.5	0
Beef, corned, boneless, medium fat, canned	20	106	4.3	—	—	—	0.02	0.24	3.4	0
Beef, corned beef hash with potato, canned	13	67	2.0	540	200	—	0.01	0.09	2.1	—
Beef, dried and chipped, uncooked	20	404	5.1	4,300	200	—	0.07	0.32	3.8	0
Beef, dried and chipped, creamed, cooked	105	140	0.8	716	153	360	0.06	0.19	0.6	Trace
Beef, potpie, home-prepared, cooked	14	71	1.8	284	159	820	0.11	0.12	2.0	3
Beef, potpie, frozen, Commercial, unheated	10	48	1.0	366	93	410	0.03	0.06	1.2	Trace

Chicken, boneless meat, canned	21	247	1.5	—	138	230	0.04	0.12	4.4	4
Chicken a la King, home recipe, cooked	52	146	1.0	310	165	460	0.04	0.17	2.2	5
Chicken fricassee, home recipe, cooked	6	113	0.9	154	140	70	0.02	0.07	2.4	0
Chicken potpie, home-prepared, cooked	30	100	1.3	256	148	1,330	0.11	0.11	1.8	2
Chicken Potpie, frozen, Commercial, unheated	11	50	1.0	411	153	910	0.10	0.14	1.4	4
Chicken and noodles, home recipe, cooked	11	103	0.9	250	62	180	0.02	0.07	1.8	Trace
Chili con carne with beans, canned	32	126	1.7	531	233	60	0.03	0.07	1.3	—
Chop Suey with meat, canned	35	116	1.9	551	138	30	0.05	0.05	0.7	2
Chow Mein, chicken without noodles, canned	18	34	0.5	290	167	60	0.02	0.04	0.4	5
Haddock, smoked, canned	—	—	—	—	—	—	0.06	0.05	2.1	—
Halibut, smoked	—	—	—	—	—	(0)	—	—	—	—
Ham, Country style, dry-cured, lean	—	—	—	—	—	(0)	—	—	—	—
Ham, commercially cured, medium fat, total edible, raw	10	162	2.6	—	—	(0)	0.72	0.19	4.1	—
Ham, commercially cured, medium fat, total edible, cooked	9	172	2.6	—	+	(0)	0.47	0.18	3.6	—
Picnic, commercially cured, medium fat, total edible, raw	10	150	2.5	—	—	(0)	0.69	0.19	3.9	—
Picnic, commercially cured, medium fat, total edible, cooked	10	182	2.9	—	—	(0)	0.52	0.20	4.0	—
Ham, canned, total contents of can	11	156	2.7	1,100	340	(0)	0.53	0.19	3.8	—
Pork and gravy (90% pork, 10% gravy) canned	13	183	2.4	—	—	(0)	0.49	0.17	3.5	—

— indicates no values available
(0) indicates probably none or too small to measure
Source: USDA Handbook No. 8

Table 2.10

MINERAL AND VITAMIN CONTENT OF SOME SAUSAGES AND CANNED MEAT ITEMS

Product—Description	Calcium mg	Phosphorus mg	Iron mg	Sodium mg	Potassium mg	Vit. A I.U.	Thiamine mg	Riboflavin mg	Niacin mg	Ascorbic Acid mg
Sausages, cold cuts, and luncheon meats:										
Blood sausage or blood pudding	—	—	—	—	—	—	—	—	—	—
Bockwurst	7	—	—	—	—	—	—	—	—	—
Bologna, all samples	—	128	1.8	1,300	230	—	0.16	0.22	2.6	—
Bologna, all-meat	—	—	—	—	—	—	—	—	—	—
Bologna with nonfat dry milk	—	—	—	—	—	—	—	—	—	—
Braunschweiger	10	245	5.9	—	—	6,530	0.17	1.44	8.2	—
Brown and Serve Sausage, before browning	—	—	—	—	—	—	—	—	—	—
Brown and Serve Sausage, after browning	—	—	—	—	—	—	—	—	—	—
Capicola	—	—	—	—	—	—	—	—	—	—
Cervelat, dry	14	294	2.7	—	—	(0)	0.27	0.23	5.5	—
Country style sausage (pork sausage smoked)	9	168	2.3	—	—	—	0.22	0.19	3.1	—
Deviled ham, canned	8	92	2.1	1,100	—	(0)	0.14	0.10	1.6	—
Frankfurters, all samples, unheated	7	133	1.9	—	220	—	0.16	0.20	2.7	—
Frankfurters, all meat, unheated	—	—	—	—	—	—	—	—	—	—
Frankfurters with nonfat dry milk, unheated	—	—	—	—	—	—	—	—	—	—

Frankfurters, heated or cooked	5	102	1.5	—	—	—	0.15	0.20	2.5	—
Frankfurters, canned	9	145	2.2	—	—	—	0.03	0.12	2.4	—
Headcheese	9	173	2.3	—	—	—	0.04	0.10	0.9	—
Knockwurst	8	154	2.1	1	1	(0)	0.17	0.21	2.6	—
Liverwurst, fresh	9	238	5.4	—	—	6,350	0.20	1.30	5.7	—
Liverwurst, smoked	10	245	5.9	—	—	6,530	0.17	1.44	8.2	—
Luncheon meat, boiled ham	11	166	2.8	1,234	222	(0)	0.44	0.15	2.6	—
Luncheon meat, chipped, spiced pork	9	108	2.2	—	—	(0)	0.31	0.21	3.0	—
Meat loaf	9	178	1.8	—	—	—	0.13	0.22	2.5	—
Meat, potted (beef, chicken, or turkey)	—	—	—	—	—	(0)	—	—	1.2	—
Minced ham	8	89	2.1	—	—	—	0.03	0.22	3.4	—
Mortadella	12	238	3.1	—	—	(0)	0.37	0.22	—	—
Polish style sausage	9	176	2.4	740	140	(0)	0.34	0.19	3.1	—
Pork sausage, link or bulk, raw	5	92	1.4	958	269	(0)	0.43	0.17	2.3	—
Pork sausage, link or bulk, cooked	7	162	2.4	—	—	—	0.79	0.34	3.7	—
Salami, dry	14	283	3.6	—	—	—	0.37	0.25	5.3	—
Salami, cooked	10	200	2.6	—	—	(0)	0.25	0.24	4.1	—
Scrapple	5	64	1.2	—	—	—	0.19	0.09	1.8	—
Souse	—	—	—	—	—	—	—	—	—	—
Thuringer	11	214	2.8	—	—	(0)	0.11	0.26	4.2	—
Vienna Sausage, canned	8	153	2.1	—	—	—	0.08	0.13	2.6	—
Turkey, meat only, canned	10	—	1.4	—	—	130	0.02	0.14	4.7	—

— indicates lack of reliable data
(0) indicates none or too small to measure
Source: USDA Handbook No. 8

and should be used in limited quantities. Meat is also a good source of most B-complex vitamins, but is usually low in the fat-soluble vitamins (A, D, E, and K) and in vitamin C. Liver and other organ meats are generally higher in B-complex and fat-soluble vitamins than muscle. Meat is a good source of phosphorus and iron, but is low in calcium. Meat also contributes significant percentages of a number of other minerals, including copper, zinc, sodium, potassium, and magnesium.

Although the carbohydrate content of meat is relatively low and may disappear completely during development of rigor mortis, the glycogen content of meat plays a key role in determining the physical properties of meat and meat products. Thus, glycogen was discussed from the standpoint of its role in glycolysis and the effects upon the properties of meat products.

BIBLIOGRAPHY

BODWELL, C. E., and McCLAIN, P. E. 1971. Proteins. *In* The Science of Meat and Meat Products, J. F. Price, and B. S. Schweigert (Editors). W. H. Freeman and Co., San Francisco, Calif.

CALLOW, E. H. 1948. Comparative Studies of Meat. II. The changes in the carcass during growth and fattening and their relation to the chemical composition of the fatty and muscular tissues. J. Agr. Sci. *38,* 174.

CHATFIELD, C., and ADAMS, G. 1940. Proximate composition of American food materials. U.S. Dept. Agr. Circ. *549*

CORNFIELD, J., and MITCHELL, S. 1969. Selected risk factors in coronary disease. Arch. Environ. Health *19,* 382.

DUGAN, L. R., JR. 1957. Fatty acid composition of food fats and oils. Am. Meat Inst. Found. Bull. *36,* Chicago, Ill.

DUGAN, L. R., JR. 1971. Fats. *In* The Science of Meat and Meat Products, J. F. Price, and B. S. Schweigert (Editors). W. H. Freeman and Co., San Francisco, Calif.

HARDINGE, M. G., and CROOKS, H. 1961. Lesser known vitamins in foods. J. Am. Dietet. Assoc. *38,* 240.

HIRSH, J. 1957. Relation of diet and nutrition to arteriosclerosis. *In* Proceedings of the Meat Industry Research Conference. Am. Meat Inst. Found., Chicago, Ill.

HORNSTEIN, I., CROWE, P. F., and HEIMBERG, M. J. 1961. Fatty acid composition of meat tissue lipids. J. Food Sci. *26,* 581.

KYLEN, A. M., McGRATH, B. H., HALLMARK, E. L., and VAN DUYNE, F. O. 1964. Microwave and conventional cooking of meat. Thiamine retention and palatability. J. Am. Dietet. Assoc. *45,* 139.

LEVERTON, R. M. 1957. The fat, protein, and caloric value of cooked meats. *In* Proceedings of the Meat Industry Research Conference. Am. Meat Inst. Found., Chicago, Ill.

LEVERTON, R. M., and ODELL, G. V. 1958. The nutritive value of cooked meats. Oklahoma Agr. Expt. Sta. Bull. *MP-45.*

LEVY, R. I., and FREDRICKSON, D. S. 1971. Dietary management of hyperlipoproteinemia. J. Am. Dietet. Assoc. *58,* 406.

LUSHBOUGH, C. H., CHUTKOW, M. R., WEIR, C. E., and SCHWEIGERT, B. S. 1958. Utilization of lysine, methionine and tryptophan from meat subjected to varying degrees of heat treatment. Am. Meat Inst. Found. Bull. *36,* Chicago, Ill.

MATSCHINER, J. T., and DOISY, E. A., JR. 1966. Vitamin K content of ground beef. J. Nutr. *90*, 331.

MEYER, B. H., MYSINGER, M. A., and WODARSKI, L. A. 1969. Pantothenic acid and vitamin B₆ in beef. J. Am. Dietet. Assoc. *54*, 122.

NOBLE, I. 1964. Thiamine and riboflavin retention in broiled meat. J. Am. Dietet. Assoc. *45*, 447.

NOBLE, I. 1965. Thiamine and riboflavin retention in braised meat. J. Am. Dietet. Assoc. *47*, 205.

PEARSON, A. M. 1971. Muscle function and post-mortem changes. *In* The Science of Meat and Meat Products, J. F. Price, and B. S. Schweigert (Editors). W. H. Freeman and Co., San Francisco, Calif.

PETERSON, E. 1972. Nutritional labeling. *In* Proceedings of the Meat Industry Research Conference. Am. Meat Inst. Found., Chicago, Ill.

RICE, E. E. 1971. The nutritional content and value of meat and meat products. *In* The Science of Meat and Meat Products, J. F. Price, and B. S. Schweigert (Editors). W. H. Freeman and Co., San Francisco, Calif.

RICE, E. E., DALY, M. E., BEUK, J. F., and ROBINSON, H. E. 1945. The distribution and comparative content of certain B-complex vitamins in pork muscular tissues. Arch. Biochem. *7*, 239.

ROSE, W. C., WIXOM, R. L., LOCKHART, H. B., and LAMBERT, G. F. 1955. The amino acid requirements of man. XV. The valine requirement, summary, and final observations. J. Biol. Chem. *217*, 987.

SCHWEIGERT, B. S., and PAYNE, B. J. 1956. A summary of the nutrient content of meat. Am. Meat Inst. Found. Bull. *30*, Chicago, Ill.

SIEDLER, A. J., KIZLAITIS, L., and DEIBEL, C. 1963. Nutritional quality of variety meats. Proximate composition, vitamin A, vitamin C, and iron content of raw and cooked variety meats. Am. Meat Inst. Found. Bull. *54*, Chicago, Ill.

TERRELL, R. N., LEWIS, R. W., CASSENS, R. G., and BRAY, R. W. 1967. Fatty acid compositions of bovine subcutaneous fat depots determined by gas-liquid chromatography. J. Food Sci. *32*, 516.

TU, C., POWRIE, W. D., and FENNEMA, O. 1967. Free and esterified cholesterol content of animal muscles and meat products. J. Food Sci. *32*, 30.

WATT, B. K., and MERRILL, A. L. 1963. Composition of foods—raw, processed, and prepared. U.S. Dept. Agr., Agr. Handbook *8*, U.S. Govt. Printing Office, Washington, D.C.

CHAPTER 3

Curing

Although salt was used for preserving fish as far back as 3500 B.C., the origin of its use in curing meat is lost in antiquity. Homer in the *Odyssey,* written about the 8th century B.C., describes sausage made by adding salt to meat. By the 5th century B.C., production of salted meat products had become commonplace. Ancient man was well aware of the preservative action of salt, which was probably discovered by accident. It is also probable the color-preserving properties of saltpeter (nitrate) were discovered as a result of its presence as an impurity in salt.

Early dry cured meat products were extremely variable in quality, often being too salty and lacking in uniformity of cure. Scientific principles were not applied to meat curing until the latter half of the 19th century, when the growing meat packing industry began to find ways of improving quality. Present rapid curing methods, such as brine injection procedures, are of more recent origin. They were not used commonly until the 1940's. Many innovations have occurred in meat curing during the last 25 years, which have been made possible by advances in equipment design and greater mechanization.

Meat curing was used originally almost entirely as a means of preserving meat during times of plenty to carry over to times of scarcity. Until the successful advent of refrigeration and its availability in the home, curing continued to be designed solely as a means of preservation. The almost universal availability of home refrigerators has, however, greatly altered the reasons for curing. Today, cured meat products are generally mild-cured and must be stored under refrigeration. This chapter deals primarily with the curing of primal meat cuts; but the cure ingredients, together with the discussion of cured meat color development, apply to sausage and cured canned meats as well.

INGREDIENTS UTILIZED IN MEAT CURING

Although a variety of compounds can be used in curing meat, the basic curing ingredients are salt, sugar or some other sweetener, and nitrite and/or nitrate, In addition, phosphates are commonly added to pickle cures in commercial operations. A number of other compounds are sometimes used in curing mixtures, such as various spices, baking soda, sodium erythorbate, hydrolyzed vegetable proteins and monosodium glutamate.

40

Salt

Salt is basic to all curing mixtures and is the only ingredient necessary for curing. Salt acts by dehydration and altering of the osmotic pressure so that it inhibits bacterial growth and subsequent spoilage. Use of salt alone, however, gives a harsh, dry, salty product that is not very palatable. In addition, salt alone results in a dark, undesirable colored lean that is unattractive and objectionable to consumers.

As a consequence of undesirable effects of salt upon flavor and appearance, it is generally used in combination with both sugar and nitrite and/or nitrate. A limited number of products still are sometimes cured with salt alone. Cuts cured in this way are strictly fatty cuts containing little if any lean tissue. Cuts such as clear plates, fat backs, jowls, or heavy bellies that are intended for seasoning of other food products, including pork and beans, may occasionally be cured with salt alone. Even in the case of such fatty cuts, nitrite and/or nitrate is sometimes used. When salt is used alone, it is added in excess since the extreme saltiness is commonly modified by cooking with other food products.

Only food-grade salt should be used in curing, since impure salt can cause flavor and color problems. Although dry salt curing utilizes salt in excess, the amount used in other dry-curing methods and pickles is variable, depending upon the end product desired. Pickle cures vary from 50 to 85°, 65° pickles being most common. An acceptable level of salt in hams has been reported to be about 3% and about 2% for bacon. Of course, higher and lower salt levels are common and are a matter of personal preference.

Sugar and Corn Syrup Solids

The addition of sugar to cures is primarily for flavor. Sugar softens the products by counteracting the harsh hardening effects of salt by preventing some of the moisture removal and by a direct moderating action on flavor. Sugar also interacts with the amino groups of the proteins and, upon cooking, forms browning products which enhance the flavor of cured meats. In some instances, the browning reaction may become too pronounced and burned flavors result. Sugar substitutes have been used in bacon cures to prevent excessive browning during cooking. Corn syrup, molasses, and other natural sugar substitutes are sometimes used in place of sugar. The extent of substitution is largely a matter of cost after determining the relative effects upon flavor and color.

Sugar, also, is an effective preservative and will retard bacterial growth. However, the level used in meat curing is so low it is doubtful sugar has any major influence on the bacteria. Some people have claimed that sugar supports the growth of desirable flavor producing bacteria, but there is no evidence to support this viewpoint.

The proportion of sugar used in curing varies widely in commerical operations. Most processors use only 20 to 30 lb per 100 gal. of brine. At this level, sugar probably plays only a minor role in flavor development. Carefully controlled studies have suggested that consumers prefer about 2% sugar in cured hams. This would require about 160 lb sugar per 100 gal. brine. Unfortunately, similar data are not available for other products.

Corn syrup or corn syrup solids are frequently substituted for sugar. As the names imply, corn syrup solids consist of corn syrup from which most of the water has been removed, while corn syrup contains a higher level of moisture. Either corn syrup or corn syrup solids may be purchased in bulk quantities. Since they differ only in the amount of moisture, they will be considered together without differentiation.

Corn syrup is composed of a mixture of sugars formed by breakdown of starch and contains dextrose, maltose, higher sugars, dextrins, and polysaccharides. Corn syrup is not as sweet and is less soluble than sugar. However, both corn syrup solids and corn syrup are used widely in curing meat because they cost considerably less. The amount of corn syrup solids is limited to 50 lb per 100 gals brine under Federal inspection regulations. Furthermore, the amount of corn syrup or sugars present in any seasonings added to the cure must also be considered in the total.

Nitrite and/or Nitrate

The function of nitrite in meat curing is fourfold: (1) to stabilize the color of the lean tissues, (2) to contribute to the characteristic flavor of cured meat, (3) to inhibit growth of a number of food poisoning and spoilage microorganisms, and (4) to retard development of rancidity. Although color stabilization was originally the primary purpose of adding nitrite to curing mixtures, its effects upon flavor and inhibition of bacterial growth are even more important. Nevertheless, the attractive pink-red color of cured meat adds to its desirability. The effect of nitrite on the flavor of cured meat has only recently been demonstrated. However, the most important reason for adding nitrite to meat cures appears to be its effect on microbial growth. It has been clearly demonstrated that nitrite is effective in preventing the growth of the *Clostridium botulinum* organism. Evidence also suggests the levels of nitrite found in cured meat may also aid in preventing the growth of other spoilage and food poisoning organisms.

Nitrate serves principally as a source of nitrite.

Nitrosamines.—The reaction of nitrous acid (which is formed by the breakdown of nitrite) with secondary amines to produce nitrosamines is a well-known reaction in organic chemistry. The reaction of nitrous acid with dimethylamine is shown below:

$$CH_3 \diagdown \!\!\!\! {>} NH \;+\; HONO \longrightarrow \; CH_3 \diagdown \!\!\!\! {>} N\text{-}NO + H_2O$$

dimethylamine   nitrous acid   dimethylnitrosamine

Until recently, nitrosamines were not of concern in meat curing. However, demonstration that nitrosamines are carcinogenic compounds has raised the question as to their occurrence in cured meats. Since nitrite is present in the cure and meat contains an abundance of secondary amines, it was assumed that nitrosamines may be present in cured meat. To date, results suggest that nitrosamines are not normally formed during curing, but they have been isolated from cured meats in a few instances. Work is now under way to determine the factors that control their formation. It has been shown that the structure has an influence on their stability, but the final answer is not yet available.[1]

Levels of Nitrite and/or Nitrate.—Nitrates were used as the only color-stabilizing element for meat curing until 1925. At that time, the U.S. Department of Agriculture also approved the use of sodium nitrite.

Federal meat inspection regulations permit the use of the following quantities of nitrate: 7 lb to 100 gal pickle, 3½ oz to 100 lb meat (dry cure), and 2¾ oz to 100 lb chopped meat. The same regulations permit use of nitrite at the following levels: 2 lb to 100 gal pickle at 10% pump level, 1 oz to 100 lb meat (dry cure), ¼ oz to 100 lb chopped meat. The regulations further state that the use of nitrite or nitrate, or a combination of both, shall not result in more than 200 ppm nitrite in finished products. The legal level permitted is sometimes less than the residual level allowed. This is evident in the case of the ¼ oz nitrite permitted in 100 lb chopped meat, which is only 156 ppm at the time of formulation.

Phosphates

Phosphates are added to the cure to increase the water-binding capacity and thereby the yield of finished product. The action of phosphates in improving water retention appears to be twofold—(1) raising the

[1] The FDA ordered on July 19, 1973 manufacturers of meat curing premixes which combine nitrite curing agents with seasoning to package the nitrite and seasoning separately to eliminate the possibility of nitrosamine formation in premixes. The FDA action will not affect manufacturers who use a chemical "buffer" to separate the nitrite and the seasoning in a premix. Nitrosamines have not been found in such premixes, which constitute a majority of such products now in use. As a safety precaution, however, FDA is requiring any manufacturer who wishes to market such premixes to submit a food additive petition as further assurance that the premixes are free of nitrosamines.

pH and (2) causing an unfolding of the muscle proteins, thereby making more sites available for water binding. Only alkaline phosphates are effective for improving water binding since acid phosphates may lower the pH and cause greater shrinkage.

Phosphates will improve the retention of brine, and improvements in yields have been noted. With addition of phosphates to pumping brines, it is not difficult to obtain finished yields for intact hams and shoulders of over 100%.

Because of the corrosive nature of phosphates, the equipment utilized must be made of stainless steel or plastic. Canned hams pumped with phosphates should always be placed in anodized cans, where an aluminum insert is selectively corroded and the can *per se* is protected, or wrapped in polyethylene film. Another problem sometimes encountered in utilizing phosphates has been the occurrence of crystals on the surface of the cured products. Such crystals have been identified as disodium phosphates. The excess salt appears to be due to hydrolysis of the polyphosphates by the natural phosphatase in meat. Prevention of the condition can be achieved by reducing the level of phosphate in the cure and maintaining a high relative humidity in the product environment.

Tripolyphosphates have been the most widely used of all the phosphates utilized in meat curing. Most recently, it has been shown there are advantages in using alkaline compounds in combination with tripolyphosphates in regard to increasing finished yields for hams and other cured products. Apparently, the other alkaline compounds increase the effectiveness over that of tripolyphosphate alone. Their action is probably synergistic and in some way increases water binding. The compounds utilized have not been fully described since the new combination product is patented and sold under a trade mark.

Although some claims have been made that phosphates improve color retention and flavor, there is little evidence to support such viewpoints.

Sodium tripolyphosphate, sodium hexametaphosphate, sodium acid pyrophosphate, sodium pyrophosphate, and disodium phosphate have all been approved for production of cured primal cuts, but only sodium acid pyrophosphate is permitted in sausages. Legal limits for added residual phosphates are set at 0.5% in the finished product. Since meat contains 0.01% of natural phosphate, this must be subtracted in calculating the level added during curing.

Sodium Erythorbate

The salts of ascorbic acid and erythorbic acid are commonly used to hasten development and stabilize the color of cured meat. In practice, only sodium erythorbate or sodium ascorbate are used in curing pickles, since ascorbic or erythorbic acid reacts with the nitrite to form nitrous oxide. Since nitrous oxide is dangerous in confined spaces and the nitrite is destroyed, ascorbates are always used under practical conditions. This group of compounds, which will be referred to as ascorbates during the remainder of this discussion, serves three main functions: (1) ascorbates take part in the reduction of metmyoglobin to myoglobin, thereby accelerating the rate of curing; (2) ascorbates react chemically with nitrite to increase the yield of nitric oxide from nitrous acid; (3) excess ascorbate acts as an antioxidant, thereby stabilizing both color and flavor.

Ascorbate may be used in both intact cuts and sausages, but the greatest advantage of its use is in sausages, where the time of processing can be greatly reduced; in processing frankfurters, the time can be reduced by one-third if ascorbates are added. This eliminates the waiting period normally needed for breakdown of nitrite and formation of the stable pink pigment in the absence of ascorbate. If ascorbate is added to the cure, emulsion-type products can go directly into the smokehouse after stuffing, without waiting for color development.

The antioxidant properties of ascorbate not only prevent development of rancidity, but also prevent fading of sliced meats upon exposure to light. Protection is closely associated with prevention of heme catalyzed lipid oxidation, which results in both pigment degradation and development of rancidity. As long as excess ascorbate is present, the pigments are protected against breakdown. Upon depletion of ascorbate, however, the heme pigments are degraded and apparently catalyze lipid oxidation.

Federal regulations permit addition of 0.75 oz ascorbic acid or erythorbic acid (0.875 oz sodium ascorbate or erythorbate) per 100 lb sausage emulsion, or addition of 75 oz (87.5 oz of sodium salts) per 100 gal pickle for curing primal cuts. Pickles containing both sodium nitrite and sodium ascorbate are stable for at least 24 hr when maintained at 50°F and pH 6.0 or higher. However, longer periods of storage are not advisable, and if the pickle is to be stored for extended periods, it should be analyzed and the necessary ascorbate added to bring it back to the original concentration.

Monosodium Glutamate

Monosodium glutamate (MSG) has been used in a number of products to enhance the flavor. It has not, however, been widely used in the meat industry as there is little advantage in its use in good meat products, although mixed meat dishes may profit from its meat flavor-enhancing properties.

Hydrolyzed Vegetable Proteins

Addition of hydrolyzed vegetable proteins (HVP) to sausages and other meat products has been utilized by some processors. HVP is said to improve flavor and effectively increase the protein content. Its use in meat products has, however, gained little acceptance by the processing industry. It is used most commonly in kosher sausage products. Some smaller processors have also used HVP in cured hams.

CURED MEAT COLOR

In order to understand color development during meat curing, it is necessary to have knowledge of the pigments in muscle and the chemical reactions they undergo during curing. Color develops as a result of the interaction of nitrites with the muscle pigments. Thus, the structure and importance of the pigments will be discussed in light of their reactions and their effects upon meat color.

Muscle Pigments

There are a number of muscle pigments in meat, including myoglobin, hemoglobin, the cytochromes, catalase, the flavins, and other colored substances. Quantitatively, the first two listed, myoglobin and hemoglobin, are by far the most abundant. Although the lesser pigments could play key roles in color development and stabilization, most of our knowledge about meat color deals with myoglobin and hemoglobin.

Myoglobin and hemoglobin are both complex proteins that undergo similar reactions in meat. However, their roles in living tissue are quite different. Hemoglobin is the red pigment found in blood and acts as the carrier for oxygen to the tissues. Myoglobin is the predominant pigment in muscle and serves as the storage mechanism for oxygen at the cellular level. Because of the differences in function, myoglobin has a greater affinity for oxygen. The rapid uptake of oxygen by myoglobin is evident in meat upon exposure of a freshly cut surface to the air, as manifested by the rapid brightening in color as it takes up oxygen.

Although hemoglobin is the predominant pigment in the living animal, after slaughter by bleeding, myoglobin becomes the major pigment. Myoglobin accounts for only 10% of the total iron in the live animal, but after bleeding, may account for as much as 95% of the iron in the beef skeletal muscle. Nevertheless, hemoglobin is still present in appreciable quantities and may play an important part in meat color.

The amount of myoglobin and hemoglobin in various tissues varies with (1) amount of muscular activity of the tissue, (2) blood supply, (3) oxygen availability, and (4) age of the animal. Tissues having a high degree of muscular activity tend to have greater proportions of both myoglobin and hemoglobin. For example, the heart is the most active muscle in the body and contains relatively large amounts of both hemoglobin and myoglobin by virtue of its high oxygen requirements. Tissues with a relatively good blood supply tend to have more hemoglobin and relatively less myoglobin than muscles having a poorer oxygen supply. This is evident in the wing muscles of birds where the demands for oxygen are largely supplied by an efficient circulatory system. If the tissues are able to store large quantities of oxygen, the myoglobin content is relatively high and the hemoglobin content relatively low. The whale has the ability to store large quantities of oxygen because of its extremely high myoglobin content, and thus can remain submerged for extended periods of time. In regard to age, the young animal has less myoglobin and relatively more hemoglobin than older animals of the same species. This is shown by the following values for myoglobin for fresh bovine skeletal muscle: veal, 1 to 3 mg per g; beef, 4 to 10 mg per g; and old beef animals, 16 to 20 mg per g. Pork contains 1 to 3 mg per g for young animals of slaughter weight, but may reach 8 to 12 mg per g in old animals. Lamb may vary from 3 to 8 mg per g, but old ewes and rams may reach levels from 12 to 18 mg per g.

Much of the knowledge about myoglobin was derived from earlier work by blood chemists and physiologists studying the structure and functions of hemoglobin. More recently, however, myoglobin has been extensively studied in its own right by protein chemists, who have detailed its exact amino acid sequence. Although myoglobin and hemoglobin undergo essentially the same reactions, they do have significant differences in structure. Both of these important pigments are molecules composed of a protein, known as globin, complexed to a nonprotein moiety containing iron. Although the globin portion of hemoglobin and myoglobin is similar in structure, the exact amino acid sequence is slightly different. Furthermore, there are slight differences between the globin from different species. The iron-containing fraction of the molecule is known as heme and is composed of two parts—an iron atom and a larger planar ring called porphyrin. The porphyrin is made up of four heterocyclic pyrrole rings linked together by methene bridges. When the hemes and globin are complexed together by the side chains and the iron nucleus, the resulting compounds are either myoglobin or hemoglobin. An essential difference in structure between myoglobin and hemoglobin is that myoglobin complexes only one heme group per molecule, whereas, hemoglobin contains four hemes per molecule. Thus, myoglobin has a molecular weight of 16,000 to 17,000 as compared to approximately 64,000 for hemoglobin.

The chemical structure of myoglobin is shown in Fig. 3.1. The central atom does not contribute any electrons but has accepted 6 pairs of electrons from other atoms—5 pairs from nitrogen and 1 pair from oxygen. Four of the nitrogen atoms contributing electrons are in the porphyrin ring, while the other nitrogen atom is from the imidazole group of the histidine molecule in the amino acid chain of globin. The nature of the group attached to the iron atom of the heme at the position shown to be occupied by the OH_2 radical determines the color of the pigment, both of myoglobin and hemoglobin.

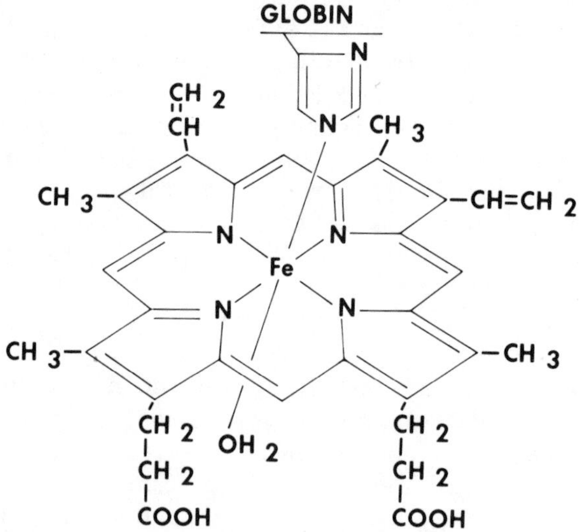

FIG. 3.1. DIAGRAM OF MYOGLOBIN MOLECULE SHOWING THE WAY THE HEME AND GLOBIN COMPLEX TOGETHER AND THE WAY IRON IS COMPLEXED WITH THE NITROGEN IN THE PYRROLE RINGS

Color of the Pigments.—In living tissue, myoglobin and hemoglobin exist in equilibrium between the reduced dull purple-red form, myoglobin and hemoglobin, and the bright red oxygenated form, oxymyoglobin and oxyhemoglobin. Upon death, the oxygen in the tissues is rapidly depleted, leaving the pigment in the dull purple-red form of myoglobin or hemoglobin. The iron can exist in the ferrous (Fe^{++}) or ferric (Fe^{+++}) forms, or as ionic (unwilling sharer of bonds) or covalent (willing sharer of bonds) bonds. The covalent form is of the greatest importance, since all the bright red pigments of both fresh and cured meat belong to this class. On the other hand, the iron in the dull red-black pigment—oxidized myoglobin and hemoglobin—exists in the ferric form. Figure 3.2 shows the nucleus of a myoglobin molecule with changes in the state of the iron and the radical attached to it, and its effects upon fresh meat color. The pigment in the oxidized form, metmyoglobin, is an undersirable brown-red, and is typical of the color observed on the exposed surface of aged meat. Although the three forms of myoglobin shown in Fig. 3.2 are interconvertible or reversible, changes from metmyoglobin to the other forms are slower and require more favorable conditions.

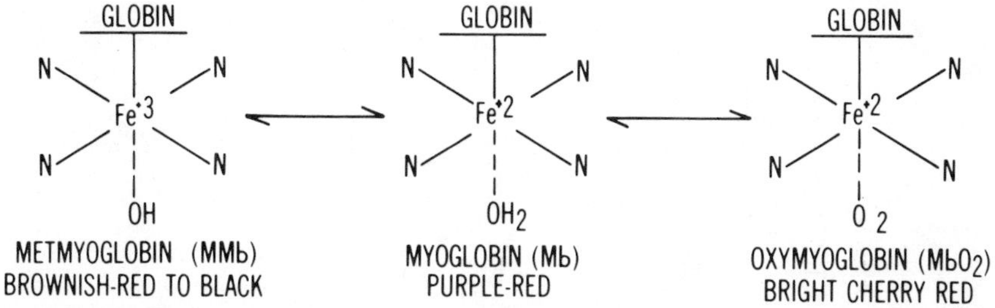

FIG. 3.2. SCHEMATIC DIAGRAM INDICATING THE IRON NUCLEUS OF THE HEME MOLECULE AND THE EFFECTS OF DIFFERENT RADICALS ATTACHED TO THE NUCLEUS UPON MEAT COLOR

The pigments containing covalent bonds are characterized spectrally by sharp peaks at 535 to 545 nm (the green portion of the spectrum) and 575 to 585 nm (blue), which gives them a bright red color. Oxymyoglobin of fresh meat, nitrosomyoglobin of cured meat and carboxymyoglobin, a combination of carbon monoxide with myoglobin, are characterized by peaks in the green and blue portion of the spectrum, and all are bright-red pigments. Myoglobin is characterized by a broad diffuse peak at 555 nm, and thus is dull red in color. In metmyoglobin, the peak is shifted to 505 nm in the blue portion of the spectrum, and has a weaker peak at 627 nm in the red part of the spectrum, the two combining to produce a brown-red color. The absorption spectra of myoglobin, metmyoglobin, and oxymyoglobin are shown in Fig. 3.3. This shows schematically the color at different parts of the spectrum, which, when combined, accounts for the color of the various products.

Myoglobin and hemoglobin can be both oxidized and oxygenated, both resulting from the presence of oxygen. The relative proportion of metmyoglobin and oxymyoglobin depends upon the partial oxygen pressure. At low oxygen pressures formation of metmyoglobin is favored, whereas high oxygen pressures favor oxymyoglobin formation. Thus, reduced myoglobin is constantly being both oxygenated and oxidized. In living tissues, and to some extent in meat, metmyoglobin is continuously reduced back to myoglobin by the action of the reducing enzymes that are naturally present in the tissues. However, the efficiency of the reducing system gradually decreases and ultimately is

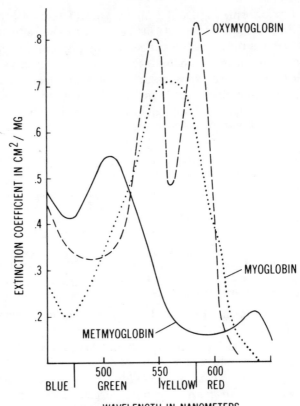

FIG. 3.3. ABSORPTION SPECTRA OF MYOGLOBIN, OXYMYOGLOBIN, AND METMYOGLOBIN FROM FRESH MEAT IN WHICH WAVE LENGTHS FOR MAXIMUM ABSORPTION AND THE PRIMARY COLOR SPECTRUM ARE DISPLAYED

depleted following death. Thus there is a gradual build-up of metmyoglobin until it predominates, and the meat color becomes a dull red or brown.

Role of Nitrite and/or Nitrate in Meat Color

Nitrite and/or nitrate are used in curing meat to counteract the undesirable effects of salt upon color. Not only is the color of fresh meat protected from degradation, but the pigments react with nitric oxide to produce the stable pigments characteristic of cured meat. These pink pigments are important to the acceptability of most processed meat products.

As indicated, both nitrite and/or nitrate are used in meat curing for color stabilization. The end result is the same in either case, although the pathway for stabilization of color by nitrite is more direct.

Nitrite requires one less step in stabilization of color, as shown in the series of reactions below:

(1) Nitrate $\xrightarrow[\text{organisms}]{\text{nitrate reducing}}$ Nitrite

(2) Nitrite $\xrightarrow[\text{absence of light and air}]{\text{favorable conditions}}$ $\underset{\text{nitric oxide}}{\text{NO}}$ + $\underset{\text{water}}{\text{H}_2\text{O}}$

(3) $\underset{\text{nitric oxide}}{\text{NO}}$ + $\underset{\text{myoglobin}}{\text{Mb}}$ $\xrightarrow[\text{conditions}]{\text{favorable}}$ $\underset{\text{metmyoglobin}}{\text{NOMMb} - \text{nitric oxide}}$

(4) NOMMb $\xrightarrow[\text{conditions}]{\text{favorable}}$ $\underset{\text{nitric oxide myoglobin}}{\text{NOMb}}$

(5) NOMb + Heat + Smoke $\xrightarrow{\hspace{1cm}}$ NO—Hemochromogen
nitroso-hemochromogen
Stable pink pigment

Since nitrate reacts quicker and less is required for color stabilization, it is being widely used in place of nitrate. Many processors prefer to use a combination of nitrite and nitrate, which gives a source of additional nitric oxide should the nitrate be depleted during curing. They believe the slower release of nitric oxide from nitrate gives them an additional safety factor over nitrite alone. Nevertheless, many highly successful operators use nitrite alone with excellent results. Trends have been toward decreased use of nitrate by the industry.

As shown by the series of reactions, nitric oxide is the active ingredient that combines with meat pigments. Although step (3) has not been proved conclusively, all evidence suggests that the original combination of nitric oxide is with the oxidized pigments, metmyoglobin and methemoglobin. The best proof for this step is the fact that the pigments in sausage become characteristically brown after adding the cure, but after heating have the characteristic pink color of cured meat, as shown in step (5). An alternate pathway for production of the stable pink pigment is possible, in which nitric oxide-metmyoglobin is not formed. In this case, myoglobin is oxidized to metmyoglobin, which is reduced back to myoglobin before combining to form nitric oxide-myoglobin. The end result is the same regardless of the pathway; nitric oxide reacts to produce the desirable and stable pink pigment of cured meat. Any hemoglobin remaining in the meat would undergo essentially the same series of reactions and also give a stable pink pigment.

Fig. 3.4 diagrammatically gives an explanation of how the various forms of myoglobin or hemoglobin fit into the total scheme to produce cured meat pigments, both desirable and undesirable.

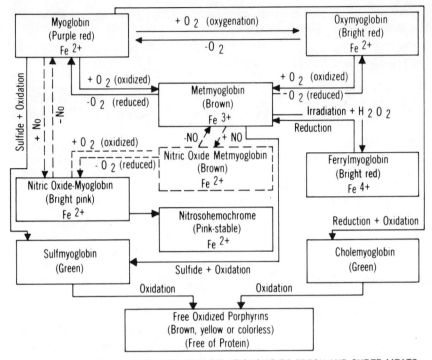

FIG. 3.4. HEME PIGMENTS IN MUSCLE IN RELATIONSHIP TO FRESH AND CURED MEATS

Broken lines indicate reactions and compounds possible but not definitely proven. Sulfmyoglobin and cholemyoglobin most frequently occur as a result of bacterial action.

CURING METHODS

Although there are a number of methods of curing primal or sub-primal cuts of meat, they are all modifications or combinations of two fundamental procedures: (1) dry curing, and (2) pickle curing. In dry curing, the curing ingredients—usually salt, sugar, and nitrite and/or nitrate—are added to meat without additional water. In this method, the curing ingredients draw enough moisture from the meat to form a brine, which serves to transport the ingredients into the meat by diffusion. In pickle curing, the ingredients are dissolved in water, which forms a brine that acts in the same general manner as that formed by the natural meat juices and the curing ingredients.

In actual practice, there are several modifications of the dry and pickle curing procedures, which are a result of combining the two methods. For example, one may start with pickle curing and end with dry curing, or vice versa. Thus, for ease of discussion the methods will not be differentiated solely upon principles, but by more specific procedures for curing, such as (1) dry salt curing, (2) conventional dry curing, (3) conventional pickle curing, (4) artery pumping, (5) stitch pumping, (6) thermal or hot cures, and (7) curing of speciality products. Each of these curing procedures will be examined in more detail.

Dry Salt Cure

The dry salt cure uses salt alone or salt in combination with nitrite and/or nitrate. As indicated earlier, the cure is primarily used in excess and mainly for fatty cuts, such as fat backs, clear plates, jowls, or heavy bellies. The advantages of dry salt curing are: (1) it is safe, that is, there is little if any spoilage, and (2) it is easy. Little special care is required to produce dry salt-cured cuts. However, dry salt curing has the disadvantages that the end product is too salty and that color is lost. Color degradation can be easily prevented by adding nitrite and/or nitrate to the cure. Since dry salt curing is used almost exclusively for fatty cuts utilized primarily for seasoning, the salty flavor is actually an advantage in practice. However, there is only a restricted and relatively low-priced market for dry salt-cured products.

Conventional Dry Curing

Dry curing in the conventional manner, which involves salt, nitrite and/or nitrate, and sugar, is sometimes utilized by the industry. However, dry curing is no longer the predominant method of curing, but is used mainly for speciality products, such as dry-cured bacon and Country-cured hams, both of which command a premium on the market. In addition, some artery-pumped hams are rubbed with a dry cure and held for a short period of time. Cuts cured by this procedure cannot be strictly classified as either dry-cured or artery-pumped, but more correctly as combination-cured. Their final properties are, however, altered by the addition of dry cure.

There are a number of modifications of the dry-curing method itself, but the procedure is essentially the same, since water is not added to the cure. These modifications depend mainly upon the container utilized in curing. Originally, much of the curing was carried out in barrels, where the brine was formed by withdrawal of natural juices from the meat by the salt. The resulting brine accumulated in the bottom of the barrel. Barrel curing, which is seldom used today, required periodic overhauling with reversal of the order with which the cuts were placed in cure each time. Use of barrels also involves unusually high space requirements, since their shape is not conducive to tight packing and efficient floor space utilization. In addition, use of space between the floor and ceiling is even less efficient.

More efficient use of space in dry curing has been achieved by using built-in shelves, which are often made of hard wood and can be made water-tight. One of the major problems encountered with this type of curing is cleaning and sanitation. Improvements in the method can be obtained by using stainless steel shelves on movable steel racks. The initial investment is high, but ease of cleaning is greatly improved.

Still another modification in the equipment used for dry curing is found in pressure boxes, which are usually made of galvanized iron or stainless steel. The boxes have a lid which can be placed on them, using a spring to generate pressure. As the pressure in the box is increased, the curing ingredients combine with the meat juices to cover the product with brine. Pressure boxes are most commonly used for bacon, jowls, and other cuts of regular shape.

There are a number of other types of equipment such as wooden and concrete vats and boxes as well as other modifications of the containers described herein. Regardless of the type of equipment, the principle of curing remains unchanged. Furthermore, the advantages and disadvantages of the procedures, although slightly altered, are essentially the same.

The time required for dry curing is usually 2 to 2½ days per lb for hams and shoulders. Bellies are commonly cured about 7 days per inch of thickness. Thus, bacon cured by this method usually requires about 10 to 14 days total time in cure. The cure is applied in 2 to 3 stages at the time of overhauling. Bacon cured in pressure boxes does not normally require overhauling, so all the cure is applied at once. The mixture of curing ingredients in dry curing varies somewhat, but a common recipe is 6.0 lb salt, 2.5 lb sugar, and 2.5 oz of nitrate or 0.25 oz nitrite per 100 lb meat, or 1 oz of curing mix per lb meat.

There are three major disadvantages to the dry curing method: (1) high cost due to poor space utilization and the amount of labor required, (2) high inventory due to slowness of curing, and (3) harsh salty flavor of the final product. Even though the salty flavor of dry cured meat is a disadvantage under average conditions, it can also be an advantage, as is found with Country-cured hams.

The advantages of conventional dry curing are: (1) a relatively high-priced specialty product is produced, and (2) cuts are less perishable because of their dryness and firmness.

Conventional dry curing is a useful procedure, but is not likely to regain any large fraction of the total cured meat market. Nevertheless, it is admirably suited to small operations, where attention can be given to the operation and high-quality products are produced. Some consumers prefer dry-cured hams and bacon and are willing to pay a premium for them.

Pickle Cure

The pickle-curing procedure uses the same ingredients as dry during, except the cure is dissolved in water to form a brine or pickle. The cuts are submerged in the pickle until the cure has completely penetrated the meat. Because the meat is packed tightly in the container, it is usually overhauled and repacked to assure uniform penetration of the brine.

All cuts can be cured by the conventional pickle-curing procedure. It is used largely by locker plant operators and other small processors. Nevertheless, some larger processors still use conventional pickle curing for certain cuts. This method is used to produce corned beef in a considerable number of plants. In this case, the method is frequently altered by stitch-pumping the larger pieces of meat to speed up the rate of curing. Since the time required for immersion pickle curing is about the same as for the dry cure, this results in an inventory reduction.

The strength of the brine is expressed in terms of degrees brine, which is essentially a measure of its density. A salometer or salinimeter is used to determine strength of the brine, and its strength is adjusted to the desired level. The water used should have a high degree of purity. It is usually cold when added, although it may be necessary to heat or add hot water to get all the curing ingredients in solution. Table 3.1 gives the necessary ingredients required to prepare brines of different salometer readings.

Hams and shoulders are normally cured from 2 to 2½ days per lb, as in dry curing. However, this will depend on the strength of the pickle and temperature of curing. The usual pickles are 60 to 70°, 70° brine being most common. As indicated earlier, most pickles contain the usual curing ingredients of salt, sugar, and nitrite and/or nitrate. Those containing sugar are sometimes referred to as sweet pickle cures.

The disadvantages, in common with those of dry curing, include: (1) poor utilization of space, and (2) slow turnover of meat inventories. Pickle cure usually gives a product with a milder flavor than dry curing, and requires less labor. However, space utilization is even poorer, since the pickle must be in a tight container.

Although pickle curing was widely used in the early part of the present century, it is now largely used in combination procedures such as artery or stitch pumping, followed by either submerging in a cover pickle or by rubbing with dry cure and holding for a short time. However, even combination procedures such as these are declining with emphasis on rapid processing.

Table 3.1

FORMULAS FOR PREPARING SWEET PICKLE CURES
OF DIFFERENT SALOMETER READINGS

Ingredients			Cold Water*		Salometer Reading at 40°F†
Salt Lb	Sugar Lb	Nitrite Gm	Gal	Lb	
10	3	28	4	33⅓	95°
9	3	28	4	33⅓	90°
10	3	33	5	41⅔	85°
8	3	28	4	33⅓	80°
8	3	33	5	41⅔	75°
6	3	28	4	33⅓	70°
7	3	33	5	41⅔	65°
6	3	33	5	41⅔	60°

* Weight of water—hot = 8.016/gal
               cold = 8.3316/gal
† Water temperature must be adjusted to 40°F to obtain an accurate salometer value.

Artery Pumping.—Artery pumping is said to have been developed by a New Zealand undertaker who decided that the principles utilized in embalming the dead could be applied in curing of meat. Thus, the method makes use of pumping a pickle or brine into the cuts through the arterial system. Since the conventional cutting procedures used to disassemble carcasses do not maintain the intact arterial system, the procedure is almost entirely limited to curing hams and to a lesser extent, picnics. Figure 3.5 shows a modern artery cure pumping operation.

The needle is usually inserted in front of the branch in the femoral artery so that the pickle goes into the entire ham. Some operators insert pickle into each branch and claim more uniformity in cure, although the operation is more time-consuming. The pumping schedule commonly calls for adding 8 to 10 percent by weight of the pump pickle. In some cases, one stitch pump (about 3 oz of pickle) is injected into the cushion. Some operators believe this minimizes undercuring and deep seated spoilage.

The curing ingredients are essentially the same as for dry curing, except the brine is dissolved in water to make a pickle. In addition to water, the pickle contains salt, sugar, and nitrite and/or nitrate. It is a common practice to also use phosphates to aid in water retention and increase yields. Nitrite has largely replaced nitrate, since the hams

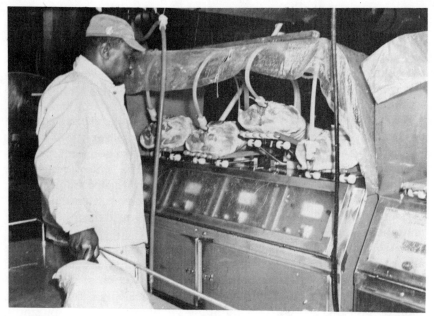

Courtesy of The National Provisioner,
Chicago, Ill.

FIG. 3.5. ARTERY CURE PUMPING OPERATION

are frequently held for very short periods before smoking, which requires rapid color development.

Some 15 to 20 years ago, hams were pumped and then placed in either brine or dry cure and held for 7 to 14 days before smoking. At present, the holding time before smoking is much shorter, many processors pumping the hams and holding for only a few hours. Some processors go directly into the smokehouse after pumping, but the majority hold them for 1 to 3 days. The use of dry cure is sometimes helpful to bring yields within legal limits. Cover pickles are also used during the holding period to complete the curing process.

The pump pickle is usually a 65 to 80° brine, 65° being the most common under commercial conditions. Sugar is usually added at a level of 20 to 30 lb per 100 gal brine; cane sugar is used most commonly. Nitrite is usually utilized instead of nitrate, and at a level of 150 ppm, or 1.5 oz per 100 gal brine. If cover pickles are used, strength of the brine is usually 55 to 60°.

The major advantage of artery pumping is the speed of curing and the attendant reduction of inventories through more rapid turnover. A second advantage is the relatively high yield, which is usually further improved by use of alkaline phosphates. The major disadvantages are: (1) it is largely limited to curing of hams and picnics and cannot be readily used for other products; (2) special care is required in cutting to maintain the artery intact; (3) hams cured by this procedure are perishable and require refrigeration. The latter disadvantage is not a serious one because the majority of consumers appear to express a preference for the mild cured product.

Single Needle Stitch Pumping.—Stitch pumping utilizes a needle having several openings, so it can be adapted to a variety of cuts. It is not dependent upon the arterial system. Usually, the operator makes 3 to 5 stitches per cut of meat, delivering about 3 oz brine per injection. However, the total amount of pickle injected is based upon adding a given weight of pickle, depending on its strength. Generally, 10% by weight of a 65° pickle containing 150 ppm nitrite plus alkaline phosphate is utilized.

Stitch pumping gives a somewhat wetter product than artery pumping and requires special care to produce a good-quality product. This is because the brine often accumulates at the injection site. As a consequence, a longer time is required for cure diffusion by stitch pumping.

Many processors use artery pumping for hams, but stitch pumping for curing picnics, shoulders, bellies, and other miscellaneous cuts. The amount of meat cured by stitch pumping and artery pumping has increased greatly in the last 20 years.

Multiple-Needle Stitch Pumping.—The regularity in shape and freedom from bone makes bellies ideally suited for curing by injection pumping. Hams, both bone-in and boneless, are also injection-cured. Mechanization of the pumping operation using the same principles as utilized in stitch pumping provided the real impetus for change. The results have been greatly reduced labor costs and a reduction in the time required for production. Pickle injection has also increased yields, all of which have contributed to lower production costs. The quality of the final product is not as high as for dry-cured bacon, since the flavor is less desirable and cooking shrinkage is greater. Nevertheless, it has been estimated that about 80% of U.S. bacon production is produced by injection-curing.

There are several models of machines for injecting the cure into bellies and hams. Most injection equipment contains a series of off-set needles. Upon activation, pickle is pumped until the desired weight is obtained. Since the pickle enters through a large number of needles spaced relatively close together, the distribution of pickle is excellent. This results in rapid curing. Figure 3.6 shows a belly stitch pumping operation.

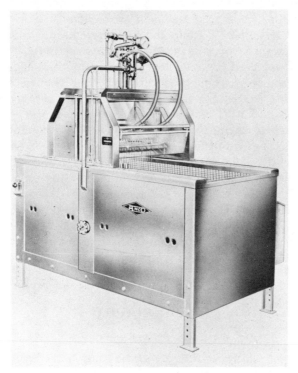

Courtesy of Allbright-Nell Co.,
Chicago, Ill.

FIG. 3.6. INJECTION PUMP

Thermal or Hot Cures

In recent years, several groups have experimented with hot cures, which can be either hot dry cures or hot pickles. The hot cures speed up the rate of curing and allow acceleration of the entire processing operation. To achieve maximum advantages from heating, the curing ingredients must be distributed into the tissues rapidly before the cure becomes cold.

Hot pickle cures can best be applied by artery pumping or stitch pumping. There are advantages in raising the temperature of the products either before or immediately after injection. This can best be achieved by placing them in the heated pickle. Best results with the hot-pickle method have been achieved using a 70° pickle at a temperature of 135 to 140°F. Hams should not be held in the hot pickle for periods longer than 1 hour, while 30 min is adequate. Following the heating period, the hams can go directly into the smokehouse. Holding overnight before smoking gives the best results.

Hot dry cure is not well adapted to large cuts but can be used to produce dry-cured bacon. One machine utilizes a series of off-set needles similar to those used for injection of brine into bellies, except they are used solely for making perforations in the tissues. The hot dry cure is then applied to the perforated bellies and rapidly penetrates the tissues; 3 to 5 lb of cure are recommended per 100 lb of bellies. A temperature of curing between 48 to 50°F is recommended, with 3 to 5 days total curing time. This curing procedure is patented. The advantages claimed for hot dry curing are: (1) rapid curing with reduction of inventory, (2) greater amounts of smoke flavor, as smoke also penetrates the perforations, (3) increased yields over dry-curing, although lower than injection-cured bellies, (4) absence of pickle pockets, and (5) improved flavor. The disadvantages include problems in heating and applying the cure and the reduced yields as compared to injection curing. Also, hot dry curing is adapted only to relatively thin cuts.

BIBLIOGRAPHY

American Meat Institute. 1944. Pork Operations. Institute of Meat Packing, Univ. of Chicago, Chicago, Ill.

BODWELL, C. E., and McCLAIN, P. E. 1971. Proteins. *In* The Science of Meat and Meat Products, J. F. Price, and B. S. Schweigert (Editors). W. H. Freeman and Co., San Francisco, Calif.

BRADY, D. E., SMITH, F. H., TUCKER, L. N., and BLUMER, T. N. 1949. The characteristics of country style hams as related to sugar content of curing mixture. Food Res. *14*, 303.

DUNKER, C. F., BERMAN, M., SNIDER, G. G., and TUBIASH, H. S. 1953. Quality and nutritive properties of different types of commercially cured hams. III. Vitamin content, biological value of protein and bacteriology. Food Technol. *7*, 288.

FAN, T. Y., and TANNENBAUM, S. R. 1972. Stability of N-nitroso compounds. J. Food Sci. *37*, 274.

GIDDINGS, G. G., and MARKIKIS, P. 1972. Characterization of the red pigments produced from ferrimyoglobin by ionizing radiation. J. Food Sci. *37*, 361.

GREENBERG, R. A. 1972. Nitrite in the control of *Clostridium botulinum*. *In* Proceedings of the Meat Industry Research Conference. American Meat Institute Foundation, Chicago, Ill.

HOAGLAND, R., *et al.* 1947. Composition and nutritive value of hams as affected by method of curing. Food Technol. *1*, 540.

KOLARI, O. E., and AUNAN, W. J. 1972. The residual level of nitrite in cured meat products. 18th Meeting European Meat Research Workers *2*, 422. American Meat Institute Foundation, Chicago, Ill.

MARQUARDT, R. A., PEARSON, A. M., LARZELERE, H. E., and GREIG, W. S. 1963. Use of the balanced lattice design in determining consumer preferences for ham containing 16 different combinations of salt and sugar. J. Food Sci. *28*, 421.

PEARSON, A. M., BATEN, W. D., GOEMBEL, A. J., and SPOONER, M. E. 1962. Application of surface-response methodology to predicting optimum levels of salt and sugar in cured ham. Food Technol. *16*, No. 5, 137.

CHAPTER 4

Smoking

It seems probable that nomadic man first discovered the preservative action and the desirable flavor imparted to meat that was hung near his fire. Regardless of its origin, smoking, like curing, of meat has been practiced since the beginning of recorded history. Curing and smoking of meat are closely interrelated and are often practiced together, i.e., cured meat is commonly smoked, and vice versa. Smoking of meat is also difficult to separate from cooking, since heat has traditionally been applied at the same time as smoke. However, the application of smoke and heat together are not necessarily closely allied, as smoke and heat can be applied either together or separately. Thus there are both hot and cold smoking of meat; however, even cold smoking usually requires some increase in temperature.

Smoking, like curing, has a preservative effect on meat. With mechanical refrigeration, the importance of preservation had declined. Today, mild-smoked, cured products are often eaten to add variety and attractiveness to the diet. Consequently, smoke serves primarily to provide variation in flavor. The highly smoked products of earlier times have largely disappeared, although consumers in some countries still prefer highly smoked meat products. Examples of this are commonly seen in northern European contries and in Iceland, where heavily smoked meat products are still preferred.

PURPOSES OF SMOKING

The primary purposes of smoking meat are: (1) development of flavor, (2) preservation, (3) creation of new products, (4) development of color, and (5) protection from oxidation. By smoking of meat and creation of new flavors, an entirely different group of meat products has been developed. Formerly, many of these products were heavily smoked; but the trend is now toward less smoke flavor, many commercial products containing only a small trace of it. In fact, it is conceivable that smoke could be completely eliminated without any serious effect on the acceptability of a great many products.

Smoking and cooking, which are generally carried out together, are also involved in development of color. This is true for the development of cured meat color, which is stabilized by heating. Furthermore, the brown color developed on the surface of many processed meat products is also enhanced by smoking.

The browning or the Maillard reaction (after the French chemist who first described browning) is **responsible for development of the characteristic brown color on the surface of smoked products.** Although the exact mechanism of browning is not fully known, it involves reaction of the free amino groups from proteins or other nitrogenous compounds with the carbonyl groups from sugars and other carbohydrates. Since carbonyls are major components of wood smoke, they play a major role in browning during smoking of meat. A proposed mechanism for the development of browning is outlined below:

$$
\begin{array}{c}
HC = O \\
| \\
(CHOH)_n \\
| \\
CH_2OH
\end{array}
+ RNH_2
\rightleftharpoons
\begin{array}{c}
RNH \\
| \\
HCOH \\
| \\
(CHOH)_n \\
| \\
CH_2OH
\end{array}
\xrightarrow{- H_2O}
\begin{array}{c}
RN \\
\| \\
CH \\
| \\
(CHOH)_n \\
| \\
CH_2OH
\end{array}
$$

Aldose   *Amine*   *Addition Product*   *Schiff's base*

$$
\begin{array}{c}
RNH \\
| \\
HC \\
| \quad\quad \rceil \\
(CHOH)_{n-1} \quad O \\
| \quad\quad \rfloor \\
HC \\
| \\
CH_2OH
\end{array}
\xrightleftharpoons{+2H^+}
\begin{array}{c}
RNH \\
| \\
CH \\
\| \\
COH \\
| \\
(CHOH)_n \\
| \\
CH_2OH
\end{array}
\xrightarrow[-NH_2]{-CO_2}
\begin{array}{c}
CH\text{---}CH \\
\| \quad\quad \| \\
C \quad\quad CCHO \\
\searrow \quad \swarrow \\
O
\end{array}
$$

N-substituted   *Enol*   *Furfural*
glycosylamine

    The first step in nonenzymatic browning is aldol condensation, which is followed by the Schiff's base formation and ultimately by Amadori rearrangement. The final step is Strecker degradation, which is not completely understood. The final reaction results in formation of furfurals or hydroxymethyl furfurals, which are brown or black in color.

    The reaction is not fully understood and involves a number of intermediate steps, which have not been fully elucidated. The important steps in the reaction then involve aldol condensation, Schiff's base formation, and Amadori rearrangement, with ultimate production of brown or black furfural compounds. These reactions occur only in neutral or acidic conditions with formation of a Schiff's base ring compound of hydroxymethyl furfural or furfural. Although there are other possible pathways for development of brown color on smoking meat, the mechanism discussed here seems to be the most logical in view of conditions present in the product. Obviously, only a few of the total reactive carbonyls and free amino groups actually participate in formation of the furfural compounds, which give the brown color to smoked meat.

One of the most important properties of smoke is its effect upon the bacterial population. Smoking of bacon has been shown to greatly reduce the number of surface bacteria and to extend its storage life. This is due to the bactericidal and bacteriostatic properties of smoke. These properties are attributable to certain components in the smoke, such as the phenols and acids which will be discussed later. Unquestionably, removal of moisture from the surface of meat during smoking also retards and reduces bacterial growth.

Smoke is also known to have a definite influence upon the development of rancidity by virtue of its antioxidant activity. This extends the shelf life of smoked meat products and helps to account for their desirability. The antioxidant activity of smoke will be discussed in greater detail under the specific components found in smoke that contribute this important property.

COMPOSITION OF SMOKE

Over 200 different compounds have been isolated from wood smoke. This does not necessarily mean that all these compounds occur in smoked meat, as the temperature of combustion, conditions in the combustion chamber, oxidative changes in the compounds formed and many other factors influence smoke composition. Furthermore, many of the compounds present in smoke are of little importance from the standpoint of either flavor or preservation. The most important components of smoke are generally considered to be phenols, acids, alcohols, carbonyl compounds, and hydrocarbons.

Phenols

About 20 different phenols have been isolated from wood smoke and identified. Among them are guaiacol, 4-methylguaiacol, phenol, 4-ethylguaiacol, o-cresol, m-cresol, p-cresol, 4-propylguaiacol, eugenol (4-allylguaiacol), 4-vinylguaiacol, vanillin, 2,6-dimethoxyphenol, 2,6-dimethoxy-4-methylphenol, and 2,6-dimethoxy-4-propylphenol. Although other phenols have reportedly been isolated from distillates of wood smoke, they have been reported in only one study and it is doubtful if they are common components of smoke. The exact importance of individual phenols in wood smoke is not known, but the somewhat variable composition reported by different investigators suggests the individual components are not as important as a number of different phenols. The effect of altering smoking conditions upon the total phenol content will be discussed later.

Phenols appear to play a threefold role in the smoking of meats and other foods: (1) they act as antioxidants, (2) they contribute a smoky note to the flavor of smoked products, and (3) they have a bacteriostatic effect, that contributes to preservation. The role of phenols in preventing oxidative changes in smoked meat is most important. Undoubtedly, the antioxidant activity of smoke is one of its most important attributes in smoked foods. Most researchers agree that phenols contribute to the smoky flavor characteristic of smoked meat. Phenols are known to possess strong bacteriostatic activity; in fact, this property has led to the use of the phenol coefficient as a standard method for expressing the effectiveness of different germicides relative to phenol.

Since smoke is largely concentrated on the surface of smoked-meat products, the total phenol concentration at varying depths has sometimes been used to express the depth of penetration and concentration of smoke. However, total phenol concentration is not always equivalent because the individual phenols are not equal in either color or flavor. Thus, the use of total phenols to measure the smoked flavor of meat is not necessarily closely related to sensory evaluation.

Alcohols

A wide variety of alcohols are found in wood smoke. The most common and simplest of these is methanol or wood alcohol, so-called because it is one of the main products obtained upon destructive distillation of wood. Although primary, secondary, and tertiary alcohols are all found in smoke, they are frequently oxidized to form their corresponding acids.

The role of alcohols in wood smoke appears to be primarily that of a carrier for the other volatile components. Alcohols do not seem to play any major part as contributors to flavor or aroma, although they may exert a minor bacteriocidal effect. Thus alcohols are probably one of the least important classes of components in smoke.

Organic Acids

Simple organic acids ranging from 1 to 10 carbons are components of whole smoke. Only 1- to 4-carbon acids are commonly found in the vapor phase of smoke, whereas longer-chain 5- to 10-carbon acids are in the particle phase of whole smoke. Thus formic, acetic, propionic, butyric, and isobutyric acids contribute to the vapor phase of smoke, whereas valeric, isovaleric, caproic, heptylic, caprylid, nonylic, and capric acids are located in the particle phase.

Organic acids have little or no direct influence upon the flavor of smoked products. They also appear to have only a minor preservative action, which occurs as the result of greater acidity on the surface of smoked meat.

Experience with artificial smoke preparations has shown that acid does, however, play an important part in coagulation of the surface proteins of smoked meat. Coagulation is essential in developing the outside covering on skinless frankfurters. Hence acids serve a most important function in peelability of skinless frankfurters and similar skinless sausages. Coagulation of the surface proteins is enhanced by heat, but acids also seem to be essential for good skin formation. Although this can be achieved rapidly by dipping or spraying with acid solutions, the same final effect upon skin formation is obtained more slowly by smoking. The volatile or steam-distillable acids are apparently the most useful fraction in skin formation.

Carbonyls

A large number of carbonyl compounds contribute to smoke. Similar to organic acids, they occur in the steam-distillable fraction and also in the particle phase of smoke. Well over 20 compounds have been identified: 2-pentanone, valeraldehyde, 2-butanone, butanal, acetone, propanal, crotonaldehyde, ethanal, isovaleraldehyde, acrolein, isobutyraldehyde, diacetyl, 3-methyl-2-butanone, pinacolene, 4-methyl-3-pentanone, α-methyl-valeraldehyde, tiglic aldehyde, 3-hexanone, 2-hexanone, 5-methyl furfural, methyl vinyl ketone, furfural, methacryaldehyde, methyl glyoxal, and others.

Although the largest proportion of the carbonyls are nonsteam-distillable, the steam-distillable fraction has a more characteristic smoke aroma and contains all the color from the carbonyl compounds. Thus, short-chained simple compounds appear to be most important to smoke color, flavor, and aroma.

Many of the same carbonyls found in smoke have been isolated from a wide variety of foods. This suggests that either certain carbonyl compounds contribute to smoke flavor and aroma, or more probably, the level of carbonyls in smoke is much higher and thus imparts the characteristic aroma and flavor to smoked products. Regardless of the mechanism or cause, smoke flavor and color seem to be largely due to the steam-distillable fraction of smoke.

Hydrocarbons

A number of polycylic hydrocarbons have been isolated from smoked foods. These include benz(a)anthracene, dibenz(a,h)anthracene, benz-(a)pyrene, benz(e)pyrene, benxo(g,h,i)perylene, pyrene, and 4-methyl pyrene. At least two of these compounds, benz(a)pyrene and dibenz-(a,h)anthracene, are recognized as being carcinogens. Both benz-(a)pyrene and dibenz(a,h)anthracene have been demonstrated to be carcinogenic in laboratory animals. Both have also been implicated in human cancer because Baltic Sea fishermen and Icelanders, who consume large quantities of smoked fish, have a high incidence of cancer compared to other populations.

Although the content of benz(a)pyrene and dibenz(a,h)anthracene is relatively low in most smoked foods, larger proportions have been found in smoked trout (2.1 mg/1,000 g wet weight) and mutton (1.3 mg/1,000 g wet weight). The concentration of benz(a)pyrene in other smoked fish amounts to only 0.5 mg for cod and 0.3 mg for red fish per 1,000 g of tissue. Although much higher levels of other polycylic hydrocarbons have been found in smoked foods, none of these have been demonstrated to be carcinogens.

Fortunately, the polycylic hydrocarbons do not appear to impart important preservative or organoleptic properties to smoked meats. Studies have shown that these compounds are removed in the particulate phase of smoke. Several liquid smoke preparations have been subjected to analysis and have been found to be free of benz(a) pyrene and dibenz(a,h)anthracene. Thus, smoke fractions can be prepared that are free of the undesirable hydrocarbons found in whole smoke.

PRODUCTION OF SMOKE

Wood consists of 40 to 60% cellulose, 20 to 30% hemicellulose, and 20 to 30% lignin. During thermal decomposition of wood or wood sawdust, a temperature gradient temporarily exists between the outer surface and the inner core. The outer surface is being oxidized and the inner surface is being dehydrated before it can be oxidized. The temperature of the outer surface is slightly above 212°F during the dehydration process. Carbon monoxide, carbon dioxide, and some volatile short-chain organic acids, such as acetic, are being released during the dehydration or distillation process. When the internal moisture level in the center of the sawdust approaches zero, the temperature rapidly rises to 570 to 750°F. Once the temperature falls within this range, thermal decomposition occurs and smoke is given off. Actually, most of the changes in wood of any consequence to smoke generation occur between 390 and 750°F. In the temperature range 390 to 500°F, the release of gases and a sharp increase in the amount of volatile acids is evident. Between 500 and 590°F, pyroligneous liquor and some tars are produced. As the temperature reaches 590°F or above, lignin is decomposed, yielding phenol and its derivatives.

Under normal smoking conditions, the entire range of temperatures is encountered, varying from 212 to 750°F or higher. This results in production of more than 200 components that have been isolated from whole wood smoke. The complexity of smoke composition is further influenced by the oxidative changes which result from introduction of oxygen during smoking. When the amount of air is limited severely, the resulting smoke is dark in appearance and contains relatively large amounts of carboxylic acids. Such smoke is generally undesirable for smoking of meat. Thus the design of a smoke generator should provide for adequate air during combustion.

Although combustion and oxidation occur simultaneously, it is possible to separate and study the influence of generating conditions on the quantity and quality of smoke. The quantity of acids and phenols increases as available oxygen increases, and production reaches a maximum when approximately 8 times the amount of oxygen required for complete oxidation is provided. Decomposition of lignin and production of phenols is greatest above 590°F, whereas acids are produced in larger quantities at lower temperatures; hence, as the combustion temperature is increased above 570°F, the ratio of acids to phenols is reduced. Thus there is a marked difference in smoke produced at temperatures less than 570°F compared to that generated at over 570°F. Temperatures favoring phenol production also oxidize them to other products, some of which adversely affect the aroma and flavor of smoke.

The best quality smoke is produced at a combustion temperature of 650 to 750°F and at an oxidation temperature of 390 to 480°F. Under actual operating conditions, it is not possible to separate the oxidation and combustion processes, since smoke generation is exothermic. However, it is possible to design smoking equipment that will give better control of smoke generation. A sawdust fluidizer has been developed in Europe which gives closer control of combustion temperature and rate of oxidation.

Although combustion temperatures of 750°F are desirable for maximum production of phenols, this high temperature also favors formation of benz(a)pyrene and other polycylic hydrocarbons. To minimize the production of carcinogenic substances, a more practical combustion temperature of 650°F appears to be a reasonable compromise.

THE NATURE OF SMOKE

Although smoke at the point of generation exists in a gaseous state, it rapidly partitions into a vapor and particle state. The vapor phase contains the more volatile components and is largely responsible for the characteristic flavor and aroma of smoke. Experiments making use of electrostatic precipitation of the particle phase have shown that 95% of the smoke flavor of meat products comes from the vapor stage. Furthermore, removal of the particle phase by precipitation also greatly reduces the content of tars and polycylic hydrocarbons, all of which are undesirable in smoke. This probably accounts for the failure of electrostatic smoking, which was once considered a promising method, but has since been abandoned by the industry.

As soon as the smoke is generated, numerous reactions and condensations occur. Aldehydes and phenols condense to form resins, which represent about 50% of the smoke components and are believed to provide most of the color in smoked meats. Polyphenols are also formed by condensation, and there are probably many more interactions and condensations. Obviously, condensation products may possess different properties than the original smoke components. Such changes could affect smoke desirability, uptake, and also penetration through sausage casings.

DEPOSITION OF SMOKE ON MEATS

The amount and rate of smoke deposition is influenced by (1) smoke density, (2) smokehouse air velocity, (3) smokehouse relative humidity, and (4) the surface of the product being smoked. The relation of smoke density to rate of deposition is obvious, since the denser the smoke the greater the smoke uptake. The air velocity in the house also facilitates uptake, since more rapid movement brings more smoke into contact with the meat surface. However, as high air velocity makes it more difficult to maintain high density, density and air velocity tend to be in opposition to each other. In actual practice, there is usually a compromise between the two, with enough air movement to achieve good contact with the product being smoked, but not rapid enough to greatly reduce density. Relative humidity can influence not only the rate of deposition but also the nature of the deposit. High humidity favors smoke deposition but limits color development. The moisture or lack of moisture on the product surface also influences smoke uptake; a moist surface favors uptake and a dry surface retards it.

In practice, smoke uptake and color development must be balanced in order to produce the desired product. Since some products must be dry and others more moist, the smoking process must be altered to produce the end product being manufactured. Furthermore, smoking is frequently also combined with cooking during production of many sausage and smoked-meat products. Smoking often becomes a secondary aim, cooking being the primary objective.

METHODS OF SMOKING

Smoking as originally practiced was a relatively simple process, but it became more complex but also more repeatable as it was industrialized. Old-style country smokehouses, such as those used for the smoking of Lebanon bologna in Fig. 4.1, had little or no control of temperature, humidity, or rate of combustion; these have largely been replaced with sophisticated equipment in which it is possible to regulate closely not only these three important factors but also smoke density. It is not the purpose of this discussion to describe modern smoking equipment in specific terms, but only in a general way.

Basically, there are three types of smokehouses, namely (1) natural air circulation, (2) air-conditioned or forced air, and (3) continuous. There are, in addition, many modifications of the three types. The first type is designed so that natural ventilation will occur. Regulation of the volume of air is controlled by the opening or closing of a series of dampers, thus providing natural circulation. The fire pit may be designed to use either logs, sawdust, or a combination of the two. Supplemental heat may be supplied by steam coils or gas. Sprinklers are usually installed to extinguish incipient fires.

A modification of the natural air smokehouse that has found some favor by the industry is the revolving smokehouse. It consists of an endless chain, to which the meat is attached. The endless chain keeps the meat in continuous motion. This system is particularly useful where curing is carried out on one level and smoking on another, since it eliminates the need for an elevator. Although the revolving smokehouse is well adapted to old multi-level packing plants, the higher labor requirements associated with this type of smoking have placed them at a marked disadvantage. A revolving smokehouse is shown in Fig. 4.2.

Air-conditioned or forced-ventilation smokehouses, as shown in Fig. 4.3, have largely replaced the natural air type. They are particularly useful where cooking or partial cooking is done and permit much more precise control of smoking. Even more important than the smoking process is control of the temperature for cooking and the resultant

Courtesy of The National Provisioner,
Chicago, Ill.

FIG. 4.1. OLD STYLE COUNTRY SMOKEHOUSE

control of shrinkage. Air circulation is controlled by a fan, so the air can be recirculated, exhausted, or a portion of the air exhausted and part recirculated. Thus this type smokehouse gives uniform air movement and good control of temperature. Forced-air smokehouses usually control not only air or smoke velocity, but usually also regulate humidity.

The continuous smokehouse comprises part of the continuous processing system and was developed specifically for frankfurter production.

Courtesy of The National Provisioner,
Chicago, Ill.

FIG. 4.2. REVOLVING SMOKEHOUSE

One type is shown in Fig. 4.4. The system usually produces about 1.5 to 5 tons of finished product per hour. It has the advantage of occupying less space than conventional smokehouses of similar capacity and also has a much lower labor requirement per unit of finished product. The continuous smoking system also permits better control of shrinkage. The smoking section of the continuous processing line must be equipped with supplemental smoke generators to allow cleaning and repair without shutting down the line.

The continuous smoking system offers some major advantages in space saving, speed of processing, labor savings, and allows more specific control of processing time, temperature, and relative humidity. However, the large capital investment and high output limit its usefulness.

TYPES OF FUEL

A variety of fuels have been used for smoking of meat, varying from animal dung (in some countries), to corn cobs, through a variety

*Courtesy of The National Provisioner,
Chicago, Ill.*

FIG. 4.3. FORCED AIR SMOKEHOUSE

*Courtesy of The National Provisioner,
Chicago, Ill.*

FIG. 4.4. CONTINUOUS SMOKEHOUSE

of soft and hard woods. Since there is considerable variation in the composition of various fuels, the components of smoke vary widely. The reactions involved in production of smoke will depend largely upon individual fuels and their composition.

As already indicated, wood is composed of cellulose, hemicellulose, and lignin. Upon heating, cellulose breaks down to form 1, 6-anhydroglucose, apparently by first forming glucose and then by dehydration to 1, 6-anhydroglucose. Further heating decomposes 1, 6-anhydroglucose into such products as acetic acid, phenols, water, and acetone. Hemicellulose is composed of pentosans and upon thermal decomposition produces furans, furfurals, and acids. The pentosans yield a larger quantity of acids than either cellulose or lignin. Furthermore, pentosans are the least heat-stable component in wood and tend to break down first. As mentioned previously, phenolic compounds are the major products of thermal degradation of lignin. Thermal decomposition of lignin also yields methanol, acetone, a variety of simple organic acids, a number of phenols, and a quantity of nonsteam-volatile components. There is also some evidence that both lignin and cellulose produce polycyclic hydrocarbons at high generation temperatures, particularly in the absence of oxygen.

Originally, smoldering cord wood was used as the fuel for producing smoke. However, it was soon learned that green or partially cured woods gave better control of temperature and a denser or heavier smoke. Today, most commercial smoking operations have abandoned cord wood and gone to sawdust, which is easier to utilize and gives a greater volume of smoke. This has resulted in designing of special smoke generation units using sawdust and forced air to accelerate smoke production. The sawdust is often wet down and used damp to control burning and density of smoke. Fig. 4.5 shows a bank of three modern smoke generators.

A special friction generator, in which a spinning disc is used to generate smoke upon contact with a solid wood block, has been used extensively for experimental studies. Friction-burning has produced some organoleptic differences in comparison to smoke from smoldering sawdust. It has been reported that friction-generated smoke has more carbonyls and acids but a lower level of phenols than sawdust smoke. Water-washing of friction-generated smoke has been demonstrated to improve its flavor and odor.

Hardwoods have generally been reported to be best for smoking, and softwoods such as pine have been largely avoided. However, liquid smoke has been produced satisfactorily from both hard and soft woods with excellent results. Hickory has come to be the standard of excellence for smoking meat, but it is almost impossible to obtain good hickory

Courtesy of the National Provisioner,
Chicago, Ill.

FIG. 4.5. SMOKE GENERATORS

sawdust in its pure form. Therefore, sawdust is most often a mixture of hardwoods.

COOKING DURING SMOKING

Cooking is often done simultaneously with smoking of meat. In fact, cooking is often more important than smoking in meat processing. Cooking requires careful control of the smoking and heating process to give best results. It is almost always carried out on cuts such as hams, picnics, and butts and on a great many processed sausage items. Cooking is accomplished by either steam or gas heat. Usually the humidity is increased during the early phases of cooking, since heat transfer is more efficient at a high humidity.

The final temperature reached depends upon the product and is expressed as the internal temperature achieved in the finished product. Smoked hams, butts, and picnics usually receive the minimum heat treatment necessary to destroy the trichinae organism. Federal regulations specify this as a final internal temperature of 137°F, but in practice most packers use 140°F. This allows some margin of safety. Federal regulations specify that fully cooked processed meat items must attain a minimum internal temperature of 148°F. A common internal temperature of frankfurters, bologna, and loaf items is about 155°F, while fully cooked hams are usually cooked to an internal temperature of 150 to 155°F.

Careful control of the entire cooking and smoking cycle results in higher yields. The humidity level, which is generally controlled in air-conditioned smokehouses by the gradient between the wet and dry bulb temperature, is particularly important in controlling final conditions. The exact schedule of temperatures, humidities, and times are worked out in detail by experimentation. Then the operator need only follow the schedule. A continuous recording of times, temperatures, and of wet and dry bulb readings should be made for each batch of product processed. Such information is extremely helpful in trouble shooting. Frequently, problems encountered in processing can be quickly located by examination of cooking schedules.

LIQUID SMOKE PREPARATIONS

Recently, several liquid smoke preparations have appeared on the market. Liquid smoke is used by some processors and has several advantages over natural wood smoke. First, it does not require the installation of a smoke generator, which usually requires a major financial outlay. Secondly, the process is more repeatable, as the composition of liquid smoke is more constant. Thirdly, liquid smoke can be prepared so the particle phase is removed, and thereby possible problems from carcinogens can be alleviated.

Liquid smoke is generally prepared from hardwoods, although soft woods can also be used if precautions are taken to remove the tarry substances. The tarry droplets and the polycylic hydrocarbons are removed by filtration. The final product is composed primarily of the vapor phase, and contains mainly phenols, organic acids, alcohols, and carbonyl compounds. Analyses of several liquid smoke preparations have shown they do not contain polycylic hydrocarbons, especially benz(a)pyrene. Animal toxicity studies have also supported the chemical analyses indicating that all carcinogenic substances in smoke are removed during production of liquid smoke.

Application of Liquid Smoke

Although there are a number of ways of adding liquid smoke, generally, it is sprayed on the product just before cooking. Commercially prepared liquid smoke solutions are diluted with water, or frequently with vinegar or citric acid. A typical liquid smoke solution prepared and used by meat processors consists of 20 to 30 parts liquid smoke, 5 parts citric acid or vinegar, and 65 to 75 parts water. Citric or acetic (vinegar) acids are used to enhance skin formation on skinless frankfurters and other small sausage products. Although skin formation can be achieved by spraying with liquid smoke alone, a higher concentration of smoke is required. Thus, acid is usually added to the smoke solution to reduce costs.

Use of liquid smoke makes it much easier to keep equipment clean, since deposition of tar and other residues from natural smoke requires frequent cleaning. Failure to clean regularly can result in spontaneous fires.

*Courtesy of Red Arrow Corp.,
Manitowoc, Wisc.*

FIG. 4.6. SMOKEHOUSE WITH LIQUID SMOKE INJECTION

Even though liquid smoke does away with the smoking process, cooking is still required for most meat items. Thus, it is necessary to provide cooking facilities even though the smoke generator is eliminated. Cooking after spraying with liquid smoke preparations is essential to give good smoke color formation. This is the reason that such smoke preparations should be added just before cooking. Several methods for adding liquid smoke other than spraying have been used. These include addition to the formula and dipping, but neither has been as successful as spraying. Fig. 4.6 shows a smokehouse with liquid smoke being injected through nozzles.

Present trends suggest that liquid smoke will largely replace natural wood smoke. The speed with which this occurs will no doubt be dependent upon automated procedures and upon the relative freedom from carcinogenic substances. Manufacturers and jobbers of liquid smoke are presently enjoying an excellent demand for their product and every indication points towards a continuation of this trend.

BIBLIOGRAPHY

ANON. 1965. Hydrocarbon residues in cooked and smoked meats. Nutr. Rev. *23*, 268.

BAILEY, E. J., and DUNGAL, N. 1958. Polycyclic hydrocarbons in Icelandic smoked fish. Brit. J. Cancer *12*, 348.

DOERR, R. C., WASSERMAN, A. E., and FIDDLER, W. 1966. Composition of hickory sawdust smoke. Low-boiling constituents. J. Agr. Food Chem. *14*, 662.

HOWARD, J. W., TEAGUE, R. T., JR., WHITE, R. H., and FRY, B. E., JR. 1966. Extraction and estimation of polycyclic aromatic hydrocarbons in smoked foods. I. General method. J. Assoc. Offic. Agr. Chemists *49*, 595.

HOWARD, J. W., WHITE, R. H., FRY, B. E., JR., and TURICCHI, B. W. 1966. Extraction and estimation of polycyclic aromatic hydrocarbons in smoked foods. II. Benz(a)pyrene. J. Assoc. Offic. Agr. Chemists 49, 611.

JENNESS, R., and PATTON, S. 1959. Principles of Dairy Chemistry. John Wiley & Sons, New York.

LOVE, S., and BRATZLER, L. J. 1966. Tentative identification of carbonyl compounds in wood smoke by gas chromatography. J. Food Sci. *31*, 218.

PORTER, R. W., BRATZLER, L. J., and PEARSON, A.M. 1965. Fractionation and study of compounds in wood smoke. J. Food Sci. *30*, 615.

WILSON, G. D. 1961. A Summary of the Technical Aspects of Smoking Meats. Am. Meat Inst. Found. Spec. Rept. #26. American Meat Institute Foundation, Chicago, Ill.

CHAPTER 5

Meat Cookery and Cooked Meat Products

The origin of meat cookery is older than civilization itself, and, like meat curing, probably first occurred accidentally upon exposure of fresh meat to fire and/or heat. This theory has some support in the classic treatise entitled "Dissertation on Roast Pig" by Charles Lamb, the famous English author who lived during the latter part of the 18th and the early part of the 19th century. According to Lamb's humorous account, the ancient Chinese kept their pigs in the houses as pets, and upon accidental burning of one house along with the pigs, they learned that "roast pig" was indeed a delicacy. In fact, Lamb satirically suggests that it became a custom to purposely set fire to their houses as a means of preparing roast pork.

Regardless of the origin of meat cookery, it not only improved palatability but also reduced the incidence of spoilage by partial destruction of the bacterial flora. Thus, cooking meat improved the keeping qualities and extended its storage life. Cooking not only contributed to the stability of meat products, but also played a most important role in providing a variety of meat products, which can be achieved solely by modifying cooking procedures. Therefore, meat cookery has contributed greatly to advances in civilization and has helped to make it possible for a limited number of people to feed the masses.

ACTION OF COOKING

Although the cooking methods used in preparing processed meat products are generally not the same as those used for fresh meats, they are based on the same principles and utilize the same basic techniques. Therefore, this discussion will consider the action of cooking in general, with special emphasis on any variation from the traditional during processing.

Cooking has the following effects on meat and meat products: (1) it coagulates and denatures the meat proteins, at the same time altering their solubility and effecting changes in color; (2) it improves meat palatability by intensifying the flavor and altering the texture; (3) it destroys considerable numbers of microorganisms and improves the storage life of meat products; (4) it inactivates indigenous proteolytic enzymes in meat and prevents development of off-flavors; (5) it decreases the water content of raw meat, especially on the surface, which in turn lowers the water activity and improves the peelability of frankfurters and extends their shelf life; (6) it stabilizes the red

78

color in cured meats, and (7) it modifies the texture or tenderness of meat and meat products.

Denaturation and Changes in Solubility

Upon cooking meat, the physical changes first became evident by coagulation on the surface. As this occurs, the color changes from red to gray or grayish brown. Coagulation is also accompanied by denaturation of the proteins, which can be measured quantitatively by determining their decreased solubility in selected solvent systems relative to their solubility prior to cooking. In cured processed meat, the color does not become grayish-brown as cooking proceeds, but the nitrite reacts with the muscle pigments to produce a stable pink color (see Chapter 3). However, denaturation and solubility changes appear to be the same as for fresh meat.

Although the exact nature of denaturation and coagulation is not fully understood, there are distinct and easily recognized physical changes in meat proteins during cooking. The solidifying of the muscle juices and the color changes are readily observable and are closely associated with the alteration in solubility. The initial changes are confined to the surface, but as time and temperature are increased, the action penetrates further into the interior of the meat. Thus, well-done meat will show the characteristic coagulated gray appearance even in the center of the cut. These changes can be easily observed in canned meat or in precooked frozen meat. In fact, on importing precooked frozen meat into the United States from countries with hoof-and-mouth disease, lack of the characteristic gray color is a basis for rejection, since the meat must be "thoroughly cooked" to destroy the causative virus. However, the more complex changes, which are manifested by decreased solubility, are not always readily observable.

Denaturation and coagulation involve changes in the protein molecule. This may be due to unfolding of the protein or the loss of its characteristic conformation, which decrease its solubility. Obviously, there could be changes in the number of lipophilic (fat-loving) and hydrophilic (water-loving) bonds, which will greatly affect the solubility in any solvent system.

Denaturation and the accompanying changes in solubility have a most important function in emulsion-type sausages. During chopping the fat is coated with protein. Myosin in particular plays a very important role in completely covering the fat particles. Once the fat is coated with myosin, it is stable only for a period of hours, or at most about a day. Heating the emulsion, however, coagulates the protein and stabilizes the emulsion, so that the protein holds the fat in suspension for an unlimited period of time. Thus cooking has an important function in the manufacture of emulsion-type sausages such as frankfurters and bologna.

Improvement in Palatability

Cooking is a most important factor in improving the palatability of meat products. Although some people like raw meat, the majority prefer the flavor and aroma of cooked meat. Cooking intensifies the flavor of meat and changes it from the "blood-like" or "serumy" taste of fresh meat to the pronounced cooked flavor and aroma.

The aroma or odor predominates after cooking, whereas taste is the major flavor component in raw meat. Although the aroma of cooked meat has a characteristic sulfury note, there appear to be a number of other components that make important contributions to the odor. Taste becomes relatively less important as the aroma develops during cooking, but the taste of cooked meat is still very important.

The sensation of flavor, which is the combined reaction to taste and odor, is variable, and depends upon the following factors: (1) species, (2) age of the animal, (3) method of cooking and addition of curing agents and seasoning ingredients, (4) amount and kind of fat in both the raw and cooked product, (5) post-slaughter aging of the meat, and (6) the characteristic flavor imparted by pre-slaughter feeding regimes. All or some of these factors may form different combinations, and thereby produce a variety of flavors.

It has been recognized for many years that there are distinctly different flavor characteristics in the meat from different species. Research suggests that the basic meaty flavor is essentially the same in all kinds of meat, and is probably associated with the amount and kind of sulfur compounds. The species-characteristic flavor, on the other hand, appears to be due to the components of the fatty tissues, probably the carbonyl compounds.

Generally speaking, older animals have a more pronounced or stronger flavor than young animals. This fact is reinforced by comparing veal with beef, or lamb with mutton. Although some people prefer stronger flavors, others show a distinct preference for the milder flavor of younger animals. There may often be a compromise between flavor and tenderness, since young animals are more tender but have less flavor.

Methods of cooking can profoundly influence the flavor of meat; in fact, it is questionable if any other factor is so important. Browning of meat, various flavor additives used in cooking, and a variety of modifications during cooking markedly affect the flavor of the end product. The contribution of browning to meat flavor was evident in early work on dielectric cooking, where prebrowning was found to be necessary to make meat cooked by this process palatable. Roasting, frying, broiling, braising, stewing, and boiling will all produce characteristically different flavors in meat products. The effects of adding salt, onions, garlic, tomatoes, spices, and other ingredients during the cooking process are well-known, and are especially important in processed meat.

Both the amount and kinds of fat present have an influence on the flavor of meat products. Mutton and lamb are generally used in limited amounts because of the flavor of the fat. Since the fat is believed to impart the characteristic species flavor, not only the kind but the percentage of fat will have a great influence on the characteristic flavor of various meat products. Boar meat, particularly the fatty tissue, should not be used in sausages to be heated before use, since an undesirable odor emanates from the fat upon heating. However, boar meat can be used in products to be eaten cold, since the undesirable odor is only evident upon heating. Recent studies in Australia using formalin-treated unsaturated fats have suggested that alteration in the proportion of saturated and unsaturated fat may be achieved, and can have a profound influence on the flavor of meat. This technique could be used to produce products with quite different flavors than those that normally occur.

Post-slaughter aging alters the flavor of meat. Some people prefer the full, rich flavor of aged meat, whereas others object to the stronger flavor and prefer fresh meat flavor. For processing, it is advisable to use meat that has not been aged. Aged meat often tends toward rancidity and creates other problems. Therefore, meat to be processed should be used as soon as possible after slaughtering.

Various feeds influence the flavor of meat. It has been demonstrated that clover, alfalfa, and rape pastures produce strong and sometimes objectionable flavors in lamb. Similarly, fish meal and certain other feeds impart off-flavors to pork. Wild onions and garlic are also known to impart undesirable flavors and aromas to beef carcasses of animals pasturing these plants during the spring of the year. Thus, off-flavors and odors can sometimes be traced to the pre-slaughter feeding regimes of the animals. In areas where such problems occur, they can usually be prevented by putting the animals on more conventional feeds for a few days before slaughter.

Tenderness can also be altered by methods of cooking. It is well-known that moist-heat cookery methods produce more tender meat than dry-heat cookery. The carcass is commonly divided into tender and less tender cuts, so that the less tender cuts can be cooked by moist heat. The tender cuts are normally cooked by dry heat, because they remain tender even when cooked by this method. Since sausages are usually chopped or emulsified, they are generally tender, and moist-heat cookery is not required. Live steam is often added to the smokehouse during cooking to accelerate the rate of temperature increase. In modern high-velocity smokehouses, the same effects can be achieved at low relative humidities, so moist-heat cookery may not be encountered.

Destruction of Bacteria and Improving Stability

Cooking performs a most important function by causing destruction of spoilage organisms. The number of organisms destroyed will depend upon the time and temperature relationship. In normal roasting, broiling, braising, or frying, the bacterial population is reduced by the influence of temperature and time. However, the meat is not sterilized, and the net effect is merely an extension of storage life. By proper handling to avoid additional contamination of the product, along with refrigeration to slow down multiplication of bacteria, the storage life is extended from a few days to a week or more. The length of storage will depend largely upon the care taken to prevent microbial growth by recontamination, or by conditions favoring the growth of the organisms still present on the meat.

Commercial sterilization of meat products can be achieved by subjecting them to high temperatures for a sufficient length of time to destroy most of the microorganisms present. This is a normal procedure in canning meat, which results in not only the destruction of the vegetative cells but also of some bacterial spores to produce a commercially sterile product.

In the manufacture of sausages and smoked meats, cooking is done primarily to produce a table-ready product. However, cooking also plays a major role in extending the shelf-life of such products. Sausages and smoked meats are normally quite stable under refrigeration (32 to 38°F), provided they are properly handled and packaged to prevent contamination after cooking. Although the raw ingredients in sausages are subject to spoilage within a few days, finished sausages can normally be stored for several weeks after cooking. This shows the importance of cooking on the stability of processed meat.

The storage life of sausages and cured meat may be limited by the growth of molds. Although vegetative molds are destroyed by cooking, at least some spores remain viable. However, as mold spores are almost universally present in the air, recontamination frequently occurs and constitutes the major problem. Proper cooking lowers the moisture content, particularly on the surface, and thus greatly reduces problems from molds. When proper packaging follows cooking, mold growth can be almost entirely eliminated.

Inactivation of Indigenous Enzymes

Enzymes present in raw meat normally do not cause marked changes in palatability, because enzymatic degradation is relatively slow in producing undesirable organoleptic changes. Under usual storage conditions, microbiological spoilage will occur before the proteolytic changes become objectionable. However, it has been found necessary to inactivate the proteolytic enzymes present in raw irradiated meat in order to prevent deleterious flavor changes due to proteolysis. After prolonged storage of irradiated raw meat at temperatures from 60 to 100°F, the flavor becomes bitter and tyrosine crystals may be isolated, all of which indicate extensive proteolysis. Heating to internal temperatures of 135 to 145°F appears to be adequate to prevent further proteolysis in irradiated meat. This heat treatment is now commonly used for all irradiated meat items.

Surface Drying

Reduction of moisture at the surface of meat and meat products serves several purposes. As already discussed, lowering of surface moisture reduces the water activity (relative vapor pressure) on the surface and thus also reduces microbial growth. The reduced surface moisture content plays a key role in preventing not only the growth of surviving bacteria, but also the growth of any other bacteria that may recontaminate the product.

Surface drying during cooking is also responsible for skin formation in production of skinless frankfurters and similar products. Coagulation of the surface proteins results in the formation of an outer layer that serves as a skin when the cellulosic casings used during sausage manufacture are removed. Thus, the skin formed during cooking is a function of the cooking time-temperature relationship. The nature of the skin is most important for peelability or removal of the casing. Drying of the surface also aids in giving the skin a dense texture and imparts the characteristic appearance of skinless products. Although the ingredients have some influence on peelability, proper cooking without excess shrinkage and wrinkling are important in imparting good peelability. The cooking process not only serves the function of producing a skin but also must be carefully controlled to make the product readily peelable and of good appearance.

Color Development

Cooking has an important function in stabilizing the red pigments formed by the action of nitrite with myoglobin and hemoglobin. The nature of the reactions and the function of heat have been discussed in detail in Chapter 3.

METHODS OF COOKING

Basically, there are only two methods of cooking meat: (1) dry heat and (2) moist heat. In actual practice, it is difficult to reduce all methods of cookery to such a simple classification system. Often cooking procedures are combinations of the two methods, i.e., part of the process may be dry heat and part moist heat. These same basic cooking methods are used for both fresh meat and processed meat.

Dry-heat Cookery

During dry-heat cooking, the meat is surrounded by hot air, such as occurs in oven-roasting or broiling. Frying in fat and pan frying are also considered to be dry-heat methods of cookery. Dry-heat cooking is recommended only for relatively tender cuts of meat. Dry heat is the common method in low-humidity cooking in smokehouses. High-velocity air-conditioned smokehouses use this method almost exclusively, since the relative humidity seldom exceeds 70%.

Moist-heat Cookery

Cooking by moist heat makes use of hot liquid or steam. Most frequently water is added during cooking. The moisture is generally kept in contact with the meat by recirculating it to prevent its loss. In fresh meats, this is usually accomplished by covering the container with a lid, which causes most of the steam to condense and to be available again for generation to steam. Stewing, braising, pot-roasting, simmering, and swissing are all commonly used moist-heat cooking procedures. The small increase in pressure which results from using a closed system gives slightly higher cooking temperatures, and is quite effective in gelatinizing collagen. If one desires an even higher temperature, this can be achieved by use of a pressure cooker, which is also a moist-heat cooking method.

Live steam is frequently injected into some of the older smokehouses to accelerate the rate of temperature rise during the final phases of processing. This is a moist-heat method, as is the use of a Jourdan cooker, in which the product is removed from the house and finished off with steam. Since the temperature is quite uniform throughout modern high-velocity smokehouses, steam is seldom injected, making it essentially a dry-heat process.

Combination Methods of Cookery

As already mentioned, cooking can be and is often accomplished by methods that combine moist-heat and dry-heat methods. These procedures can utilize the advantages of both methods. During cooking of sausages, it is not unusual to start processing with the damper open, thus using a dry-heat method. After the proper amount of drying has been achieved, the damper may be closed and live steam injected, which raises the humidity and converts the process to moist-heat. As already mentioned, using a Jourdan cooker following traditional smokehouse cookery at low relative humidity is also a combination dry- and moist-heat method.

Another example of the combination procedure is braising, where meat may be browned over high heat before adding water. During the later phases of cooking, the pan is covered. This results in a moist-heat cooking method. The braising procedure has the advantage that the flavor is developed under dry heat while the tenderizing influence of moist heat is retained. Covering a roast without adding water retains the moisture present in the meat; the humidity of the heated air is raised, which helps to hydrolyze the collagen. This is a combination of the dry-heat and moist-heat methods. Injection of live steam into older smokehouses or use of a Jourdan cooker to accelerate temperature increase during the later phases of cooking reverses the order from that applied in braising fresh meat. Thus, dry heat is used first and moist-heat methods later.

CONSIDERATIONS IN SELECTING COOKING METHODS

The characteristics desired in the final product and the nature of the raw material in a large measure determine selection of the type of cooking method. Although roasting gives a desirable flavor, some products will become too tough if cooked by dry heat. Therefore, it may be more desirable to cook by one of the combination procedures or perhaps by a moist-heat method. If the raw material will be tender enough when roasted or broiled, the processor may choose a dry-heat cooking method.

Tender Cuts.—If the cuts of meat are of sufficiently high quality, they may be cooked by dry-heat methods. Prime rib roasts of beef, steaks or roasts from the loin and sirloin, leg of lamb, and fresh or cured ham roasts are usually quite acceptable when cooked by dry heat. Good quality pork, veal, or lamb chops may also be cooked by dry-heat methods. Whole beef rounds, if from good quality carcasses (equivalent to the top portion of U.S. Good grade or above), may be cooked by roasting—a dry-heat method. Similarly, top-round steaks of U.S. Prime or Choice grade may be cooked by broiling.

Tender cuts of meat are generally quite acceptable when cooked by dry-heat methods. Thus, the more tender cuts may be cooked by oven roasting, pan frying, deep-fat frying, and broiling. Ground or comminuted meats are also sufficiently tender to permit cooking by dry-heat procedures. The amount of shrinkage is relatively low in dry heat, so it is used wherever possible because of greater yields. Combination dry-heat and moist-heat cooking methods are frequently used to reduce shrinkage and still tenderize and give good flavor. Such combination procedures are frequently used in production of precooked frozen meat items for heat-and-serve meals.

Tough Cuts.—Shank meat, heel of round, breast of lamb, and chuck roasts of beef are usually classified as less-tender cuts. They generally give best results if cooked by moist-heat or combination methods. Thus, they are commonly cooked by braising, stewing, swissing, simmering or pressure-cooking. In order to reduce shrinkage losses, these cuts are often cooked in casings or packaging materials that prevent evaporation and hold the juices lost during cooking. Phosphates may be added to some of these products to help retain the juices, thereby increasing yields.

Processed Products.—Sausages, hams, and roasts for precooked frozen meals are often cooked by combination methods to reduce shrinkage and improve flavor. Obviously, these procedures also will give tender products. Some loaves are browned in hot fat to improve appearance, flavor, and aroma. Comminuted meats are tender and do not normally require moist heat to improve tenderness, but combination dry- and moist-heat procedures are often used to speed up processing and give more throughput.

Pressure Cooking.—One of the most successful methods of tenderizing tough cuts of meat is by pressure-cooking. The use of pressure results in higher cooking temperatures; it minimizes the time required to gelatinize the collagen, and produces tender meat in a relatively short time. Meat cooked under pressure does not usually appear to be dry, but seems relatively moist. It is quite different from meat cooked to high internal temperatures in air, which is generally very dry in appearance and mouth-feel.

Cooking losses are usually higher than those for dry-heat cookery. Another serious problem in pressure cooking is the fact the meat may lose its normal texture and disintegrate into a rather homogeneous mass of disconnected fibers. To prevent the loss of texture, pressure cooking must be carefully controlled to the correct end-point.

Simmering.—Certain cuts of beef and some sausages, such as braunschweiger, may be cooked in water. Generally, these items are heated to temperatures considerably below boiling (160 to 170°F). The hot water provides for relatively fast heat penetration. Most often these products will be heated in casings or plastic bags to avoid excess shrinkage losses. If cook-out accumulates in the bags or casings, it may be saved and utilized.

Specific Cooking Methods

A number of methods will be considered with more specific recommendations for their use. It should be borne in mind that the recommendations apply only to products and cuts and not to specific temperatures and procedures. Some specific methods of making processed meat items will be given in more detail later in this chapter.

Broiling.—This is a dry-heat procedure that can be used for more tender steaks from beef, chops of lamb, and cured ham steaks. The meat is usually supported by a wire grill and the heat may come from above as in an electric or gas oven, usually at full heat, or from below as with a charcoal broiler. After the side exposed to the heat is sufficiently done, the meat is turned over and finished on the other side. It usually requires about ⅔ of the total time on the side cooked first and ⅓ on the last side. However, the degree of rareness or doneness desired will determine the timing to some extent.

Some broilers may have reflectors on the opposite side from the heat; this will permit simultaneous cooking on both sides, which should cause both sides to be done at the same time. One merely cooks the meat until the desired degree of doneness is reached in the center. However, most professional cooks prefer to turn the meat, feeling that this gives better control.

Broiling is not normally used in processing of meats. It may, however, be used as the heating method just prior to eating processed products, such as cured ham slices, precooked frozen meat in the form of steaks or roasted slices, or for heating various types of sausages. Frozen meat patties or hamburgers are also frequently cooked by this procedure before eating.

Roasting.—This is another dry-heat method of cookery that is adapted to more tender cuts of meat. Prime rib roasts of beef, beef sirloin, top round, sirloin tip, veal leg, veal rump, veal shoulder, pork loin, pork shoulder, leg of lamb, shoulder of lamb (whole or rolled), lamb loins and racks, and cured hams are commonly cooked by roasting. Entire beef rounds can also be cooked in this manner if of high enough quality.

The roast should be at least 2½ in. thick. It is placed in an open roasting pan with fat side up, so that it will be self-basting. The roast should be left uncovered and liquid should not be added. The roast is placed in a hot-air oven at a temperature of about 250 to 350°F. Lower oven temperatures require longer cooking times but materially reduce shrinkage. High temperatures (400°F) may be used for a short time to brown the roast and improve the flavor during the last 15 to 20 min of cooking.

Roasting may be used in preparing precooked frozen beef. However, these products are more commonly cooked in water, usually in plastic bags, to retain the juices and reduce shrinkage. Roasting as the final step in preparing various precooked frozen meat items for eating is common.

Frying.—Frying is classified as a dry-heat method. It may be accomplished by either pan frying in a small amount of fat or in a large amount of fat in a deep-fat fryer. It is suitable for relatively small cuts of meat, such as thinly sliced steaks, chops, bacon, veal chops, or lamb chops. It may also be used for chicken parts cut into relatively small pieces. Batter or bread crumb coverings may be used to impart a desirable flavor. This method of cookery is not used for production of processed loaf items, bacon, or ham slices.

Braising.—This procedure is a combination of dry-heat and moist-heat cooking. It is commonly used for less-tender cuts, such as the rump of beef, chuck roasts of beef, heel of round, breast of lamb, and lamb shanks. It may also be used for pork spareribs, veal chops and steaks, and pork chops and steaks. The meat is usually braised by browning in hot fat in a pan, which constitutes dry-heat cookery. Moisture as water, vegetable stock, milk, or gravy is then added, together with seasoning. The pan is tightly covered and the meat is simmered by adjusting the heat to just below boiling, which is the moist-heat phase. Vegetables may be added at a time just sufficient to cook them.

Braising is not normally used for processed meat products, although they may be prepared for the table by this method. However, consumers generally prefer faster methods.

Pot Roasting.—This method is essentially the same as braising. It is commonly used in preparation of the same cuts as discussed under braising. Pot roasting nearly always makes use of vegetables, which are added at the proper time to be ready to eat with the meat. Otherwise, the procedure is similar to braising.

Stewing.—This is a moist-heat procedure. The cuts of meat are the less-tender ones and are almost always boneless. The meat is cut into small pieces and is usually browned in a small amount of fat, as in braising; however, stews may not always be browned. The meat is then covered with water or tomato juice. The container is covered and the meat is allowed to cook at a simmering temperature. The vegetables are added just long enough before the meat is done so they will be tender but not overdone. The liquid is reduced during cooking to give the stew a slightly thickened consistency.

Stew is a popular canned-meat item. The procedures used in its production are given in complete detail under canned meat items, chapter 12.

Simmering.—As discussed earlier, simmering is a moist-heat method of cookery. It is commonly used in producing various beef items, including precooked frozen products and corned beef. Braunschweiger is also often cooked by simmering.

Often these products are cooked in plastic bags to prevent juice losses during cooking and also to prevent flavor losses. If the items are cooked directly in water, the stock may be concentrated and added back to the original products, or it may be used for other purposes.

COOKED MEAT PRODUCT RECIPES

A number of methods of producing some cooked or frozen meat items are given. The list of products is by no means complete. The recipes are given only as guides, and modifications may be developed to suit individual processors.

Roast Beef

Raw Materials.—Well-trimmed cow rounds (insides, outsides, or knuckles), shoulder clods, or sirloin butts are used.

Seasoning.—The exposed surfaces may be rubbed with salt and other seasoning as desired, or a seasoned pumping solution may be used instead.

Stuffing.—Use #8 × 30 fibrous casings. Stuff with a press through a 3¾ in. o.d. (outside diameter) stuffing horn.

Cooking.—Transfer the rolls into an oven preheated to 300°F and roast until the internal temperature reaches 140 to 165°F. The choice of final temperature is dependent upon the degree of doneness desired. Approximately 4½ hr are required to reach an internal temperature of 155°F.

Chilling.—The rolls should be chilled in running tap water until the internal temperature reaches 100 to 120°F. The excess liquid in the rolls may be removed and the rolls repacked under pressure.

Yield.—The final yield is dependent upon the cooking temperature, final internal temperature, and casing size.

Cooked Veal Rolls

Raw Materials.—Veal rib eyes, shoulder clods, or other cuts high in lean content may be used. Cuts having 85 to 95% lean should comprise at least 75% of the mixture. Veal trimmings containing not less than 60% lean are used for preparing the binder and should comprise approximately 25% (but no more) of the mixture. Tendons and excess fat should be removed.

Preparation of Meat.—The veal trimmings (60% or more lean) should be chopped coarsely or else ground through a ⅛ to ¼-in. plate. Add 5 to 10% water if desired. This forms the binder for the larger pieces of veal. The chunks of veal (85 to 95% lean) are ground through a 1 to 2-in. plate. This portion should comprise at least 75% of the total mixture.

Seasoning.—Salt 1 to 2% depending on preference; phosphate, 8 oz per 100 lb total meat (maximum legal limit of 0.5%); other seasonings as desired.

Mixing.—Place the lean veal trimmings (binder) and the veal chunks together in a mixer. Start the mixer and add a phosphate-water solution (8 oz phosphate dissolved in 1 lb water to every 100 lb of meat). Add 1 to 2% salt according to taste. Mix thoroughly. Then the mixture should be vacuum-mixed for 4 min or until it is tacky and sticks to the fingers when handled. Vacuum mixing produces a roll with fewer internal air pockets or spaces and results in a smoother surface. Thus vacuum mixing permits better portion control. The maximum vacuum obtainable should be used, which normally is about 28 in.

Although larger chunks can be used in making veal rolls, the size recommended gives a more uniform color. Larger pieces take longer to cook than the binder, and thus result in a gradation in color. The binder is not necessary to prepare veal rolls, but it fills any voids and permits better portion control. The binder also gives a smoother surface and 1 to 2% better cooking yields.

Stuffing.—The meat-binder mixture is stuffed in the desired type and size fibrous casing by means of press, air stuffer, or other suitable equipment. Vacuum stuffing provides some of the advantages of vacuum mixing.

Processing.—Veal loaf can be processed by water-cooking or by dry-processing. If water-cooking is employed, a moistureproof fibrous casing should be used, usually a No. 8 or 9 size.

When dry-processed, veal rolls can be cooked in forced-air convection ovens, smokehouses, or equivalent equipment at temperatures up to 350°F. The rolls can be cooked in either moistureproof or conventional fibrous casings. However, browning does not occur in moistureproof casings. Blanching for 5 to 10 min in 190°F water or in the dry-processing equipment will make it possible to remove the moistureproof casing without the roll falling apart. Removal of the casing will allow browning to occur during the later phases of cooking. The rolls in either type of casing can be cooked from the frozen state, but require longer cooking times. The cooking times for a No. 9 fibrous casing are shown in Table 5.1.

Table 5.1

COOKING TIME FOR VEAL ROLLS IN NO. 9 FIBROUS CASINGS

Cooking Method	Cooking Temperature °F	Cooking Time to Internal Temp. of					
		140°F		145°F		150°F	
		Hr	Min	Hr	Min	Hr	Min
Water or steam	160	2	30	2	50	3	25
	150	2	30	4	20	—	—
	145	5	—	—	—	—	—
Oven	250	3	—	3	15	3	30

Cooling.—Rolls cooked in water can be cooled to an internal temperature of 100°F by showering with cold water or placing in slush ice. They may then be frozen or stored at 32 to 36°F. Dry-processed rolls can be partially cooled at room temperature and then placed in a 32 to 36°F cooler. If the casing is not moistureproof, an additional overwrap is needed to prevent moisture loss.

Frozen Boneless Pork Loin Roasts and Chops

Raw Materials.—Use boneless pork loins weighing 5½ to 10½ lbs. Bone-in loins weighing 12 to 18 lb will give boneless loins of the weights desired and will meet military specifications for these products. In addition, powdered egg white (low whip–*Salmonella* free) is needed for binding.

Preparation and Stuffing.—The loins are boned and trimmed. Then each loin is cut in half and opposite ends are placed together, i.e., blade end to ham end. After cutting but before putting the loins together, each section is dipped in egg white. Stuff the loin into No. 7 casings, using 401 can lids, if the loins are going to be cut into chops. After the loin is stuffed, it should be pressure-packed until it is approximately ½ in. less than the recommended stuffed casing circumference. This allows for expansion due to freezing. To minimize casing breakage during freezing, the loins should be individually wrapped in thin polyethlene sheets.

Cutting Loin into Chops.—If the loin is to be cut into chops, it can be sliced with a frozen meat slicer as soon as it reaches 26 to 28°F. This firms the meat up sufficiently for slicing, but minimizes the problems encountered on slicing at low temperatures.

Government Specifications.—Military procurement specifications for frozen chops call for each chop to weigh 5 oz plus or minus ½ oz. Individual chops must not exceed ⅞ in. or be less than ½ in. thick.

Storage.—Frozen loins should be stored at no higher than 0°F, and a temperature of −25°F or lower is preferable. Loins should be moved into commercial outlets or military procurement routes as soon as possible after freezing. They should never be stored over 6 months, and preferably no more than 3 months. The loins are subject to development of rancidity, and the lower temperatures and shorter storage times tend to prevent this.

Cooking.—The loins are cooked by roasting; the sliced chops are generally broiled, pan-fried, or grilled.

Frozen Boneless Pork Shoulder and Ham Rolls for Roast or Chops

The product described is largely intended for large-volume institutional kitchens. Boneless rolls are versatile, excellent for portion control, and have a uniform composition.

Raw Materials.—This product can be prepared from pork picnics, skinned shoulders, Boston butts, and skinned hams. According to U.S.D.A Institutional Meat Purchase Specifications, the weight limits are no larger than 8 lb for picnics, 14 lb for skinned shoulders, 6 lb for Boston butts, and 16 lb for skinned hams. The bones and skin are removed, leaving all fat on the boneless cut. The shank meat and heavy fat deposits should be removed.

Preparation.—The shank meat and excess fat trimmings should be ground through a ⅛-in. plate and the lean cuts through a 1 to 2 in. plate. The lean cuts should make up at least 70% of the meat block, while the ground shank and fat trimmings should never exceed 30% of the total.

Mixing.—Place all the ground meat, both finely and coarsely ground, in a mixer. Add 1 to 1.5% salt. Mix for 4 min. Although vacuum mixing gives the most uniform product and best portion control, it is not an absolute requirement.

Stuffing.—The product is stuffed into moistureproof fibrous casings using a piston-type or else a continuous-type stuffer. U.S.D.A. Institutional Meat Purchase Specifications call for 7 lb. rolls packaged 8 to a box to give a total of 56 lb. To meet these requirements, the casing used is usually a No. 5N by 28 in. The rolls should be pressure-packed to approximately ¼ in. less than is recommended by the casing manufacturer, which allows for expansion during freezing.

Freezing and Storage.—Rolls should be frozen as soon as possible after stuffing. Rapid freezing and low-temperature storage provides better stability. The rolls should be handled the same as the frozen pork loins and chops.

Cooking.—The frozen chops may be fried, grilled, or broiled. They are also sometimes braised, but generally dry-heat methods are employed. If roasts are preferred, the roll should be placed in an oven at 250 to 300°F and cooked to an internal temperature of 170°F. If diced meat is preferred, the rolls should be tempered at 25 to 29 °F and the casing removed. The roll should be cut into 1-in. thick slices and then cut into small pieces with a knife. The cubed meat can be used for chop suey and stews or ground and used in ground-pork recipes.

Frozen Boneless Beef Rolls for Grilling or Broiling

The product described is a comminuted fresh beef product having the taste and textural properties of beef steak. It eliminates trimming waste, gives careful portion control, and is uniform in composition.

Raw Materials.—Boneless beef rounds are used from U.S.D.A Prime, Choice, Good, or Standard carcasses. The top, bottom, or knuckle sections of the round may be used.

Preparation.—Heavy fat deposits and connective tissue are removed. The poorer parts should be discarded, while the sound material is ground through a ⅛-in. plate. The trimmed lean muscle should be ground through a large plate (either a 1- or 2-in. hole plate, or a 1- to 1.5-in. kidney shaped hole plate). The amount of trimmings should not exceed 15% of the total weight, while the large lean muscle portion should comprise at least 85%.

The entire meat block should be placed in a mixer and 1 to 1.5% salt added. It should be mixed for 4 min. Vacuum mixing is desirable from the standpoint of uniformity and portion control, but is not absolutely necessary.

Stuffing and Pressure Packing.—Stuff the product into moisture-proof fibrous casings (using No. 6 to 9) with a piston or continuous stuffer. The rolls should be pressure-packed to a circumference approximately ¼ in. smaller than that recommended for the casing to allow for expansion during freezing. A precision sizer can be used to eliminate the pressure-packing step and improve efficiency and portion control.

Table 5.2 gives the weight that can be expected per linear inch for different moisture-proof fibrous casing sizes. This information is useful in selecting the desired size casing.

Freezing.—Rolls should be frozen as quickly as possible after stuffing. Low-temperature freezing and storage improve stability. Storage should be limited to a maximum of 5 to 6 months.

Slicing Instructions.—Rolls may be sliced into portion-controlled pieces of the desired thickness. In the frozen state, a power meat saw can be used, or if tempered to 25 to 29°F, an electric slicer will be effective. Thawing for 20 min prior to cutting will make it possible to remove the casing before slicing. If the casing is not removed before slicing, it should be removed before cooking.

Cooking.—Slices may be grilled or broiled from the frozen or tempered state. The frozen meat will require slightly longer cooking times.

Cooked Beef Rolls

Ingredients.—Beef rounds, knuckles, or sirloin butts of 85 or 95% lean comprise the basic meat ingredients. Beef trimmings of 60% or more lean are used as a binder, in combination with phosphates and seasoning. The binder (trimmings) should not constitute over 25% of the total meat block, while the beef rounds or sirloin butts should comprise at least 75% of the total.

Trimming and Cutting.—Tendons and undesired fat should be trimmed from the rounds, knuckles, or butts. The high-quality trimmings should be kept and cut into small pieces, while the undesirable portions should be discarded. Table 5.3 shows the approximate yields for different types and grades of meat prepared for cooked beef rolls.

Preparation of Meat Mixture.—Boneless beef rounds, knuckles, or butts are passed through a 1- to 2-in grinder plate. This portion should not be less than 75% of the total meat block. The binder is prepared by chopping the lean trimmings (60% lean) coarsely, or by passing through a ⅛- to ¼-in. grinder plate. Between 5 and 10% water should be added during chopping or grinding. The binder should be limited to a maximum of 25% of the total meat.

The ground chunks and the ground trimmings (binder) are placed in a mixer and blended with a phosphate-water solution (8 oz phosphate in 1 to 1½ lbs water for every 100 lb meat) and 1 to 2% salt (according to taste). Federal regulations limit the level of phosphate to 0.5% of the total meat weight. After the salt and phosphates are thoroughly dispersed, the blend should be vacuum-mixed for 4 additional min. The mixture will be tacky and will stick to the fingers when handled. The efficiency of the mixer may slightly alter mixing times. Although

Table 5.2

PRODUCT WEIGHT PER LINEAR INCH FOR FIBROUS CASINGS OF DIFFERENT SIZES

Casing Size	Weight Per Inch Oz
6	8
7	9
8	11
9	12

Table 5.3

YIELDS AND TRIM LOSSES FOR VARIOUS CUTS AND GRADES OF BEEF
PREPARED FOR COOKED BEEF ROLLS

Cut and Grade of Meat	Yield* %
Inside cow rounds, U.S. Utility or Cutter	86
Outside cow rounds, U.S. Utility or Cutter	84
Inside rounds, U.S. Choice	70
Outside rounds, U.S. Choice	70
Knuckles, U.S. Utility or Cutter	90
Sirloin butts, U.S. Utility or Cutter	76
Sirloin butts, U.S. Choice	63

* Proportion of the cut that is available after removing the fat, bone, and tendons.

vacuum mixing and the use of small chunks of meat (1 to 2-in. pieces) are not absolutely necessary, better portion control and appearance will result from their use. Similarly, the binder is not essential, but in its absence there are void spaces and portion control is more difficult.

Stuffing and Pressure Packing.—The meat and binder mixture is stuffed into the desired type and size of fibrous casing, using a press, air stuffer, or other suitable equipment. Vacuum stuffers provide some of the advantages of vacuum mixers. The rolls should be packed to the recommended sizes for the casings.

Cooking.—Cooked beef rolls can be processed by either water-cooking or dry-processing. Water-cooking should be done only in moistureproof fibrous casings. Usually No. 8 or 9 casings are used. The water temperature is usually 10°F higher than the desired internal temperature of the meat, which is usually 140 to 150°F. Table 5.1 shows a schedule of times and cooking temperatures required to produce different degrees of doneness.

Dry-processing of beef rolls can be carried out in forced-air convection ovens, smokehouses, or equivalent equipment at temperatures up to 350°F. The rolls can be cooked in moistureproof or conventional fibrous casings. However, browning will not take place in moistureproof casings.

The moistureproof fibrous casings can be removed by soaking the rolls for 5 to 10 min in 190°F water. Once the casings are removed, browning will take place on heating. Rolls in either type of casing can be cooked from the frozen state, but require more time for cooking.

Cooling.—Water-cooked rolls can be cooled by showering with cold water or in slush ice. They should be cooled to 100°F or below, and may then be frozen or stored at 32 to 38°F. Dry-processed rolls may be cooled at room temperature or by placing in a cooler at 40°F until the internal temperature is less than 100°F. After cooking, the product in fibrous casings should be placed in polyethylene sheets to prevent moisture losses during freezing or refrigeration. Moistureproof fibrous casings may be frozen or refrigerated without additional packaging.

Smoked, Chopped Turkey Loaf

Raw Materials.—All-white meat and all-dark meat turkey rolls are made from boneless turkey breast and boneless turkey thighs, respectively. Both contain the respective kinds of turkey skin and broth. Part of the meat is pickled, ground into coarse chunks and is then mixed with a finely chopped emulsion of skin, meat, and other additives. The mixture is stuffed into fibrous casings and formed into squares under pressure. This product is smoked in an air-conditioned smokehouse to an internal temperature of 170°F, chilled in water, and stored overnight at 40°F.

Formulation.—

Ingredients	White Meat Loaf Lb	Oz	Dark Meat Loaf Lb	Oz
turkey breast meat	88			
turkey thigh meat			88	
defatted turkey broth	15		15	
turkey skin	12		12	
sodium caseinate	3	8	3	8
chicken roll seasoning	1	4	1	4
monosodium glutamate		8		8
sodium nitrite		⅛		⅛

Preparation.—Whole eviscerated frozen tom turkeys weighing 20 to 24 lb are thawed and boned. The skin is removed. Only the breast meat, thigh meat, and skin are used. The yield on eviscerated weights should be approximately 54%. One half of the breast meat or thigh meat is left intact and placed in the following pickle for 16 hr at 40°F:

Pickle Formula

Ingredients	Amount Gal	Lb
water	100	
salt		52
phosphate		35
nitrite		1

The pickled meat is removed from the phosphate solution, allowed to drain well, and ground through a 1-inch plate. After grinding, the pickled meat is set aside until needed.

The turkey skin and 1 lb defatted broth are chopped together into a smooth paste. The remaining portion of the unpickled meat, either white or dark as the case may be, is then added to the chopper along with the remainder of the broth, caseinate, and spice. It is then chopped until it is smooth in consistency. The finished emulsion is then transferred to a mixer along with the coarse-ground pickled meat and blended.

Stuffing.—The mixture is stuffed into No. 8 x 28-in. fibrous casings using a conventional pneumatic stuffer at 80 lbs line pressure. The stuffed casings are placed in 3⅛ by 3⅜-in. wire cages and compressed. Unpressed casings may be used if a round shape is acceptable.

Processing.—The wire cages or unpressed product, as the case may be, are suspended from smokesticks and processed in an air-conditioned smokehouse. The following schedule is suggested:

Time Min	House Temperature °F	Relative Humidity %	Smoke Added
15	140	40	yes
15	150	40	yes
15	160	40	yes
15	170	40	yes
120	180	80	yes
60	190	95	no

The smoking process requires a total of 4 hr, and the internal temperature of the product should be 170°F at the end. After processing, the rolls should be chilled in cold water for 45 min or placed in cooler storage at 40°F for 16 hr. The chilled product is removed from the cages and the casings are stripped off before slicing.

Process-storage shrinkage amounts to approximately 6.5 to 8%. In some areas, products of this type are packaged for commercial sale in 3-oz packets, containing 14 to 20 slices each. White-meat rolls sell at a somewhat higher price than dark-meat rolls.

Turkey Roll

Raw Materials.—Boneless, skinless turkey meat (either white or dark meat) and an emulsion made of skin or a binder are used.

Formulation.—

Ingredients	Amount	
	Lb	Oz
turkey meat, boneless	90	
and skinless (white or dark)		
emulsion or binder*	10	
salt	1	8
prepared seasoning	1	8
phosphate		8

* The emulsion can be made from body skins, wing meat, and wing skin. Part of the emulsion can be replaced by a binder made of soy protein concentrate and sodium caseinate. The binder may replace a maximum level of 3½% of the meat and skin weight.

Emulsion Preparation.—Grind skins (body and wing skins) and wing meat through a ⅜-in. plate; then put them through a 1.7-mm plate in a Mincemaster or chop into a fine emulsion. If an all-dark-meat roll is prepared, one can use automatically deboned turkey meat or emulsified dark meat in the emulsion. This will prevent a grainy appearance, which occurs if emulsified skins are used in dark-meat emulsion rolls.

Meat Preparation.—Tendons and blood vessels are removed. The remainder of the meat is cut into the desired size pieces. Place meat in mixer and add a phosphate slurry (composed of 1 part phosphate and 3 parts water). Add salt and continue mixing until the meat becomes tacky. Add the skin emulsion, seasoning, and binder. Continue mixing for 1 to 2 additional min.

Stuffing.—Stuff into moistureproof or conventional fibrous casings with a pneumatic stuffer. Pressure-pack on conventional closing equipment. A combination white and dark meat roll can be prepared by layering alternate white and dark meat portions to give both white and dark meat in each slice.

Cooking.—Rolls can be cooked in 180°F water to an internal temperature of at least 160°F. Cooking time is about 2½ hr in a No. 6 fibrous casing. Rolls should be cooled in cold running water for approximately 15 min and then be placed in slush ice overnight. They can be frozen the following day.

Rolls can be dry-roasted in conventional fibrous casings. They are cooked in a 300°F rotary oven or smokehouse to an internal temperature of 160°F. To ensure complete browning, the rolls should be rotated 1 or 2 times during cooking. They are chilled the same as water-cooked rolls.

Turkey Ham

Raw Materials.—Boneless, skinless turkey thigh meat and automatically deboned turkey meat is used to produce turkey ham.

Curing.—Boneless thigh meat is trimmed of excess fat, blood vessels, and tendons. It then is placed in a curing pickle for a maximum of 24 hr at 40°F.

The pickle is composed of the following ingredients and amounts:

Ingredients	Amount		
	Lb	Oz	Gal
water			100
phosphate	50		
salt	12	8	
erythorbate	3		
nitrite	2		

Ten gallons of pickle will cover 225 lb meat, 25 gal 550 lb, and 50 and 100 gal 1,200 and 2,500 lb meat, respectively. The gain in weight while in the pickle falls within a range of 7 to 10%.

Mixing.—After curing, remove the thigh meat from the pickle and drain for 5 min. Place in mixer, add 1% salt and continue mixing until the meat becomes tacky. Add 20% of deboned meat and seasonings as desired. Mixing is continued for an additional 1 to 2 min. Total mixing time will depend on the efficiency of the mixer.

Stuffing.—The mixture is stuffed into prestuck fibrous casings using a conventional pneumatic stuffer or other suitable stuffing equipment. The product is pressure-packed on conventional closing equipment and placed on flat ham screens.

Processing.—The product is placed on a smokehouse tree, put in an air-conditioned smokehouse, and processed as follows:

Temperature °F	Relative Humidity %	Time Min
cold smoke (about 100)	—	5
140 to 180	40	60
180	40	to 155°F internal temperature or above

Total time in the smokehouse depends upon the size of casing, but the internal product temperature should reach at least 155°F. The smoked product should be chilled in a cold-water shower for 30 to 45 min and then be placed in a 40°F cooler overnight. The casing is then removed and the product sliced. An 80 to 90% yield can be expected after processing.

Turkey White Meat—Turkey Ham Combination Roll

Raw Materials.—The product is composed of 2 layers, 1 being made of turkey white meat and emulsified skin and the other of turkey ham. The turkey ham is composed of cured turkey thigh meat and automatically deboned turkey meat.

Formulation.—

Ingredients	Amount Lb	Oz
turkey white meat, boneless and skinless	90	
skin emulsion*	10	
salt	1	8
prepared seasoning	1	8
phosphate		8

* The emulsion is made from body skins, wing meat, and wing skin. A binder composed of soy protein concentrate and sodium caseinate may be mixed with the skin emulsion to the extent of 3½% of the weight of the meat and skin.

Emulsion Preparation.—Pass the skins (body and/or wing) and wing meat through a ⅜-in. grinder plate. Chop to a fine emulsion or put through a 1.7-mm plate of a Mincemaster.

Meat Preparation.—Trim the white meat free of tendons, blood vessels, and excess fat. Cut into desired size pieces. Place meat in mixer, add phosphate slurry (1 part phosphate to 3 parts water) and begin mixing. Add salt and mix until surface becomes tacky. Add emulsion, seasoning, and binder. Continue mixing for an additional 1 to 2 min.

Prepare turkey ham from whole thigh meat as described in the previous formulation. After the thigh meat is cured and mixed, and 20% of deboned turkey meat added and mixed, the turkey ham is ready for stuffing.

Stuffing.—The turkey white meat and the turkey ham are stuffed into fibrous casings to give 2 distinct layers. A half-shell horn or other suitable equipment places a layer of turkey white meat and turkey ham in each slice. Plans for constructing a half-shell horn are shown in Fig. 5.1. The product is pressure-packed and closed with conventional equipment.

Processing.—The rolls are placed on a smokehouse tree, put into an air-conditioned smokehouse and processed as follows:

Temperature °F	Relative Humidity %	Time Min
cold smoke (not over 100)	—	5
140 to 180	40	60
180	40	to at least 155°F internal temperature

Total cooking time depends on the casing size, but should result in an internal temperature of at least 155°F. The processed product is chilled in a cold-water shower for 30 to 45 min and placed in a 40°F cooler overnight. The chilled product is ready for slicing after removing the casing.

Turkey Rolls

Turkey rolls for institutional use are made from breast, thigh, or mixed breast and thigh meat, and are packed in moistureproof fibrous casings. They are made for institutional use or as consumer rolls.

Raw Materials.—Breast and thigh meat are used alone or in combination to make a mixed roll. Either fresh or frozen turkeys in a weight range of 20 to 30 lb are the basic starting material. The skin may be removed intact before boning and scraped free of adhering fat, or

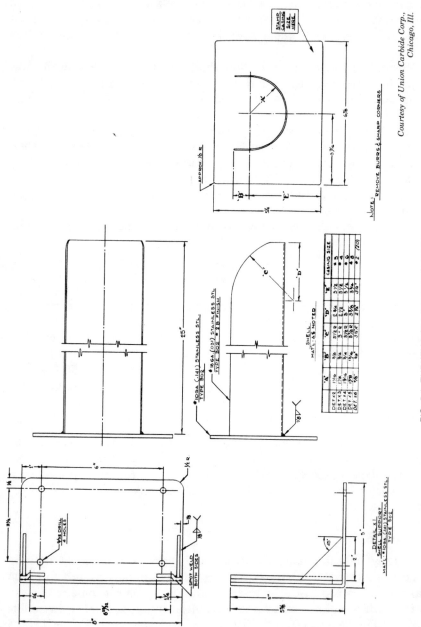

Courtesy of Union Carbide Corp.,
Chicago, Ill.

FIG. 5.1. TURKEY ROLL STUFFING SHELL

it may be left intact on the breasts and thighs during boning. The breasts and thighs should be boned out with as little tearing or cutting as possible, so as to maintain the integrity of the muscles.

Types of Turkey Rolls.—A 9-lb mixed roll is made for the institutional trade. They are stuffed into No. 8 or No. 80 by 27-in. long moistureproof casings. They contain 60 to 70% white meat and 30 to 40% thigh meat. The dark meat is layered over the white meat so that each roll contains white and dark meat. The ingredients are preweighed and gelatin is used as a binder. Spices are added to taste. Since the juices are taken up by the gelatin during cooking, the finished weight should be identical with the weight of the ingredients. The moistureproof casings prevent losses or gains in weight.

All-white-meat institutional-type rolls are also made to weigh 9 lbs. Except for the fact they are made only from breast meat, they are handled the same as 9-lb mixed rolls.

Improved 9-lb Turkey Roll.—Formulations are the same as for the two types just described. Thus they can be either mixed or all-white-meat rolls. They are made more solid by draining some of the cook-out juice. This is done by chilling the roll to 120°F or less. The excess juice is drained off by making a slit about 1 in. long parallel to the long axis of the roll and just inside the second clip. The casing is not cut off at the clip, but the drained roll is repressure-packed. A single uncushioned clip is used to make the final closure. The amount of juice drained off is from 10 to 14 oz for the 3 to 4-lb roll or to 24 to 36 oz for the 9-lb roll. This gives a shrinkage of 20 to 25% during processing.

Consumer rolls are prepared from mixed or all white meat in the same way as described above. Consumer rolls should be of the improved type in which the cook-out juice is partially or completely removed, as described above. A No. 6 by 26-in. long moistureproof casing is commonly used.

Methods of Preparation.—A half-shell horn attached to a press is used to assemble the roll (Fig. 5.1). In assembling the roll, 2 pieces of breast meat are placed at the bottom of the shell horn. Seasoning and dry powdered gelatin are sprinkled over the surface of the white meat. Then dark meat is placed on top of the white meat. A pre-tied and pre-soaked casing of suitable size is then slipped over the horn. The meat is then forced into the casing, either by hand or with the press. The assembled roll is then pressure-packed and clipped.

If the skin is left attached to the meat, the meat is placed so the skin will be on the outside of the roll. If the skin is removed, it is used to line the casing before adding the meat.

The type of seasoning is optional and a number of kinds are available on the market. Salt should be added to a level of 1½ to 2 lb per 100 lb meat. Monosodium glutamate may be added to a level of 0.5% by weight. Gelatin is added in the amount of 3 to 4 oz for 9-lb rolls and 1½ to 2 oz for 3 to 4-lb rolls.

The first tie may be applied to the casing either dry or after soaking. The casing should be folded back about ½ in. and the first clip applied to the doubled portion. This furnishes a shoulder to prevent the clip from slipping off during cooking. The second clip is then applied.

Processing Instructions.—Rolls are processed by immersion in hot water (175 to 180°F) until the internal temperature reaches a minimum of 160°F, which is required under United States government regulations. During cooking, rolls should be completely covered with water.

Institutional-type rolls are chilled in ice water to 35 to 45°F (internal temperature) and transferred to a blast freezer. Blast freezer temperatures of −45°F have been used. They should then be held at 0 to − 10°F, the latter temperature being preferred.

Special Considerations.—Addition of sodium phosphate is permitted, but the maximum level allowed is 0.5%. It may be injected by stitch pumping, in which case a solution of 6% should be used. The pumping level is limited to 10% or less by weight.

The following brine is recommended, where a cover brine is used:

Ingredients	Amount	
	Lb	Gal
water		100
salt	100	
phosphate	50	

If the meat is to be treated with the phosphate-brine before making the rolls, this can be done using the same formula. The meat should remain in the phosphate-brine not less than 6 hr and not over 18 hr.

Oven-roasted Boneless Turkey Breasts

Raw Materials and Preparation.—Raw turkey breasts with or without first joint wing meat and skin are used. Whole turkey breasts are first boned, and the tendons, blood vessels, and excess fat are removed. The meat and skin should be trimmed so as to leave the product as nearly intact as possible. The meat and skin up to the first joint of the wing can be left attached to the breast, if desired.

Curing.—The boneless, trimmed breasts are either pumped or submerged in a curing pickle. They should be held in the pickle for 12 hr. A suggested formula for the pickle is given below.

Ingredients	Amount		
	Lb		Gal
water			100
salt	125		
phosphate	50		
dextrose	50		
monosodium glutamate	1	4	

Forming the Product.—One whole breast (skin on) and one half breast (skin removed) are used. The half breast is placed under the whole breast and they are stuffed into a plastic bag of suitable size. The bag is closed with conventional closing equipment.

Processing.—The product is oven-roasted at a temperature of 300°F to an internal temperature of at least 160°F. It is then partially cooled to approximately 120°F. The cooking bag is removed and the product repacked in another plastic bag. A clear gelatin solution or part of the cook-out juices can be added back to the bagged product to improve its appearance. The bag is evacuated under vacuum, clipped, and shrunk in the conventional manner.

Cooking yields are generally about 75%. Cooking times will vary widely according to the weights, cooking method, and temperature.

Boneless Turkey Roasts

Raw Materials.—Although tom turkeys in the weight range of 20 to 24 lb are preferred, one may also use heavy (16 to 18 lb) breeding turkey hens.

Preparation of Meat.—The necks and giblets are first removed from the body cavity. The tail is cut off and the excess tail fat remaining on the carcass is removed. The wings are removed next to the body, and the drumsticks at thigh joints. The neck flap is cut in half to expose the keel bone. Beginning at the keel bone, one-half of the breast with the thigh attached is removed while leaving the skin in one piece. The entire procedure is repeated on the other side. The thigh is then removed from the breast, leaving as much skin as possible attached to the breast. This gives the greatest amount of skin for covering the roast. All the bone from the thigh is removed and the tendons on the breast are exposed.

Tying the Roast.—The roast may be hand-tied by using a metal pan (similar to a bread pan) 5 by 3 by 10 in. One string (about 36 in. long) is placed at the bottom of and parallel to the long axis of the mold. Four strings (about 24 in. long) are positioned about 2 in. apart and at right angles to the long axis of the mold. One half breast should be placed skin down in the mold, and thigh meat should be positioned skin up on top of the breast meat. All meat masses are then covered with the skin. All strings should then be tied.

A tying machine or a shaping-tying machine can be used to form and tie the roasts. The roast may be seasoned, if desired, by distributing suitable spice ingredients over the meat surfaces.

Processing.—The raw roast can be frozen and sold in that form, or it can be cured and/or smoked.

Cooking.—The roasts are not normally cooked by the processor. However, they may be roasted by the purchaser to an internal temperature of 160°F in an oven at 250 to 300°F.

BIBLIOGRAPHY

ANON. 1961. Merck Products for the Meat Industry. Merck Chemical Div., Merck and Co., Rahway, N.J.

ANON. 1965A. Instructions for the proper use of Devro sausage casings for fresh pork sausage. Prod. Bull. 2. Devro, Inc., Somerville, N.J.

ANON. 1965B. Service Manual. Union Carbide Corp., Films & Packaging Div., Chicago, Ill.

BATZER, O. F., SANTORO, A. T., LANDMANN, W. A., and SCHWEIGERT, B. S. 1960. Precursors of beef flavor. J. Agr. Food Chem. 8, 498.

BENDALL, J. R. 1964. Meat proteins. In Symposium on Foods—Proteins and Their Interactions, H. W. Schultz, and A. F. Anglemier (Editors). Avi Publishing Co., Westport, Conn.

BOWERS, J. A., HARRISON, D. L., and KROPF, D. H. 1968. Browning and associated properties of porcine muscle. J. Food Sci. 33, 147.

COLVIN, J. R. 1964. Denaturation: A requiem. In Symposium on Foods—Proteins and Their Interactions, H. W. Schultz, and A. F. Anglemier (Editors). Avi Publishing Co., Westport, Conn.

CONNELL, J. J. 1964. Fish muscle proteins and some effects on them of processing. In Symposium on Foods—Proteins and Their Interactions, H. W. Schultz, and A. F. Anglemier (Editors). Avi Publishing Co., Westport, Conn.

COVER, S., KING, G. T., and BUTLER, O. D. 1958. Effect of carcass grades and fatness on tenderness of meat from steers of known history. Texas Agr. Expt. Sta. Bull. 889.

HOSTETLER, R. L., and LANDMANN, W. A. 1968. Photo-micrographic studies of dynamic changes in muscle fiber fragments, 1. Effect of various heat treatments on length, width, and birefringence. J. Food Sci. 33, 468.

LAW, H. M., YANG, S. P., MULLINS; A. M., and FIELDER, M. M. 1967. Effect of storage and cooking on qualities of loin and top round steaks. J. Food Sci. 33, 637.

LOWE, B. 1955. Experimental Cookery, 4th Edition. John Wiley & Sons, New York.

MACY, R. L., NAUMANN, H. D., and BAILEY, M. E. 1970. Water-soluble flavor and odor precursors of meat. 4. Influence of cooking on nucleosides and bases of beef steaks and roasts and their relationship to flavor, aroma, and juiciness. J. Food Sci. 35, 81.

PAUL, P., BRATZLER, L. J., FARWELL, E. D., and KNIGHT, K. 1952. Studies on tenderness of meat. I. Rate of heat penetration. Food Res. *17*, 504.

PRICE, J. F., and SCHWEIGERT, B. S. 1971. The Science of Meat and Meat Products, 2nd Edition. W. H. Freeman and Co., San Francisco.

RAMSBOTTOM, J. M., and STRANDINE, E. J. 1949. Initial physical and chemical changes in beef as related to tenderness. J. Animal Sci. *8*, 398.

ROGERS, P. J., GOERTZ, G. E., and HARRISON, D. L. 1967. Heat induced changes of moisture in turkey muscle. J. Food Sci. *32*, 298.

SCHOCK, D. R., HARRISON, D. L., and ANDERSON, L. L. 1970. Effect of dry and moist heat treatments on selected beef quality factors. J. Food Sci. *35*, 195.

SMITH, G. C. *et al.* 1968. The effects of freezing, frozen storage conditions and degree of doneness on lamb palatability characteristics. J. Food Sci. *33*, 19.

ZAIKA, L. L., WASSERMAN, A. E., MONK, C. A., Jr., and SALAY, J. 1968. Meat flavor. 2. Procedures for the separation of water-soluble beef aroma precursors. J. Food Sci. *33*, 53.

ZIEGLER, P. T. 1952. The Meat We Eat, 3rd Edition. Interstate Printers & Publishers, Danville, Ill.

CHAPTER 6

Raw Materials

Of basic importance to the manufacture of all processed meats is selection of proper raw-meat materials. Quality of these meats as determined by their chemical and microbiological age should be high, for it is certainly a truism that a finished product can be of no higher quality than the ingredients it contains. When producing smoked meats, the concern is only with primal and subprimal cuts. However, when manufacturing sausage and canned meats, trimmings resulting from fabrication of primal cuts, as well as boneless whole carcass meat from carcasses which do not find a ready market as block meat, are utilized.

SAUSAGE AND CANNED MEATS

For the manufacture of sausage and canned meats, lean skeletal beef and pork are the most desirable raw-meat materials. Veal and mutton are also used, but in much smaller quantities than beef and pork. This is particularly true of mutton which, if used in excessive quantities, imparts an undesirable flavor to the finished products. Comminuted processed meat products tend to be quite dry and tough unless sufficient fat is present. Generally, pork and, to a lesser extent, beef trimmings provide most of the fat in sausage and canned-meat formulations.

Federal meat inspection regulations classify animal tissues used for preparation of comminuted meat products as either meat or meat by-products. To classify as meat, tissues must be of skeletal origin and for purposes of labeling need only be referred to as beef, pork, veal, or mutton. Nonskeletal or smooth muscle tissues, such as lips, tripe, pork stomachs, and cardiac muscle are referred to as meat by-products, and must be listed individually in the ingredient statement printed on packages.

Tissues vary in moisture-protein ratio, fat-lean ratio, and amount of pigment, as well as in their ability to bind moisture and emulsify fat. These two properties are collectively referred to as the binding ability of a meat. In the trade, sausage ingredients are classified as either binder or filler meats. Binder meats are further subdivided into high, medium, and low categories depending on their ability to bind water and emulsify fat. Meats with high binding properties are lean skeletal tissues, such as whole-carcass bull and cow meat, lean pork trim, and whole-carcass mutton. Beef and pork cheek meat, beef shanks, and veal are of medium value as binders. Low-binding meats contain a large proportion of (1) fat, (2) smooth muscle, or (3) cardiac muscle tissue. These meats include regular pork trimmings, jowls, tongues, and hearts. Another category, meats with very poor binding properties, is referred to as filler meat. While these materials, such as tripe, snouts, lips, skin, and partially defatted tissues, are nutritionally acceptable, their use in comminuted meat products should be limited if overall quality of sausage or canned meat products is to be maintained.

The moisture-protein ratios of various tissues are important in preparing sausage formulas because they provide guidelines in predicting composition of finished products. Approximate moisture-protein ratios of some common sausage ingredients are presented in Table 6.1.

Fat content of meat used for comminuted meat products is influenced primarily by carcass grade and particular cut or type of trimming from the carcass. Variations in fat content greatly exceed those of moisture and protein. If moisture and protein are known, fat content may be approximated by difference, allowing about 0.8% for ash. When selecting meats for comminuted meat products, consideration should also be given to the percentage of myoglobin present in the raw material, principally because of the effect this pigment has on the color of the finished product. Heart and cheek meats are good sources of myoglobin and may be used to advantage in products which tend to be pale in color. A detailed list of raw materials most commonly used in·making comminuted meat products is shown in Table 6.2.

There are no generally observed standards for boneless processing meat. However, on occasion, meat graded as number one or number two by the seller is available for purchase. Meat graded number one is of higher quality and usually provides more lean meat.

Table 6.1

MOISTURE-PROTEIN RATIOS

Meat Type	Moisture %	Protein %	Moisture-Protein Ratio
Beef hearts	77	16	5
Bull meat	74	21	4
Beef tripe	73	15	5
Beef chucks	72	20	4
Pork cheek meat	72	20	4
Pork head meat	63	16	4
Beef flanks	59	15	4
Pork belly trimmings	54	14	4
Regular pork trimmings	38	9	4
Pork fat	6	1	6

PROCESSED MEATS

Table 6.2

RAW MEAT MATERIALS USED FOR PREPARATION OF COMMINUTED PROCESSED MEATS

Cattle	Hogs	Veal	Sheep
Boneless primal cuts (chucks, plates, flanks, and navels)	Boneless primal cuts (hams, loins, shoulders, and bellies)	Boneless primal cuts	Boneless primal cuts
Trimmings from primal cuts	Trimmings from primal cuts	Hearts	Hearts
Cheeks	Cheeks	Cheeks	Cheeks
Head meat	Head meat	Tongues	Tongues
Hearts	Hearts		
Tripe	Stomachs		
Livers	Livers		
Tongues	Tongues		
Lips	Skins		
Giblet meat	Snouts		
Weasand meat	Giblet meat		
	Weasand meat		

Beef

The following cuts of boneless processing beef are usually quoted in market price sheets which serve the meat industry: whole-carcass bull meat, whole-carcass cow meat, boneless beef (90% lean), boneless chucks, trimmings (85 to 90%), trimmings (75 to 85%), insides, outsides, and knuckles. In addition, the following meat by-products are sometimes used for the manufacture of comminuted meat products: head meat, hearts, lips, weasand, and giblet meat. When cheeks are trimmed of overlying glandular and connective tissue, the resultant product is called cheek meat, to differentiate it from the untrimmed product referred to only as cheeks. When cheek meat is used in a comminuted-meat formulation, Federal inspection regulations require it to be labeled as either beef or pork, but it need not be referred to as beef or pork cheeks. If, however, the cheeks are not trimmed, they must be listed separately as beef cheeks or pork cheeks. Beef-head meat is removed from the poll of the head. Weasand and giblet meats are used for the cheapest grades of processed meat products. Weasand meat is the muscular tissue surrounding the esophagus. Giblet meat refers primarily to the diaphragm muscle.

Pork

Pork used in comminuted processed products comes from two sources: (1) boned primal cuts, usually from heavy hogs, and (2) trimmings obtained during preparation of primal cuts for curing or merchandising as fresh pork.

Pork trimmings may be either fresh or cured. When primal pork cuts that have already been injected with curing pickle are trimmed, the resultant meat is referred to as sweet pickled trim. Fresh pork trimmings are divided into lean and fat trim. Lean pork trimmings consist of (1) special lean (80%) and (2) extra lean (90%). Fat trim consists of (1) regular and (2) 50% trimmings. Regular pork trim contains 55 to 60% fat, whereas 50% pork trim contains 45 to 55% fat.

Veal and Mutton

Veal used in comminuted processed meats is either whole-carcass or veal trimmings. Because veal comes from young animals, there is little fat on the carcass. Therefore, both whole-carcass veal and veal trimmings are quite lean. On occasion, mutton, usually in the form of whole-carcass meat, is used in processed meat products. Mutton is usually quite dark in color and contributes desirable pigment to comminuted sausage or canned meat formulations. Mutton has good binding properties, but because of pronounced flavor, its usage is usually restricted to 20% or less of the total meat block.

Variety Meats

Variety meats are used in many comminuted processed meat products. Government regulations specify that variety meats must be labeled specifically as to origin. Those finding greatest use in processed meat products are tongues, livers, hearts, tripe, and pork stomachs. Three types of tongues or tongue trimmings are available: (1) tongues, (2) tongue trimmings, and (3) tongue meat. Federal inspection regulations require that all glandular and connective tissue obtained when long-cut tongues are converted to short-cut tongues be identified as tongue trimmings and further identified according to species. Trimmings from the tongue itself must be referred to as tongue meat and identified according to species. Tongue meat, however, may not include tongue trimmings. Tongues are scalded to remove the mucous membrane.

Most beef, calf, and lamb livers are sold fresh, but hog livers are used primarily for the manufacture of liver sausage and braunschweiger. Regardless of ultimate use, the gallbladder is always removed from the liver immediately after the liver is cut from the carcass. Livers are not generally scalded, but some processors of braunschweiger do use scalded livers.

When heart or heart meat is used for the manufacture of processed meats, the label must indicate species. Hearts are classified as either heart or heart meat. Heart meat refers to the trimmed heart with the cap removed.

Beef tripe is obtained from the paunch. The paunch is trimmed free of adhering fat, opened, and the contents removed. It is then washed and scrubbed. The mucous membrane covering the inner surface of the tripe is removed during the scrubbing operation. For use in processed meats, tripe is frequently scalded and cooked.

Pork stomachs are prepared similar to beef tripe. The stomachs are opened and washed and the mucous membrane removed during the washing operation. They also may be scalded before being used.

Partially Defatted Tissue

Partially defatted beef and pork tissues are subjected to low-temperature rendering to remove fat without denaturing the protein. Two types of partially defatted tissues are available: (1) chopped and (2) fatty. Chopped tissues can be used in meat sausages in unrestricted amounts, but fatty tissues cannot be used in meat products and are limited to a level of 15% by Federal inspection regulations.

SMOKED MEATS

Hams

Fresh or green hams, as they are often called in the packing industry, are not sold according to quality grades but rather according to weight grades. Market prices are generally quoted on the basis of the following weight grade classifications: below 14, 14 to 17, 17 to 20, 20 to 25, 25 to 30, and over 30 lb. Lighter-weight hams, those below 20 lb, are generally of higher quality than heavier hams. Hams weighing in excess of 20 lb come from more mature hogs, frequently sows. Heavy hams usually are darker in color, coarser in texture, and less tender than lighter hams. If they are not used in comminuted meat products, heavy hams are frequently boned and sectioned. Individual sections are canned or processed in stockinettes, casings, or metal molds for sale as individual ham units. Heavy hams are often made into cooked or boiled hams. Since these hams are sliced thin and eaten cold, problems of coarse texture, toughness, and sex odor are minimal.

Since very little ham is consumed fresh, most hams are traded within the packing industry between slaughterer and processor. In addition to weight grade, the value of green hams is affected by (1) trim style, (2) length of shank, and (3) length of butt.

Hams are classified according to trim style as (1) rough, (2) regular, (3) skinned, and (4) skinless. Market prices are quoted for skinned hams unless otherwise specified. Rough hams are untrimmed hams with only the foot removed. No additional trimming is done. Regular hams are produced by removing the tail bone and flank in addition to the foot. Skinned hams have the foot, tail bone, flank, and half of the skin removed. Skinless hams are trimmed like skinned hams, except that all skin is removed. Both skinless and skinned hams have excess surface fat removed and are beveled toward the butt end. Hams represent from 22 to 28% of a carcass, or about 17 to 19% when prepared as skinned hams.

Green hams are sold with the foot removed at the hock. However, they can be purchased as short-shanked hams with the foot cut off close to the body. In another case, the foot is removed below the hock. Such hams are referred to as long-shanked hams and are used primarily for preparation of Country hams.

Hams are usually separated from the loin by cutting between the second and third sacral vertebrae parallel to the angle of the hock joint. Depending on the market for pork loins, hams can be separated from the loin closer to or farther from the aitch bone. The closer a ham is cut to the aitch bone, the smaller the ham butt.

The anatomical structure of a ham lends itself to division into either two or three primary sections. Bones in a ham are shown in Fig. 6.1. It is necessary to understand the position of these bones before a ham can be sectioned properly.

One method of division separates a boneless ham into two sections—(1) cushion and (2) knuckle. Most of the butt and shank meat remain with the cushion. The cushion section comprises 75 to 80% of the total boneless ham weight, the knuckle—called cap in certain areas of the country—accounting for the remainder. Prior to sectioning, all bones are removed in the conventional manner. Fig. 6.2 shows a ham with all bones positioned and an approximate point of division used to section a boneless ham.

Another method of sectioning a boneless ham is to subdivide the cushion into top and bottom sections corresponding to (1) top or inside and (2) bottom or outside rounds of a beef carcass. Together with the

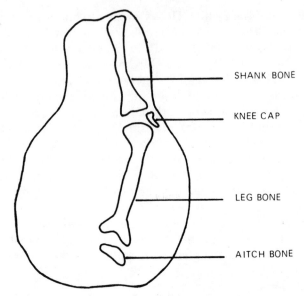

SHANK BONE

KNEE CAP

LEG BONE

AITCH BONE

FIG. 6.1. POSITION OF BONES IN HAM

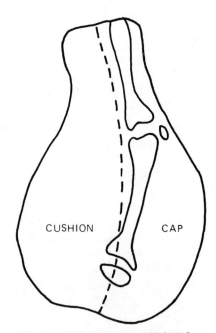

CUSHION   CAP

FIG. 6.2. BONELESS HAM SECTIONING

knuckle, inside and outside sections constitute the major natural muscle groupings of a ham. When reviewed as component pieces of a center-cut ham slice, the muscle groupings appear as shown in Fig. 6.3.

Because of widespread reluctance on the part of consumers to purchase pork products with even moderate amounts of fat and connective tissue, sectioned hams are usually well trimmed. A well-trimmed boneless ham has a boning yield of approximately 60% based on pumped weight. When a boneless ham is sectioned, approximately 25% is top, 27% is knuckle, 30% is bottom, and 18% is shank and butt meat.

Bellies

Rough bellies refer to untrimmed bellies with the spareribs in place. Trimmed bellies with the spareribs removed and the ends and sides trimmed constitute about 14% of carcass weight. Trimmed bellies can be purchased with the skin or rind either on or removed. Processors using bellies from their own slaughter operations to produce bacon for slicing derind them prior to processing. Fresh belly skins have more market value than processed skins. In either case, bellies are sold according to weight grade. Prices for the following weight grades of skin-on bellies are quoted on most markets: 8 to 10, 10 to 12, 12 to 14, 14 to 16, 16 to 18, 18 to 20, and 20 to 25 lb. The grades for derind bellies are as follows: 7 to 9, 9 to 11, 11 to 13, 13 to 15, 15 to 17, and 17 to 19 lb. Approximately 9 to 11% of the belly is in the skin. As is true with all lean primal cuts of pork, heavier bellies have less quality and more fat than do lighter bellies. This statement is generally true, but does not take into account skippy bellies. Highest-quality bacon is made from skin-on bellies weighing 10 to 16 lb. Bellies used for dry salting usually weigh at least 20 lb and generally in excess of 25 lb.

Teats do not accompany quality bellies but are removed in the trimming operation. Likewise, care is taken to remove small pieces of car-

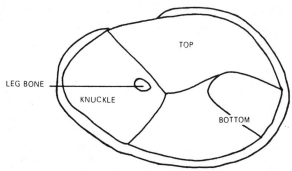

FIG. 6.3. MUSCLE GROUPINGS OF CENTER CUT HAM SLICE

tilage which may remain when the spareribs are removed. Bacon prepared from bellies with teats left in place is referred to as seedy bacon, while that prepared from bellies with pieces of cartilage remaining is known as bony bacon. Bellies that are excessively thick contain larger amounts of fat in relation to lean. However, some bellies are too thin to produce quality bacon. Excessively thin bellies are referred to as skippy bellies. Skippy bellies come from either very young hogs or poorly developed hogs of any age. They lack firmness and produce very narrow bacon slices. Skippy bellies are usually used for sausage or number two bacon.

Pork Shoulders

Pork shoulders can be processed as complete shoulders but, in most cases, they are divided into two primal cuts: (1) Boston butts and (2) picnics. Both Boston butts and picnics are sold according to weight grade, as are other primal pork cuts. Pork shoulders represent about 23% of the hog carcass, or about 14 to 16% when trimmed. The trimmed shoulder refers to the shoulder with neck bones, ribs, breast flap, and foot removed and one-third collar of skin left on the picnic.

Boston butts are the upper halves of pork shoulders. The usual market weight grades are 4 to 8 lb and 8 lb and over. Boston butts that have been boned and trimmed are called boneless butts. They are commonly referred to as CT or cellar-trimmed butts, and are sold according to 3 weight grades: 1½ to 3, 3 to 4½, and 4½ to 6 lb.

The term picnic or less frequently, cala, is commonly applied to the lower half of pork shoulders. Picnics are cut from skinned shoulders which have had the rib, neck bone, and breast flap removed and foot cut off at the knee or 1 in. above. Picnics have all skin removed to within 4 in. of the base of the shank, and the fat is beveled to approximately ½ in. thickness. Green picnics are traded on the market graded according to the following weights: 4 to 6, 6 to 8, and 8 lb and over.

As with hams, heavier butts and picnics generally come from larger, more mature hogs. These heavier cuts tend to be somewhat darker in color, coarser in texture, and less tender than similar cuts from younger hogs.

Pork Loins

Pork loins are used to produce two smoked-meat products: (1) smoked pork loins, which are merchandised in the form of either chops or roasts, and (2) Canadian bacon. Approximately 20% of a hog carcass is in the untrimmed loins, while trimmed loins represent 14 to 17% of the carcass. Bone-in pork loins are sold on the market graded according to the following weight classes: 14 and below, 14 to 17, 17 to 20, and 20 lb and over. They are classified as regular loins. Regular loins have excess fat removed from the tenderloin and not more than ½ in. of fat left covering the outside of the loins. Both blade and ham ends remain on the loin.

Canadian bacon is manufactured from boneless pork loins. The largest muscle in the pork loin, commonly referred to as the strip or sirloin muscle, is removed from heavy loins and sold as a Canadian back, generally weighing 5 to 9 lb.

Processed Beef Cuts

Beef plates comprised of a brisket and short plate are used to prepare beef bacon and most corned beef. Lean corned beef is also produced from muscles of the round and the shoulder clod. Primal cuts from low-grade carcasses can be used, but the finished products reflect the original raw materials utilized.

Dried beef is generally processed from muscles of the round of lean cattle. On occasion, shoulder clods are also used. The sub-primal cuts utilized are usually removed from carcasses that would find little acceptance for block beef cuts.

STORAGE OF RAW MATERIALS

The life of any raw meat material is related to (1) sanitation and (2) refrigeration. All raw materials should be handled under the most sanitary conditions possible. Unless they are to be used warm directly from the kill floor, meats should be chilled as rapidly as possible to approximately 30°F and maintained at this temperature until used. If trimmings are not to be used within 5 days, they should be frozen immediately and held at 0°F or below. Primal cuts, such as hams and bellies, can be held for longer periods of time before they need to be frozen. Frozen primal cuts such as loins, bellies, and hams must be thawed before being cured. Thawing is done in a cooler operating at less than 50°F, or in cold running water. Trimmings used in comminuted products are sawed or chopped into pieces small enough to be fed into a grinder or cut in a sausage chopper. It is not necessary to thaw trimmings before use.

CERTIFIED PORK

To ensure that processed meat products that are usually eaten without being cooked by the consumer and that have not been cooked by the processor to at least 137°F are free of trichina, pork certified by Federal inspection authorities to be free of trichina should be used. To be certified, pork must be subjected continuously to a temperature not higher than that specified in Table 6.3. The duration of refrigeration at the specified temperature is dependent on the thickness of the meat or the inside dimensions of the container.

Federal inspection regulations relating to freezing meat to kill trichina, as specified in Table 6.3, read as follows:

"Group 1 comprises product in separate pieces not exceeding six inches in thickness, or arranged on separate racks with the layers not exceeding six inches in depth, or stored in crates or boxes not exceeding six inches in depth, or stored as solidly frozen blocks not exceeding six inches in thickness.

"Group 2 comprises product in pieces, layers, or within containers, the thickness of which exceeds 6 inches but not 27 inches, and product in containers including tierces, barrels, kegs, and cartons having a thickness not exceeding 27 inches."

If the pork is not described in Table 6.3, the meat must be frozen to a minimum temperature of −30°F in the center.

UNDESIRABLE CONDITIONS

Processed meat products reflect the quality of raw materials used in their manufacture. Aside from meat deterioration due to development of rancidity or microbiological contamination, the suitability of meats for use in manufactured products depends in part on their freedom from the following undesirable conditions: (1) PSE musculature, (2) two-toning, (3) sex odor, and (4) mutton flavor.

Pale, Soft, Watery Pork

Pale, soft, watery or exudative pork, referred to as PSE pork, is a major concern of meat processors. Normal pork is grayish-pink

Table 6.3

FREEZING REQUIREMENTS FOR TRICHINA-FREE PORK*

Temperature °F	Group 1 Days	Group 2 Days
5	20	30
−10	10	20
−20	6	12

* In accordance with Federal meat inspection regulations.

tinged with red in color, firm, and dry. PSE pork is quite pale, soft, and watery. Generally, there is very little evidence of marbling, and muscles are pulled loose from connective tissue attachments. The incidence of PSE pork is related to the following variables:

(1) Season: it is highest when environmental temperatures are high or fluctuating markedly.

(2) Breed of hog: Poland Chinas, Landrace, Hampshires, and Yorkshires are most susceptible. Chester Whites, Durocs, and Berkshires are most resistant.

(3) Sex: slightly higher incidence in gilts than in barrows.

(4) Muscling or lack of fat: highest incidence is in meaty hogs and those with little backfat.

The problem is associated with rapid accumulation of acid in muscular tissues after slaughter, which results in tissues with low pH. Low pH tissues are characteristically light in color, soft, and bind water poorly. Whenever possible, PSE pork should be avoided as a raw material for both sausage and smoked meats. When PSE pork is used for the manufacture of smoked-meat products, such as hams, picnics, and bacon, the end products are usually dry because PSE pork has poor water-binding ability. Cured primals made from PSE pork average 3 to 5% more shrink in the smokehouse than those made with normal pork. Additionally, when PSE pork is used, the finished products, whether primal or comminuted, will usually be light in color. PSE pork is not a desirable component of comminuted meat products because of its poor ability to bind water and emulsify fat.

Two-Toning

Two-toning is associated with muscular tissues of swine. It refers to light and dark color in the same surface or muscle. All primal cuts from pork carcasses can be affected, but the condition is most commonly associated with hams. The normal color of fresh pork is referred to as grayish-pink tinged with red. Pork primals that are too dark are also undesirable, just as are two-toned primals. Pale-colored muscles can be produced by feeding iron-deficient rations to pigs. Both pale and dark colors are associated with pH and the content of myoglobin. High-pH meats are dark in color and have good water-binding and emulsifying properties. On the other hand, low-pH meats are pale in color and have poor water-binding and emulsifying properties. The reason for light and dark colors in the same surface is not known. It may be related to metabolic activity of individual muscles or in the various portions of single muscles. The condition is minimized in cured pork products, but it is present. Two-toning does not appear to affect consumer acceptability for such factors as tenderness, juiciness, and flavor to any marked extent. Its effect is primarily from a visual or aesthetic viewpoint.

Sex Odor

Sex odor refers to the objectionable odor which on occasion emanates from pork when heated. Until recent years, this odor was referred to as boar odor. However, research workers have shown the odor to be associated with barrows, gilts, and sows, as well as with boars and stags. Nonetheless, the incidence has been shown to be much greater in boars than in other classes of swine. Sex odor is present in fat but not in lean tissues. It can be detected when fat is heated to high temperatures, but odor intensity varies from one carcass to another. Federal inspection regulations specify that meat with pronounced sexual odor must be condemned and cannot be used for food products or for rendering. Meat which has less than a pronounced sex odor can be used only in comminuted cook meat food products, or for rendering. The exact cause of sex odor is unknown, but at least one responsible compound, a steroid, 5α-androst-16-ene-3-one, has been identified. Raw materials suspected of having sex odor can be checked by heating a small sample and sniffing the odor emanated during cooking.

Mutton Flavor

Because of a distinct somewhat strong flavor associated with mutton, meat from mutton carcasses is less marketable than lamb. As with sex odor, there is a wide difference in the ability of people to identify mutton flavor. Although mutton usually contributes highly desirable lean to processed-meat formulations, use should be limited to no more than approximately 20 to 25% of the total meat block to avoid significant contribution to product flavor. Mutton carcasses are recognized by the round joint on their forelegs, but mutton flesh is distinguished from lamb chiefly by color. Mutton flesh tends to be dark red in contrast to the pink color of lamb. In addition, the texture of mutton is somewhat more coarse. Textural differences may not always be detectable visually. Cause of mutton flavor is not known definitely, but is related to the age of the sheep.

BIBLIOGRAPHY

ANON. 1971. The Yellow Sheet. The National Provisioner Daily Market & News Service, National Provisioner, Chicago, Ill.

BATCHER, O. M., BRANT, A. W., and KUNZE, M. S. 1969. Sensory evaluation of lamb and yearling mutton flavors. J. Food Sci. *34*, 272.

BEERY, K. E., SINK, J. D., PATTON, S., and ZIEGLER, J. H. 1971. Characterization of the swine sex odor components in boar fat volatiles. J. Food Sci. *36*, 1086.

BRISKEY, E. J., and KAUFFMAN, R. G. 1971. Quality characteristics of muscle as a food. *In* The Science of Meat and Meat Products, J. F. Price and B. S. Schweigert (Editors). W. H. Freeman and Co., San Francisco, Calif.

HOFSTRAND, J., and JACOBSON, M. 1960. The role of fat in the flavor of lamb and mutton as tested with broths and depot fats. Food Res. *25*, 706.

KRAMLICH, W. E. 1971. Sausage products. *In* The Science of Meat and Meat Products, J. F. Price and B. S. Schweigert (Editors). W. H. Freeman and Co., San Francisco, Calif.

MacKENZIE, D. S. 1966. Prepared Meat Product Manufacturing, 2nd Edition. American Meat Institute, Chicago, Ill.

PATTERSON, R. L. S. 1968. 5α-androst-16-ene-3-one: Compound responsible for taint in boar fat. J. Sci. Food Agr. *19*, 31.

PEARSON, A. M., THOMPSON, R. H., and PRICE, J. F. 1969. Sex odor in pork. *In* Proceedings of the Meat Industry Research Conference. Am. Meat Inst. Found., Chicago, Ill.

SAFFLE, R. L., and GALBREATH, J. W. 1964. Quantitative determination of salt-soluble protein in various types of meat. Food Technol. *18*, 119.

U.S. Dept. of Agr. 1970. Meat inspection regulations. Federal Register, Part II, *35*, No. 193.

WILSON, G. D., GINGER, I. D., SCHWEIGERT, B. S., and AUNAN, W. J. 1959. A study of the variations of myoglobin concentration in "two-toned" hams. J. Animal Sci. *18*, 1080.

ZIEGLER, P. T. 1956. The Meat We Eat, 9th Edition. Interstate Printers & Publishers, Danville, Ill.

CHAPTER 7

Sausages

Sausages are meat products that are salted and usually seasoned. The name is derived from the Latin term *salsus* meaning salt. Today, they are one of the most popular meat products in the U.S. From ancient times to the present day the sausage mixture has been encased, assuming a cylindrical form. This shape has become traditionally the sausage shape, and in most instances, is one of the characteristics that differentiate sausages from other meat products. Meat products sold to the consumers in cylindrical form must meet the compositional requirements for sausage. This is in contrast to loaves, which must be in rectangular or loaf form. Sliced loaves, however, can be made in a round form, provided the slices are unit-packaged at the point of manufature and labeled appropriately, or are packaged at warehouses under regulatory inspection.

CONSUMER ACCEPTANCE

Sausages are often products of local preference. For example, by observing the kind of frankfurters an individual consumes, you can make a reasonable guess as to his geographical origin. Frankfurters in Texas are of a deep red hue and of a hot spicy flavor, whereas frankfurters in New England or Cincinnati are more likely to be a pale pink and of a mild flavor. Of course it is difficult to establish precise market patterns, since one of the most successful manufacturers of nationally distributed sausages has stressed uniformity of color, flavor, and texture. On the other hand, the U.S. Army Quartermaster has had difficulty in developing specifications for sausage. The ingreditents, composition, and quality assurance demanded by the Army specifications are excellent. However, individuals within the heterogeneous military group often yearn for the product back home. The nostalgia for back-home products has defied our most capable scientific groups when developing specifications for food products for the Armed Forces. As a marketing concept, the desire for old-time, back-home, old-country farm products leads one to believe that considerable nostalgia may be sold with each pound of this type product.

Consumers today are interested in sausages from the standpoints of nutrition, economy, and versatility or adaptability. Sausages can be served for breakfast, lunch, dinner and for snacks. The satiety factor of sausages is high. Furthermore, sausages are quite good nutritionally, since the animal proteins supply amino acids of the right type and in the proper proportions. Consumers often associate the color, flavor, and textural qualities of sausages with brand names. "Buy a pound, serve a pound" is a well established phrase for developing consumer interest in most types of sausage.

CLASSIFICATION

The term sausage covers such a large number of diversified products that no single system of classification is completely satisfactory. One system separates sausages into (1) ground and (2) emulsion-type products. In some parts of the U.S., sausage is ground pork, and the emulsified items are designated by specific names, such as frankfurters, wieners, bologna, and braunschweiger. In other areas sausage is a generic term that includes all sausage items. The latter will be used throughout this text.

At times the meat components, cure, spices, or casings are used to further define sausages. Beef casing or B. C. salami, garlic bologna, and beef wiener are common trade terms used to characterize sausages.

The classification shown in Table 7.1 is used in this text. This classification is based on physical differences and the properties of sausage that are imposed by operational procedures.

Ground sausages show discrete particles of meat. In the case of emulsion-type sausages, fat is emulsified and stabilized by the lean components. Both types can be chilled, cured, cooked, dried, frozen, or smoked. Coarse-ground and emulsion-type sausages can be prepared with the same type equipment in many instances. However, differences in structure of the sausage mass require different types and degrees of handling and processing to yield acceptable products. The principles of the equipment are essentially the same, but it does vary in size depending on the volume to be produced. Selection of equipment by

Table 7.1

SAUSAGE CLASSIFICATION

Coarse-ground	Emulsion
Smoked	Smoked
Cooked	Cooked
Chilled	Chilled
Frozen	Frozen
Dried	Dried
Cured	Cured

sausage manufacturers is tempered by a number of factors, such as space, labor, price, volume, and time. In many instances it is purchased and added to an existing operation. New equipment can markedly aid in the successful growth of an operation, or act as a bottleneck to impede the existing process.

An important concept to recognize is that processing of sausages is a continuous sequence of events in which it is not practical to consider any one step separately or to assign more importance to one step than to another. Each step in the proper sequence, therefore, is important to a successful operation. Nevertheless, in studying the sausage process, it is convenient to separate the process into definite categories. The operational handling starts with grinding the meat ingredients.

GRINDING

The grinder components are illustrated in Fig. 7.1. Meat chunks of variable size and shape and with variable fat contents are ground to form uniform cylinders of fat and lean. The worm or screw feed in the barrel of the grinder conveys the meat and presses it into holes of the grinder plate. The rotating blade cuts the compressed meat and aids in filling the grinder plate holes. The size of the holes in the grinder plate determines the diameter, and the thickness of the plate determines the length of the cylindrical particles. Particles of lean and fat passed through a ⅛-in. plate which is ⅝ in. thick will give approximately 35 million small cylinders per 1,000 lb meat. Proper mixing of these particles is extremely important to obtain a uniform

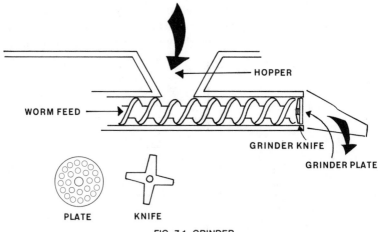

FIG. 7.1. GRINDER

blend, which is a necessary requirement if the pre-mix or pre-batching technique is to be used.

MIXING

Cylinders of fat and lean obtained by grinding are tumbled in a mixer to give a uniform distribution of fat and lean particles. This can be used for coarse-ground sausages or for emulsion-type sausages by utilizing a chopper or emulsifier, and with suitable additions of required ingredients to obtain the desired texture and uniformity of composition. Components of the mixer are illustrated in Fig. 7.2. The mixer should never be overloaded, since this prevents good mixing. Filling the mixer to the top of the paddles or blades only is a means of assuring proper mixing.

CHOPPING

A chopper is illustrated in Fig. 7.3. It is composed of a revolving metal bowl that contains the meat, while knife blades rotating on an axle cut through the revolving meat mass. A chopper is often used as a means of batching the sausage mix, the mixed batch being transferred to an emulsifier for acquiring the desired texture. A chopper is basically a knife on an axle; speed of the knife, rpm of the bowl, and sharpness of the blades are all factors in its performance. The chopper is also called a silent cutter or a flyer. The latter is the descriptive

CHAMBER

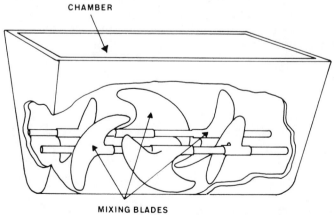

MIXING BLADES

FIG. 7.2. MIXER

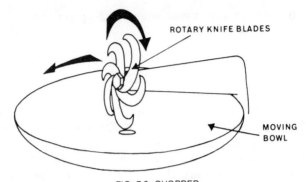

FIG. 7.3. CHOPPER

term in New England, where chopping is sometimes called flying the meat. The temperature of the meat mass during chopping will rise 10 to 20°F in 10 to 15 min of chopping. About 25 to 30% of the heat used in processing is contributed by the chopper or emulsifier.

EMULSIFYING

An emulsifier is illustrated in Fig. 7.4. This machine combines the principles of grinding and chopping. Emulsifiers handle large volumes of meat rapidly to produce a desired texture. The emulsifier should be fed uniform mixes because it rapidly passes increments of meat mixes through an orifice that may hold 2 lb or less of product. In the course of a few seconds, 100 lb of meat pass through an emulsifier, with a rise in temperature of 8 to 15°F. The heat formed at the contact surfaces must be extremely high; however, accurate determinations of the amount and distribution of heat have not been made. The advantage in its use has been the speed of handling materials, the high degree of disintegration of meat tissues, and the ease of obtaining desired textures.

STUFFING

The sausage emulsion, also known in the trade as mix, sausage dough, or batter, is transferred to stuffers for extruding the mix or emulsion into casings. At this point, the size and shape of the product is determined. Three types of stuffers are used: (1) piston, (2) pump, and (3) one that combines the features of the piston and pump in a single unit.

An illustration of the components of a piston stuffer is given in Fig. 7.5. The piston-type stuffer is essentially a large barrel or cylinder

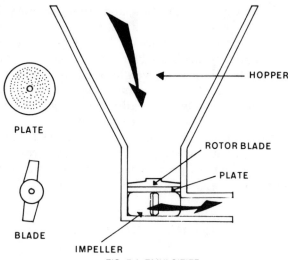

FIG. 7.4. EMULSIFIER

that has a moving plate. The plate is usually raised by air pressure and pushes the meat mixture through a stuffing lock and finally through a tubular structure called a stuffing horn. The horn size is selected in relation to the size and type of casing to be used. Usually a horn of as large a diameter as possible is used to reduce smearing of the emulsion.

The piston-type stuffer is recommended for coarse-ground sausages and those having fat chunks, olives, pimento, and pickles, because these items may be damaged by impeller-type pumps. These usually

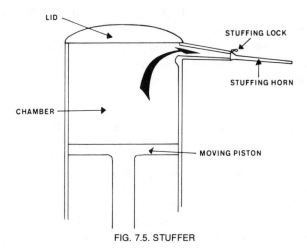

FIG. 7.5. STUFFER

have feed-back and pop-off connectors, and are satisfactory for stuffing other emulsion-type products such as frankfurters or bologna.

The stuffer that combines features of the piston and pump usually has a volumetric delivery and is used for small sausages and for stuffing uniform-weight rather than catch-weight products. Air pressure of 125 psi is used with many stuffers. The pumps, however, frequently work on a continuous basis, the by-pass valve handling the cycling of the emulsion when stuffing is not being carried out.

A special system for stuffing and linking skinless frankfurters has been developed which allows automatic handling of casings. Approximately 3,000 lb or more of product per hr can be stuffed and linked with this machine.

LINKING AND TYING

After the emulsion is stuffed into casings, the encased mass is tied with thread or fastened with metal clips. In the case of small sausages, such as frankfurters, stuffed casings are twisted or drawn together to produce links, either by hand or with mechanical devices.

Large sausage items are tied or clipped at one end with a hanging tie and suspended from a smoke stick or hook so the entire surface is free from contact with the equipment. This permits a good flow of air around the sausages in the smokehouse and prevents touch marks and spotting due to contact with adjacently hanging products. With long bologna, 48 to 60 in. in length, the tendency is to process in uniform cellulosic casings, and place the encased bologna on a screen in a horizontal position. This horizontal processing aids in retaining a uniform cylinder of meat. If the heat capacity of the smokehouse is adequate, an increase in overall productivity results; 25 to 30% more product can be placed in the smokehouse, in contrast to the amount held in the vertical hanging positions. This has considerable interest where sliced bologna or sliced luncheon meats are prepared.

For frankfurters and other small sausages, hand-linking is rarely done today. Machines that stuff and link are now the accepted practice. For 10-to-the-lb frankfurters, hand-linking of 100 lb per hr was considered excellent. Present machines will link from 600 to 3,600 lb per hr. The 3,600 lb per hr is the amount of product simultaneously stuffed and linked with modern equipment. These high-speed linkers set the production economics of the sausage industry today.

Sausage links of the 10-to-the-lb size are draped on smokesticks, 8 or 9 links forming a loop. For example, frankfurter emulsion stuffed to 25 mm in casings 84 ft long gives 186 links and 18.6 lb of finished sausage. This corresponds to approximately 23 loops of 8 links or 21 loops of 9 links.

SMOKING AND COOKING

The draped smokesticks are placed on smoketrees or trolleys with 12 to 18 sticks per tree. Fig. 7.6 shows a smoketree with a stick of frankfurters. The average tree holds a 42-inch stick and measures 48 by 48 by 72 in.

The filled trees are transferred to the smokehouse, and while houses of 2 or 4 trees may be used, the trend is to larger houses holding at least 10 trees. In the continuous type of smokehouse the sausages are draped on hooks, or the smokestick is conveyed on a double belt or a moving-screen conveyor carrying the product without use of sticks.

The smokehouse operation is essentially a specialized drying and cooking operation in which sausage emulsion is coagulated. The important factors relating to smokehouse performance are as follows: (1)

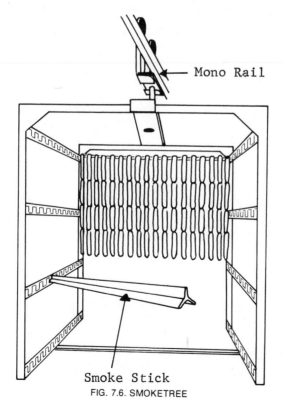

Mono Rail

Smoke Stick

FIG. 7.6. SMOKETREE

dimension, (2) time cycle, (3) temperature range, (4) thermal requirements (Btu), (5) relative humidity, (6) air flow, (7) air flow pattern, and (8) smoke density. These factors control the environment to which the sausage will be exposed during smoking and cooking.

Encased sausage at the time of introduction into the smokehouse usually has an internal temperature of 60 to 70°F. During cooking, this rises to 155 to 160°F. A rise of approximately 100°F is usually required, indicating that at least 10,000 Btu are needed for each 100 lb sausage to be cooked.

The rate at which sausages cook is influenced to a large extent by the air velocity in the smokehouse. As noted in Fig. 7.7, the greater the velocity, the faster the internal temperature of the sausage will rise. The cooking rate is much less affected by the level of humidity in the smokehouse, as indicated by Fig. 7.8 and 7.9. At high air velocities (4000 fpm), there is practically no difference in the heating rate of frankfurters cooked in both high- and low-humidity atmospheres. However, at lower air velocities (2000 fpm), frankfurters do cook slightly faster in a high-humidity atmosphere. The internal and surface heating rates of frankfurters are shown in Fig. 7.10.

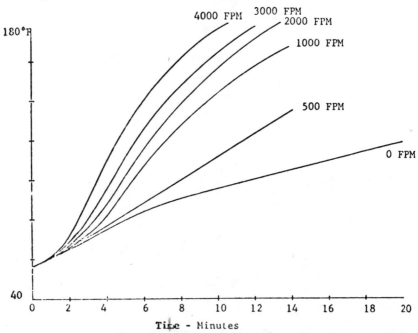

FIG. 7.7. INTERNAL HEATING RATES OF FRANKFURTERS PROCESSED IN SIZE 25 CELLULOSIC CASINGS (23 MM DIAMETER)

The frankfurters were cooked in an oven at 210°F with low relative humidity and various air velocities.

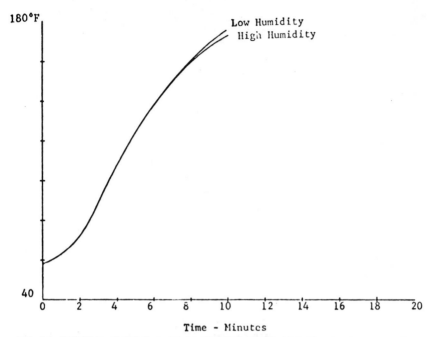

FIG. 7.8. INTERNAL HEATING RATE OF FRANKFURTERS COOKED AT LOW AND HIGH
RELATIVE HUMIDITIES

The frankfurters were stuffed in size 25 cellulosic casings (23 mm diameter) and cooked
in an oven at 210°F and an air velocity of 4000 FPM.

A 4-cage smokehouse, 9 ft long, 9 ft wide, and 8 ft high with a
smoke-producing unit attached has a 600,000 Btu per hr rating, 40,000
Btu being supplied by the smoke generator. This smokehouse holds
from 1,000 to 2,000 lb of product, and with 8 to 11 changes of air
per minute cooks and smokes frankfurters in 1 hr or less, and large-
diameter bologna in 6 to 8 hr. The 4 cages, totaling 1,000 lb of sausage,
require 100,000 Btu. However, the high heat-exchange potential is
important when rapid heating of the environment within the
smokehouse is required. After the temperature level of the smokehouse
is reached, only 15 to 20% of the heat is required to maintain this
temperature level.

Air-flow patterns are important to production performance when
the variables in size, shape, and methods of holding within a
smokehouse are considered. Ham, bacon, bologna, and frankfurters,
because of the size and shape differences, may require different air
velocities to achieve optimum heat exchange.

Smoke-density control is necessary to obtain uniformly smoked products. Smoke density can be measured with an electric eye instrument;
30 or 40% transmission of light as recorded on the instrument has

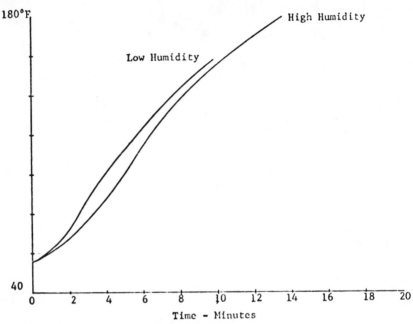

FIG. 7.9. INTERNAL HEATING RATE OF FRANKFURTERS COOKED AT LOW AND HIGH
RELATIVE HUMIDITIES

The frankfurters were stuffed in size 25 cellulosic casings (23 mm diameter) and cooked
at 210°F and an air velocity of 2000 FPM.

been demonstrated to provide an acceptable level of smoke on frankfurters made in continuous processing ovens.

CHILLING

After smoking and cooking the product is showered with cold water
and then chilled by refrigeration. On large-volume, continuous operations chilling is frequently done with a brine solution by dipping or
spraying the products. A 6% salt brine is reasonably close to osmotic
balance with the sausage. This brine permits lower chill temperatures
and rapid cooling of the product. A 10-to-the-lb size frankfurter can
be chilled to an internal temperature of 40°F in 7 to 8 min. The balanced
brine inhibits leaching of salt from the sausage and imbibing of water
by the sausage. The increased rate of chilling obtained when a brine
is used is illustrated in Fig. 7.11.

PEELING AND PACKAGING

After properly chilling the product, usually to an internal temperature of 35 to 40°F, the cellulosic casings on frankfurters and slicing

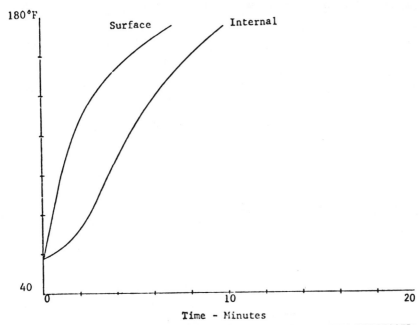

FIG. 7.10. INTERNAL AND SURFACE HEATING RATES OF FRANKFURTERS PROCESSED IN SIZE 25 CELLULOSIC CASINGS (23 MM DIAMETER)

The frankfurters were cooked in an oven at 210°F with low relative humidity and an air velocity of 4000 FPM.

bologna are removed. This constitutes the peeling operation. In the past, hand removal of cellulosic casings from frankfurters was slow; removal of the casings from 100 to 125 lb of sausage per hr was considered a good rate. Modern machines remove the casings from 5,000 lb of frankfurters per hr.

Peeled frankfurters are unit-packed, usually in 1-lb units, by special packaging machinery; 6- to 10-lb bulk packages are assembled by hand. Large slicing bolognas are peeled, sliced, and packaged, 6-oz to 1-lb packages being the most popular sizes.

COARSE-GROUND SAUSAGES

The manufacture of coarse-ground products such as fresh pork sausage, semi-dry, and dry sausages is described here in detail. Formulations for these products are given in Chapter 9.

The various basic handling procedures and equipment used in preparing sausages have been described. This section describes the use of this information in making various sausages characterized as either coarse-ground or emulsion-type.

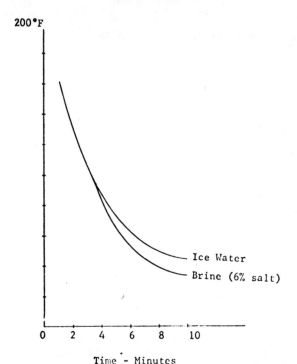

FIG. 7.11. INTERNAL COOLING RATE OF COOKED FRANKFURTERS IN ICE WATER AND
BRINE

The frankfurters were stuffed in size 25 cellulosic casings (23 mm diameter) and cooked
to an internal of 155°F.

Fresh Pork Sausage

Pork sausage is prepared by selecting fresh, chilled pork trimmings
approximately 65% lean and grinding the trimmings through a ½- to
1-in. plate. To 100 lb trimmings, add 1½ lb salt, 3 oz cane sugar,
2 oz sage, ¼ oz ginger, and 4 oz white or decorticated pepper. These
are blended in a mixer and finally passed through a ¼-in. plate. The
ground mixture is transferred to a piston stuffer and stuffed into sheep,
hog, or collagen casings. Cloth bags, cellulosic casings, and plastic
pouches are used at times for 1- to 6-lb units. Hog casings are stuffed
and coiled in units for Country-style pork sausage.

A formulation of the type described above can be prepared as a
skinless-type pork sausage by stuffing into cellulosic casings of ¾-in.
diameter and 40 to 50 ft in length. The casing may be shortened or
lengthened as required to fit on the stuffing horn. The important point
is to reduce or prevent fat smearing. The stuffed casing is linked on
a Ty-linker with thread, the links draped on a smokestick and showered
with 140 to 150°F hot water for 5 sec to melt any fat adhering to

the casing inner wall. The product is placed in a blast chill to freeze. When the internal temperature reaches 10 to 15°F, the sausage is peeled by splitting the casing with a knife blade and removing the split casing. Score marks on the sausage surface are removed by holding the peeled sausage in a cooler for a few hours. This type of skinless sausage is popular in Canada where a cereal binder is included in the formula to produce a breakfast-type sausage.

A common practice today is to package pork sausage in plastic tubes using a mechanical dispenser. The tube is formed from a plastic sheet and then clipped to give a cylindrical unit pack; 3000 1-lb units or more can be prepared per hour with this type of unitized handling on a single machine.

Encased or packaged pork sausage is marketed either frozen or refrigerated. The lower temperatures, 0 to −10°F for frozen and 28 to 36°F for chilled, permit longer shelf life and flavor retention.

Semidry Sausage

Semidry sausage is usually made from pork or beef or a mixture of the two and is characterized by a moisture content averaging 40 to 45%.

A variety of sausages are included in this category such as summer sausage, goteberg, cervelat, thuringer, and holsteiner. They have excellent keeping qualities with little refrigeration because (1) some reduction in microbiological contaminants is achieved in the cooking process, (2) a high salt-to-moisture ratio contributes to retarding bacterial growth, and (3) a low pH (5.3 or less) provides the tangy flavor and serves a protective function. Good keeping quality is achieved with a pH of 4.8 to 5.0 and with a total acidity of 0.75 to 1.0% calculated as lactic acid.

Summer sausage is a good example of the handling and processing required for semidry sausages. Grind pork trimmings through a ¼-in. plate and beef trimmings through a ⅛-in. plate. Place the ground meats in a mixer, add the salt, sugar, spices, cure, and starter culture, and mix for 2 to 3 min. Then regrind the mix through the ¼-in. plate. Hold the mix for 12 to 72 hr at 40°F. Then stuff into animal or cellulosic casings of approximately 4.5- to 5-lb capacity, using casings 3.5 in. in diameter and 22 in. long. Follow stuffing with a warm water shower for 2 min to wash the sausage surface free of any adhering particles. Smoke the encased sausage for 16 hr at 110°F. Then shower with cold water for about 15 min. Allow to stand at room temperature so the surface dries and then chill to 40°F. Semidry sausages have improved shelf life if stored refrigerated rather than at room temperature.

Dry Sausage

Semidry sausages are smoked and cooked to varying degrees, whereas dry sausage is not cooked, and only with some products is smoke applied. The manufacture of dry sausages is more difficult to control than that of semidry or more conventional type sausages. Overall processing time may require up to 90 days. As a result of this prolonged holding the sausage is vulnerable to chemical and microbiological degradation. However, when prepared properly, the finished sausages are usually stable and can be held with little or no refrigeration. The salt, acid, and moisture content, as well as specific types of organisms associated with the product, make for the characteristic flavor and texture of dry sausages. The raw materials and the sequence of events must be carefully controlled. Dry sausages are the "ne plus ultra" of the industry and the dry sausage maker is truly an artist.

The initial dry-sausage mixes are held under specified conditions of refrigeration to establish a medium for bacterial culture. After this, the mixture is stuffed into casings of suitable size. With animal casings the sausage is usually held in a stockinette through at least one-third to one-half the drying cycle, or until the dry casing can retain the weight of the sausage without stretching at the hanging tie. With cellulosic casings it is not necessary to use stockinettes for support. During the drying cycle the products will lose about 25 to 30% of their weight. The temperature, relative humidity, and air flow must be controlled so that drying proceeds properly. Air flow may vary from 15 to 20 changes per hour in the drying room. If drying is too slow the texture may be soft, the surface may discolor, and some molds or yeast may develop on the product. If drying is too fast, a surface crust develops and a brown or dark ring appears under the surface and at times marked ridges or invaginations occur at the sausage surface.

The proper ratio of fat to lean is important to give good conformation to the sausage. It is important to use well-trimmed meat to avoid glandular tissues. Lipase in glands often splits or liquefies fat; as a result, fat drains from the sausage later in the process, producing a series of small honeycombs or pin-holes in the body of the sausages. It is important to eliminate or reduce air pockets during stuffing since the meat around these pockets will discolor. Upon continued drying, large pockets may develop in the sausage body, or a cobweb-like structure may form. Any of these conditions makes for an unattractive dry sausage. As a guide for drying conditions the Meat Inspection Service of the U.S.D.A. defines the time and type of drying depending on the diameter of the sausage.

Formulations for hard salami, Genoa salami, and pepperoni are given in Chapter 9. Hard salami is cooked; Genoa is simply air-dried, while pepperoni may be either cooked or air-dried. These sausage mixes should be stuffed as cold as possible and with a minimum of pressure. This keeps the fat particles intact and reduces smearing. Fat smearing can markedly increase the incidence of rancidity and surface discoloration.

Mortadella, a dry sausage prepared in a beef bladder, illustrates very precisely the problems and limitations imposed on sampling dry sausages. The surface or periphery is considerably different in composition from the center of the product. This condition occurs in sampling all types of sausages, but is more pronounced in dry sausages.

The mortadella analyzed was a pear-shaped product with a 2.5-in. diameter at the small end and 4.75-in. diameter at the large end, and measured 11 in. in length. This analysis, which is given in Table 7.2, also illustrates some of the mechanisms operating during production of dry sausages. Drying occurs from the outside inward, with pronounced surface drying. Some fat may render from the surface during the drying process. Also, it is obvious that the small end of the mortadella dries to a much greater degree than does the larger-diameter area under essentially the same conditions of drying.

The equipment used to manufacture dry sausages is relatively simple. Nevertheless, considerable control is needed, and some basic understanding of the fundamentals of raw material composition and of processing and handling is important for achieving this control. The problems associated with drying a meat mass to give a smooth cylinder and an organoleptically acceptable product have been discussed. The long processing time required to manufacture dry sausages makes it difficult to define the various factors involved in manufacture.

Table 7.2

MORTADELLA ANALYSIS

	Moisture %	Protein %	Fat %	Ash %
Large Diameter				
Center	49.2	18.4	24.1	6.6
Surface	33.5	27.4	30.4	5.2
Small Diameter				
Center	35.3	21.8	32.8	7.1
Surface	26.7	29.1	33.1	6.3

EMULSION-TYPE PRODUCTS

The manufacture of emulsion-type products, such as frankfurters, bologna, and liver sausage, is described here in detail. Formulations for these products are noted in Chapter 9.

The steps in preparing emulsion sausages such as bologna and skinless frankfurters are listed in Table 7.3. These steps are common to either small products such as frankfurters or large items such as bologna. The main difference is that after peeling, frankfurters are unit-packed, whereas bologna is often sliced before packaging.

Emulsion-type sausages are formed by solubilizing the meat proteins and suspending the fat particles in the protein solution. On subsequent heating the fat particles are entrapped within the protein matrix that has formed a little sac around the fat particle. In the process of forming the solution and coating the particles in a chopper or an emulsifier, considerable heat is generated, which must be absorbed to prevent coagulation of the protein at the emulsifying stage. Ice or cold water is added to aid emulsification of the fat and to impart good flow characteristics to the emulsion, important to the stuffing of meat emulsion into casings. The concept of emulsification is useful in understanding some of the problems related to sausage stability. The problems associated with emulsion stability are overchopping, short meat, rapid heating, and excessive heating. An analysis of these problems using the concepts of emulsion chemistry provides an understanding of the corrective measures needed and their application.

Emulsion

In Figure 7.12, a sausage emulsion is schematically presented with the broken stripes, illustrating the lean muscle fiber with a high myosin

Table 7.3

STEPS IN PREPARATION OF EMULSION SAUSAGES

(1) Selection of ingredients	(10) Shower
(2) Grind	(11) Chill
(3) Mix	(12) Peel or slice
(4) Chop or emulsify	(13) Package
(5) Stuff	(14) Scramble
(6) Link or tie	(15) Assemble
(7) Hang	(16) Package
(8) Smoke	(17) Ship
(9) Cook	(18) Display
	(19) Market

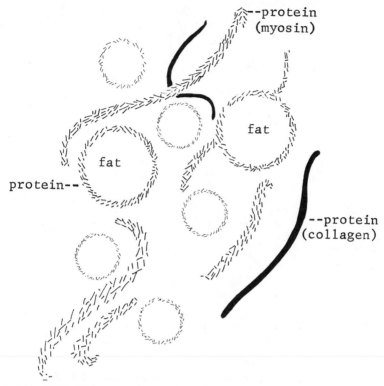

FIG. 7.12. SCHEMATIC REPRESENTATION OF AN EMULSION, SHOWING SOLUBILIZED
PROTEIN AND FAT GLOBULES COATED WITH PROTEIN

content. The term myosin is used collectively to represent the salt-soluble, heat-coagulable proteins and the water-soluble proteins associated with muscle. These proteins coagulate by heating at 130 to 135°F. The solid stripes represent the connective tissues which are rich in collagen-type proteins. Collagen fibers shrink to about one-third of their length on heating to 148°F, and with continuing heat, form gelatin. Collagen, under the conditions of sausage manufacture in the chopper, will imbibe considerable quantities of water. On heating later in the process, shrinkage occurs and the moisture is squeezed from the swollen fibers. The discs are representative of the fat particles, and the broken stripes on the rim surrounding the disc or globule of fat are the salt-soluble, heat-coagulable protein of the lean muscle.

Overchopping.—Figure 7.13 shows an isolated fat globule coated with the myosin-type protein. This globule, for illustration of the principle, arbitrarily measures 5 units in diameter. When this globule is chopped to give particles 1 unit in diameter, at least 125 units are formed from the 5 unit diameter fat globule. The volume remains

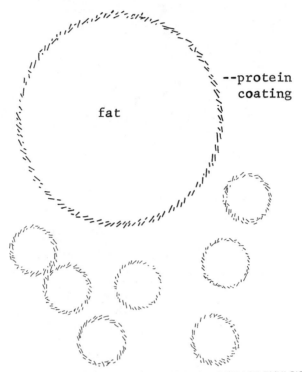

FIG. 7.13. ILLUSTRATION OF OVERCHOPPING A SAUSAGE EMULSION

the same; however, the surface of the fat increases 5-fold. As chopping is continued, the fat particles become smaller and smaller in diameter and the surface of the fat increases enormously. Eventually the fat surface becomes of such magnitude that the protein solution cannot adequately coat all of the fat particles, and uncoated or partially coated fat surfaces result. The uncoated fat renders from the mixture during heating and causes fat pocketing or greasing out of the emulsion. An unsightly and unsatisfactory sausage results. The corrective measure involves reviewing the chopping technique.

Short Meat.—Short meat is a condition occurring during preparation of sausages that is usually ill-defined. The problem is related to an imbalance of myosin to collagen in the meat components, or to a low content of lean meat in the formula. In Figure 7.14, the fat particles covered with myosin and those covered with collagen-type protein seem identical. However, on heat-processing the collagen shrinks, converts to gelatin, and drains from the fat surface, thereby giving an uncoated fat particle and a droplet of a gelatin solution. This is very serious and results in a most unsatisfactory product with a fat cap at the

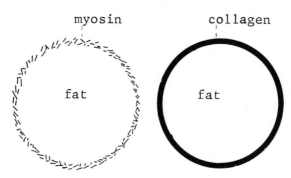

FIG. 7.14. FAT PARTICLES WITH MYOSIN AND COLLAGEN TYPE PROTEINS

top of the sausage and a jelly pocket at the bottom (Fig. 7.15). When this occurs it is necessary that a thorough check be made of the formulation and the meat supply.

Heat Breakdown.—Although the formulation and handling techniques are satisfactory, a problem of fat separation may arise as a result of heating too rapidly or at too high a temperature. During rapid heating the protein coating sets solid and entraps the fat particle. The fat particle expands on continued heating, whereas the protein coating has a tendency to shrink. With the outer portion of the particle shrinking and the innermost portion expanding, the coagulated protein sac ruptures, and entrapped fat separates or renders (see Fig. 7.16). This is encountered at times with frankfurters, and results in a small tip of fat at the smokestick mark. The surface of the frankfurter may have only a small amount of grease. This condition is not as unsightly as that resulting from overchopping or from short meat. When this

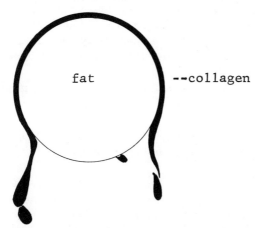

FIG. 7.15. SCHEMATIC REPRESENTATION OF FAT GLOBULE, DEMONSTRATING COLLAGEN
PROTEIN CONVERTED TO GELATIN AND DRAINING AWAY

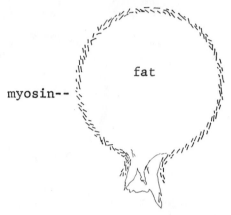

FIG. 7.16. SCHEMATIC REPRESENTATION OF A FAT GLOBULE WHICH SHOWS RUPTURED
MYOSIN COATING AND FAT DRAINING AWAY

type of fat separation occurs, it is necessary to review and correct the smoking and cooking schedules.

Casings

Casings are needed to make most sausages. They determine sausage sizes and shapes. Casings may serve as processing molds, as containers during handling and shipping, and as merchandizing units for display. Casings, to perform functionally, must be sufficiently strong to contain the meat mass but have shrink and stretch characteristics that allow contraction and expansion of the meat mass during processing and storage. Casings must not only be able to withstand the forces produced during stuffing but also the forces of linking or closure.

Casings for the sausage industry are obtained from two basic materials, cellulose and collagen. Four specific types—(1) animal, (2) regenerated collagen, (3) cloth, and (4) cellulosic casings—are produced from these basic materials.

Years ago, sausage production was limited by the amount of available animal intestines. Since the advent of cellulosic casings, sausage production is limited only by the available meat supply. Originally, animal casings played an important role in establishing sausage production techniques in the United States. Today, cellulosic casings are the major types used.

Cellulose and collagen are the two materials used for structure by nature. Essentially, cellulose occurs in all plants and collagen in all animals. There are only a few rare exceptions to this general observation. A brief description of each of the four categories listed follows.

Animal.—The gastrointestinal tract from the gullet to the anus is used for casings. In some instances, bladders are used for special types of sausage. The structures are washed, scraped, treated with chemicals to remove soluble components, and salted. The various anatomical structures, such as the esophagus, stomach, small and large intestines, appendix, and rectum, are all separated, cleansed, salted, graded as to size and condition, and packaged in suitable containers for shipment and storage.

The commercial designation for casings is somewhat different from the anatomical characterizations. Commercial terminology is shown in Table 7.4.

Sheep casings average 30 yards of rounds. Ideally the whole casing is coiled from one strand. However, during cleaning and handling some breakage may occur and the final coil may contain several strands. Casings under 18 mm diameter are listed as narrow, and the others are graded from 18 to 20, 20 to 22, 22 to 24, and over 24 mm. It is the practice to report small casing diameters in millimeters and lengths in feet. This practice has carried over into the cellulosic and regenerated collagen casing industry.

Properly prepared animal casings may return up to 25% of the value of the live animal. Much of the preparation requires hand labor and skills that are not readily available in large urban areas of the world today. The high price and relatively limited supply of animal casings has been a factor in the development of substitute casings such as cellulosic and regenerated collagen.

Table 7.4

ANIMAL CASINGS

Casing	Source
Rounds	Small intestine of cattle, sheep, goats, and pigs
Runners	Small intestines of cattle
Middles	Large intestines of cattle and pigs
Beef bungs	Caecum (blind gut)
Hog bungs	End of the intestinal tract, usually 5 to 6 ft of intestines, starting from the anus
Caps	Caecum or blind gut of the hog
Weasands	Esophagus of cattle
Bladders	Urinary bladder of cattle or hogs
Stomachs	Hog stomach, often called maws
Small casings	Small intestines of hogs, sheep, or goats

Examples of some typical sausage products manufactured in animal casings are shown in Fig. 7.17 and 7.18.

Regenerated Collagen.—Regenerated collagen casings have many of the physical properties of animal casings and the uniformity and cleanliness of cellulosic casings.

Collagen casings are prepared by acquiring a suitable collagen source such as the corium layer of beef hides. The corium is extracted with an alkaline solution to remove soluble components and washed with potable water. The collagen is then swollen with acid to give a viscous mass of acid collagen that is pushed through an annular die to form a tube. The tube is fixed by moving through an alkaline bath and the neutralized collagen returns to a reasonable approximation of its original state. The tube is dried and cut to size. For small sausage products, it is shirred into sticks in the same manner as small cellulosic casings. The small casings are edible and are used for fresh pork sausage links. Large collagen casings for other types of sausage are often treated with aldehydes to cross-link the collagen and increase the strength of the casing. This type of casing is removed from the sausage rather than eaten by the consumer.

Cellulosic.—Cellulosic casings include those made from cotton bags and those derived from processed cotton linters. Cloth bags made from various sizes of cotton thread have a small but well-defined acceptance for fresh pork sausage, smoked sausage, and some specialty items such as Taylor roll. Cloth bags were developed during the Civil War when Dr. Horsford suggested the use of cotton bags as substitutes for animal casings in his report on the Army Ration of 1864. Cloth bags give a high degree of uniformity to the encased product.

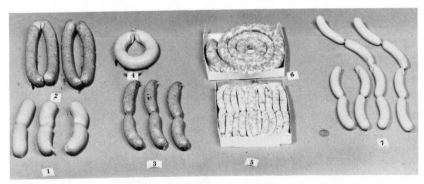

FIG. 7.17. SMALL SAUSAGES IN HOG AND SHEEP CASINGS

1—Knockwurst in hog casing. 2—Polish sausage in hog casing. 3—Thuringer in hog casing. 4—Ring bologna in beef casing. 5—Pork sausage links in sheep casing. 6—Country style or rope pork sausage in hog casing. 7—Frankfurters in sheep casing. The half-dollar indicates general size of these products.

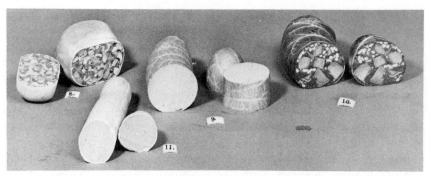

FIG. 7.18. LARGE SAUSAGES AND SPECIALTY ITEMS IN ANIMAL CASINGS

8—Head cheese in a hog stomach. 9—Bologna in a beef bung. 10—Blood and tongue sausage in a beef bung. 11—Liver sausage in a sewed hog bung. The half-dollar serves to indicate product size.

Cloth bags have good functional qualities. One-, 2-, and 5-lb bags are tightly stuffed with ground pork in such a manner that some of the fat oozes through the seams and mesh of the bag. This degree of tight stuffing reduces air pockets in the product. When the bag is smoked at slightly elevated temperatures the oozed fat melts and seals the surfaces, acting as an impermeable coating which retards drying out of the sausage during storage.

Cotton fibers that are the source of the thread for the aforementioned bags have an associated item, cotton linters, a fine fuzz-like material that is removed from cottonseed after the cotton fiber and seed have been separated at the cotton gin. Linters are an excellent source of high-grade alpha-cellulose. Since the linters are so finely divided and have very little associated products, they make for ease of handling without degrading the quality of the cellulose. Linters are cleaned mechanically, cooked in dilute alkali to remove soluble components, and washed to remove any traces of salts. The resulting cotton has a degree of purity rarely attained in cellulosic materials. This chemical cotton is treated with caustic to produce alkali cellulose, a moist, granular white material. Mixing this with carbon disulfide results in formation of a yellow-orange viscous mass called cellulose xanthate. The xanthate is mixed with a dilute caustic solution, filtered, and the resulting liquid is viscose solution. Viscose is extruded through nozzles into an acid solution and the cellulose is regenerated as the carbon disulfide is split from the complex. The tubes can be controlled in wall thickness and in tubular diameter. These finished tubes or casings are composed of pure cellulose, food-grade glycerine, and water.

Advantages of these tubes for sausage casings are their uniformity, cleanliness, and ease of handling. They can be printed or pigmented to give an attractive appearance for retail display. Cellulosic casings are available in many sizes and types; however, this great variety can be categorized in four basic subdivisions.

Small Cellulose.—Small-diameter cellulosic casings are most often supplied as shirred sticks, varying from 40 to 160 ft. in length. Existing mechanical stuffing equipment stuffs these tubes at a rate of 250 to 300 fpm. After processing, the cellulose casings are removed from the sausage at the manufacturing plant as a convenience for the consumer.

Large Cellulose.—Large-diameter casings are chemically identical with small casing tubes. Large cellulosic casings are supplied in flat bundles of 100 pieces. They must be soaked in water prior to use. The soaked casing is readily stretched, and on stuffing and tying the encased product acquires the characteristic sausage shape of a cylinder with hemispheral ends. A variety of bologna and large sausage products prepared in this manner are merchandized with the casings intact, or the casings may be removed at the retail level.

Fibrous.—Fibrous casing is prepared from a formed cellulosic matrix to which regenerated cellulose has been added. The resulting tubes are quite strong and very uniform when stuffed. Their primary use is for production of sausages for slicing. A special type of fibrous casing is the so-called easy-release; these are similar to regular fibrous casings except they have been treated internally to facilitate their removal from large sausages. Another type of fibrous casing is covered with a plastic coating to give a moistureproof barrier. This is often used with water-cooked items such as liver sausage. The plastic coating on moisture-impermeable fibrous casings also serves as a barrier to oxygen.

Dry Sausage Fibrous.—Dry sausage fibrous casings are manufactured in such a manner they adhere to the sausage surface. This is important for the preparation of dry and semidry sausages.

Several typical sausages produced in cellulosic casings are shown in Fig. 7.19.

Clips and Thread Closures.—For closing sausage casings, a soft cotton thread from 2 to 16 ply is often used; 2-ply is used for frankfurters and other small sausages while 12- to 16-ply thread is used for bologna, salamis, and other large sausages.

Large sausage casings are usually tied dry and then soaked prior to stuffing. The stuffed casing is tied wet. Metal clips are used for the first closure on dry large cellulose casings and a string is used for the second closure. However, fibrous casings, because of their strength, can be clipped at both ends, either in the dry or wet state.

Fig. 7.20 shows a variety of unstuffed cellulosic casings.

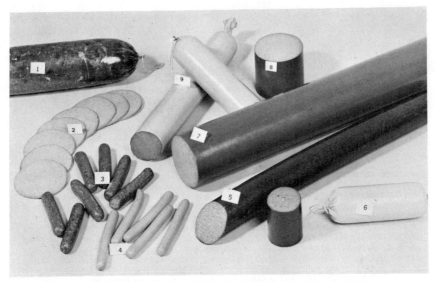

FIG. 7.19. SAUSAGES MANUFACTURED IN CELLULOSIC CASINGS

1—New England sausage in large cellulosic casing. 2—Bologna slices from bologna in fibrous casing. 3—Smoked pork sausage links prepared in small cellulosic casing. 4—Skinless frankfurters prepared in small cellulosic casing. 5—Summer sausage in fibrous casing. 6—Small catch weight product in an opaque fibrous casing. 7—Large bologna in fibrous casing for slicing. 8—Chunk bologna in fibrous casing. 9—Liver sausage in moisture-proof fibrous casing.

Spices

Spices are such important contributors to sausage flavor that standardization is often necessary to control seasoning formulations. Besides contributing to flavor spices provide, in some instances, bacteriostatic and antioxidant properties. Either natural spices or the oils and oleoresins extracted from them may be used for flavoring sausages. Oils and oleoresins are solvent-extracted and transferred to a salt or sugar base. This mixture is identified as a soluble spice. As an example, black pepper contains an oil and oleoresin accounting for 5 to 12% of the content of the peppercorn. Pepper also contains a nitrogenous base, piperine, which is the characteristic tang or bite principle in black pepper. The piperine is usually transferred or extracted with the oleoresin fraction and may be as much as 8% of the weight of the peppercorn. Incorporation of the oleoresin at a predetermined level such as 4% in a sugar or salt base permits control of the pepper used in sausage.

Soluble spices are frequently used with canned meats, whereas natural spices are used most frequently for dry or semidry sausages. Canned meats made with natural spices may darken when heated

FIG. 7.20. TYPES OF CELLULOSIC CASINGS, CLIPS AND TIES

1—Large cellulosic casings used for bologna and other large sausages and smoked meats. 2—Fibrous casings used for slicing products; casings available in moisture-proof, easy release, and dry sausage types. 3—Shirred fibrous casings used for various chub sausages; available in types described under 2. 4—Butcher thread, hanging ties, and clips. 5—Shirred small cellulosic casings from 55 to 160 ft in length and 14 to 40 mm in diameter. Available with or without stripes and either uncolored or colored with a self-coloring food dye; the stripes are for product identification and as an aid in some peeling operations where the plain casings may present some difficulty in recognizing peeled from unpeeled product. 6—Clipped fibrous casings. 7—Clipped large cellulosic casings. 8—Self-coloring shirred cellulosic casing with a portion of the casing pulled from the intact shirred strand. 9—Uncolored shirred cellulosic casing with a portion of the casing pulled from the intact shirred strand.

as a result of the presence of other components in the spice, such as anthocyanins and flavones. Soluble spices are low in these compounds and give a brighter appearance to canned meat products.

Natural spices may at times acquire a high bacterial content by their very nature and because of the collection and storage conditions to which they are subjected. Some type of sterilization of natural spices is usually desirable.

The meat industry is reported to be the biggest single user of spices, black pepper being the largest single item used. Others used include allspice, basil, bayleaf, cardamom, cloves, ginger, mace, nutmeg, mustard, paprika, pimento, cayenne pepper, white pepper, caraway, coriander, celery seed, cumin, marjoram, thyme, savory, sage, anise, cinnamon, capsicum, onion, garlic, sesame, and fennel.

Spices may be used whole, cracked, or ground. Some spices are rubbed to disintegrate the structure, and others are finely milled. White pepper is used in products where black pepper particles may detract from appearance of the sausage, such as in veal sausage or light-colored loaf items. Spices are a small portion of the total ingredient cost of sausages.

Technological descriptions of spices are available in specialized food handbooks or in the U.S. Dispensatory. The Dispensatory lists the botanical source of a spice and its chemical composition; it also provides some information on the biology of the specific plants associated with the spices.

To assure proper control of the flavor complex, a good procedure is to prepare a sausage with a spice mixture and evaluate the product with a trained taste panel. While chemical standards are helpful, the final result depends on flavor or taste, which requires a periodic review of the product line by taste panels.

Additives

The processing, handling, and storage of sausages for today's markets has required the use of additives to meet the demands of modern consumers. Some of the common additives are water or ice, curing salts, and chemical stabilizers such as antioxidants. All additives should be food-grade quality. The Food Chemical Codex is a good reference for the quality requirements of these items.

Ice or Water.—Water or ice added to the meat mass provide considerable functional qualities. The ice or water chills the meat during the chopping or mixing operations. This chilling permits longer and more efficient churning of the meat mass without mechanically overheating. This is accomplished by lowering the initial temperatures and by lubricating the meat mass. Added water aids in dissolving sodium chloride and curing salts to give better distribution in the mass. Of equal importance, water imparts fluidity to the emulsion or meat mixture that aids in proper filling of the casings. Texture and tenderness of the finished sausages are markedly affected by the added water content.

Salt.—Salt for sausages must be of food-grade quality. Salt (sodium chloride) serves three functions in sausage: (1) it dissolves in water to form a brine which acts to retard microbiological growth; (2) it aids in solubilizing the myosin-type proteins of comminuted muscle for emulsifying the fat in emulsion sausages; and (3) it contributes to basic taste characteristics.

Curing Salts.—In the general concepts of curing or preservation all the additives contribute to preservation. However, specifically, the term "curing salt" refers to sodium or potassium nitrate and nitrite. These ingredients are added so that no more than 200 ppm sodium nitrite will be present in finished sausages. Some exceptions have been made for special products, but the trend is to control and possibly reduce the presence of these compounds to a workable minimum.

Nitrates and nitrites are discussed in Chapter 3. However, it may be well to emphasize the importance of nitrite in sausages. Nitrite used at the level of ¼ oz per 100 lb will result in 156 ppm nitrite being added to the product. This small quantity of nitrite, in combination with moisture level, pH, added salt, and final internal processing temperature, has a general bacteriostatic effect in the finished sausage. Nitrite produces a flavor that has become characteristic.

The formation of a characteristic cured color in meat is often indicated as the primary need for curing salts, but this is not really true. The red or pink cured color becomes an indicator showing that the proper sequence of events has been satisfactorily carried out. Besides acting as an indicator of initial acceptable quality, color also serves as a signal when incipient spoilage is under way or when active spoilage has occurred. The spoiled product will discolor. It is common to note off-flavor and off-odors when the normal cured color changes to gray or brown.

Ascorbates-Erythorbates.—The ascorbates and the erythorbates are closely related chemicals that can be used interchangeably in sausage mixes. They are active reducing agents that react with nitrite to give nitric oxide. In the acid form they must be used cautiously in making solutions, since nitric oxide gas in concentrated form is toxic. These compounds ensure development of the desired color in cured meats, and in this regard they have value. A very specific action of ascorbic acid or its salt has been noted in relation to limiting the formation of green discolorations that occur at times under the metal smoke sticks. This property is not observed with erythorbate.

Sugars.—The use of sugars in the curing of meat is common. However, in most instances, sugar is used as an adjunct to provide flavor, mask the salt flavor, or to provide a reservoir for an acid-forming substance. Sugars are used at levels from 8 oz to 2 lb per hundredweight of meat. A variety of sugars, such as sucrose, corn syrup and solids, dextrose, and sugar derivatives such as sorbitol, are used.

Sugars in some of the sausage mixes are important to acid formation so the proper pH of the sausage product is developed and maintained. This is especially important for dry and semidry sausages.

Phosphates.—Sodium acid pyrophosphate is the only phosphate permitted in sausages in the United States, although phosphates have been allowed in some European countries. It is permitted at 0.5% in the finished product. It is used principally to accelerate development of cured color in frankfurters processed in a continuous cooker.

Acids and Liquid Smoke.—The use of acids and liquid smoke has become popular especially for small sausages such as frankfurters. The acid is sprayed prior to smoking or cooking. It reduces surface pH of sausages and either coagulates proteins at the surface or permits coagulation at a lower temperature. Usually the use of an acid spray gives a better surface and helps development of surface color. Almost any food-grade acid can be used. Acetic acid or vinegar is used extensively. However, they are volatile and the odor is objectionable to some individuals. Volatile acids can accumulate on equipment by condensation and corrode the trackings, trolleys, and other areas in the plant.

If an acid spray is used primarily for improving peelability, an alternative is the use of specially treated cellulosic casings.

Liquid smoke has a prior history of about 100 to 150 years. However, the present products are better controlled than soot and chimney tar extracts described in the older literature. Liquid smoke, when sprayed, dipped, or atomized onto sausage surfaces, imparts flavor, improves color, and aids peeling in some instances. Because of recent demands for improving environmental quality, liquid smoke is finding increased usage.

Binders or Extenders.—Meat processors have a wide variety of nonmeat products available to incorporate in sausages. These are often referred to as binders or extenders and less frequently as fillers, emulsifiers, or stabilizers. They are added to basic meat formulations for one or more of the following reasons: (1) to improve emulsion stability, (2) to improve cooking yields, (3) to improve slicing characteristics, (4) to improve flavor, and (5) to reduce formulation costs.

The content of these materials permitted in sausage products is controlled by Federal meat inspection regulations. Individually or collectively, up to 3.5% of cereal, starch, vegetable flour, soy flour, soy protein concentrate, nonfat dry milk, and calcium-reduced nonfat dry milk are permitted in finished sausage products. Isolated soy protein, however, is restricted to 2%. Sausages containing more than 3.5% of these nonmeat ingredients or more than 2% isolated soy protein are referred to as imitation, and must be labeled as such. For meat products known as loaves, Federal inspection regulations recognize two different types. Regulations governing the amount of extender materials allowed in finished products differ depending upon the type loaf. Products identified as meat loaves are restricted to the percentage of extender materials allowed in other sausage products. Those referred to as nonspecific (the word meat does not appear in the name), such as pickle and pimento, macaroni and cheese, and luxury loaves are not restricted in respect to their content of extender materials.

BIBLIOGRAPHY

ANON. 1953. Meat Products, Bull *804*. American Dry Milk Institute, Chicago, Ill.

ANON. 1964. Service Manual. Union Carbide Corp., Food Products Div., Chicago, Ill.

BORCHERT, L. L. *et al.* 1967. Electron microscopy of the meat emulsion. J. Food Sci. *32*, 419.

CARPENTER, J. A., and SAFFLE, R. L. 1965. Some physical and chemical factors affecting the emulsifying capacity of meat protein extracts. Food Technol. *19*, 1567.

DUDLEY, R. P. 1965. Sausage—a $2 billion market. V. Additives. Meat *31*, 34.

GERRARD, F. 1959. Sausage and Small Goods Production. Leonard Hill, London.

GHINELLI, I. 1950. The Preservation of Meat. Casanova, Parma, Italy. (Italian)

GRUTTNER, F. 1956. Handbook of Meat Processing, 5th Edition. Serger & Hempel, Braunschweig, Germany. (German)

HANSEN, K. L. 1960. Emulsion formation in finely comminuted sausage. Food Technol. *14*, 565.

HARTLEY, D. 1964. Food in England. MacDonald, London.

MacKENZIE, D.S. 1966. Prepared Meat Product Manufacturing, 2nd Edition. American Meat Institute, Chicago, Ill.

MANN, I. 1962. Processing and utilization of animal by-products. Food and Agricultural Development Paper 75. Food and Agriculture Organization of the United Nations. (Italian)

MILLS, F. *et al.* 1958. The effect of sodium ascorbate and sodium isoascorbate on the quality of frankfurters. Food Technol. *12*, 311.

NAGHSKI, J. 1971. By-Products—hides, skins, and natural casings. *In* The Science of Meat and Meat Products, J. F. Price, and B. S. Schweigert (Editors). W. H. Freeman and Co., San Francisco, Calif.

SHANNON, W. J. 1966. Modern sausage production. Meat Process. *6*, 33.

SWIFT, C. E., and ELLIS, R. 1957. Action of phosphates in sausage products. Food Technol. *11*, 450.

SWIFT, C. E., and SULZBACHER, W. L. 1963. Comminuted meat emulsions: factors affecting meat proteins as emulsion stabilizers. Food Technol. *17*, 224.

SWIFT, C. E., LOCKETT, C., and FRYAR, A. J. 1961. Comminuted meat emulsions—the capacity of meat for emulsifying fat. Food Technol. *15*, 468.

SWIFT, C. E., TOWNSEND, W. E., and WITNAUER, L. P. 1968. Comminuted meat emulsions: relation of the melting characteristics of fat to emulsion stability. Food Technol. *22*, 775.

SWIFT, C. E., WEIR, C. E., and HANKINS, O. G. 1954. The effect of variations in moisture and fat content on the juiciness and tenderness of bologna. Food Technol. *8*, 339.

VISCORA. 1968. Automatic and continuous processes of making small sausages, Bull. *6*. Viscora, Paris.

WANG, H. 1954. Histology of beef casings. Am. Meat Inst. Found. Bull. *17*, Chicago, Ill.

WANG, H. 1955. Histology of pork casings. Am. Meat Inst. Found., Bull. *25*, Chicago, Ill.

CHAPTER 8

Least-Cost Formulation and Preblending of Sausage

Two relatively recent developments of great importance to the sausage industry are preblending and the application of computerized linear programming to least-cost formulation. These two developments have grown out of demands for more accurate control of costs, uniformity in composition, and maintenance of quality. Many processors, both large and small, are using one or both of these procedures in their manufacturing operations.

Although both preblending and computerized least-cost formulation are relatively new concepts, they did not develop simultaneously and are not interdependent. Thus, a processor may elect to use preblending, or he may decide to use computerized least-cost formulation, or even utilize both procedures in his operation. The choice of procedure and the degree of implementation is a decision that each operator must make in view of his own capabilities and problems.

Both preblending and computerized least-cost formulation will be discussed. Although preblending will be considered first, this does not imply that it is the more important of the two. Preblending makes possible analysis prior to final formulation. Thus it permits adjustment of formulas to meet specifications and required standards, whether they are strictly based on cost alone, solely on quality, or on a combination of cost and quality. On the other hand, selection of raw ingredients and their approximate proportions must be determined even earlier in the operation. Therefore, computerized linear programming to obtain least-cost formulas may be used before preblending.

Neither computerized least-cost formulations nor preblending are panaceas for the sausage industry, but must be applied with judgement and use of the best information possible to achieve maximum advantage. Each will be discussed separately and their interrelationship in combined programs will be considered.

PREBLENDING

Preblending first achieved prominence in the mid 1960's. Preblending consists of the grinding and mixing of separate meat ingredients with part or all of the cure (salt and nitrite and/or nitrate) in proportion to the amount of meat. This permits sampling and chemical analysis before the final blending or mixing of all ingredients. Some operators also add the seasoning at the same time as the cure. Other processors who make a variety of products prefer to add only the cure and then vary the seasoning to provide several different products.

Preblending has the following advantages: (1) it permits control of composition by adjusting the final blend to a known fat content; (2) addition of the cure stabilizes the meat and helps to control meat spoilage; (3) it can be used on hot boned meat, where addition of the cure results in the maximum amount of salt-extractable protein and improves emulsification; (4) preblending with the cure allows the meat to be cured while the emulsifiers and other equipment are used for other products, or even while the meat is en route from one processing operation to another; and (5) preblending retards oxidation of the raw materials since it allows curing to begin earlier.

Preblending and Control of Composition

One of the major advantages of preblending is the close control of composition made possible by analysis of the meat mixture. Immediately after the individual meat items are preblended, a sample is removed for chemical analysis. This sample is usually analyzed for fat and moisture content by one of the rapid methods discussed in Chapter 13. In some instances, although not commonly, the meat samples are also analyzed for protein content. While the analysis is being carried out, the meat is also curing through the action of the salt, nitrite and/or nitrate.

Once the composition of the samples from different preblends is known, it is possible to determine the exact combination of each ingredient to give the desired composition. As the fat content is the most variable and since both moisture and protein are inversely related, in practice, fat is most often the only component considered. Thus, the fat content can be balanced to the desired level by adding the necessary amount of the different meat components. If the fat content is well below the desired level, a known amount of a product containing a greater amount of fat can be added to balance off the product to the desired fat composition, or vice versa.

For example, it two preblended meat blocks have fat contents of 20% and 40%, mixing them together in the proportion of 1 : 1 will result in 30% fat content. However, the calculation is not quite this simple, as one must also consider cooking losses to obtain the final fat content. Furthermore, the processor usually adds a safety factor in order to comply with regulations. Federal meat inspection regulations specify a maximum of 30% fat for frankfurters, so that one must determine both shrinkage and cooking losses before calculating the final formulation.

Calculation of the proportion of each meat block needed to give the desired composition can also be determined by using the computer. Since some 4 or 5 different types of meat may be used in a single formulation, the advantages in using a computer to calculate the best combination of ingredients can be easily seen. Although the major decisions as to the kind of meat to be used must be determined before procurement, the computer still is a major time-saver in producing a final formula. However, one must still bear in mind that certain restrictions on the level of various ingredients must be imposed if quality is to be maintained.

Control of Meat Spoilage by Preblending

Almost, if not just as important as the control of composition made possible by preblending are the advantages gained by cure stabilization of the preblended mixture, and thus preventing or retarding spoilage. Once the prebatched meat begins to cure, it becomes more stable and its storage life is greatly extended. Thus, preblending changes relatively unstable fresh meat to a more stable product, in which the storage life is lengthened from a few hours or days in the fresh state to a matter of a week or so after curing. Nevertheless, it is generally desirable to limit the time before final blending to a few hours, or a day or two at most, because of inventory reduction, space requirements, and ultimate storage life. Following curing, there is a gradual decline in shelf-life as a result of microbial growth. Thus there is an added advantage of getting the product into distribution channels while storage life is at a maximum.

Preblending of Hot Boned Meat

There are distinct advantages in curing hot boned meat. Pre-rigor meat has a greater emulsifying capacity, since the salt-soluble protein is easier to extract before the actin and myosin combine to form actomyosin, which occurs during development of rigor mortis. Although there are good reasons for using hot boned meat in all processed products, the advantages are maximal in emulsion-type products where the greater emulsifying capacity can be utilized.

Processors who also do their own slaughtering may find it advantageous to bone at once and immediately add the cure. When the meat is ground hot, the cure having been added during or before grinding, as with any other preblended meat, the content of extractable salt-soluble protein is greatly increased. The advantage of using hot boned bull meat in sausage emulsions has long been recognized. An explanation for its effectiveness lies primarily in the increased extraction of the salt-soluble proteins, resulting in an increase in emulsifying capacity.

The advantages of curing hot boned meat apply not only to intact cuts and emulsion-type sausages, but also to the preparation of hot boned fresh pork sausage. The latter product has been widely accepted, not only because of its good color, stability, and flavor, but also because of reduced inventory due to rapid turnover. When producing hot boned fresh pork sausage, some small processors have found it advantageous to use the same crew first for slaughtering and then for cutting and further processing immediately afterward. In some of these operations, the entire hog carcass is used to produce whole hog fresh pork sausage.

Preblending Allows Better Use of Equipment

Some large processors have found it feasible to preblend their meat in the boning room and to cure it while in transit to other stages of the processing operation. Since the meat is curing while in transit to the processing plant or room, there is more efficient use of certain pieces of equipment, such as the smokehouse, cook tank, and retort. Thus total output through certain pieces of equipment can actually be increased during the working day.

At least one large processor has found it possible to cure meat while it is being trucked to their processing plants at different locations. As already explained, the meat is relatively stable after adding the cure. Undoubtedly, this permits more variation in operations.

Some processors offer preblended meat for sale to other processors and will also furnish a rapid analysis of fat content. Thus, there may be a trend toward specialized processing, one company furnishing raw products, another preblending and adding the cure, and still another serving as the final blender and processor. Although the above example of specialization is probably an extreme, within-company specialization is indeed a reality.

Preblending and Retardation of Oxidation

Rancidity is one of the most serious flavor problems of the meat industry. Sausages would be especially vulnerable to rancidity or oxidative deterioration except for addition of the cure. As has already been explained in Chapter 3, the nitrite and possibly the nitrate have an important function in improvement of flavor. The better flavor after curing seems to be closely related to prevention of oxidative rancidity, although little concrete information is available at this time. Circumstantial evidence suggests that preblending reduces rancidity in sausages, probably as a result of inhibition of oxidation by the nitrite and/or nitrate. Thus, curing of hot boned meat may be expected to retard rancidity development and give a more desirable flavor. This does, in fact, appear to be real.

Use of Preblending in Least-Cost Formulation

As already indicated, preblending may be separate from least-cost formulation using computerized linear programming, but they are most often used together. The general formulas are arrived at by the processor on the basis of cost. The amounts of various meat blocks required are then arrived at and the amount desired is purchased. In order to make the manufacturing process more precise and the product of constant composition, each meat block is now preblended with part or all of the cure, and possibly with the seasoning. At this time, one or more samples are removed from each preblended meat block and analyzed for fat, and possibly for moisture content. After curing and analysis, the preblended ingredients are then blended together to give the final composition, the remaining cure and seasoning being added, if this has not already been done during preblending.

Special Considerations in Preblending

Although the discussion of preblending has stated that the meat be chopped, the fineness has not been specified. The fineness of chopping will depend upon the uniformity of the raw meat block, desired distribution of cure, and the difficulty of obtaining a representative sample for analysis. Lean meat can be chopped coarser than the fatter ingredients and still give a uniform sample with respect to fat content.

The consistency of the meat can also influence the uniformity of the chopped material. For example, rework sausages require especially fine grinding to give a product that can be quickly and easily mixed into the final blend. If tripe or other by-products are used, they generally require especially fine chopping. In cases where the variation in composition is great and the meat items are hard to sample, emulsification of the raw product may need to be substituted for chopping. However, the latter practice should be used only as a last resort.

Raw materials for preblending should always be of good sound quality. Even though the meat is to be cured at once, quality should not be sacrificed. If the meat is rancid or partially spoiled before preblending, a lower-quality finished product can be expected.

The product should be kept at temperatures that inhibit bacterial growth. Cleanliness and good sanitation practices are required. Good raw materials and sound handling practices are just as essential in preblending as in normal processing. Quality of the finished product will be determined by the quality of the raw materials and by the type processing methods at all stages of the operation.

LEAST-COST FORMULATION

Least-cost formulation is not a new process, as meat processors have utilized it for many years. There are, however, extreme limitations to the number of meat items that can be employed, if one uses simple machine or pencil computations. The amount of time required for simple computation with as few as 3 or 4 meat ingredients places extreme restrictions on simple calculation procedures. Thus, processors were inclined to use simple formulas involving only a few raw materials. Such formulations were obviously not necessarily of the least cost, but were those that the processors knew could be used with good results.

About 1958, a few ingenious operators began exploring the possible use of linear programming with high-speed computers as a means of calculating least-cost sausage formulas. As is the case with preblending, most of the emphasis has been placed on emulsion-type sausages where large volume production is common. Many processors have regarded computerized least-cost formulations as a modern marvel that would make the sausage business extremely profitable. Unfortunately, such has not been the case, as computer programming of least-cost formulations requires even more basic information and skill than traditional sausage formulation. Understanding of the scientific principles involved in emulsion chemistry and the functional properties of meat raw materials has become far more important as the number of raw materials available has been increased by rapid computations. As a result, development of limitations or constraints has been necessary in order to maintain quality in the finished product. Consideration of these factors will be discussed later in this chapter.

Linear Programming—A Managerial Tool

A linear programming model is developed to solve four types of managerial problems: (1) a single-formula model can be used to determine the least-cost formula of one product, for example of frankfurters; (2) a composite-formula model can be used for determining least-cost formulas for many products, one at a time; (3) a multi-formula model may be used where the availability of certain raw material is limited; and (4) a multi-formula model may be used to analyze the manufacturing operation in which there are certain production and procurement restrictions.

Single-Formula Model.—The single-formula model is designed to determine the least-cost formula for available ingredients that will meet predetermined product specifications. It is the simplest method and provides a starting point for understanding programmed analysis of meat products. Three types of information are needed: (1) a list of available ingredients with the cost of each, (2) the composition of each ingredient, and (3) formula specifications for the product.

Composite-Formula Model.—The composite-formula model greatly increases computational efficiency. One to several composite models are used to generate formulas for the entire line of products. Each composite model represents a group of products that contain essentially the same ingredients and formula specifications. Thus one composite model may be used to generate least-cost formulas for several products, for example, to give two frankfurter formulas and one bologna formula. This model can then be used to obtain the least-cost formula for an all-beef frankfurter, for an all-meat frankfurter, and for bologna.

Multi-formula Models.—Multi-formula models can be utilized whenever there are limitations in supplies of ingredients, in production capacity, or in any other component of the processing operation. In such situations, it is necessary to allocate the limited resources among the alternative products. Under these conditions, multi-formula models can produce competitive least-cost formulas for several products.

The multi-formula model can also be used as a management guide for decisions relative to product mix and pricing strategy, as well as to predict future profits. Thus it can serve as a guide in formulation, raw material procurement, plant and labor utilization, product lines, and sales promotion.

Advantages of Computerized Least-Cost Formulations

By use of linear programming, the meat processor can determine the specific allocation of ingredients required for a given product at a minimum cost. The product can be manufactured subject to any restrictions on composition or ingredient availability. Obviously, linear programming for least-cost formulation is aimed at improvement of profitability.

Specifically, least-cost linear programming has the following advantages: (1) it will give the most economical combination of ingredients for a given product within the limitations placed upon each ingredient in the formula; (2) its extreme rapidity permits calculations that would not otherwise be possible; (3) it makes possible a saving in time alone over the more laborious traditional calculation (pencil or machine) that can be devoted to concentration on other production problems; (4) it permits adjustment of formulas on the basis of analysis, using values obtained from preblending or other sources; (5) it maximizes the use of available ingredients; (6) it reduces inventory and waste; (7) it supplies accurate procurement information; and (8) it can be utilized for making management decisions on production, promotion, pricing, and labor utilization policies.

The principal advantage of computerized least-cost formulation is that of minimizing ingredient costs of raw materials. However, the processor must first develop limitations in order to maintain product quality. This will be discussed later in this chapter under the subject of constraints. Once these limitations or constraints have been developed, the computer will give the least-cost formula. Obviously, such information can be used in procurement of raw materials, whether through intra- or inter-plant transfer or by purchase from other suppliers.

A competent worker with a desk calculator can find the most economical blend of raw materials, if allowed adequate time for calculation. In fact, prior to the use of computers for least-cost sausage formulation, a calculator was commonly used to ascertain the best combination of ingredients. However, the operator was necessarily limited to a very few ingredients, and the operation was extremely time-consuming. To illustrate the problem of manual calculation, the following example is shown:

First, assume that one has the following information on cost and composition of bull meat, cow meat, pork trimmings, and pork fat:

Ingredients	Cost/lb	Fat	Protein	Moisture	Ash
	$	%	%	%	%
bull meat	0.47	8	20	71	1
cow meat	0.45	15	18	66	1
pork trimmings	0.30	50	10	39	1
fat pork	0.11	70	5	24	1

Then, assuming that restrictions on composition amount to a minimum fat content of 24%, a maximum of 28% fat, and a minimum of 14% protein, one can calculate the various combinations of ingredients and their cost. The difficulties are obvious in calculating costs where the number of ingredients is limited to only 4, and where the only restrictions are for fat and protein content. Even with this simple formula, the time and effort involved in arriving at a least-cost formula are tremendous. However, computer linear programming revealed that the least-cost formula and its composition within the restrictions imposed are as follows:

Ingredients	Weight lb	Fat lb	Protein lb	Cost $
cow meat	76.4	11.46	13.75	34.38
fat pork	23.6	16.52	1.18	2.60
	100.0	27.98	14.93	36.98

The above blend complies with the restrictions on fat and protein and gives the lowest product cost. The problem of selecting the least-cost formulation from the 25 to 45 ingredients available to the processor, together with the 10 to 15 restrictions on the blend of a single product, cannot in practice be solved without using computer linear programming.

The computer may also be utilized to adjust final blends on the basis of analysis. Information on composition obtained by analysis of preblended materials or other compositional data allows the processor to carefully adjust the final composition to comply with product specifications such as the meat inspection regulations. This results in closer tolerances with less product "give-away" in terms of protein, which is usually the most expensive component in the blend. Similarly, one can also come closer to maximum levels of fat in the final product, which is generally the least expensive of the meat components in a sausage mixture. The net effect is a uniform product in terms of composition, although not necessarily in quality.

Disadvantages of Computerized Least-Cost Formulations

Although there is little argument about the principles of computerized application for obtaining least-cost formulations, there are a number of weaknesses or disadvantages in linear programming for least-cost sausage formulas. Some of these are listed below: (1) the usefulness of least-cost linear programming is limited by the accuracy of the data fed to the computer; (2) the data generated cannot be substituted for good judgement, sound scientific principles, and knowledge of the functional behavior of the raw materials; (3) limitations must be developed for all possible combinations of raw materials; (4) limitations on raw materials change with composition; and (5) a computer requires considerable capital outlay.

Computers are not sales gimmicks installed to impress people on plant tours or even the plant labor force as to the sophistication and science of the sausage industry. They are only valuable when they are used, and used properly. The presence of a computer is not a substitute for knowledge of emulsion chemistry, the functional properties of the raw meat ingredients, or sound processing. A computer is only a tool, and the information coming back is no better than that going into it. Although the computer will tell you the most economical or least-cost formulation of the ingredients, it has no knowledge of their functional properties. Thus the processor must use his knowledge in developing constraints or limitations for the various ingredients in order to maintain product quality. Only when the operator develops and utilizes such information in feeding the computer will the computer return meaningful information on cost. For these reasons operators with limited knowledge will not find a magic answer with a computer.

As already indicated, the limitations on the use of various ingredients must be fed to the computer for it to generate useful information. These limitations vary with composition and must be changed to compensate for alterations in composition. Since composition of the same meat raw materials is highly variable, especially in terms of fat and water content, the development and utilization of limitations is extremely important. Furthermore, there is marked variation in the composition of the same meat components from plant to plant, and even within the same plant. Although blending in larger quantities will help by reducing this variation, it must be considered in using computers for calculating least-cost formulations. Analysis of each meat ingredient is almost mandatory, which obviously requires a laboratory with competent personnel for obtaining the necessary analytical data.

The capital investment for a computer is considerable, even small units costing $25,000 and up. Self-contained larger units normally cost $100,000 or more. These are only initial outlays, because up-dating and changes in computer design make older models obsolete with surprising regularity. The computer also requires maintenance by a manufacturer's representative or, alternatively, by an electronic technician on the plant maintenance staff. In addition, a computer programmer is usually desirable, and is absolutely essential if maximum use is to be made of a computer facility.

Although a number of specialized computer companies provide service on least-cost formulations, the formulas are normally based on an average composition. Thus there must necessarily be great leeway of the built-in factors for safety purposes, which greatly limits the usefulness of the formulas. To further compound the problem, small companies making use of such services seldom have analytical data on composition, and most often operate without analytical laboratories for obtaining the required information. Furthermore, small operators find it difficult to compete with larger ones on cost alone, and are more likely to be on a sounder basis in producing a high-quality premium product.

Information Required for Linear Programming

In order to use linear programming effectively in a meat-processing program, an operator must perform two basic functions: (1) define the problem, and (2) collect data and formulate the model.

Defining the Problem.—This consists of deciding which function is to be optimized. In least-cost formulation, the total cost of raw materials is minimized by selecting the lowest-cost ingredients after placing restrictions on their use to maintain quality. One must also ascertain what products will be produced and how large the quantities are to be blended. Since sausage production is a batch operation, the quantities in each batch are needed.

Collection of Data and Formulation of Model.—Interrelationships among ingredients, restrictions on the final composition, and any other limitations must be expressed as linear equations. Ingredient costs and compositional data are perhaps the easiest information to obtain. A good analytical laboratory is necessary as a continuing part of linear programming. Knowledge of the behavior of different ingredients in a blend and their effects on the finished product is essential. Pilot-plant studies or small experimental batches should be made before going to full-scale commercial production. Constraints or limitations on raw materials must be developed on the basis of experimental data or with "educated guesses" from practical experience with sausage products. An experienced sausage man can often look at a formula and tell whether it will make an acceptable product.

Types of Constraints

The basic elements of a linear programming model are the equations or inequalities that express the restrictions on the solution. These inequalities or equations are called constraints. Constraints used in blending sausages may be due to cost limitations (objective function), ingredient limitations, composition limitations, or capacity limitations. A model linear program for least-cost sausage formulation will always contain at least one of each type of constraint. Thus it is imperative that restrictions for every relationship be incorporated into the linear program.

Cost Constraints.—The objective function or cost constraint is an equation expressing the total cost of the formulation. It takes the following form, assuming there are n different ingredients that may be used in the formulation:

Minimum $Cost = C_1 \times M_1 + C_2 \times M_2 + C_3 \times M_3 \ldots + C_n \times M_n$

where M_1 is the weight of ingredient 1, M_2 is the weight of ingredient 2 and etc., and $C_1, \ldots, C_n$ are the respective ingredient costs per pound. The per pound costs ($C_1, \ldots, C_n$) are constant coefficients supplied as input data for the model. The ingredient weight ($M_1, \ldots, M_n$) is the unknown to be computed. Since price and limitations are considered in the model, the least-cost formula will probably not contain all possible ingredients. The linear program then computes the optimal formulation and gives the weight for each ingredient.

To illustrate this principle assume there are 5 possible ingredients ($n = 5$) with following costs:

C_1 = \$0.20/lb C_3 = \$0.22/lb C_5 = \$0.40/lb

C_2 = \$0.44/lb C_4 = \$0.80/lb

Then assume that the computer returns the following optimal formula:

M_1 = 10 lb M_3 = 0 lb M_5 = 0 lb

M_2 = 88 lb M_4 = 2 lb

The total cost is then calculated by substituting the above values in the equation:

(10) (0.20) + (88) (0.44) + (0) (0.22) + (2) (0.80) + (0) (0.40) = \$42.32

Thus, a cost of \$42.32 would be the lowest possible cost for a formula satisfying the constraints in this problem.

Ingredient Constraints.—These constraints are used to control the amount of an ingredient or a combination of ingredients in the blend. Such constraints can be used to limit either the minimum or maximum, to give a fixed level or a specific range (inequalities) for the ingredient. The limitations imposed may be due to poor texture (rework), taste (mutton), color (pale vs. red) or poor binding qualities (shank meat). Ingredients can be constrained singly, in pairs, or in any other combination.

An example of a single constraint is the cure, seasoning, and other dry ingredients, which may be 5 lb and must be used regardless of the type of meats. On the other hand, a multiple equality may be used, such as a combination of beef and pork hearts. Some processors add hearts for color and, in order to take advantage of the best buy, use both names on the label. Thus they must use some of each. Assuming a total of 10 lb in any combination together, beef hearts plus pork hearts equal 10 lb. If beef hearts equal 5 lb, then pork hearts equal 5 lb, but if beef hearts equal 1 lb, then pork hearts equal 9 lb.

Inequalities can also be used to specify either an upper or lower limit for an ingredient or combination of ingredients. For example, bull meat plus cow meat plus lean beef trimmings $\geq$ 60, or at least 60 lb bull meat, cow meat, and lean beef trimmings must be used. In another example, pork trim (50% fat and 50% lean) plus skinned pork jowls $\geq$ 30, or at least 30 lb pork trim (50/50) and/or skinned jowls must be used. In another example, beef cheek meat plus pork cheek meat $\leq$ 15 lb, or no more than 15 lb beef cheek meat and/or pork cheek meat may be used in the formula.

Bounding inequalities specify both an upper and lower limit for an ingredient. For example, mutton is usually limited on the low end by labeling requirements and at the upper end by flavor limitations.

Thus, mutton ≥ 5 and mutton ≤ 20, or at least 5 lb mutton must be used, and the maximum must be no greater than 20 lb.

Composition Constraints.—Constraints for composition are used to specify the required final composition of the blend. The specifications for such constraints are in several instances based on legal requirements plus a safety factor. In other cases, they are based on limitations on ingredients necessary to maintain quality. Since meat inspection regulations specify that the maximum fat content in frankfurters must not exceed 30%, the constraint for fat may be set at 28% to provide the necessary margin for safety.

Assuming a restriction on fat content of 28% and a formula containing cow meat, pork trim (50/50), skinned jowls, and 80% lean pork trim with an analysis of 10, 50, 70, and 20% fat, respectively, these values can be used to calculate a formula meeting the fat restriction. These constraint inequalities are then used to express the restrictions: 0.10 (lb cow meat used) + 0.50 (lb 50/50 pork trim used) + 0.70 (lb jowls used) + 0.20 (lb pork trim used) ≤ 28.

Next, one may assume that the optimal computerized formula contains the following amounts of each ingredient:

cow meat $= 38$ lb
pork trim (50/50) $= 15$ lb
skinned jowls $= 16$ lb
80% lean pork trim $= 25$ lb
(assume cure and seasoning $= 6$ lb)

These values may then be substituted in the above equation to give the following:
0.10 (38) + 0.50 (15) + 0.70 (16) + 0.20 (25) = 27.5, which is less than the 28% restriction and therefore satisfies the fat restriction. If one finds the unrestricted lower limit is too low in fat, one could establish bounding inequalities for fat and say: fat ≤ 28 and fat ≥ 26. In this case, fat content would be greater than 26%, but no more than 28%.

Constraints similar to the above illustration for fat content must be developed for all other composition restrictions, which may include protein content, added moisture, color, binding qualities, and other factors associated with composition.

Capacity Constraints.—A capacity constraint may be incorporated into the model to limit the quantity of production to the capacity of the plant. The capacity constraint can then be expressed in the following equation: $M_1 + M_2 + M_3 + M_4 \ldots M_n =$ Maximum capacity, where $M_1, M_2 \ldots, M_n$ are the actual weights of the n possible ingredients used in the mix. If the capacity of the system is 6,500 lb, the individual components must be computed to equal 6,500 lb. There are, however, many advantages to placing the total on a 100-lb basis since fat, protein, and moisture can then be read directly in percentages. In addition, use of a 100-lb base also gives costs directly in dollars and cents per 100 lb.

The weight or percentage of each ingredient can then be multiplied by a constant factor to obtain the actual ingredient weights needed to produce the total quantity of the blend.

Developing Constraints.—Some of the limitations associated with ingredients and composition have already been briefly discussed. However, it is not possible to discuss each limitation, since this will depend upon the product, legal requirements, the ingredients, and the properties of each. In addition, the limitations on added moisture content and shrinkage during processing must be considered. Some of these will be discussed briefly from the standpoint of how they can be used and some of the factors or considerations in their development. Some points to be considered will be stressed, but the list is by no means complete; the constraints pointed out are only examples and should not be taken as actual even where numbers are arbitrarily assigned. All processors must determine their own constraints based on actual experimental information and use of their own sound judgement. It is always best to try out these constraints on small batches instead of changing an entire operation, at least until the constraints have been shown to be correct.

Some of the better-known constraints include fat and protein content, which have already been discussed. Other compositional constraints are added moisture and shrinkage, which will be discussed together, color, binding quality, flavor, and the use of frozen meat. Each of these will be covered briefly to point out some of the considerations that must be taken into account.

Moisture and Shrinkage Constraints.—One of the government restrictions on sausages specifies that the moisture content of the finished product shall not exceed 4 times the percentage of protein plus 10% of the finished weight. In actual practice, many meat ingredients have protein-to-moisture ratios less than 4 times percent protein, while a number of other meat ingredients have moisture ratios greater than 4 times percent protein. Generally speaking, lean cuts have low protein-to-moisture ratios (% moisture/% protein), while fat cuts have high protein-to-moisture ratios.

In setting up a moisture constraint, it is necessary to calculate a moisture coefficient for each ingredient because each has a different protein-to-moisture ratio. The moisture coefficient is obtained simply by using the following equation:

% actual moisture − 4 × % actual protein content. Thus, bull meat containing 68% moisture and 19.8% protein would have a moisture coefficient of −0.112 or [0.68 − 4(0.198) = −0.112]. For beef navels with 40.2% moisture and 10.0% protein, the moisture coefficient would be +0.002 or [0.402 − 4(0.100) = +0.002]. If bull meat and beef navels were the only two meat ingredients used in the formula, the moisture constraint inequality would be: −0.112 (lb bull meat) + 0.002 (lb beef navels) ≤ 10. This shows that the maximum amount of moisture to be added is 10 + 0.112 × lb bull meat (to be computed) − 0.002 × lb beef navels (to be computed).

Assuming the least-cost formula under these restrictions consisted of 46 lb bull meat and 38 lb beef navels, the calculation for the amount of water to be added is as follows: 0.112 (46 lb bull meat) + −0.002 (38 lb beef navels) + 10 = 15.07% added water.

The maximum amount of moisture under governmental regulations, as already stated, is 4 times the protein content + 10. The average protein content of the blend is 12.908%, which is calculated as follows: 0.198 (46 lb bull meat) + 0.100 (38 lb beef navels) = 12.908%. Substituting this in the following equation for moisture restrictions: 4 (protein content) + 10% = % water allowed, a value of 61.63% [4 (12.908) + 10% = 61.63%] is obtained. This means that 15.07% water can be added and the formula will still comply with Federal regulations, which allow 61.63% total water.

To compensate for shrinkage, one can add the amount of water lost during processing, i.e., from the time of chopping until packaging. Temperature, relative humidity, time in the smokehouse, and internal processing temperatures influence shrinkage. Although shrinkage can be adjusted by linear programming, the simplest way is to add the amount of water lost in processing. This must be obtained from actual records and then the necessary water is added. Simply stated, if 8 lb water is lost during processing, then 8 lb can be added to the formula. This amount is in addition to that added to adjust the protein-to-water ratio.

In the example above using bull meat and beef navels, the formula then is composed of 46 lb bull beef, 38 lb beef navels, and 23.07 lb water. The water allowance includes 8 lb for shrinkage and 15.07 lb to adjust the protein-to-moisture ratio to comply with Federal regulations. This practice of adjusting for shrinkage is simpler than the use of linear programming, since the amount of water lost during processing may vary within smokehouses. This being the case, the processor can readily add more or less water to a batch, depending on which house will be used for processing.

Binding Constraints.—The amount of fat that can be emulsified to form a stable emulsion is a measure of the binding qualities of the meat ingredients. Since the salt-soluble proteins are the principal emulsifying agents, lean muscle with a low content of connective tissue provides the most effective binding qualities. On the other hand, fatty tissues and lean meat with a high connective tissue content are generally poor binding components. Although protein content indicates something concerning the capability to emulsify fat, a high proportion of connective tissues would indicate poorer binding qualities and should be avoided unless allowances are made for this. Thus beef and pork cheek meat, tripe, tongue trimmings, partially defatted tissue, liver, beef hearts, pork snouts and lips, pork ears, and other materials high in connective tissues are poor emulsifiers, and must have limitations placed on their use.

Tables 8.1 and 8.2 give data on the binding qualities of a number of sausage ingredients, using one system of relative rankings. The system is based on scores of 1.00 to 0.00 for excellent to poor binding qualities. This is only one method of ranking various ingredients. The values presented are averages, so do not always apply to individual cases. However, they do give some idea as to the ranking of different ingredients. Since there is considerable variation in composition and binding qualities of the same meat ingredients, some processors find it desirable to develop ranking systems of their own. Table 8.3 gives a ranking system for binding, connective tissue, and residue as used by one company.

Not only do fat and connective tissue contents alter binding qualities, but bacterial growth and freezing both have adverse effects on binding. Thus any one or all of these factors may modify the binding qualities of the meat ingredients, and should be considered in developing constraints. Furthermore, other factors may also influence binding, and if so, should be considered in developing formulations.

Color Constraints.—Appearance is an important consumer requirement, color being the most important attribute. Natural meat color is due to the combined effects of the red pigments in muscle (myoglobin and hemoglobin) blended into the other meat components. In other words, the percentage of myoglobin and hemoglobin in combination with muscle, fat, and connective tissue determines meat color. The blending effect is more important in emulsion-type sausages, where the color is diluted by blending the components.

Tables 8.1 and 8.2 show comparative color rankings for various meat ingredients. This system is based on using bull meat as an index of 1.00 and pure white as 0.00. Values given in Tables 8.1 and 8.2 are then relative to these standards. The contribution of each component is obtained by multiplying the weight by the factor from the table. As with binding values, the color ranks are averages and do not reflect

Table 8.1

CHARACTERISTICS OF SAUSAGE INGREDIENTS FROM PORK

Ingredients, Pork	Fat Level %	Color*	Bind†	Protein %	Moisture/ Protein Ratio %	Added Water %
Bacon ends	70	0.10	0.05	8.8	2.40	26.5
Backfat, untrimmed	80	0.20	0.30	4.2	3.83	11.9
Backfat, trimmings	62	0.25	0.15	8.1	3.71	13.6
Belly, trimmings	70	0.20	0.30	6.3	3.75	12.8
Blade meat	8	0.80	0.95	19.2	3.76	16.2
Cheek meat, trimmed	15	0.65	0.75	17.8	3.79	15.2
Ears	10	0.10	0.20	22.5	3.00	36.0
Ham, boneless	19	0.60	0.80	16.9	3.80	15.2
Head meat	25	0.50	0.80	16.1	3.60	11.8
Hearts	17	0.85	0.30	15.3	4.40	4.2
Jaw meat	8	0.80	0.80	20.9	3.40	24.9
Jowls, skinned	70	0.20	0.35	6.3	3.72	13.1
Lips	31	0.05	0.10	20.1	3.42	23.8
Liver	8	0.80	0.00	20.6	3.47	23.1
Neckbone, trimmings	25	0.60	0.70	15.9	3.55	19.0
Nose meat	15	0.45	0.70	17.9	3.74	16.2
Picnic, trimmings	25	0.60	0.80	15.6	3.80	14.4
Skin	32	0.05	0.20	28.3	1.40	92.6
Skirts	30	0.50	0.45	14.2	3.90	12.6
Snouts	35	0.05	0.10	14.6	3.45	19.9
Spleens	15	0.60	0.00	15.9	4.33	5.2
Stomachs, scalded	13	0.20	0.05	16.7	4.20	7.3
Tissue, partially defatted	35	0.15	0.20	14.0	3.63	16.8
Tongues	19	0.15	0.20	16.3	3.95	11.9
Tongue, trimmings	32	0.15	1.10	15.6	4.34	5.1
Trimmings, lean, 95%	10	0.70	0.90	18.9	3.73	16.8
Trimmings, lean, 50%	55	0.35	0.55	9.7	3.64	15.0
Trimmings, regular	60	0.30	0.35	8.4	3.77	13.1
Weasand meat	17	0.80	0.80	16.4	4.05	10.1

* 0.00 = white and 1.00 for bull meat
† 1.00 to 0.00 in order of decreasing desirability

the range within a product; neither do they make any allowance for poor color due to bacterial action or pigment degradation.

Table 8.4 shows a color constant value for 4 meat ingredients. This value was developed by chemically determining the pigment content (myoglobin plus hemoglobin) of the tissue and expressing it as a constant color value, or as milligrams pigment per 100 g protein. To apply this value to the same meat ingredient of a different chemical composition, one multiplies the constant color value by the percentage protein. This gives a value that can be used for each product. The processor then ascertains the minimum color score that is acceptable

Table 8.2

CHARACTERISTICS OF SAUSAGE INGREDIENTS FROM
BEEF, VEAL TRIMMINGS, AND BONELESS MUTTON

Ingredients, Beef	Fat Level %	Color*	Bind†	Protein %	Moisture/ Protein Ratio %	Added Water
Beef fat	85	0.10	0.05	3.3	3.55	11.3
Bull meat	8	1.00	1.00	20.8	3.40	24.8
Cheeks	15	0.90	0.85	18.3	3.59	19.4
Chucks, boneless	10	0.85	0.85	19.5	3.57	20.4
Clods, shoulder	10	0.95	1.00	20.0	3.50	19.9
Cow meat, domestic	12	0.95	1.00	18.8	3.65	18.4
Cow meat, imported	10	0.95	1.00	19.0	3.65	18.6
Flanks, boneless	55	0.55	0.50	9.9	3.54	16.2
Head meat	25	0.60	0.85	16.4	3.54	19.4
Hearts	21	0.90	0.30	14.9	4.30	6.0
Lips	20	0.05	0.20	15.9	4.00	11.0
Liver	9	0.80	0.00	20.7	3.40	23.6
Lungs	12	0.75	0.05	17.5	4.00	11.0
Navels, boneless	52	0.65	0.55	10.5	3.55	16.3
Shank meat	12	0.90	0.80	16.8	4.20	7.2
Spleens	12	0.95	0.20	16.9	4.20	7.2
Tissue, partially defatted	25	0.30	0.25	18.9	3.20	15.2
Trimmings, lean, 85/90%	15	0.90	0.85	18.9	3.45	22.7
Trimmings, lean, 75/85%	25	0.85	0.80	16.9	3.41	22.2
Tongues	20	0.25	0.20	15.5	4.15	8.4
Tongue trimmings	40	0.15	0.15	12.6	3.75	14.6
Tripe	11	0.05	0.10	12.8	5.90	16.2
Weasand meat	6	0.75	0.80	17.8	4.20	7.1
Other						
Veal, trimmings	10	0.70	0.80	19.4	3.62	19.3
Mutton, boneless	15	0.85	0.85	18.1	3.70	17.1

* 0.00 = white and 1.00 = bull meat
† 1.00 to 0.00 in order of decreasing desirability
Source: Anderson and Clifton 1967

and incorporates it into the model. This constraint will then give a least-cost model using a minimum color score.

Using the data in Table 8.4 for constant color values and composition, one can then obtain a practical solution for color in the linear program. For example, the color coefficients are as follows: bull meat = 4.72 (23.5 × 0.201), cow meat = 3.68 (20.7 × 0.178), pork trim (50/50) = 0.31 (3.4 × 0.091), and pork cheek meat = 1.94 (11.3 × 0.172). The color constraint can then be incorporated into the linear program by multiplying the color coefficients and the weight of each respective ingredient together and adding the results. If one uses a color constraint of ≥ 150, then one obtains the following equation: 4.72 (weight of bull meat) + 3.68 (weight of cow meat) + 0.31

Table 8.3

RANKING SYSTEM FOR SOME COMPOSITIONAL CONSTRAINTS USED IN A
COMMERCIAL OPERATION WITH VALUES FOR VARIOUS PRODUCTS

Products	Fat %	Protein %	Moisture %	Binding*	Connective Tissue†	Residue†
Beef cheek meat, fresh	14.8	18.5	65.7	0.513	0.323	0.164
Beef cheek meat, two days	14.8	18.4	65.8	0.232	0.450	0.326
Beef cheek meat, frozen	14.8	18.5	65.7	0.413	0.413	0.264
Beef hearts	18.0	15.0	66.0	0.222	0.153	0.622
Beef lips	19.4	16.1	64.0	0.388	0.540	0.160
Beef skirt meat	14.0	14.0	66.0	0.389	0.348	0.264
Beef tripe	6.0	14.0	79.2	0.030	0.725	0.250
Cow beef, fresh	17.6	17.8	63.6	0.650	0.200	0.160
Cow beef, frozen	6.2	20.4	72.4	0.502	0.190	0.290
Mutton, boneless	15.2	19.0	64.8	0.405	0.262	0.382
Navels, beef	46.2	12.9	41.1	0.443	0.260	0.297
Picnic, trimmings	27.1	14.8	57.1	0.540	0.154	0.299
Picnics, rough boneless	23.4	15.6	60.0	0.488	0.234	0.300
Picnics, rough boneless, frozen	14.8	18.5	65.7	0.413	0.323	0.264
Pork cheeks, fresh	25.0	15.0	59.0	0.490	0.272	0.248
Pork cheeks, frozen	25.0	15.0	59.0	0.370	0.304	0.316
Pork blade meat	14.5	18.0	57.0	0.456	0.294	0.256
Pork, fat backs	78.0	3.2	18.8	0.276	0.577	0.147
Pork, ham scraps, S.P.	35.1	10.9	53.0	0.481	0.319	0.200
Pork, head meat	10.7	18.3	70.0	0.430	0.268	0.300
Pork hearts, fresh	22.5	16.5	61.0	0.273	0.119	0.608
Pork hearts, frozen	22.5	16.5	61.0	0.034	0.202	0.774
Pork jowls	60.6	7.5	30.8	0.355	0.319	0.326
Pork lean trimmings	26.0	16.0	57.0	0.582	0.181	0.236
Pork neckbone lean	34.0	14.5	51.0	0.485	0.210	0.305
Pork, regular trimmings	55.0	9.6	34.9	0.455	0.220	0.339·
Pork, snouts	36.2	15.5	46.7	0.151	0.580	0.269
Pork, stomachs	9.4	17.8	72.0	0.020	0.544	0.485
Pork, partially defatted chopped	33.0	14.7	51.3	0.268	0.206	0.388
Pork, partially defatted fatty tissue	26.0	17.4	55.0	0.079	0.607	0.326

* Values given for binding are based on scoring system of 1.000 to 0.000 in order of decreasing binding ability.
† Values are from 0.000 to 1.000 in order of decreasing desirability. In other words, high values indicate a high residue and high connective tissue content.

(weight pork trim −50/50) + 1.94 (weight pork cheek meat) ≥ 150.
Assuming the computer comes up with a formula of 20 lb bull meat, 40 lb cow meat, 25 lb pork trim (50/50), and 9 lb pork cheek meat, the color score would be calculated as follows: 4.72 (20) + 3.68 (40) + 0.31 (25) + 1.94 (9) = 266.8, which is well above the minimum acceptable score of ≥ 150.

The two systems of considering color scores in developing color con-

Table 8.4

CONSTANT COLOR VALUES AND PERCENTAGE PROTEIN
FOR FOUR MEAT INGREDIENTS

Ingredient	Constant Color Value*	Protein %	Color Coefficient†
Bull meat	23.5	20.1	4.72
Cow meat	20.7	17.8	3.68
Pork trim (50/50)	3.4	9.1	0.31
Pork cheek meat	11.3	17.2	1.94

* Mg meat pigment/100 g. protein
† Constant color value x % protein
Source: IBM 1966

straints for least-cost computerized formulations should be useful in setting up guides for color constraints. Examination of the color scores in Tables 8.1 and 8.2 does indicate the importance of considering color in any linear program. Bacon ends, backfat, belly trimmings, pork ears, jowls, lips, skin, stomachs, partially defatted tissue, tongues, and tongue trimmings are all very poor in color, whereas lean meat is relatively high. Thus consideration must be given to developing a minimum acceptable color score if linear programming is to be used for least-cost formulations.

Flavor Constraints.—Flavor is probably the most important single sensory property of meat. Although people have wide differences in flavor preferences, each sausage product has a characteristic flavor made to appeal to a certain segment of the population. Consequently, flavor constraints must be carefully developed for all products. Certain meat items have characteristic flavors, some of which are not detectable until they reach a certain level. For example, it is possible to use a certain proportion of mutton in frankfurters or other products. Since lean mutton may be a good buy, bounding inequalities are often utilized, where minimum and maximum levels are specified. The minimum value of mutton ≥ 5 would be to meet labeling requirements, and the maximum level of mutton ≤ 30 would be to limit the upper level to avoid flavor problems. Thus, the lower level is a labeling constraint and the limiting upper level a flavor constraint.

Tables 8.1 and 8.2 give some flavor ratings for various meat ingredients. As indicated earlier, these are averages and are probably based upon emulsion-type sausages Different constraints may be necessary as one alters the formula to yield different products. For example, boar meat is very evident in frankfurters at low levels but may be utilized at moderate levels in liver sausage and braunschweiger. Some ingredients may be so bland in flavor that constraints must be made to keep a maximum amount of flavor.

Once the limitations have been determined, the constraints are used just as in binding or color. Thus one arrives at a value for each ingredient and then, by multiplying the value for each ingredient by the weight and adding the values a total flavor score is obtained. Once a minimum acceptable score is determined, it can be used as a constraint and will be considered in linear programming.

Frozen Meat Constraints.—Some processors develop special constraints for using frozen meat. Freezing decreases binding qualities and may also cause rancidity with some decrease in the desirability of flavor. It can also cause some decrease in the desirability of color score. Consequently, all these problems may be considered by simply limiting the amount of frozen meat to be utilized in the formula. Obviously, this may require different limitations for different ingredients and for different products.

As the constraints for frozen meat are applied in the same way as for color or binding qualities, they will not be considered further. Suffice it to say that one may need to develop different limitations depending on the temperature and length of time in freezer storage, as temperature and time of storage can have profound effects upon the properties of meat ingredients.

Poultry Meat Constraints.—Federal regulations permit the use of poultry meat in sausages. With development of mechanical boning devices, large quantities of boneless meat are now available. Because of its susceptibility to oxidation, differences in flavor, and emulsification properties, poultry meat must be limited in most sausages. Unless used within a few hours after mechanical boning, poultry meat is subject to oxidative deterioration; hence constraints must be developed for sausages that contain it. The exact nature of the products being made will determine the nature of the constraints.

Other Constraints.—A wide variety of other constraints may be needed in production of various types of sausages. The extent of constraint must be determined by research and by use of common sense. Some other possible areas where constraints may need to be developed include: use of partially defatted tissue, addition of cereals, use of nonfat dried milk, use of soy proteins (concentrates, spun fibers, and other soy-protein extenders), and similar compositional areas.

Once an area is known to be a limiting factor in the production or quality of sausages, it can be easily incorporated into a constraint by a series of trials to determine the best levels. Once the minimum or maximum is known, the constraints are used in the same way as outlined earlier in this chapter.

Some Examples of Least-Cost Formulations

Thus far the principles involved in arriving at least-cost formulations have been considered. To further illustrate the use of least-cost formulation for several frankfurter and bologna formulas, Table 8.5 shows data from a computer printout. The formula given is for an all-meat frankfurter. The information at the top of the table indicates some possible restrictions and their use in the formula. Immediately underneath this information, the printout indicates that label restrictions are for beef and pork, water added, and pork hearts. Next the optimum formulation using the various restrictions is printed out, giving the weights, indredients (and their input numbers), cost, and analysis. The weight and cost of the meat block, the weight of added water, and of the dry ingredients is given next. The weight and cost of the emulsion and the weight loss due to processing shrinkage then gives the weight and cost of the finished product, together with the yield and total cost of the batch. The last information in the printout from the computer gives the other available ingredients (and their input numbers), which were fed to the computer for consideration in the formulation.

The data at the top of Table 8.5 show the actual values for each possible restriction and actual restrictions used in arriving at the formula. The minimum restrictions show that the protein content must be at least 9%, color at least 15 (on the scale utilized) and emulsifying power at least 32 (based on the system used). Both beef and pork were also restricted to a minimum of 30% and combined to a minimum of 70% to meet labeling requirements. Maximum restrictions were 10% for added water, 30% for total fat, and 43% for collagen protein. Actual values for the formula show that all restrictions were met by the computerized formulation.

The optimum formula shown in Table 8.5 shows that the processor wants to incorporate a minimum of 150 lb beef plates and a maximum of 60 lb pork hearts into each batch, since both beef plates and pork hearts are on his inventory. In addition, 40 lb dry ingredients must be incorporated into each batch.

The processor must also add 107.9 lb water to the meat block (Table 8.5) in order to adjust the protein-moisture ratio and to compensate for losses during processing. In this example, the processor has decided upon 8% shrinkage, which gives the finished product weight and cost for ingredients. Given the final and beginning weights, the computer also gives a printout for product yield.

For future planning, the printout (Table 8.5) from the computer also gives the other ingredients considered in the linear program for least-cost formulation. The actual value of each of these ingredients is given, together with the penalty or cost for using them. The penalty represents the difference between the cost and the actual value in the formula. For example, pork blade meat costs $59.00 per cwt but is worth only $51.65, so the penalty for using pork blade meat is $7.35 per cwt ($59.00 − $51.65 = 7.35). The processor can.use these data for adjusting his inventory by buying or selling as the situation may demand. Thus, he would probably sell any ingredients with a high cost penalty and buy those with a low penalty in anticipation of his needs.

Table 8.6 gives essentially the same data as Table 8.5 except for the arrangement of the material. The formulation can be used for either frankfurters or bologna. The limitations call for a maximum of 29.5% fat and 43% collagen protein, while minimum restrictions specify 10% protein and 32 for emulsifying power. The least-cost formulation (Table 8.6) meets all these restrictions. The labeling limitations also require that beef and pork, water added, and mutton be utilized.

Calculations for yield, shrinkage during processing, and costs of per pound and per batch are made and included in the printout. Similarly opportunity and penalty costs are given for all products available for least-cost analysis. It is interesting to note that no value or penalty is given for pork stomachs, since they could not be used and maintain the constraints for quality.

These two examples of computer printouts for least-cost formulations illustrate the nature of the information given to the processor (Tables 8.5 and 8.6). The restrictions used are those for a specific processor, and thus may not work for other systems, but they do illustrate how constraints are used in least-cost formulations. As indicated earlier in this discussion, computerized least-cost formulation can be very useful to a processor provided adequate constraints are developed and accurate analytical data are fed to the computer.

SUMMARY

Preblending and computerized least-cost formulation have been discussed. Both offer certain advantages and disadvantages. They can be very useful if properly applied, but if improperly utilized they can be a source of serious problems. Preblending results in a more stable product and allows a processor to determine and adjust composition to meet any predetermined standard. Least-cost formulation by computer linear programming can result in substantial savings in product cost. However, development of constraints is necessary to avoid poor

Table 8.5

LEAST COST FORMULA FOR AN ALL MEAT FRANKFURTER

PRINTOUT INFORMATION FROM COMPUTER

Product Specification—Emulsion Type

Restriction	Units	Min.	Actual	Max.	Cost Restriction	Units	Min.	Actual	Max.
Protein	%	9.00	10.37		Total fat	%	30.00	30.00	30.00
Moisture	%		51.47	10.00	Bind	SAF		9.60	
Color	HEME	14.00	15.93		Beef	%	30.00	30.15	
Pork	%	30.00	23.81		Beef fat	%		12.06	
Pork fat	%		17.94		Coll./Prot.	%		42.85	43.00
Water added	%		21.40		Meat	%		79.36	
Pork hearts	%		11.90		Pork cheeks	%		13.49	
Seasonings	%		7.94		Beef & Pork	%	70.00	67.45	
Emuls. power	EMS	32.00	32.00		Heart Flavor	%		11.90	

Labels—Beef & Pork, Water Added, Pork Hearts

Optimum Formulation

Weight lb	Percentage Green	Percentage Final	No.	Ingredient	Cost	Inventory Min.	Inventory Max.	Analysis Prot.	Coll.	Fat	Moist.	Bind	Color	Optimum Cost Range Low	High
152.0	38.00	30.15	33	Beef plates	29.00	150.0		13.1	42.0	40.0	46.7	16.3	25.2	26.17	29.28
111.3	27.83	22.08	7	Pork trimmings 50%	18.00			9.7	34.0	55.0	35.3	11.7	9.0	17.46	24.03
68.0	17.00	13.49	21	Pork head meat	37.00			16.1	69.0	25.0	58.0	7.5	15.6	30.69	38.23
60.0	15.00	11.90	19	Pork hearts	29.50		60.00	15.3	27.0	17.0	67.3	6.1	33.2		39.49
8.7	2.17	1.72	10	Boneless picnic meat	41.00			16.3	23.0	23.0	60.7	20.1	15.9	40.46	44.97

400.0 lbs of Meat Block @ $27.64/cwt.

107.9   12.71   99   Water   10.00   40.00 40.00   100.0   12.32
40.0   7.94   98   Dry ingredients
547.9 lbs. of Emulsion @ $20.91 per cwt.
43.9 lbs Weight Loss due to 8.0% Shrinkage
504.0 lbs. of Finished Product @ $22.72 per cwt.
126.0% Yield. Total Cost of Batch is $114.54.

Opportunity—Penalty Costs

No.	Ingredient	Cost	Value	Penalty	Analysis					
					Prot.	Coll.	Fat	Moist.	Bind	Color
35	Beef trimmings—85/90	59.00	48.07	10.93	18.9	27.0	15.0	65.2	24.4	38.6
14	Pork blade meat	59.00	51.65	7.35	19.2	23.0	8.0	72.2	23.7	20.0
44	Beef head meat	38.50	37.28	1.22	16.4	73.0	25.0	58.1	7.8	26.4
38	Boneless beef chucks	64.50	47.49	17.01	18.4	30.0	15.0	65.7	24.0	38.1
37	Cow meat	66.50	49.31	17.19	18.8	21.0	12.0	68.6	24.5	38.9
17	Pork cheek meat—trim	46.50	43.54	2.96	17.8	72.0	15.0	67.5	8.6	28.7
32	Beef trimmings—50%	26.00	18.03	7.97	9.8	42.0	55.0	35.0	12.3	19.0
10	Boneless picnic meat	46.00	41.00	5.00	16.3	23.0	23.0	60.7	20.1	15.9
36	Bull meat	70.00	52.87	17.13	19.8	20.0	9.0	70.7	30.0	46.5

Table 8.6

LEAST COST FORMULATION FOR FRANKFURTERS AND BOLOGNA
PRINTOUT INFORMATION FROM COMPUTER

Product Specification—Emulsion Type

No. Restriction	Units	Min.	Actual	Max.
2 Protein	%	10.00	10.31	
3 Total fat	%		29.50	29.50
4 Moisture	%		50.72	
5 Bind	SAF		10.22	
17 Coll./Prot.	%		43.00	43.00
43 Emuls. Power	EMS		34.64	

Labels—Beef & Pork, Water Added, Mutton

Optimum Formulation

Weight lb	No.	Ingredient	Inventory Min.	Max.	Cost	Analysis Prot.	Fat	Moist.	Optimum Cost Range Low	High
223.7	32	Pork snouts			18.00	9.6	56.3	32.6	1.03	22.69
180.0	60	Boneless mutton			46.50	18.1	15.0	67.0		49.34
101.6	34	Beef trimmings—75/85			43.00	16.9	25.0	57.6	41.57	48.35
78.4	32	Beef trimmings—50			36.00	9.8	55.0	35.0	30.90	37.43
16.3	7	Pork trimmings—50			33.50	9.7	55.0	35.3	31.54	34.29

600.0 lbs. of Meat Block @ $33.56 per cwt.

197.6   Water
70.0   Dry ingredients   10.00   70.00   70.00
867.6 lbs. of Emulsion @ $24.01 per cwt.
86.8 lbs. Weight Loss due to 10.0% Shrinkage
780.8 lbs. of Finished Product @ $26.68 per cwt.
130.1% Yield. Total Cost of Batch is $208.34.

Opportunity—Penalty Costs

No.	Ingredient	Cost	Value	Penalty	Analysis		
					Prot.	Fat	Moist.
44	Beef head meat	48.75	14.74	34.01	16.4	25.0	58.1
17	Pork cheek meat-trim	52.00	17.94	34.06	17.8	15.0	67.5
14	Pork blade meat	69.00	50.41	18.59	19.2	8.0	72.2
8	Pork trimmings-80	55.50	45.12	10.38	15.8	25.0	58.8
21	Pork head meat	52.00	17.25	34.75	16.1	25.0	58.0
45	Beef heart meat	52.50	40.27	12.23	14.9	21.0	64.1
38	Boneless beef chucks	64.50	49.70	14.80	18.4	15.0	65.7
35	Beef trimmings-85/90	68.50	52.01	16.49	18.9	15.0	65.2
29	Pork stomachs—scalded	14.00			16.7	13.0	70.1
15	Skinned pork jowls	29.00	28.30	0.70	6.3	70.0	23.4
36	Bull meat	71.00	58.10	12.90	19.8	9.0	70.7

quality in the finished product. Computerized formulas must be developed with good judgment and sound knowledge about the functional properties of each ingredient and how they interact.

BIBLIOGRAPHY

ACTON, J. C., and SAFFLE, R. L. 1969. Preblended and prerigor meat in sausage emulsions. Food Technol 23, 367.

ACTON, J. C., and SAFFLE, R. L. 1970. Stability of oil-in-water emulsions. 1. Effects of surface tension, level of oil viscosity and type of meat protein. J. Food Sci. 35, 852.

ACTON, J. C. 1972A. Effect of meat particle size on extractable protein, cooking loss and binding strength in chicken loaves. J. Food Sci. 37, 240.

ACTON, J. C. 1972B. Effect of heat processing on extractability of salt-soluble protein, tissue binding strength, and cooking loss in poultry meat loaves. J. Food Sci. 37, 244.

ANDERSON, H. V., and CLIFTON, E. S. 1967. How the small plant can profitably use least-cost sausage formulation. Meat Processing 2, 17.

ANON. 1966. Linear programming. Meat blending. I.B.M. Technical Publications Dept., I.B.M., White Plains, N.Y.

BORTON, R. J., WEBB, N. B., and BRATZLER, L. J. 1968A. The effect of microorganisms on the emulsifying capacity and extract release volume of fresh porcine tissue. Food Technol. 22, 94.

BORTON, R. J., WEBB, N. B., and BRATZLER, L. J. 1968B. Emulsifying capacities and emulsion stability of dilute meat slurries from various meat trimmings. Food Technol. 22, 506.

BORTON, R. J., BRATZLER, L. J., and PRICE, J. F. 1970A. Effects of four species of bacteria on porcine muscle. 1. Protein stability and emulsifying capacity. J. Food Sci. 35, 779.

BORTON, R. J., BRATZLER, L. J., and PRICE, J. F. 1970B. Effects of four species of bacteria on porcine muscle. 2. Electrophoretic patterns of extracts of salt-soluble protein. J. Food Sci. 35, 793.

BROUMAND, H., BALL, C. O., and STIER, E. F. 1958. Factors affecting the quality of prepackaged meat. II. E. Determining the proportions of heme derivatives in fresh meat. Food Technol. 2, 65.

BUTLER, O. D., BRATZLER, L. J., and MALLMAN, W. L. 1953. The effect of bacteria on the color of prepackaged retail beef cuts. Food Technol. 7, 397.

CALLOW, E. H. 1948. Comparative studies on meat. II. The changes in the carcass during growth and fattening and their relation to the chemical composition of the fatty and muscular tissues. J. Agr. Sci. 38, 174.

CARPENTER, J. A., and SAFFLE, R. L. 1964. A simple method of estimating the emulsifying capacity of various meats. J. Food Sci. 29, 774.

CARPENTER, J. A., and SAFFLE, R. L. 1965. Some physical and chemical factors affecting the emulsifying capacity of meat protein extracts. Food Technol. 19, 1567.

CARPENTER, J. A., SAFFLE, R. L., and CHRISTIAN, J. A. 1966. The effects of type of meat and level of fat on organoleptic and other qualities of frankfurters. Food Technol. 20, 693.

CHRISTIAN, J. A., and SAFFLE, R. L. 1967. Plant and animal fats and oils emulsified in a model system with muscle salt-soluble protein. Food Technol. 21, 1024.

DuBOIS, M. W., ANGLEMIER, A. F., MONTGOMERY, M. W., and DAVIDSON, W. D. 1972. Effect of proteolysis on the emulsification characteristics of bovine skeletal muscle. J. Food Sci. 37, 27.

FOX, J. B., TOWNSEND, W. E., ACKERMAN, S. A., and SWIFT, C. E. 1967. Cured color development during frankfurter processing. Food Technol. 21, 388.

FRANK, S. S., and CIRCLE, S. J. 1959. The use of isolated soybean protein for nonfat, simulated sausage products, frankfurter and bologna type. Food Technol. *13*, 307.

FRONING, G. W. 1970. Poultry meat sources and their emulsifying characteristics as related to processing variables. Poultry Sci. *49*, 1625.

FRONING, G. W., and JANKY, D. 1971. Effect of pH and salt preblending on emulsifying characteristics of mechanically deboned turkey frame meat. Poultry Sci. *50*, 1206.

GRUNDEN, L. P., MacNEIL, J. H., and DIMICK, P. S. 1972. Chemical and physical characteristics of mechanically deboned poultry meat. J. Food Sci. *37*, 247.

HANSEN, L. J. 1960. Emulsion formation in finely comminuted sausage. Food Technol. *14*, 565.

HEGARTY, G. R., BRATZLER, L. J., and PEARSON, A. M. 1963. Studies on the emulsifying properties of some intracellular beef proteins. J. Food Sci. *28*, 663.

HUDSPETH, J. P., and MAY, K. N. 1967. A study of the emulsifying capacity of salt-soluble proteins. Food Technol. *21*, 1114.

MANDIGO, R. W., and HENRICKSON, R. L. 1966. Influence of hot processing pork carcasses on cured ham. Food Technol. *20*, 538.

MAURER, A. J., and BAKER, R. C. 1966. The relationship between collagen content and emulsifying capacity of poultry meat. Poultry Sci. *45*, 1317.

MILLER, W. O., SAFFLE, R. L., and ZIRKLE, S. B. 1968. Factors which influence the water-holding capacity of various types of meat. Food Technol. *22*, 1139.

OCKERMAN, H. W. *et al.* 1969. Comparison of sterile and inoculated beef tissue. J. Food Sci. *34*, 93.

PEARSON, A. M., SPOONER, M. E., HEGARTY, G. R., and BRATZLER, L. J. 1965. The emulsifying capacity and stability of soy sodium proteinate, potassium caseinate, and nonfat dry milk. Food Technol. *19*, 103.

ROBACH, D. L., and COSTILOW, R. N. 1961. Role of bacteria in the oxidation of myoglobin. Appl. Microbiol. *9*, 529.

SAFFLE, R. L., CHRISTIAN, J. A., CARPENTER, J. A., and ZIRKLE, S. B. 1967. Rapid method to determine stability of sausage emulsions and effects of processing temperatures and humidities. Food Technol. *21*, 784.

SWIFT, C. E., and SULZBACHER, W. L. 1963. Comminuted meat emulsions: Factors affecting meat proteins as emulsion stabilizers. Food Technol. *17*, 224.

SWIFT, C. E., LOCKETT, C., and FRYAR, A. J. 1961. Comminuted meat emulsions—The capacity of meats for emulsifying fat. Food Technol. *15*, 468.

SWIFT, C. E., WEIR, C. E., and HANKINS, O. G. 1954. The effect of variations in moisture and fat content on the juiciness and tenderness of bologna. Food Technol. *8*, 339.

TSAI, R., CASSENS, R. G., and BRISKEY, E. J. 1972. The emulsifying properties of purified muscle proteins. J. Food Sci. *37*, 286.

VADEHRA, D. V., and BAKER, R. C. 1970. Physical and chemical properties of mechanically deboned poultry meat. Poultry Sci. *49*, 1446.

WILLIAMS, L. D., PEARSON, A. M., and WEBB, N. B. 1963. Incidence of sex odor in boars, sows, barrows, and gilts. J. Animal Sci. *22*, 166.

CHAPTER 9

Sausage Formulations

In sausage processing, each step depends on what was done before, and influences each succeeding step. Careful selection of the meat for sausage formulation is important in obtaining quality products. Whole-carcass beef should contain no more than 10 to 12% fat, and plates, flanks, and shanks should be trimmed carefully and appear in the same ratio as in the carcass. Trimmings should be free of bone, sinews, cords, and membranes. Beef trimmings may contain up to 25% trimmable fat, but should also be free of clots and bruises. Regular pork trimmings are acquired from primal cuts and trimmings removed when shaping hams, shoulders, loins, butts, and bellies. Regular trimmings should not contain more than 55% fat by analysis.

All the formulas are based on a 100 lb meat block. All additives used are based on this weight rather than on percentage. For example, the salt, sugar, spices, water, or ice are simply added and sausage yields are calculated based on the meat block rather than on the emulsion weight. The formulations will be divided in 3 sections: (1) ingredients, (2) instructions, and (3) notes.

GROUND SAUSAGES

The preparation of ground fresh sausages requires relatively few operational steps. In a manufacturing operation it is best to prepare these items first to avoid contact with cured products. All equipment must be scrupulously clean and preferably cold. If necessary, flush the equipment with ice water.

FRESH PORK SAUSAGE

Formulation No.	Ingredients	Amount lb oz
1	pork trimmings (65% lean)	100
	salt	1 10
	white pepper	5
	sugar	4
	sage	2
	mace	1
2	pork trimmings (65% lean)	85
	fresh belly trimmings	15
	salt	1 12

FRESH PORK SAUSAGE (*Continued*)

Formulation No.	Ingredients	Amount lb	oz
	white pepper		4
	sugar		3
	sage		2
	ginger		0.5
3	pork trimmings (65% lean)		70
	neck-bone trimmings		30
	salt	1	12
	white pepper		4
	sugar or dextrose		3

Instructions.—Grind the chilled trimmings (38°F maximum temperature) through a ⅜-in. plate. Mix in mixer 2 to 3 min with the salt, sugar, and spices. Pass the mix through a 3/16-in. plate. Fill stuffer and tamp the mix tightly to minimize air pockets. Use 90 to 120 lb line pressure for stuffer. Stuff into animal, cellulose, or collagen casings or suitable bulk containers.

Note.—If animal casings are used, prepare casings 16 hr before use. Select 18- to 22-mm diameter casings. Wash the casings in cold water to remove salt and store in ice water. Flush just before use with 60°F water and shirr on stuffing horn. Squeeze gently on the horn to remove excess water. Hand- or machine-link.

Cellulosic or collagen casings are stuffed as removed from the package. These casings are conditioned and the moisture content is controlled by the manufacturer. They can be machine-linked. Cellulosic casing products should be dipped or sprayed for 10 to 15 sec with hot water (160°F) and then placed in a blast freezer until an internal temperature of 10 to 15°F is reached. Remove cellulosic casings and package.

Hold product at lowest possible temperature if prolonged storage is required. For short-term storage 22 to 26°F is recommended.

CANADIAN PORK SAUSAGE OR BREAKFAST SAUSAGE

Formulation No.	Ingredients	Amount lb	oz
1	pork jowls	55	
	pork trimmings (80% lean)	45	
	ice	10	
	corn flour	3	
	salt	2	

CANADIAN PORK SAUSAGE OR BREAKFAST SAUSAGE *(Continued)*

Formulation No.	Ingredients	Amount lb	oz
	white pepper	4	
	nutmeg or mace	1	
	thyme		0.5
	sage		0.5
2	jowls or regular trimmings	50	
	pork skirts	20	
	beef trimmings	15	
	back fat	15	
	ice	15	
	corn flour	4	
	dry skim milk	4	
	salt	2	
	sugar		8
	white pepper		4
	ginger		1
	mace		1

Instructions.—The meat ingredients are ground through a ⅜-in. plate, placed in a chopper with the spice, salt, flour, and ice, and chopped finely, usually 1 to 2 min. The chopped mixture is stuffed into animal, cellulosic, or collagen casings and handled as described in the instructions and notes for fresh pork sausage.

CHINESE SAUSAGE

Formulation	Ingredients	Amount lb	oz
Goin Chong	pork trimmings (80% lean)	50	
	pork back fat (diced)	30	
	pork livers	20	
	salt	2	8
	sugar	1	
	soy sauce		4
	cinnamon		1
	sodium nitrate		0.25
	sodium nitrite		0.125
Bok Yu Chong	pork trimmings (75% lean)	75	
	back fat (diced)	25	
	salt	2	8

CHINESE SAUSAGE (*Continued*)

Formulation	Ingredients	Amount lb oz	
	sugar	1	
	soy sauce		4
	cinnamon	1	
	sodium nitrate		0.25
	sodium nitrite		0.125

Instructions.—Grind pork trimmings through a ½-in. plate and dice the chilled back fat into ¼-in. cubes. For Goin Chong pass the livers through a ⅛-in. plate. Mix in mixer with the salt, sugar, soy sauce, spices, and curing salts. Stuff into size 26 cellulosic casings or equivalent-sized animal casings. Link at 4-in. intervals. Heat in smokehouse at 120°F for 48 hr with no smoke added. Hold at 60 to 65°F for 24 to 48 hr prior to packaging.

Note.—These are essentially raw pork products and unless made with certified pork, the products must be heated to 137°F in a smokehouse. Usually these products shrink 30 to 35% during processing and storage.

ITALIAN PORK SAUSAGE

Formulation No.	Ingredients	Amount lb oz	
1	pork trimmings (65% lean)	100	
(hot)	salt	1	8
	white pepper		4
	fennel		4
	crushed red pepper (mild)		4
	coriander		2
	paprika		2
2	pork trimmings (65% lean)	100	
(sweet)	salt	1	8
	white pepper		4
	fennel		4
	paprika		2

Instructions.—Grind the chilled trimmings through a ¼-in. or ⅜-in. plate. Sift the salt and spices into the coarsely ground pork while mixing, preferably with a large fork to achieve good mixing with a minimum of smearing. Stuff into hog casings, size 30 to 36 cellulosic or collagen casings. The stuffed product may be linked or rolled into rope-type sausages.

Note.—Either of these types can be prepared in bulk for pizza operations.

SKINLESS SMOKED LINKS

Formulation No.	Ingredients	Amount lb oz
1	pork stomachs	25
	regular pork trim	25
	veal	25
	pork hearts	10
	beef trimmings	5
	pork cheeks	5
	bacon ends	5
	ice	10
	salt	1 8
	corn syrup	8
	white pepper	4
	sodium nitrite	0.25

Instructions.—Grind the selected chilled meat products through a ⅜-in. plate. Mix in a mixer with the ice, salt, spices, and regrind through an ⅛-in. plate. Stuff into 22-mm sheep casings or collagen casings or into size 21 or 22 cellulosic casings. Link at 4-in. intervals. Drape on smokesticks and smoke using either hickory or hard maple wood. A representative smoke schedule follows:

100°F for 2 hr with dampers closed, smoke on;
120°F for 15 min with dampers open, smoke on;
120°F for 15 min with dampers closed, smoke on;
145°F for 15 min with dampers closed, smoke on;
160°F for 20 min or until 146°F internal temperature is
  reached.

Steam cook for 3 min at 165°F. Cold shower for 3 min, leaving some residual heat in product so no spotting occurs on transfer to a holding cooler. Cut and package animal or collagen casing products. Peel cellulosic casing and package skinless type product into 1 lb units.

SKINLESS POLISH SAUSAGE

Formulation No.	Ingredients	Amount lb	oz
1	beef trimmings (75% lean)	40	
	pork cheeks	35	
	regular pork trimmings	25	
	ice	10	
	salt	2	
	corn syrup	1	8
	ground black pepper		2
	marjoram		1
	sodium nitrate		0.5
	sodium nitrite		0.25
	garlic		0.25
2	pork cheeks	40	
	beef trimmings (75% lean)	30	
	regular pork trimmings	30	
	ice	10	
	salt	2	
	corn syrup	1	8
	ground black pepper		2
	marjoram		1
	sodium nitrate		0.5
	sodium nitrite		0.25
	garlic		0.25

Instructions.—Grind the beef trimmings and pork cheeks through an ⅛-in. plate. Grind the pork trimmings through a ¼-in. plate.

Chop the beef trimmings and 10 lb pork cheeks with the ice, salt, spice, and cure to achieve a smooth paste. Mix the pork trimmings into the paste either in a mixer or with a few turns of the chopper. Stuff into size 32 to 36 cellulosic casings. For short links, link to 5 to 5½ in. Long links are made 14 to 15 in., or if being prepared for a pickled sausage, 27 to 30 in. Drape linked product on smokesticks with 1½ in. between loops to permit good movement of air during the smoking process. Shower with 160°F water prior to smoking to remove grease and meat particles from the encased sausage.

Start the smokehouse at 130°F for 3 hr, then increase the temperature to 150°F for ½ hr and then 170°F for ½ hr. This will result in an internal product temperature of 150 to 152°F. Shower with cold water to an internal temperature of 90°F. Place in a holding cooler of 34 to 38°F until the sausage is well chilled. Peel and package. The long type is usually packed 2 pieces to a unit package. The 27- to 30-in. lengths are cut into 1-in. cylinders and placed in a vinegar-brine solution—40 grain vinegar—with 5 lb salt added to each 100 lb vinegar. For 1 lb sausage, use ½ lb vinegar brine. Place in 1-gal wide-mouth jars. Sausage held at 40°F will keep for 2 months or more but will keep only a couple of weeks at room temperature.

Note.—If a vinegar of greater strength is used, the sausage may turn brown on storage. If microbiological growth occurs in jars stored at room temperature, the packaged jars may be cooked in 150°F water for 1 hr or more depending on the size of the container; 30 min may be adequate for small jars.

The sausage may gain 5% or more in weight in the vinegar brine.

SEMIDRY OR SUMMER SAUSAGES

Semidry sausages are coarse-ground, fermented products requiring considerable knowledge of the art. They can be prepared using starter cultures comparable to those used in the cheese industry, or they can be held under specific conditions that preferentially promote the growth of organisms that impart flavor, texture, and preservative qualities.

THURINGER

Formulation No.	Ingredients	Amount lb	oz
1	pork trim (75% lean)	55	
	whole carcass beef	45	
	salt	2	8
	dextrose	1	
	ground black pepper		4
	starter culture		2
	whole mustard seed		2
	coriander		1
	sodium nitrate		0.25
	sodium nitrite		0.125

Instructions.—Grind all meats through a ¼-in. plate. Mix the ingredients in a mixer and pass the mixture through an ⅛-in. plate. Stuff into No. 2 × 16 fibrous casings. Wash the surface of the encased product with a hot shower for ½ to 2 min. Hang at room temperature for 2 hr and transfer to a smokehouse at 110°F for 12 hr. Maintain a dense smoke in the house. Finish at 120°F for 4 hr. Remove from the smokehouse and allow to stand at room temperature for 2 hr. Transfer to a holding cooler. The finished product should have a salt content of 3% and pH of 4.8 to 5.0.

Note.—The pork must be certified pork trimmings, or an internal temperature of 137°F must be obtained during smoking. The use of the starter culture markedly reduces the processing time.

CERVELAT

Formulation No.	Ingredients	Amount lb	oz
1	beef trimmings	70	
	regular pork trimmings	20	
	pork hearts	10	
	salt	3	
	sugar	1	
	ground black pepper		4
	sodium nitrate		2
	whole black pepper		2
2	beef trimmings	80	
	regular pork trimmings	20	
	salt	3	
	sugar	1	
	ground black pepper		4
	whole black pepper		2
	sodium nitrate		2

Instructions.—Grind the beef trimmings and hearts through a ¼-in. plate. Grind the pork trimmings through a ⅜-in. plate. Mix the ground materials with the salt, sugar, ground pepper, and nitrate, withholding the whole black pepper. After mixing, regrind through an ⅛-in. plate and add the whole black pepper. Mix with a kneading action for 2 min. Transfer to an 8-in. deep pan and hold at 38 to 42°F for 48 to 72 hr. Remix after removal from the pans and stuff into No. 2 or 2½ size fibrous casings. Hang in a drying room for 24 to 48 hr at 55°F and then place in a smokehouse for 24 hr at 80°F. Slowly increase the temperature of the smokehouse to 115°F and hold for 6 hr or more until a good color develops on the sausage. Cool by holding at room temperature for several hours prior to transfer to a holding cooler.

Note.—The pork must be from certified trimmings, or the internal temperature of the sausage must reach 137°F during smoking.

LEBANON BOLOGNA

Formulation No.	Ingredients	Amount lb	oz
1	whole carcass cow meat	100	
	salt	1	8
	sugar	1	
	mustard		8
	white pepper		2
	ginger		1
	mace		1
	sodium nitrate		1

Instructions.—Whole-carcass cow meat is salted with 2% salt and held for 8 to 10 days at 34 to 38°F. The beef is ground through a ½-in. plate and mixed in a ribbon mixer with the salt, sugar, spices, and sodium nitrate. The mixture is then passed through an ⅛-in. plate and stuffed into No. 8 fibrous casings. The filled casings are tied and stockinetted for support. The product is transferred to a smokehouse for a 4- to 7-day cold smoke, usually 4 days in the summer months and 7 days in the late fall and winter months.

Note.—Lebanon bologna is traditionally made under conditions that call for little or no refrigeration. The finished product is extremely stable even though the moisture content may be as high as 55 to 58%. The salt content of the finished product is usually 4.5 to 5.0% and the pH ranges from 4.7 to 5.0.

The sausage is processed traditionally in outdoor wooden smokehouses using a wood fire inside the house and a metal baffle plate to direct the heat. The ventilator doors at the top of the house are opened or closed at the discretion of the smokehouse operator.

CHORIZOS

Formulation No.	Ingredients	Amount lb	oz
1	pork trimmings (85% lean)	35	
	regular pork trimmings	35	
	neckbone trimmings	30	
	salt	2	8
	sugar		8
	sweet red peppers		6
	chili powder		6

CHORIZOS (*Continued*)

Formulation No.	Ingredients	Amount lb	oz
	red pepper (hot)	2	
	sodium nitrate	2	
	garlic powder		0.25

Instructions.—Grind the chilled pork trimmings through a ¼-in. plate. Mix in a mixer with the salt, sugar, sodium nitrate, and spices. Stuff into animal or collagen casings of 24 to 26 mm, or into size 27 cellulosic casings. Link at 4-in. intervals. The sausage may be packaged at this stage as a fresh chorizo. If it is to be processed further, it is dried at 54 to 58°F for 10 days or lightly smoked and dried for 15 to 20 days at 55 to 58°F. The product is sometimes packaged in lard somewhat comparable to sausage in oil products.

Note.—The term hot in relation to spicing is difficult to define, consequently, more or less hot red pepper may be used at the discretion of the sausage producer.

DRY SAUSAGES

The manufacture of dry sausages is steeped in art. However, the art is slowly yielding to the advancement of science.

GENOA (BEEF AND PORK)

Formulation No.	Ingredients	Amount lb	oz
1	beef chucks	40	
	pork shoulder trimmings	30	
	regular pork trimmings	30	
	salt	3	8
	sugar	2	
	burgundy wine		8
	white ground pepper		3
	whole white pepper		1
	sodium nitrate		0.5
	garlic powder		0.25
2	lean pork trimmings (85% lean)	60	
	regular pork trimmings	40	
	salt	3	8
	sugar	2	

GENOA (BEEF AND PORK) (*Continued*)

Formulation No.	Ingredients	Amount lb	oz
	burgundy wine	8	
	white ground pepper	3	
	whole white pepper	1	
	sodium nitrate	0.5	
	garlic powder	0.25	

Instructions.—Grind the lean meats through an ⅛-in. plate and the fat pork through a ¼-in. plate. Mix the salt, sugar, spices, wine, and sodium nitrate in a mixer for 5 min, or until a satisfactory mix is obtained. Hold the mix in trays 8 to 10 in. deep for 2 to 4 days at 38 to 40°F.

Stuff into a No. 5 by 22 fibrous casing or a sewed bung or suitably sized collagen casing. Hold in a green room at 70°F and 60% relative humidity for 2 to 4 days, or until the sausage stiffens and a pink color develops on its surface. Store in drying rooms at 53°F and 60% relative humidity for 90 days. A minimum moisture loss of 24% in the dry room is desirable for obtaining a good product.

Note.—Good color, no yeasty or rancid surface flavor, a moist texture in the center and a minimum of surface crusting are requirements for good dry sausage.

Control of the air flow in the drying room is important but difficult, since products of varying moisture are present and the air-flow pattern is not well defined. Usually, 15 to 20 air changes per hr is a good rate. The shifting of product is important for maintaining good drying. The rooms should be kept dark; low-intensity ruby lamps can be used, since intensity of lighting can be a factor in surface discoloration. Product may be bunched or spread on a stick, or the stick may be shifted from the bottom to the top of a rack, depending on the drying pattern. Low fat-content products and small-diameter products will shrink more readily than higher-fat and large-diameter products.

B. C. SALAMI (HARD)

Formulation No.	Ingredients	Amount lb	oz
1	beef chucks	40	
	pork jowls, glands trimmed	40	
	regular pork trimmings	20	
	salt	3	8
	sugar	1	8

B. C. SALAMI (HARD) *(Continued)*

Formulation No.	Ingredients	Amount lb	oz
	white pepper	3	
	sodium nitrate	2	
	garlic powder	0.25	

Instructions.—Grind the beef through an ⅛-in. plate and the pork through a ¼-in. plate. Mix all the ingredients in a mixer for 5 min, or until a good distribution of the fat and lean is apparent.

Store the mix in trays 8 to 10 in. deep for 2 to 4 days at 40 to 45°F. Stuff into No. 5 by 22 fibrous casings, sewed bungs or suitable-sized collagen casings. Hold stuffed product for 9 to 11 days at 40°F and 60% relative humidity.

Note.—If product molds in the drying room, some correction of the relative humidity is needed. The molded product should be wiped with an oiled rag to remove mold. The dry room may require a thorough cleanup.

In animal casings, the sausage is usually held in stockinettes for the first half of the drying cycle. After this period of drying, the encased sausage can be suspended from the tying string for the remainder of the drying period without stockinettes.

PEPPERONI

Formulation No.	Ingredients	Amount lb	oz
1	regular pork trimmings	45	
	beef chucks	30	
	pork hearts	15	
	pork cheeks	10	
	salt	3	8
	sugar	1	
	sweet paprika		12
	decorticated ground pepper		6
	capsaicin		4
	whole fennel seed		4
	sodium nitrate		1

Instructions.—Grind all the meat ingredients through a ½-in. plate, and then through an ⅛-in. plate. Add the spices, salt, sugar, and nitrate and mix for 5 min, or until a good distribution of the ingredients is apparent. Stuff into 38 to 44mm animal casings, or if for slicing product, No. 1 × 32 fibrous casings. Hold for 9 to 11 days at 38°F. Transfer to a green room maintained at 65°F and 69% relative humidity and hold for 48 hr.

Smoke for 60 hr at 90°F. Use a dry smoke until red color develops then adjust relative humidity to 80% and finish smoking.

Hold for 21 days in a drying room at 53°F and 69% relative humidity. Shrinkage is about 35%.

Note.—The traditional Italian-style pepperoni is not smoked. Smoke-flavored pepperoni is objectionable to the Italian trade.

The pizza trade requirements are frequently met by supplying the pepperoni as a cooked product where the product is held at 120°F for several hours and finally processed in a 145° smokehouse with smoke until the internal temperature reaches 137°F.

EMULSION-TYPE SAUSAGES

Emulsion products have a high degree of acceptance resulting from the texture and flavor achieved in processing. The formulations have been used by a large number of sausage companies throughout the United States. Federal inspection regulations governing the moisture to protein ratios and fat levels in emulsion type sausages have tended to promote a degree of uniformity in formulas.

BOLOGNA

Formulation No.	Ingredients	Amount	
		lb	oz
1	whole-carcass beef	60	
	regular pork trimmings	40	
	ice	25	
	salt	2	12
	sugar		8
	ground white pepper		4
	coriander		1
	mace		1
	sodium erythorbate		0.85
	sodium nitrite		0.25

Instructions.—Grind the beef through a ¼-in. plate and the pork through a ⅜-in. plate. Mix in a mixer with the spices, salt, sugar, erythorbate, and nitrite. Add ice or equivalent weight of ice and water depending on the temperature of the mix. Pass through a double-plate emulsifier to acquire the desired texture. The temperature rise of the mix passing through the emulsifier is usually 8 to 15°F.

If the emulsion is prepared in a conventional chopper, place the ground beef in the chopper with half the ice. Add the salt, erythorbate, and sodium nitrite and chop to a smooth paste, approximately 5 min. Add the remaining ice, spice, sugar, and pork trimmings and chop to the desired texture, usually for an additional 5 min, or until a temperature of 55 to 58°F is achieved.

Transfer the finished emulsion to a stuffer and stuff into casings. It is important to use as large a horn on the stuffer as is compatible with the casings. This permits lower stuffing pressures. A line pressure on the stuffer of 70 to 110 psi is usually required. A No. 8 by 36 in. fibrous casing gives a bologna of approximately 18 lb with a 15-in. circumference.

This size product will require approximately 8 hours in the smokehouse. It is best to start at a house temperature of 130°F with the damper open. Cook for 30 min and then close the damper and raise the temperature 10°F an hr to 170°F. Continue to heat at 170°F until an internal temperature of 156°F is reached. Cold shower for 35 to 40 min. Hold for at least 30 min at room temperature prior to placing the sausage in a 36 to 40°F holding cooler.

Note.—Bologna prepared for slicing and pre-packaging requires careful control of size. It is preferable to use a casing that has been specially treated for easy release from the bologna surface.

BOLOGNA (MILK POWDER)

Formulation No.	Ingredients	Amount lb	oz
1	regular pork trimmings	60	
	carcass beef	40	
	ice	25	
	dry skim-milk	4	
	salt	2	12
	sugar	1	
	white pepper		2
	coriander		1
	mace		1
	sodium erythorbate		0.85
	sodium nitrite		0.25
2	carcass beef	50	
	fat back	25	
	regular pork trimmings	25	
	ice	25	

BOLOGNA (MILK POWDER) (*Continued*)

Formulation No.	Ingredients	Amount lb	oz
	dry skim-milk	4	
	salt	2	12
	sugar	1	
	white pepper		2
	coriander		1
	mace		1
	sodium erythorbate		0.85
	sodium nitrite		0.25
3	regular pork trimmings	40	
	beef trimmings	30	
	carcass beef	20	
	fat back	10	
	ice	25	
	dry skim-milk	4	
	salt	2	12
	sugar	1	
	white pepper		2
	coriander		1
	mace		1
	sodium erythorbate		0.85
	sodium nitrite		0.25
4	beef trimmings	60	
	regular pork trimmings	40	
	ice	25	
	dry skim-milk	4	
	salt	2	12
	sugar	1	
	white pepper		2
	coriander		1
	mace		1
	sodium erythorbate		0.85
	sodium nitrite		0.25

Instructions.—Follow the same instructions for manufacture used for meat bologna.

BOLOGNA (IMITATION)

Formulation No.	Ingredients	Amount	
		lb	oz
1	beef weasand meat	30	
	beef trimmings	25	
	pork tongue trimmings	20	
	beef cheeks	10	
	pork stomachs	10	
	pork fat	5	
	ice	30	
	wheat flour	14	
	salt	3	
	sugar	1	
	white pepper		4
	garlic powder		1
	sodium nitrite		0.25
2	beef trimmings	20	
	beef weasand meat	20	
	pork tongue trimmings	15	
	mutton	15	
	beef cheeks	10	
	pork stomachs	10	
	pork hearts	5	
	pork fat	5	
	ice	30	
	wheat flour	14	
	salt	3	
	sugar	1	
	white pepper		4
	garlic powder		1
	sodium nitrite		0.25
3	beef trimmings	40	
	beef lips	20	
	mutton	10	
	sweet pickle trimmings	10	
	beef weasand meat	10	
	pork hearts	5	
	pork fat	5	
	ice	30	
	wheat flour	14	

BOLOGNA (IMITATION) (*Continued*)

Formulation No.	Ingredients	Amount lb	oz
	salt	3	
	sugar	1	
	white pepper		4
	garlic powder		1
	sodium nitrite		0.25
4	beef trimmings	25	
	beef hearts	20	
	beef tripe	20	
	back fat	20	
	pork stomachs	10	
	pork fat	5	
	ice	30	
	wheat flour	14	
	salt	3	
	sugar	1	
	white pepper		4
	garlic powder		1
	sodium nitrite		0.25

Instructions.—Grind beef, beef cheeks, and mutton through an ⅛-in. plate and the pork fat through a ¼-in. plate. Emulsify the other ingredients to give a smooth paste. For the remainder of the manufacturing follow instructions given for meat bologna.

Small-diameter emulsion-type sausage are the most popular sausages manufactured in the United States.

FRANKFURTERS (MEAT)

Formulation No.	Ingredients	Amount lbs	oz
1	whole-carcass beef	60	
	regular pork trimmings	40	
	ice	30	
	salt	3	
	corn syrup	2	
	white pepper		4
	nutmeg		1
	sodium erythorbate		0.85

FRANKFURTERS (MEAT) (*Continued*)

Formulation No.	Ingredients	Amount lb	oz
	sodium nitrite		0.25
2	whole-carcass beef	50	
	pork jowls	50	
	ice	40	
	salt	3	
	corn syrup	2	
	white pepper		4
	nutmeg		1
	sodium erythorbate		0.85
	sodium nitrite		0.25
3	pork jowls	55	
	whole-carcass beef	45	
	ice	40	
	salt	3	
	corn syrup	2	
	white pepper		4
	nutmeg		1
	sodium erythorbate		0.85
	sodium nitrite		0.25
4	pork jowls	50	
	whole-carcass beef	30	
	pork trimmings (80% lean)	20	
	ice	35	
	salt	3	
	corn syrup	2	
	white pepper		4
	nutmeg		1
	sodium erythorbate		0.85
	sodium nitrite		0.25

Instructions.—For all 4 formulas, grind the beef and pork trimmings through a ¼-in. plate. Chop the beef with half the ice, nitrite, erythorbate, salt, and corn syrup to a smooth paste. Add the remaining pork, ice, and spices, chop to 56 to 60°F, or until desired texture is achieved. Transfer to a stuffer and stuff into size 25 cellulosic casings. Link at 5¼-in. lengths to give 10 to the pound finished frankfurters. Hand-link the product on smokesticks in loops with 8, 9, 10, or 12 frankfurters to a loop, and 21 to 22 loops to a 42-in. smokestick. The smokesticks are transferred to cages and the sticks spaced to permit good air flow when the product is cooked.

A suggested schedule for processing follows:

130°F for 15 min with the dampers open, smoke on;
140°F for 15 min with dampers closed, smoke on;
160°F for 30 min with dampers closed, smoke on;
170°F for 30 min or until 155°F temperature is reached.

Cold shower for 5 min and chill to approximately 90°F. Allow to stand for 15 min minimum to dry surfaces before placing in a holding cooler. After chilled frankfurters have reached approximately 40°F internal temperature, they are peeled and packaged in 1 lb units.

Note.—Introduction of continuous frankfurter lines and high-velocity smokehouses that process frankfurters in from 40 to 60 min has resulted in changes in conventional manufacturing systems. With

Table 9.1

MEAT BLOCK, 35% FAT

(lb lean/lb fat trim)

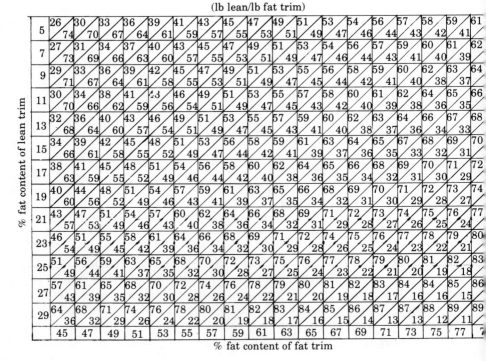

% fat content of fat trim

large-volume operations pre-blending of the meat ingredients has become a standard practice. These trimmings are separated by visual inspection into fat and lean trimmings. The fat content of the lean and fat meat trimmings is determined. Table 9.1 shows the pounds of each type of trimming to give 100 lb blend with a 35% fat content. A production test run should be made to establish the processing shrink. Then appropriate moisture additions (Table 9.1) can be made on subsequent batches. Some of the continuous units process, shower, and brine chill the product for immediate peeling of the frankfurters.

FRANKFURTERS (MILK POWDER)

Formulation No.	Ingredients	Amount lb	oz
1	regular pork trimmings	70	
	pork trimmings (80% lean)	20	
	lean beef chucks	10	
	ice	30	
	dry skim-milk	3	
	salt	3	8
	pepper		2
	paprika		2
	capsaicin		1
	nutmeg		1
	sodium erythorbate		0.85
	sodium nitrite		0.25

Instructions.—Chop the lean pork and beef with half the ice, salt, sodium nitrite, and erythorbate to give a smooth paste. Add the milk powder, spices, and remainder of the ice and chop about 6 min to a temperature of 52 to 55°F. Stuff into size 25 cellulosic casings and link at 5¼ in. Heat at 120°F for 30 min, raise the smokehouse temperature to 140°F for 30 min and finally 160 to 165°F until a 152°F internal temperature is reached. Cold shower for 5 min. Allow the surface to dry and place the frankfurters in a cooler at 34 to 38°F. Peel and package.

FRANKFURTERS (GERMAN STYLE)

Formulation No.	Ingredients	Amount lb	oz
1	beef trimmings	40	
	pork jowls	25	
	beef head meat	20	

FRANKFURTERS (GERMAN STYLE) (*Continued*)

Formulation No.	Ingredients	Amount lb	oz
	regular pork trimmings	15	
	ice	30	
	dry skim-milk powder	4	
	salt	3	
	white pepper		4
	nutmeg		1
	garlic powder		0.25
	sodium nitrite		0.25
2	whole-carcass beef	40	
	regular pork trimmings	30	
	pork trimmings (60% lean)	20	
	veal	10	
	ice	30	
	dry skim-milk powder	4	
	salt	3	
	white pepper		4
	nutmeg		1
	garlic powder		0.25
	sodium nitrite		0.25

Instructions.—Follow instructions given for preparation of meat frankfurters.

FRANKFURTERS (MILWAUKEE)

Formulation No.	Ingredients	Amount lb	oz
1	pork trimmings (60% lean)	40	
	regular pork trimmings	35	
	cow trimmings	10	
	lean veal	10	
	pork neck bone trimmings	5	
	ice	30	
	salt	2	8
	corn syrup	1	
	sugar		8
	white pepper		4
	monosodium glutamate		2

FRANKFURTERS (MILWAUKEE) (*Continued*)

Formulation No.	Ingredients	Amount	
		lb	oz
	nutmeg	1	
	ginger	1	
	sodium nitrite	0.25	

Instructions.—Chop the beef, veal, and neck bone trimmings with the ice, salt, sugar, and sodium nitrite to a smooth paste. Grind the pork trimmings through a ¼-in. plate. Mix the emulsion with spices in a mixer for 5 to 6 min.

Transfer to a stuffer and stuff into size 25 cellulosic casings. Link at 4-in. intervals. Heat at 120°F for 30 min, raise the smokehouse temperature to 140°F for 30 min and finally 160 to 165°F until a 152°F internal temperature is reached. Cold shower for 5 min. Allow the surface to dry and place the frankfurters in a cooler at 34 to 38°F. Peel and package.

WHITE HOT FRANKFURTER (NO NITRITE CURE)

Formulation No.	Ingredients	Amount	
		lb	oz
1	regular pork trimmings	50	
	lean veal	25	
	whole carcass beef	25	
	ice and water	60	
	cracker ·meal	12	
	salt	4	
	corn syrup	2	
	white pepper		6

Instructions.—Grind beef and veal through an ⅛-in. plate and pork through a ¼-in. plate. Place all ingredients in the chopper and chop to a fine texture. Stuff in size 26 cellulosic casings, link at 4-in. intervals. Hold at room temperature for a maximum of 1 hr to dry slightly. Cook in a Jourdan cooker or steam cabinet at 160 to 165°F for 15 min, or until an internal temperature of 155°F is reached. Cold shower and then transfer to a holding cooler. Peel, package, and hold in a 30 to 34°F cooler.

Note.—This item is quite perishable and care should be exercised so as not to increase spoilage development.

BOCKWURST

Formulation No.	Ingredients	Amount	
		lb	oz
1	veal trimmings	40	
	regular pork trimmings	40	
	beef trimmings	20	
	wheat flour	3	
	salt	2	8
	white pepper		4
	nutmeg		1
	fresh eggs	2 dozen	
2	pork trimmings (65% lean)	65	
	veal clods	35	
	fluid milk (skim or whole)	8	
	ice	4	
	salt	2	8
	sugar		4
	mace		1.5
	eggs	1 dozen	
3	veal trimmings	50	
	regular pork trimmings	50	
	fresh milk	12	
	onions (juice only)	3	
	salt	2	8
	sugar		8
	white pepper		4
	sage		0.5
	thyme		0.5
	cardamom		0.5

Instructions.—Grind the meat ingredients through a 1-in. plate and then through an ⅛-in. plate. Place in a cutter and chop for 3 to 4 min after adding the milk, salt, and spices. Stuff into casings. Chill in cooler to 26 to 30°F.

Note.—The product should have a smooth texture and very pale color. It is very palatable but is also readily perishable and has a short shelf life. Keep well refrigerated.

Liver Sausage and Braunschweiger

These are emulsion-type sausages that are usually water-cooked; in the case of braunschweiger, the cooked product may be lightly smoked at the end of the cook cycle. In some instances, smoked bacon is used in the product to produce a smoked flavor. Some producers call their top-grade product braunschweiger and their economy grade liver sausage.

LIVER SAUSAGE

Formulation No.	Ingredients	Amount	
		lb	oz
1	pork livers	50	
	pork jowls	50	
	salt	2	8
	ground white pepper		4
	coriander		1
	nutmeg		1
	sodium nitrate		0.5
	sodium nitrite		0.25
2	pork livers	50	
	regular pork trimmings	40	
	veal trimmings	10	
	fresh onions	5	
	milk powder	3	8
	salt	2	8
	white pepper		4
	sodium nitrate		0.5
	sodium nitrite		0.25
3	pork livers	50	
	jowls	30	
	veal trimmings	15	
	bacon ends	5	
	milk powder	3	8
	salt	2	8
	dry onion flakes (toasted)		8
	white pepper		4
	monosodium glutamate		2
	sodium nitrate		0.5
	sodium nitrite		0.25

LIVER SAUSAGE (*Continued*)

Formulation No.	Ingredients	Amount lb	oz
4	pork livers	35	
	cooked tripe	25	
	cooked pork skins	15	
	sweet pickled ham fat	15	
	pork jowls	10	
	dry skim-milk	3	8
	salt	2	8
	white pepper		4
	ground clove		1
	sodium nitrate		0.5
	sodium nitrite		0.25

Instructions.—For all the above formulas, grind the jowls or pork trimmings through a ½-in. plate. Grind tripe and pork skins through an ⅛-in. plate. Chop livers and other meat ingredients together with the spices, cure, salt, and dry skim-milk. Chop all ingredients to a paste or use the chopper as a mixer for several passes and then run the emulsion through the fine plate of an emulsifier. Stuff tightly into No. 3 by 32 inch moistureproof fibrous casings using a large horn, usually 1-in. diameter, with a line pressure of 35 to 70 psi. Place the sausage in a 165°F water tank for 1½ hr. Chill rapidly, preferably in a tank or truck with slush ice.

Note.—Adjust inventories of raw materials so that at least 50% of the livers are fresh. When only frozen livers are used, it is well to use some fresh trimmings. Fresh livers usually result in more stable emulsions than frozen livers.

The internal temperature of liver sausage should be between 150 and 152°F. Higher temperatures may produce a bitter flavor in the finished sausage. Lower temperatures may not give the desired shelf-life.

Gray-colored liver sausage can be achieved by leaving the nitrite out of the sausage.

LIVER SAUSAGE (10 OZ UNIT PACKS)

Formulation No.	Ingredients	Amount lb	oz
1	pork livers	45	
	skinned pork jowls	45	

LIVER SAUSAGE (10 OZ UNIT PACKS) (*Continued*)

Formulation No.	Ingredients	Amount lb	oz
	beef trimmings	5	
	smoked bacon ends	5	
	dry skim-milk	3	8
	salt	2	8
	corn sugar	1	
	dehydrated onions		4
	white pepper		4
	coriander		1
	sodium nitrite		0.25

Instructions.—Grind the jowls, bacon, and beef through an ⅛-in. plate. Place the livers in the chopper and chop with the dry skim-milk, salt, sugar, spices, and cure to obtain a free-flowing paste. Add the ground meats and chop to the desired texture, usually 6 or 8 min. Liver sausage emulsion should be handled as little as possible. Transfer to a stuffer, attach a Rockford filler, adjusted to deliver 10 oz. Stuff tightly into 3 by 11-in. plastic tubes. Place stuffed and tied product into 160°F water and hold for 1 hr, or until the sausage reaches an internal temperature of 152°F.

Chill in ice water, and hold overnight in a cooler, or until the sausage has an internal temperature of 35°F. Dip the chilled sausage for 5 to 10 sec in 195 to 200°F water to shrink the plastic film to the contracted sausage surface. This gives a tight, smooth package. Hold in 30 to 34°F cooler.

COTTO SALAMI

Formulation No.	Ingredients	Amount lb	oz
1	beef trimmings (75% lean)	25	
	cow meat	20	
	pork cheek meat	20	
	pork hearts	20	
	regular pork trimmings	15	
	ice	10	
	salt	2	8
	sugar		12
	whole black pepper		3
	white pepper		2
	sodium erythorbate		0.85

COTTO SALAMI *(Continued)*

Formulation No.	Ingredients	Amount oz	Amount lb
	garlic powder	0.5	
	sodium nitrate	0.5	
	sodium nitrite	0.25	
2	cow meat		30
	regular pork trimmings		30
	pork cheek meat		20
	pork hearts		15
	pork stomachs		5
	ice		10
	salt	2	8
	sugar		12
	whole black pepper		3
	white pepper		2
	sodium erythorbate	0.85	
	garlic powder	0.5	
	sodium nitrate	0.5	
	sodium nitrite	0.25	

Instructions.—Grind the pork meat items through a ¼-in. plate and the beef through an ⅛-in. plate. Chop the beef trimmings, ¼ of the cow meat, and the pork stomachs with the ice, salt, sugar, cure, and erythorbate to a smooth paste. Mix with the spice and ground meat in a mixer for about 5 min. Hold for 6 to 8 hr at 40°F. Stuff into No. 8 by 22-in. fibrous casings.

Place 6 pieces to a 42-in. smokestick and space to prevent touching or crowding so good circulation of air can be obtained in the smokehouse. A suggested schedule for cooking is as follows:

1 hr at 140°F, with smoke;
2 hr at 160°F, with smoke;
3 hr at 170°F, with smoke;
1 hr at 180°F or until 153°F internal temperature is reached, with smoke.

Shower with cold water for 40 min. Then rinse with hot water for 10 to 20 sec to remove grease. Chill at 28 to 32°F until 40°F internal is obtained. Hold at 38 to 40°F.

SPECIALTY ITEMS

Specialty items are often prepared from meat products other than skeletal meat and are formed in a variety of loaf shapes: (1) rectangular,

(2) traditional, (3) old-fashioned, and (4) cylindrical (if sliced and packaged at plant level). Note Fig. 9.1.

These loaf items are some of the most nutritious products of the sausage trade and are of interest economically since they frequently utilize meat by-products to the best advantage.

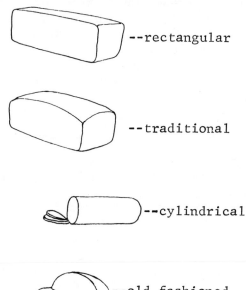

--rectangular

--traditional

--cylindrical

--old fashioned

FIG. 9.1. LOAF STYLES

FAMILY LOAF

Formulation No.	Ingredients	Amount	
		lb	oz
1	beef trimmings (90% lean)	50	
	pork trimmings	50	
	ice	30	
	wheat flour	12	
	dry skim-milk	4	
	salt	2	12
	corn syrup	1	
	chopped onions	5	
	white pepper		4
	sage		2
	celery seed		1
	sodium nitrite		0.125

Instructions.—Grind the beef through an ⅛-in. plate and the pork through a 3/16-in. plate. Chop the beef, ice, flour, milk powder, spices, and sodium nitrite for 2 to 3 min. Add the pork trim and chop for an additional 2 to 3 min.

Stuff into stainless steel loaf pans 10 by 5 by 4 in. that have been coated with lard on the inner surface. Stuff with a loaf stuffing horn on a piston stuffer with 80 lb air pressure. Stuff to top of the pan. Then level off the top of the pan with a flat knife or spatula. Cooking can be done in a bake oven or a smokehouse. The oven should be kept below 220°F. Loaves are heated to an internal temperature of 152 to 155°F. In a smokehouse the following schedule can be used:

1 hr at 150°F;
1 hr at 170°F;
3 hr at 190°F, or until an internal temperature of 152 to 155°F is reached.

Cool loaves at room temperatures for 2 hr, then dip in hot cottonseed oil at a temperature not to exceed 425°F. Dip for 20 to 30 sec, or until the loaf takes on a reddish-brown baked appearance. Chill to an internal temperature of 45°F. Stuff into plastic tubes 7½ by 18 in. and store at 32 to 34°F.

This loaf can be prepared in No. 8 by 40-in. fibrous casings by processing in the smokehouse for 8 hr, starting at 130°F for 30 min and then raising the temperature to 150°F for 1 hr, and finally heating for 6 hr or more at 170°F. Cold shower for 40 min and then chill to an internal temperature of 42°F. Strip the casing and slice the loaf for pre-packaged items. In this manner, the product can be produced in a cylindrical form and still be merchandised as a loaf item in accordance with Federal meat inspection regulations.

VEAL LOAF

Formulation No.	Ingredients	Amount lb oz	
1	lean veal trimmings	40	
	regular pork trimmings	40	
	cooked tripe	20	
	ice	45	
	dry skim milk	12	
	fresh chopped onions	5	
	salt	3	
	mustard flour	1	
	white pepper		4

VEAL LOAF (*Continued*)

Formulation No.	Ingredients	Amount lb	oz
	lemon extract		2
	garlic powder		1
	sodium nitrite		0.125

Instructions.—Grind the meat products through a ¼-in. plate. Transfer to the chopper and chop all the ingredients to a smooth paste. Follow the instructions outlined for preparation of the family loaf.

LUXURY LOAF

Formulation No.	Ingredients	Amount lb	oz
1	extra lean pork (95%) lean)	80	
	cow meat	20	
	ice	15	
	dextrose	3	8
	salt	2	8
	sodium nitrate		1
	sodium nitrite		0.25
2	extra lean pork (95% lean)	80	
	cow meat	10	
	pork shank meat	10	
	ice	15	
	dextrose	3	8
	salt	2	8
	sodium nitrate		1
	sodium nitrite		0.25

Instructions.—Grind the cow meat and pork shanks through an ⅛-in. plate and the lean pork through a 1-in. plate.

Chop the cow meat and pork shanks with the ice, salt, sugar, nitrate, and nitrite for about 5 min to a smooth paste. Transfer to a vacuum mixer and add the lean pork. Mix under vacuum for 2 min. Hold for 24 hr at 36 to 40°F. Vacuum-mix for 3 to 5 min. Stuff in 11 by 4 by 4-in. metal molds with parchment liners. Use a large loaf stuffing horn and a piston air stuffer with 60 to 70 lb line pressure. Stuff compactly and slowly from the bottom to the top of the mold. Fold the parchment liner over the top surface. Use ratchet lids for covering the mold. Place the molds in 160°F water and cook for 3½ hr, or until an internal temperature of 152°F is reached. Chill with tap water to 90°F and then place in tubs with cracked ice. Remove from molds and stuff the loaves into plastic tubes and store at 30 to 34°F. This product can be processed in suitably sized fibrous casings and squared into the rectangular shape by compressing the encased product in a wire cage.

Note.—The meat should be selected and trimmed with care to remove any connective tissue or tendons and any excess fat, since these items would show as particles in the loaf and detract from its quality.

CURED BEEF LOAF

Formulation No.	Ingredients	Amount lb	oz
1	lean beef	100	
	ice	5	
	salt	3	
	sugar	1	
	sodium nitrate		1
	sodium nitrite		0.125

Instructions.—Grind the beef through a ½-in. plate. Mix all the ingredients in a mixer for 5 min. Transfer to a cooler and hold for 24 hr at 36 to 40°F. Grind the mix through an ⅛-in. plate, mix for 5 to 6 min, and transfer to a stuffer. Stuff in parchment-lined metal molds or suitable-sized fibrous casings. Heat in a water cooker to an internal of 152 to 155°F; usually 3½ hr at 160°F is sufficient for 4-in. rectangular loaves. Chill in a tank of slush ice. Remove from molds and wrap in plastic wrappers. If product is sliced thin, it has many of the characteristics of chipped beef.

HAGGIS

Formulation No.	Ingredients	Amount lb	oz
1	pork hearts	50	
	pork livers	20	
	beef suet	20	
	pork spleens	10	
	oatmeal	35	

HAGGIS (*Continued*)

Formulation No.	Ingredients	Amount lb	oz
	fresh onions	5	
	salt	2	
	white pepper		6
	nutmeg		3

Instructions.—Cook the hearts, livers, and spleens in 180 to 190°F water. Remove the cooked items and grind with the suet through a ¼-in. plate. Chop onions to a fine pulp. Bring the broth separated from cooking to a boil and sift in the oatmeal. Stir vigorously. To the hot mass add the cooked meats, onions, salt, and spices. Stuff into No. 8 moisture proof fibrous casings and cook for 3 hr in 170°F water until an internal temperature of 160°F is reached. For a traditional product, a sheep stomach is filled and cooked. The item is highly nutritious but quite perishable. Keep chilled at 30 to 34°F.

BLOOD PUDDING

Formulation No.	Ingredients	Amount lb	oz
1	beef blood	35	
	pork back fat	20	
	pork skins	15	
	pork snouts	10	
	pork ears	5	
	pork weasand meat	5	
	pork hearts	5	
	pork stomachs	5	
	dry skim-milk	10	
	white corn meal	5	
	fresh onion	2	
	salt	1	4
	sugar	1	
	black pepper		4
	marjoram		2
	fresh garlic		1
	clove		1
	cinnamon		0.5
	sodium nitrate		0.5
	sodium nitrite		0.25

Instructions.—The pork ingredients are obtained from vat-cured pork. Snouts from white pigs are often separated and used in souse or head cheese. The cured pork items are cooked until tender and then ground through an ⅛-in. plate. The backfat is scalded and diced into ¼-in. cubes.

Place the ground materials in a mixer, add blood, diced fat, salt, spices, and curing salts and mix for 6 to 8 min. Transfer to a stuffer and stuff into No. 6 fibrous casings or into ring casings.

Cook at 160°F in water for 3 hr, or until a 152°F internal temperature is reached. Cold shower or chill in slush ice. Dry the surface of the product at room temperature prior to placing in 34 to 38°F holding cooler.

Note.—Blood can be whipped with a paddle or a bundle of small sticks to remove fibrin. Store the defibrinated blood at 36°F or lower. Salt used at 2½ lb per 100 lb blood together with ¼ oz sodium nitrite and 1 lb sugar aids in preservation.

An excellent anticoagulant for blood collection can be prepared by dissolving 3 oz sodium citrate and 3 oz salt in 1 qt water. Pour this solution into the holding container for the blood and stir gently. Store the blood in a 32 to 36°F cooler. If desired, 2 lb salt and ⅛ oz sodium nitrite can be added to the blood after chilling.

BLOOD AND TONGUE LOAF

Formulation No.	Ingredients	Amount lb	oz
1	pickled lamb or pork tongues	65	
	cured beef blood	20	
	pork back fat	15	
	dry skim-milk	12	
	fresh onions	5	
	salt	1	
	white pepper		4
	fresh garlic		2
	marjoram		2
	clove		1
2	pickled lamb or pork tongues	35	
	cured beef blood	25	
	pickled back fat	25	
	pickled pork skin	15	
	dry skim-milk	12	
	fresh onions	5	

BLOOD AND TONGUE LOAF (*Continued*)

Formulation No.	Ingredients	Amount	
		lb	oz
	salt	8	
	white pepper	4	
	garlic	2	
	marjoram	2	
	clove	1	
	cinnamon		0.5

Instructions.—Scald and clean the tongues and cut into 1-in. cubes. Cut backfat into ¼-in. cubes. Rinse cubed back fat in water before using. This prevents the fat from sticking together. Grind the onions through an ⅛-in. plate and press garlic in a garlic press.

Place all the ingredients in a mixer and mix for 6 to 8 min. Stuff into No. 6 fibrous casings or place in greased loaf pans. Water cook for 3 to 3½ hr at 165°F, or until an internal temperature of 155°F is reached. Chill in ice water and transfer to a holding cooler at 34 to 38°F.

Note.—Back fat should be held in pickle brine prior to cubing. This hardens the fat and facilitates cutting in the cuber.

BLOOD SAUSAGE

Formulation No.	Ingredients	Amount	
		lb	oz
1	cured beef blood	85	
	diced pork fat	15	
	fresh onions	5	
	salt	2	
	white pepper		4
	nutmeg		1
	cinnamon		0.5

Instructions.—Chop the onions to a fine pulp. Add diced pork fat, onions, salt, and spices to the blood. Fill size 26 cellulosic casings. Place the filled casings in 165°F water for 30 min, or until an internal temperature of 152 to 155°F is reached. Chill in ice water. Cut cooked, chilled sausage into 4-in. lengths and package.

KISZKA

Formulation No.	Ingredients	Amount	
		lb	oz
1	sweet pickle ham skins	45	
	cured pork snouts	25	

KISZKA (*Continued*)

Formulation No.	Ingredients	Amount	
		lb	oz
	pork liver	15	
	cured lips	5	
	tripe	5	
	cured beef blood	5	
	water	50	
	barley	25	
	onions	5	
	salt	1	
	pepper		4
	thyme		1
	nutmeg		1
	marjoram		1

Instructions.—Grind the cured ingredients through an ⅛-in. plate. Chop the liver, onions, and spices with the ground materials to a smooth paste. Sift barley into boiling water and stir. The barley will swell and absorb most of the water. At this time, add the lard and stir until the lard is well incorporated. Add the blood and chopped paste and stir until the mass is mixed.

Stuff into beef rounds and tie into rings or stuff into No. 30 fibrous casings. Place the sausage in boiling water for 20 to 25 min. Remove from cook tank. Allow to dry at room temperature for at least 30 min and place in a refrigerator at 32 to 38°F.

Note.—Buckwheat or rice may be substituted for the barley.

PICKLE AND PIMIENTO LOAF

Formulation No.	Ingredients	Amount	
		lb	oz
1	pork trimmings (70% lean)	60	
	veal trimmings	30	
	beef trimmings (85% lean)	10	
	ice	40	
	dry skim-milk	12	
	sweet pickles	5	
	pimientos	5	
	fresh onions	5	
	salt	3	
	dextrose	1	
	white pepper		4
	marjoram		1

PICKLE AND PIMENTO LOAF (*Continued*)

Formulation No.	Ingredients	Amount lb	oz
	sodium erythorbate		0.85
	sodium nitrate		0.5
	sodium nitrite		0.25

Instructions.—Grind the meats through an ⅛-in. plate. The pickles are passed through a ¼-in. plate and the pimientos through a ½-in. plate of a vegetable chopper. Chop the meat ingredients with the onions, spices, salt, cure, milk powder, and ice to give a smooth paste. Add the pickles and pimiento and run for 2 or 3 revolutions of the bowl to get a good mix.

Stuff into parchment-lined metal molds or into No. 7½ easy-release fibrous casings for in-plant slicing. The product in molds is water-cooked at 165°F until an internal temperature of 152 to 155°F is reached, usually 3½ to 4 hr. The product in casings is best cooked in a high-humidity, high-velocity smokehouse.

The product is well chilled, the casing removed by stripping, and the loaf sliced. A loaf temperature of 28 to 30°F facilitates handling while slicing. Loaf items in molds are removed after chilling and can be stuffed into a cellulosic or plastic film for shipping and display.

Baked loaves can be prepared in the mold by heating at 225 to 250°F, until a 155°F internal temperature is reached. They are then handled as are water-cooked loaves.

Note.—Pimientos are sweet bell-shaped Spanish peppers and should not be confused with pimento which is related to allspice.

OLIVE LOAF

Formulation No.	Ingredients	Amount lb	oz
1	lean veal	50	
	pork trimmings (50% lean)	40	
	beef trimmings (85% lean)	10	
	ice	45	
	dry skim-milk	12	
	stuffed olives	6	
	salt	2	12
	sugar	1	
	white pepper		4
	marjoram		1
	sodium nitrate		0.5
	sodium nitrite		0.25

Instructions.—Grind the meat ingredients through a ¼-in. plate. Chop the ice, milk powder, salt, sugar, spices, and cure for 6 to 8 min to a smooth paste. Drain the olives. Sprinkle the drained olives with a light layer of powdered gelatin and work into the emulsion with a large spatula or paddle. Stuff into loaf pans or into No. 7½ easy-release fibrous casings. Process as indicated for pickle and pimiento loaf.

SCRAPPLE

Formulation No.	Ingredients	Amount	
		lb	oz
1	cured pork head meat	65	
	cured pork skins	20	
	pork livers	15	
	water	65	
	corn meal	35	
	salt	2	8
	pepper		4
	sage		2
	nutmeg		1

Instructions.—Cook the head meat, skin, and liver in water in a steam-jacketed kettle. Remove the meat products and grind through a ⅛-in. plate. Add the ground meat products back and continue cooking in boiling water. Stir in the corn meal, salt, and spice with a paddle and continue to cook for at least 30 min to a thick consistency. Pour the sausage into greased molds or into No. 8 fibrous casings and chill rapidly. Hold overnight. Slice in thick slices and package.

SOUSE

Formulation No.	Ingredients	Amount	
		lb	oz
1	cured pork tongues	35	
	cured pork snouts (white pigs)	20	
	cured pork cheeks	20	
	cured lean ham trimmings	15	
	cured pork lips	10	
	pickles (diced)	6	
	pimientos	6	
	high-bloom gelatin	3	8
	100-grain vinegar	3	
	salt	1	
	whole pepper		2
	whole cloves		2

Instructions.—Place the meat ingredients in sufficient water to cover. Bring the water to a boil and simmer until tender. Remove the cooked meat and grind through a 1-in. plate. Reheat the broth with the added spices and then filter through cloth to remove particles of meat and spice. To 2 gal broth, add the vinegar, salt, and gelatin. Reheat this mixture to 165°F and pour over the meat mass to which the pickles and pimientos have been added. Chill in cooler overnight. Remove from molds and wrap in cellulosic or plastic tubes. Store at 32 to 36°F.

HEAD CHEESE

Formulation No.	Ingredients	Amount lb	oz
1	cured pork snouts (white pigs)	20	
	cured pork lips	20	
	cured pork hearts	20	
	cured pork cheek meat	15	
	cured pork skins	15	
	cured pork ears	10	
	broth from cooking water	45	
	onions	5	
	gelatin	4	
	vinegar	3	
	salt	1	
	mustard		8
	white pepper		4

Instructions.—Place the various meat ingredients in separate cooking nets. Cover with water and cook at 170 to 180°F until tender, usually 2 to 3 hr. Hearts usually require longer heating than the other items. Grind the onions, ears, and skins through a 1/16-in. plate. Cut the snouts, lips, hearts, and cheeks into ¾-in. pieces. Place the meat ingredients in a mixing vat and add the heated broth with the spice, salt, gelatin, and vinegar. Stuff into pork stomachs or into No. 60 fibrous casings. Cook at 165°F for 2½ hr and then chill in ice water. Store at 35 to 40°F.

SUMMARY

The sausage art is yielding to technology as production moves from small back of the store shops to large 100,000 lb per day operations. While the principles of manufacture are essentially the same for both, a considerable number of problems based on the volume or bulk of material and the scheduling and handling of this material have arisen. Successful sausage production now depends on selection of proper raw materials, controlled processing, and uniformity of workmanship. This combination will produce superior sausages.

CHAPTER 10

Smoked Meats

Smoked meat is an all-encompassing term that has gradually changed meaning over the years. It refers primarily to primal cuts of pork which have been cured, smoked, and often cooked. The principal smoked-meat products are ham and bacon. It is common practice among meat processors to separate ham production and marketing from bacon production and marketing. Consequently, processing companies often have smoked meat as well as sliced bacon departments. This division is made simply because the bacon market is so large that it is desirable to place individual management responsibility for bacon apart from other smoked meats.

With few exceptions, smoked meats are both cured and smoked. Years ago, most smoked meats were simply smoked and not cooked. This is no longer the case. Many smoked meats are cooked, usually at the same time they are smoked. The two processes usually go hand-in-hand. While reference is made to the smokehouse, today it would be more accurately referred to as a cookhouse or oven, for less smoking and more cooking of smoked meats is being done. However, there are exceptions, probably the most notable being Country hams. Corned beef and cooked hams are examples of cured meat products that are not smoked. Additional exceptions are smoked fresh beef, pork, and lamb sometimes used for banquets or barbecuing. These products are smoked but not cured. It is common to think of smoked meats as being primarily pork products, but cured, smoked beef and, to a much lesser extent, lamb products are also produced.

HAMS

Federal meat inspection regulations form a basis for differentiating hams in two ways: (1) according to the highest internal temperature they reach during cooking, and (2) according to the amount of added substance they retain after processing. In effect, these regulations control product recognition and labeling and, in so doing, form the basis for a system of classification.

Internal Temperature

Federal inspection regulations recognize two classes based on the internal temperature that hams achieve in the smokehouse. The classes are (1) smoked (140 to 147°F), and (2) fully cooked or ready-to-eat (148°F and above). The terms cooked, thoroughly cooked, fully cooked, ready-to-serve, and ready-to-eat are synonymous. To ensure destruction of trichina, the microscopic parasite responsible for trichinosis, Federal inspection regulations specify that hams must reach an internal temperature of at least 137°F. Country hams are not cooked, but are rendered safe to eat by being subjected to a prolonged curing process. Country hams are usually cooked before being eaten. Hams classified by the Federal government as smoked should also be cooked further before being eaten. To increase palatability, these hams are generally cooked to internal temperatures above 160°F by consumers. Moreover, fully cooked hams, which are required to reach at least 148°F, are generally cooked by meat processors to at least 152°F to increase palatability of hams that might be eaten without additional cooking by consumers.

Prior to incorporation of nitrite in the cure and introduction of the arterial pumping technique, the internal temperature of hams cooked in smokehouses seldom exceeded 137 to 140°F. With these two technological innovations, hams were cured faster. They tended to be more mildly flavored, and it became a fairly common practice for ham processors to exceed 137°F internal temperature in the smokehouse. Such hams became commonly known as tendered. Tendered hams were processed more rapidly because they were arterial-cured and were more moist and mildly flavored. In time, processors produced even more moist and more mildly cured, as well as, more tender hams. To accomplish this, hams were pumped with additional pickle, placed directly in the smokehouse and subjected to even higher temperatures, but less smoke. From this series of changes emerged the so-called ready-to-eat or fully cooked hams. Today, the trend is toward production of more and more fully cooked hams.

Added Substance

Most hams today are cured by pumping with solutions in which the cure ingredients are dissolved in water. For this reason Federal meat inspection regulations recognize three ham categories depending on the amount of added substance remaining in hams after processing. Added substance refers to water and salt present in the cured product in excess of the normal amount occurring in the uncured product. Labeling restrictions are shown in Table 10.2.

Basically, government control is expressed in terms of weight, that is, the weight of the finished product cannot exceed its fresh, uncured weight unless labeled appropriately. In actuality, control is exercised through calculation based on chemical analysis. There are inevitable differences between actual and calculated yields, but inspection procedures recognize these variances with a scale of tolerance. Tolerances are expressed in the form of statistically validated ranges based on

Table 10.1

PROCESSING PROCEDURES

Product	Cured	Smoked	Cooked
Bacon	yes	yes	partially *
Canadian bacon	yes	yes	yes†
Jowl bacon	yes	yes	partially
Breakfast bacon	yes	yes	partially
Fat-back	yes	no	no‡
Smoked ham	yes	yes	yes
Fully cooked ham	yes	yes	yes
Country ham	yes	yes	no
Smithfield ham	yes	yes	no
Scotch ham	yes	no	no
Prosciutto	yes	yes	no
Cooked ham	yes	no	yes
Baked ham	yes	yes /no	yes
Picnic	yes	yes	yes
Shoulder butt	yes	yes	yes
Smoked pork loin	yes	yes	yes
Corned beef	yes	no	yes/no
Dried beef	yes	yes/no	no
Smoked tongue	yes	yes	yes
Pickled pigs feet	yes	no	yes
Smoked lamb	yes	yes	yes
Smoked fresh meat	no	yes	yes

* partially: more than 100°F but less than 140°F
† yes: 140°F internal temperature or above
‡ no: less than 100°F internal temperature

the number of samples analyzed. Control by chemical analysis is based on calculation according to the following formula:

estimated yield = % moisture + % salt − k × % protein + 100

The protein multiplier or k factor is an average figure representing the approximate ratio of moisture to protein. The k factor differs among products. Factors recognized by Federal inspection authorities are shown in Table 10.3.

Table 10.2

HAM LABELING ACCORDING TO ADDED SUBSTANCE

Federal Labeling Restriction	Added Substance in Finished Ham
No labeling restrictions	None
Labeled "Water Added"	Up to 10%
Labeled "Imitation"	Over 10%

Table 10.3

PROTEIN MULTIPLIERS

Product	k Factor
Smoked picnics, butts, and miscellaneous products	4.00
Canned picnics	3.93
Canned hams and other canned pork products	3.83
Smoked hams	3.79

Presence of Bone

Except for some long-cut hams which may contain part of the back-bone, whole intact hams contain three bones—(1) aitch, (2) body, and (3) shank. The presence or absence of one or more of these bones in a processed ham forms the basis for still another method of grouping hams, as shown in Table 10.4.

Whole bone-in hams are comprised of three segments—(1) butt, (2) center, and (3) shank. Bone-in hams can be sold whole or cut into sections. When cut in half, the sections are referred to as a butt half or shank half. If one or more center slices are removed after hams are cut in half, the remaining butt and shank sections are called portions, either butt or shank. Once the center slices are removed, they are no longer half hams.

Semiboneless hams are designed to provide convenience to the consumer while retaining some of the appeal of the bone-in product. Aitch and shank bones are removed. This leaves only the femur or body bone, which facilitates carving by the consumer. A few semiboneless

Table 10.4

HAM CLASSIFICATION ACCORDING TO PRESENCE OF BONES

Type	Bone		
	Aitch	Body	Shank
Bone-in	present	present	present
Semi-boneless	absent	present	absent*
Boneless	absent	absent	absent

* A limited number of semi-boneless hams are produced with both body and shank bones left intact.

hams are produced in which only the aitch bone has been removed, leaving the body and shank bones intact.

The anatomical structure of hams lends to division into 2 or 3 primary sections. Preparation of these sections is discussed in detail in Chap. 6. Generally, heavier hams weighing 18 lb and up are used for preparation of sectioned ham products.

With increased emphasis on consumer convenience, boneless hams have grown in popularity during recent years. They are manufactured in either round or flat shapes. Round boneless hams are made in cellulosic casings. In the last few years, the fastest growing segment of the boneless ham market has been flat hams, produced by pressing boneless hams between wire screens. Prior to pressing, hams are stuffed into either stockinettes or cellulosic casings. The hams are then fully cooked in a smokehouse. Because they are cooked, the flat shape is retained when the screens are removed.

One of the most recent developments in the production of boneless hams is binding of ham chunks by tumbling to extract salt-soluble protein, compressing the small sections in metal molds, and cooking. The end result is a solid piece of meat produced from smaller pieces. This patented process is used to manufacture chunked-and-formed ham slices.

Commercial Ham Curing

Whether classified as smoked or fully cooked, whether bone-in or boneless, whether flat or round in shape, most commercially produced hams are cured in a similar manner. Since the middle 1930's most have been pickle-cured. A typical curing pickle consists of salt, sugar, sodium nitrate, sodium nitrite, and phosphate. In addition, corn syrup and sodium erythorbate are used frequently. Government regulations restrict amounts of corn syrup, nitrate, nitrite, phosphate, and erythorbate that can be used. Restrictions, based on a 10% pump level, are as follows:

Corn syrup: Corn syrup may not exceed 60 lb per 100 gal pickle; corn syrup solids are limited to 50 lb per 100 gal.

Phosphate: Finished products may not contain more than 0.5% of an approved phosphate.

Erythorbate: Pickles may not contain in excess of 87.5 oz per 100 gal pickle.

Nitrate: Pickles may not contain more than 7 lb per 100 gal and finished products may not contain more than 500 ppm.

Nitrite: Pickles may not contain in excess of 2 lb per 100 gal and finished products may not contain more than 200 ppm.

An example of a curing formula is shown in Table 10.5. The salometer strength of this pickle is about 65°, depending on pickle temperature. This formulation can be used for hams pumped to 110% of green weight. For hams pumped in excess of this, modifications are required; otherwise, the hams (1) are too salty, and (2) do not conform with Federal regulations relating to ingredients. For example, hams pumped to 120% require reducing all ingredients by 50%, except water. Commercial processors generally prepare 100° stock pickles and dilute with water to the strength pickle they wish to pump. Because of their low solubility in brine, phosphates are dissolved in water and then combined with the pickle. Erythorbate is best added with a minimum of agitation shortly before the pickle is to be used.

Because injection machines allow for increased automation, their use is gaining in popularity. Curing pickle is injected directly into the ham musculature by a multiple-stitch needle machine, or through an artery-injection needle into the arterial system from where it diffuses into the muscle tissue. Either method allows curing ingredients to diffuse throughout hams much faster than is possible by dry rubbing or immersion in pickle. Curing pickle was first injected into ham muscles through individual-stitch needle injections. The injection process was improved upon when it was learned that curing pickle could be introduced via the arterial system. Many packers still use the arterial pumping system for curing hams, but many others now use multiple-needle injection machines. When needles are attached to the machine with a flexible coupling, bone-in products can be injected.

The amount of cure injected into hams depends on (1) the type of ham being cured, that is, whether regular, water-added, or imitation, and (2) the amount of moisture lost by the hams during processing. Processing loss includes pickle released by hams shortly after pumping, smokehouse shrink, and cooler shrink.

After hams are pumped, they are sometimes placed directly in the

Table 10.5

CURING FORMULA

Ingredient	Amount		
	Lb	Oz	
Salt	1	8	
Sucrose		6	
Phosphate		8	
Sodium erythorbate		0.5	
Sodium nitrate		0.3	
Sodium nitrite		0.3	
Water	8	5	(1 gal)

smokehouse or held in a cooler for up to 24 hr. To achieve maximum quality, hams are placed in cover pickle for 3 to 7 days. Hams cured in cover pickle have better color development, better color stability, fewer uncured spots, more uniform distribution of salt, better flavor, and improved water-binding.

The next step in manufacture is to smoke and cook hams in the smokehouse. A typical cook schedule starts at 130 to 140°F. After 2 hr, the temperature is raised to 150 to 160°F, and then after an additional 2 hr it is further increased to 170 to 180°F. When smokehouses have provisions for controlling relative humidity, hams should be cooked in an atmosphere of 30 to 40% relative humidity. Although graduated schedules are still in common usage, more processors are turning to single-temperature schedules. Such schedules call for starting and maintaining one temperature, generally 170 to 180°F, from beginning to end of the cook schedule. The length of time hams remain in the smokehouse is dependent upon (1) size of ham, (2) the final internal temperature desired, (3) air velocity in the smokehouse, and (4) the cook schedule employed. Hams are generally subjected to a natural wood smoke.

Cooked Ham

Cooked hams are sometimes referred to as boiled hams. However, the term "boiled ham" is a misnomer. Federal inspection regulations forbid labeling hams as boiled unless they are actually cooked in boiling water. Cooked hams are boned and stuffed into metal molds. They are not boiled but are cooked in tanks in 165 to 180°F water to internal temperatures of 152 to 160°F. These hams are seldom subjected to smoke and are invariably sold sliced for sandwiches.

Baked Ham

Federal regulations specify the termed "baked" shall apply only to products which have been cooked by direct action of dry heat for sufficient time to permit them to assume the characteristics of baked items. Baked hams must reach an internal temperature of at least 170°F. To avoid the great expense associated with manufacture of baked hams, processors produce baked-style hams. These are usually prepared from conventional cooked hams. Chilled cooked hams are dipped in a gelatin-based glaze. Frequently the top surface of these hams is decorated with pineapple slices and maraschino cherries. A glaze formula is shown in Table 10.6

A procedure that can be used to prepare baked-style hams is as follows: Disperse the gelatin in cold water and heat. Incorporate all other ingredients. When the mixture has cooled to 120°F, immerse

Table 10.6

BAKED STYLE HAM GLAZE

Ingredient	Amount	
	Lb	Oz
Corn syrup	5	
Brown sugar	2	
Finely ground paprika		6
Soluble clove		4
Gelatin	2	
Water	4	2
Pineapple juice	4	5

the hams. Remove immediately and let chill. Decorate the surface before the gelatin solidifies.

Country Ham

The only uncooked hams produced in the United States of any commercial significance are Country hams. "Country" or "Country Style," when applied to hams and shoulders, is a generic term which indicates characteristics, and not the location of manufacture.

Federal regulations require products that are not actually produced in the country to be labeled Country Style. Country and Country Style hams and shoulders must be free of trichinae, be dry-cured, have a salt content of at least 4%, and shrink a minimum of 18% during processing.

The appearance and most certainly the flavor of Country hams differ dramatically from common pickle-cured hams. The salty, somewhat dry, rather hard, highly flavored product known as a Country ham is produced primarily in southern regions of the United States. Its history dates back to colonial times when early settlers allowed hogs to roam living on acorns and nuts. In the fall, when the pigs returned home for food, they would be turned into the peanut fields. The colonists developed a method of curing hams so they would be preserved through the hot summers. This tradition has continued ever since.

The first Country hams came from hogs grown in the peanut belt in Virginia and North Carolina. The best known Country hams are Smithfield hams produced in Smithfield, Virginia. In 1925, the Virginia State Legislature passed an Act stating that Smithfield hams must be processed in Smithfield to be called Smithfield. While processors in a number of southern states use essentially the same curing method as that used for Smithfield hams, connoisseurs disagree as to which

Country hams are best—those produced in Virginia, North Carolina, Tennessee, Kentucky, Georgia, or Missouri.

Production of Country hams can generally be divided into three phases. First is the curing period, during which curing ingredients are rubbed on all ham surfaces. During this time, generally about 30 to 40 days depending on size of the hams, they should be held under refrigeration. In large commercial operations, hams are cured in stacks. Layer after layer of hams is put down. A mixture of salt, sodium nitrate, and often sugar is shoveled on the hams. Then another layer of hams is placed on top of the preceding layer, and so on until the ham stacks reach about 4 ft in height. The hams are then left to cure. Some processors elect to let hams cure an additional month to allow for more complete salt equalization. Hams are generally overhauled 2 to 3 times during the curing period.

During the second phase, hams are hung in the smokehouse and subjected to a cool smoke. They can be hung in stockinettes, but are frequently hung from hooks in the smokehouse by pieces of twine inserted through the skin at the hock. As Country hams are not cooked, the smokehouse temperature is kept between 70 and 90°F. Internal temperature of the hams usually ranges about 10°F lower than the smokehouse temperature. To guard against internal spoilage, smokehouse temperatures are not allowed to exceed 100°F. When smoke is applied continuously, 2 or 3 days are usually required to reach a desirable amber or mahogany color. When smoke is generated intermittently, hams usually remain in the smokehouse for 5 to 8 days.

After smoking, the third phase, the long aging process begins. Country hams are aged for 6 to 9 months. Aging is not conducted under refrigeration. It is during this time that the full flavor characteristic of Country ham develops, probably as a result of enzymatic action. To encourage enzymatic activity, hams are usually aged between 70 and 85°F. Production of Country hams is less controlled than that of modern, mildly flavored, sweet pickled hams. However, experimental work conducted at several state universities has shown it is possible to produce finely flavored Country hams under controlled conditions. Such a procedure is as follows:

Apply a mixture of 8 lb salt, 3 lb sugar, and 3 oz sodium nitrate to the surfaces of carefully trimmed hams. Use approximately 1¼ oz of this curing mix per lb ham. The total amount of curing mix should be applied at 3 intervals. This will allow for more uniform salt penetration. The first application is rubbed on the fresh meat as quickly as possible after slaughter. The second application is made about 3 days after the first, and the third application on the tenth day or about a week after the second. It is not necessary to rub hams hard, just enough to distribute the curing ingredients over the surface. The ideal temperature for dry-curing hams is 38°F. One of the main objections to country-cured hams is their saltiness. Such objections can be minimized by following this curing schedule:

15-lb ham stays in cure 2 days per lb or 30 days;
20-lb ham stays in cure 1¾ days per lb or 35 days;
25-lb ham stays in cure 1½ days per lb or 40 days;
To allow for more complete equalization of salt, it is desirable to hold hams under refrigeration for an additional 3 to 4 weeks. Hams should be soaked in cold water for about 1 hr after being removed from cure to remove surface salt. This prevents salt-streaking during smoking and gives the final product a more attractive appearance. The small amount of moisture picked up during soaking is soon removed in the smokehouse. The length of time required to produce the desired amber or mahogany color depends on smoke density. It has been shown that there is no difference between hams subjected to continuous smoke and those subjected to smoke for intermittent periods.

Occasionally, Country hams are not smoked but are put directly into the aging room. Such hams, however, lack smoke flavor. Under controlled conditions with an aging room temperature of 70°F and a relative humidity between 60 to 65%, it is possible to produce flavorful hams with no more than 4 months aging. However, under these conditions, it is necessary to control air flows at 30 to 35 fpm. Because Country hams tend to become progressively harder and their flavor accentuated as aging continues; they should not be aged for more than 9 to 12 months.

As Country hams have not been cooked, they should be parboiled before being eaten to make them (1) less hard and (2) less salty. Today some commercial processors of Country hams make fully cooked Country hams. To prepare fully cooked hams, aged hams are water cooked at about 180°F for 8 hr and the skin peeled. These hams are then decorated with cloves and burnt sugar. Fully cooked Country hams can be sliced and eaten cold if desired, or served reheated.

The lean of Country cured hams is dark red and very firm, while the fat is quite yellow. Flavor is intense and distinctive. Most Country hams are rubbed with finely ground black pepper. Some processors rub their hams prior to smoking while others do not apply pepper until the hams are aged and ready for sale.

In addition to Country hams, three other uncooked hams are sold in the United States, principally to meet the demands of limited ethnic markets. These hams are Westphalian, Scotch, and Prosciutto.

Westphalian Ham

Westphalian hams are produced in Germany. These uncooked hams have a distinctive flavor produced by smoking with juniper twigs and berries spread over a beechwood fire. Westphalian hams are sliced thin and eaten uncooked. They are prepared as follows:

Hams with the aitch bone and shank removed are rubbed with a mixture consisting of 16 lb salt and 2 oz sodium or potassium nitrate. This amount of curing mix is sufficient to cure 100 lb of green ham. They are then placed on shelves or stacked on concrete floors and allowed to cure for 10 to 14 days, after which they are placed in a 90°F pickle and cured for an additional 2 weeks. They are then removed from the brine and stacked layer upon layer in a cool, dry basement where they ripen for approximately 1 month. Hams are then soaked in water for about 12 hr in preparation for the smokehouse. Finally, they are hung in the smokehouse for about 7 days and exposed to cool smoke generated from beechwood logs. From time to time, juniper twigs and berries are thrown on the smoldering fire.

Scotch Ham

Scotch hams are cured but neither smoked nor cooked. Fresh hams are skinned and most of the fat removed. The hams are then dry cured similar to dry-cured hams manufactured in the United States. The cured hams are boned and either rolled and tied or stuffed into casings. Similar hams produced in the United States must be termed Scotch style.

Prosciutto

These dry-cured Italian hams are somewhat similar to Country hams. The long curing and drying process results in about a 35% shrink in weight. The following procedure can be used for manufacturing prosciutti (plural):

Select good-quality fresh hams weighing from 12 to 18 lb. Since prosciutti hams are customarily eaten without being cooked, they must be manufactured from hams that have been certified to be free of trichina. The foot should be cut off below the hock so the shank is left extra long. The aitch bone is removed to allow the ham to be flattened. The following curing formula will cure approximately 100 lb of green ham:

	lb	oz
salt	3.5	
cane sugar	1	4
dextrose	1	4
allspice		8
white pepper		5
black pepper		2
nutmeg		2
mustard seed		0.5
coriander		0.5
sodium nitrate		0.5
sodium nitrite		0.25

The hams are placed on platforms approximately 12 in. off the floor. The platforms should be in a dry cooler at approximately 36 to 38°F. Hams should be rubbed thoroughly with the curing mixture. They are then piled 4 high on the platform with the skin side down, and some of the curing mixture is sprinkled over the top of each layer. The pile is overhauled in 10 days and the hams on top are placed on the bottom. Each ham is rerubbed with the curing mixture. The hams are then overhauled a second time in another 12 days. The hams should be left in cure for a total of approximately 45 days. Hams handled in this manner will come out flat and dry. However, if after the curing period still flatter hams are desired, they can be laid on planks and then planks and additional weight placed on top of them. A ham thickness of about 2 in. is considered desirable for prosciutti hams. Some processors place the hams in pressure molds during the cure to ensure that they reach the desired flatness. After the hams come out of cure, they are soaked in 80 to 90°F water to soften the skin, and scrubbed with a soft-fiber brush so they will not show salt streaks when they come out of the smokehouse. Next, the hams are strung with twine. The twine is not forced through the meat; instead, a double loop is made, the shank encircled, and the knot tied. The hams are then placed in a smokehouse at 130°F and allowed to remain there for 48 hr. The temperature is raised gradually to 140°F and kept there for about 2 hr. Then the temperature is dropped to 120°F for 8 hr. From 120°F, the temperature is gradually reduced so that when the hams are ready to come out of the smokehouse, the house temperature should be 95 to 105°F. To ensure firmness, the hams should be hung outside of the smokehouse to cool for approximately 8 hr. Finally, the hams are rubbed on the meat side with a mixture of equal parts of white and black pepper. This should be done carefully to avoid getting any pepper on the skin. The meat side of the hams should look almost black when the rubbing has been completed. The hams are then aged for 30 days at a temperature of 70 to 75°F and a relative humidity of 65 to 75%. Prosciutti hams manufactured in a packinghouse in this manner are very similar to those which have been made for centuries in Italian homes. Italians eat the ham cold but Americans frequently fry or warm it.

BACON

Since there are no quality grades for bacon, it does not readily lend itself to classification. Processors usually grade bacon in-plant on the basis of weights of the green bellies used in manufacture. These grades are strictly individual processor grades and are translated to the consuming public only in terms of brand names and prices. Generally, the heavier the bellies used for curing, the fatter, less tender, and darker color the bacon.

One of two methods is used to cure bacon: (1) dry cure or (2) pickle cure. In the case of dry-cured bacon, a mixture of curing ingredients is rubbed on all surfaces of the green bellies. Bellies are placed in a cooler to cure for 10 to 14 days before cooking and smoking.

Most commercially processed bacon today is pickle-cured. Pickle is introduced by a needle injection machine similar to that used for hams and other smoked meats. Bellies destined to be sliced in-plant are derinded before being stitched. After pickle is injected, the belly is combed (pierced with a multipoint hanger) and hung in a smokehouse. The length of time bacon remains in the smokehouse depends on (1) size of the belly, (2) smokehouse air velocity, (3) cook schedule temperatures, and (4) internal temperature desired. Bacon is usually cooked in the smokehouse according to a three-step cook schedule. First, smokehouse temperatures usually range between 115 and 125°F. Dampers are open and the bacon is dried. Drying may last for 1 to 2 hr. During the second phase, lasting approximately 2 hr, dampers are closed and the temperature increased 5 to 10°F. Dampers remain closed during the third phase, and the temperature is increased an additional 5 to 10°F to as high as 140°F, or, as is the case with some processors, temperature is adjusted to 128 to 130°F. Whichever the case may be, this temperature is maintained until the internal temperature desired is achieved, usually 126 to 132°F. Today, it is common to find bacon processors cooking with a one-temperature schedule—generally 130 to 140°F. Cooking bacon to higher internal temperatures helps develop and stabilize the cured meat color. When air-conditioned smokehouses are used to cook bacon, relative humidity is maintained between 25 and 40%. Bacon is subjected to smoke during all or part of the cooking period depending on the requirements of individual processors.

After bacon is cooked and smoked, it is chilled and derinded, if the slab had not been derinded before being cured. Prior to slicing, bacon slabs are held in tempering coolers where internal temperature of the bacon is reduced to 26 to 28°F. This is done to (1) allow bacon to retain its shape when it is subsequently pressed, and (2) to facilitate slicing. Prior to slicing, chilled bacon slabs are pressed or blocked. The pressing operation consists of placing slabs in a large forming machine which compresses the bacon to a relatively uniform width and thickness. Before pressing, bellies lack dimensional uniformity to such an extent that slicing yields suffer greatly. After being pressed, bacon slabs are sliced on high-speed slicers which automatically shingle slices into selected weight units. Bacon slabs are sliced to 3 different thicknesses: (1) thin, (2) regular, and (3) thick. Thin-sliced bacon, sometimes referred to as hotel or restaurant sliced, is sliced approximately 1/32nd, regular is 1/16th, and thick about 1/8th in. thick. The shingled bacon is then conveyed on a belt to a packaging machine where it is placed in either vacuum or nonvacuum packages, the former having longer shelf-life.

Canadian Bacon

Canadian bacon differs markedly from bacon manufactured from bellies because it is produced from the large muscle of pork loins, the strip or sirloin muscle. The predominant feature of Canadian bacon is leanness. As it is comprised primarily of one large muscle, very little intermuscular fat is encountered. Since most of the external fat is trimmed off, the finished product is quite lean.

Boneless loins are stitch-pumped and placed in cover pickle for 2 to 5 days. After being removed from cover pickle, loins are washed with cold water, stuffed into cellulosic casings or stockinettes, and hung in a smokehouse, where the loins are smoked and cooked to an internal temperature between 150 and 155°F. Smokehouse schedules used to cook Canadian bacon are similar to those for cooking hams. Either graduated or single-temperature schedules can be used. If relative humidity is controlled during cooking, it is generally maintained between 25 and 40%. Canadian bacon is sold either sliced or in chunk form.

Wiltshire Bacon

In much of Europe, and Great Britain in particular, bacon generally refers to a Wiltshire side. Wiltshire sides are made from selected hogs weighing between 150 and 200 lb live weight. The most desirable sides weigh 50 to 60 lb and have a backfat thickness of 1¼ to 1½ in. The shoulder, loin, belly, and ham are left as 1 piece. The foreleg is removed at the knee and the hind leg at the hock. The tenderloin, ribs, neck bone, back bone, aitch bone, skirt, and loose fat are also removed. Hind legs are sometimes removed from Wiltshire sides and sold separately. These are referred to as gammons. Shoulders, known as fore ends, are also frequently sold as separate cuts, but the remainder of the side is normally sliced for sale. Wiltshire sides are cured by pumping and are then placed in cover pickle, in which they generally remain for 7 to 10 days. They are then removed from the pickle and stored under refrigeration for from 2 days to 2 weeks. This is sometimes referred to as a maturation period. Following maturation, the sides may be smoked or sold without further processing.

Beef Bacon

Beef bacon, usually referred to as breakfast bacon, is made from boneless beef short plates. The short plates are cured and processed similar to pork bellies. Beef bacon is much less widely marketed than is bacon made from pork bellies or Canadian bacon.

Jowl Bacon

Fresh, trimmed jowls, sometimes called bean pork, are squared and subjected to the same curing, cooking, and smoking procedures as is bacon made from bellies. The resultant product is known as jowl bacon, or bacon squares. Jowl bacon is generally fatter than bacon made from bellies.

Fat Backs and Heavy Bellies

Fat backs, the heavy layer of fat removed from pork loins, and heavy bellies, weighing at least 20 lb, are cured by either the pickle or dry-salt cure method. This product is commonly referred to as salt pork. When the dry-cure procedure is used, the pork is rubbed with salt and stacked 3 to 4 ft high in coolers. The meat is overhauled after 8 to 10 days, rubbed again, and restacked. Heavier cuts are overhauled once again about the 20th day. Total curing time depends on thickness of the cut, but generally is from 20 to 30 days. Some processors add nitrate or nitrite to the cure; others use salt alone. Products that are pickle-cured are usually stitch-pumped and immersed in 90° salometer pickle. Such pickles may, but do not necessarily, contain nitrate or nitrite. As a rule of thumb, bellies, both dry- and pickle-cured, remain in cure 1 day for each pound of belly weight.

SMOKED PORK LOIN

Pork loins can be dry-cured but are usually pickle-cured. Commercially prepared, smoked pork loins are stitch-pumped with a pickle similar to that used to cure other pork primals. Stitched loins are then placed in cover pickle for 3 to 5 days. After curing, loins are smoked and cooked to 142 to 152°F. Pork chops cut from smoked pork loins are sometimes referred to as Windsor chops.

PICNIC

Picnics are cured, smoked, and cooked in a manner similar to hams. They may be artery-pumped, but in most cases are stitched with an injection-needle machine. Picnics are subject to the same Federal inspection regulations with regard to added moisture and internal temperature that apply to hams. Because of their greater proportion of bone, fat, and connective tissue and lack of one or more large muscles, picnics are of less economic value than hams, so are marketed under more competitive circumstances.

SHOULDER BUTT

Pork shoulder butts or Boston butts, as they are commonly known, are usually boned and trimmed, cured, smoked, and cooked in a manner similar to picnics and hams. Butts are manufactured according to the same Federal regulations that apply to hams and picnics. They may be placed in pickle in a curing vat for 7 to 10 days, but more frequently are stitch-pumped with curing pickle. After removal from the pickle, butts are stuffed into stockinettes or cellulosic casings, hung in smokehouses, and cooked to an internal temperature between 142 and 152°F. They are generally sold as cured and smoked pork shoulder butts. In the New England area, they are referred to as cottage rolls. For those who prefer a somewhat leaner bacon than is generally produced from bellies, butts may be sliced and fried as bacon.

CORNED BEEF

Corning refers to the preservation of beef by the use of salt. The word corn comes from the Latin "corne," meaning a horn or a hardened and thickened portion of cuticle. The word corn was equivalent to grain, and in Britain, generally meant any small hard particle. The term "corned" thus came to apply to meat preserved by sprinkling with grains or corns of salt. Large amounts of corned beef are sold in the United States today. Some is taken from pickling barrels and refrigerators of small independent butcher shops. However, the largest portion is prepacked and sold in supermarkets. A consumer desire for leaner meat products has led some processors to prepare corned beef from muscles of the round instead of the traditional brisket. Regardless of which cuts are used, the basic corning process is the same. The principal means of curing corned beef is to inject pickle into the beef. The old-fashioned method was to put beef cuts into pickle in curing crocks and cure for varying periods of time, depending on thickness of the cut.

The basic curing pickle used to produce corned beef does not differ from that used to cure hams or other smoked meats. However, it is not unusual to include in corned beef pickle an assortment of spices and herbs, such as laurel leaf, allspice, or garlic. On occasion, celery and onions are also put in the pickle.

Federal regulations permit briskets to be pumped to 120% of green weight, but other cuts, such as sections of the round, may only be pumped to 110%. The meat should then be placed in cover pickle for a few days. For beef corned by simply immersing in pickle, approximately 2 weeks retention in pickle is necessary for cuts 3 in. or less in thickness. If corned beef is to be sold ready-to-eat, it is cooked in water or steamed to an internal temperature of 152 to 160°F.

Cooked corned beef is usually red, but there is a particular type produced in the New England region which is gray-brown in color, as a result of omitting nitrite from the curing formula.

Corned beef briskets can be bought prepackaged. They can be purchased either uncooked or cooked and sliced. The chunk of beef is removed from the bag and simmered until tender. This serves as the basis for the traditional corned beef and cabbage meal.

SMOKED FRESH MEAT

Smoking of fresh meats has achieved no commercial significance, probably because of the lack of shelf-life associated with any fresh meat product, thus creating problems in distribution. However, caterers serving large groups occasionally offer fresh, smoked beef or pork in sandwiches. Cuts selected are usually high-quality beef rounds and loins and pork hams and loins. The meat may be completely cooked in the smokehouse as it is being smoked, or subjected only to cold smoke. When meat is cold-smoked, the temperature of the smokehouse does not exceed 100°F. Smoking is continued until the desired amount of smoke is deposited on the product. Meat that has been cold-smoked is then cooked in a conventional oven before serving.

DRIED BEEF

Dried beef is cured, dried, and sometimes smoked, but not cooked. It is low in moisture, containing 25 to 35%. Either the dry or pickle cure procedure can be used, although most commercially produced dried beef is cured in pickle. A typical curing formula is shown in Table 10.7. If the meat is dry-cured, 1 oz per lb of meat of the curing mix is applied to the meat surface. The curing mix should be applied in 2 rubbings at 5-day intervals. If the pickle cure is used, the cure ingredients are dissolved in 4 gal water. This provides sufficient pickle to cover approximately 100 lb meat.

The length of time the meat remains in cure depends upon the size of cuts being cured. Generally, muscles of the round—top, bottom, and knuckle—are used for manufacture of dried beef, but shoulder clods are also used. As a rule of thumb, dry- or pickle-cured meat should remain in cure a minimum of 2 and a maximum of 3 days per lb. After being removed from cure, the meat is rinsed with cold

Table 10.7

DRIED BEEF CURING FORMULA

Ingredient	Amount Lb	Oz
Salt	6	
Sugar	3	
Nitrate		2.75
Nitrite		0.25

water and allowed to dry. When produced in a commercial establishment, the beef is generally dried in a smokehouse for 2 to 3 days.
Smokehouse temperatures range between 90 and 100°F. Depending
on the desires of individual processors, smoke is applied during part
of the drying period.

SMOKED AND CURED LAMB

Both lamb and mutton legs and shoulders lend themselves to curing
and smoking. However, these products are of no commercial significance in the United States. Curing formulations and procedures, as
well as cooking and smoking schedules, are quite similar to those
used for curing primal pork products.

SMOKED TONGUE

Tongues are cured similar to other smoked meat products. Although
beef tongues are generally used, pork, sheep, and calf tongues are
also smoked on occasion. They are stitch- or artery-pumped. Curing
pickles and cooking and smoking schedules are similar to those used
for processing hams, picnics, and butts. Tongues are usually soaked
over night in a strong pickle solution to loosen the mucous coating.
They are then washed, cured, and cooked to an internal temperature
of at least 152°F in the smokehouse. Not all tongues are cooked. Some
are only cured and sold raw.

PICKLED PIGS FEET

Pickled pigs feet are processed according to 1 of 2 procedures, usually
referred to as long and short cures. The long cure calls for preparation
of an 80 to 90° salometer brine to which conventional amounts of nitrate
and nitrite are added. The feet are immersed in the pickle and remain
for 10 to 14 days. They are then removed, skinned, cut from toes to
shank, and the entire foot cooked in 180 to 200°F water until the
meat is tender, usually 3 to 4 hr. After cooking, the feet are chilled
in running water, then placed in a refrigerator to complete chilling.
Chilled feet are split and semi-boned. They are then packed in 40
to 75 grain vinegar in jars. Pepper, bay leaves, and other spices may
be added to the jar for appearance and flavoring.

The short curing procedure is sometimes referred to as the hot cure, because feet can be cured as they are cooked. Properly cleaned and chilled feet are immersed in pickle for 3 to 6 hr. Temperature of the pickle is raised gradually to approximately 180°F. The feet are cooked until tender, usually 3 to 4 hr, and then cooled in running water and packed in vinegar in jars.

BIBLIOGRAPHY

BARD, J., and TOWNSEND, W. E. 1971. Cured meats. *In* The Science of Meat and Meat Products, J. F. Price, and B. S. Schweigert (Editors). W. H. Freeman and Co., San Francisco, Calif.

BARNETT, H. W., NORDIN, H. R., BIRD, H. D., and RUBIN, L. J. 1965. A study of factors affecting the flavour of cured ham. *In* Proc. 11th European Meeting of Meat Research Workers. Belgrade, Yugoslavia.

BRADY, D. E., SMITH, F. H., TUCKER, L. N., and BLUMER, T. N. 1949. Characteristics of country-style hams as related to sugar content of curing mixture. Food Res. *14*, 303.

BRANDLY, P. J., MIGAKI, G., and TAYLOR, K. E. 1966. Meat Hygiene, 3rd Edition. Lea & Febiger, Philadelphia, Pa.

CARPENTER, Z. L., KAUFFMAN, R. G., BRAY, R. W., and WECKEL, K. G. 1963. Factors influencing quality in pork. B. Commercially cured bacon. J. Food Sci. *28*, No. 5, 578.

CHRISTIAN, J. A. 1960. Curing hams country style. N. Carolina State Coll., Agr. Ext. Serv. Cir. *405*. N. Carolina State Univ., Raleigh, N.C.

CROSS, H. R., SMITH, G. C., and CARPENTER, Z. L. 1971. Effect of quality attributes upon processing and palatability characteristics of commercially cured hams. J. Food Sci. *36*, 982.

FIELDS, M. D., and DUNKER, C. F. 1952. Quality and nutritive properties of different types of commercially cured hams. I. Curing methods and chemical composition. Food Technol. *6*, 329.

JENSEN, L. B., and HESS, W. T. 1941. A study of ham curing. Food Res. *6*, 273.

JOHNSON, V. K., and BULL, S. 1952. An accelerated cure for bacon. Food Technol. *6*, 354.

KARMAS, E., and THOMPSON, J. E. 1964. Certain properties of canned hams as influenced by conditions of thermal processing. Food Technol. *18*, 126.

KOMARIK, S. L. 1959. Meat-curing process. U.S. Patent 2,902,369. Sept. 1.

KOMARIK, S. L., and HALL, L. A. 1951. Curing process for bacon. U.S. Patent. 2,553,533. May 15.

MacKENZIE, D. S. 1966. Prepared Meat Product Manufacturing, 2nd Edition. American Meat Institute, Chicago, Ill.

OCKERMAN, H. W., BLUMER, T. N., and CRAIG, H. B. 1964. Volatile chemical compounds in dry-cured hams. J. Food Sci. *29*, 123.

SKELLEY, G. C., KEMP, J. D., and VARNEY, W. Y. 1964. Quick aging of hams. J. Animal Sci. *23*, No. 3, 633.

U.S. DEPT. OF AGR. 1970. Meat inspection regulations. Federal Register, Part II, *35*, No. 193.

WATTS, B. M. 1956. Freeze-curing of bacon. Food Technol. *10*, 101.

WISMER-PEDERSEN, J. 1960. Effect of cure on pork with watery structure. II. Effect on quality of canned hams. Food Res. *25*, 799.

WISTREICH, H. E., MORSE, R. E., and KENYON, L. J. 1959. Curing of ham: A study of sodium chloride accumulation. I. Method, effect of temperature, cations, muscles and solution concentration. Food Technol. *13*, 441.

WISTREICH, H. E., MORSE, R. E., and KENYON, L. J. 1960. Curing of ham: A study of sodium chloride accumulation. II. Combined effects of time, solution concentration, and solution name. Food Technol. *14,* 549.

ZIEGLER, P. T. 1956. The Meat We Eat, 9th Edition. Interstate Printers & Publishers, Danville, Ill.

ZWART, S. 1965. Method of curing bacon slices. U.S. Patent 3,220,854. Nov. 30.

CHAPTER 11

Canned Meats

The major reason for canning meat is to provide safe products from both public health and spoilage loss standpoints, and in so doing, preserve as much as possible desirable flavor, texture, and appearance qualities. The considerations are similar to those of the entire commercial canning industry. However, the problems of meat canners are often more acute because meat products are low-acid foods. This chapter describes canning of both sterile and pasteurized meat products. In practice, complete sterility is seldom achieved. Usually, the thermal processing required to assure absolute sterility is so severe that the organoleptic characteristics of canned meat products are affected adversely. In many cases, microorganisms survive thermal processing temperatures, but remain dormant or are inhibited from germination by some other factor. In the trade, the terms commercially sterile or shelf-stable products are in common usage. A safe commercial process does not necessarily require complete destruction of microbial life.

Successful production of commercially sterile canned meat products requires that all viable microorganisms be either destroyed or rendered dormant. Also, the process must inactivate raw material enzyme systems. Commercially sterile canned meat products generally reach an internal temperature of at least 225°F, but this temperature may be as low as 215°F, depending on salt and nitrite content. This severe heat treatment may result in noticeable changes in flavor, texture, and color. It is true generally that physical as well as chemical changes are functions of both the time and temperature to which the meat is subjected. To assure product safety Federal inspection regulations require samples of each processed lot be held at 95°F ± 2° for a minimum of 10 to 30 days before the cans leave the plant. Incubation time depends on the product. One can must be incubated from every retort load and for each 1,000 cans cooked in a hydrostatic cooker. At the end of the incubation period cans are examined for evidence of spoilage, as noted by end distortion of the cans. If none is found, the canned products are permitted to enter commercial distribution channels. The quality of canned meat products is highly dependent upon condition of the raw meat materials. Even though microorganisms that cause deterioration may be destroyed during processing, any flavor changes they induce cannot be reversed.

In contrast, some meat products merchandised in cans receive only a pasteurization process and are commonly referred to in the trade as perishable, which means they must be kept refrigerated. Even then, their shelf-life is usually considerably less than that of shelf-stable canned meat products.

242

Pasteurized canned meats are a compromise. Perishable or pasteurized canned meats are cooked to an internal temperature of at least 150°F, as required by Federal inspection regulations. This results in canned products being free from any public health hazard, but does not result in complete destruction of all microbial contaminants. Therefore, pasteurized canned meats must be held under refrigeration. If they have been processed under sanitary conditions and properly refrigerated, it is quite possible for pasteurized canned meats to be both palatable and safe to eat for at least two years. Salt and nitrite present in the curing pickle contribute significantly to the safety of pasteurized canned meats.

The canning of meats or other products in which meat is a constituent, except pork and beans, if intended to be offered in interstate commerce, can be done only with approval of Federal meat inspection authorities. During 1970, approximately 2.4 billion lb of meat and meat products, exclusive of soups, were canned under Federal inspection. Of this, about 1.5 billion lb were in the 7 product categories shown in Table 11.1.

Canned hams, the only perishable product listed, accounted for the largest share. Primarily for reasons of convenience, canned hams have increased in popularity in recent years.

CANS

Five principal types of cans, as shown in Fig. 11.1, are used in the meat industry: (1) square and pullman base, (2) pear-shaped, (3) round sanitary, (4) drawn aluminum, and (5) oblong.

Square and Pullman Base.—These containers are used primarily for pasteurized meats. The principal meats packed are chopped products such as spiced luncheon meat and chopped ham, corned beef for govern-

Table 11.1

PRINCIPAL MEAT PRODUCTS CANNED UNDER FEDERAL INSPECTION, 1970

Product	Amount Million lb
Canned hams	352
Spaghetti meat products	267
Luncheon meat	257
Chili con carne	247
Meat stews	195
Vienna sausage	100
Beef hash	98

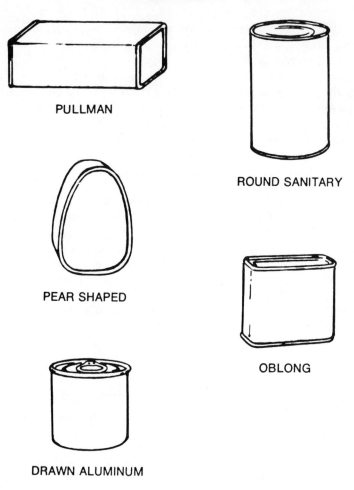

PULLMAN

ROUND SANITARY

PEAR SHAPED

OBLONG

DRAWN ALUMINUM

FIG. 11.1. CAN STYLE

ment contract packs, and boneless hams, particularly in the pullman style.

Pear-shaped.—These containers are used to pack pasteurized hams and picnics. They are anodized and enameled, as are the square and pullman base containers. Recently, plastic containers constructed of high-density polyethylene have been used commercially. Some containers are manufactured with a barrier material to lower the oxygen transmission and so increase product shelf-life.

Round Sanitary.—Cylindrical or round sanitary cans, as they are generally called, are available in a variety of diameters and heights to fit the broad line of canned meat products. They range in size from the 208 x 108 to the number 10 cans used for institutional canned meat products. The major products packed in sanitary cans are chili, stews, hashes, and a variety of entree meat-base products.

Drawn Aluminum.—Drawn aluminum cans are used principally for Vienna sausage, potted meats, and meat spreads.

Oblong.—Oblong cans are used for sterile canned luncheon meats, generally in the 12-oz size, although some 7-oz cans are also packed. Luncheon meat cans are available in either tinplate or aluminum.

Can Materials

Tinplate cans are made of thin sheets of steel coated with a very thin film of tin. The tin coating serves two purposes: (1) it covers the face of the steel sheet to prevent rusting, and (2) it acts as a medium by which parts of the sheet may be made to adhere by soldering. Can production is a high-speed operation. Can-making machines, when linked together by mechanical conveyors, produce complete cans with side seams soldered and one end seamed at a rate of 5 per sec. Tables 11.2 and 11.3 show names of some of the more commonly used cans in the meat-canning industry.

The first number of the dimension of a round can denotes diameter and the second denotes height. The first digit of either number represents number of whole inches and the last two digits represent inches in sixteenths. Thus, a 401 x 411 can is 4 1/16 in. in diameter and 4 11/16 in. high. In the case of a pear-shaped can, the first number indicates length, the second width, and the third height.

To prevent interaction between a meat product and the metal, cans are generally coated on the inside with an organic material. The terms

Table 11.2

CAN DESCRIPTIONS

Dimensions		Round Sanitary	Nominal Capacity
Diameter	Height	Use	Fl Oz Water
208 x 109		potted meat	3.2
208 x 207		spreads, Vienna sausage	5.3
211 x 400		chili, meat sauces	10.5
300 x 407		chili, hash	14.6
401 x 411		USDA chopped meat, boned turkey	28.6
404 x 309		stew, chili, hash	23.9
404 x 509		stew, chili, hash	38.9
603 x 700		various meat products for institutional use (known as number 10 can)	105.1

Table 11.3

CAN DESCRIPTIONS

Luncheon Meat and Pear-Shaped Cans

Dimensions			Use	Nominal Capacity	
Length	Width	Height		Lb	Oz
202 x	314 x	304	oblong luncheon meat		12
400 x	400 x	602	rectangular luncheon meat	3	
400 x	400 x	1110	rectangular luncheon meat	6	
310 x	402 x	1208	rectangular luncheon meat	6	
*410 x	414 x	1100	pullman luncheon meat or whole ham	8	
512 x	400 x	212	miniature base pear-shaped ham	1	8
*710 x	506 x	300	No. 1 base pear-shaped ham	3	
*904 x	606 x	308	No. 2 base pear-shaped ham	5	
*1011 x	709 x	400	No. 4 base pear-shaped ham	8	

* Containers made in various heights to accommodate several weight ranges of product.

enamel and lacquer are used interchangeably with organic coating. These coatings are solutions of resins in organic solvents. Two general kinds of organic coatings are used in the food industry, (1) acid-resistant and (2) sulfur-resistant. Acid-resistant coated cans are used primarily for fruits. Meat products are generally packed in cans which have been lined with a sulfur-resistant material. This is necessary because during the retorting operation, sulfur released from meat proteins will stain tinplate an unsightly black. Because solid meat products are frequently difficult to remove from cans, coatings containing a release agent are used to facilitate product removal. Pear-shaped and pullman base containers used for hams and other pasteurized canned products are lined with an organic coating containing a release agent. A reclinched or welded aluminum anode is also placed in each can used for cured meats. The aluminum corrodes preferentially and, in so doing, minimizes product discoloration as well as internal can corrosion caused by curing salts. An aluminum anode is seldom used for sterile products because the hydrogen evolved during high-temperature retorting and storage may reduce shelf-life.

Aluminum cans are not used as extensively as tinplate cans in the meat-canning industry. However, they are used by canners for certain products packed in shallow drawn cans, such as potted meats, meat spreads, and Vienna sausage. Although aluminum cans are more costly than tinplate, they offer certain advantages, such as lower shipping costs, resistance to sulfide and rust discolorations, and easier opening. They are especially popular when an easy-open, pull-type top feature is desired. The easy-open lid feature is probably the strongest selling point for aluminum cans. However, the development of steel cans with steel easy-open lids, with their slight economic advantage, is likely to detract from the popularity of aluminum cans. Meat products containing sodium chloride cannot be canned in bimetallic cans because of corrosion problems that result from electrolytic action.

RETORTS

The single most important phase of a sterile canning operation is retorting. The retort operation serves two purposes: (1) products are subjected to a high temperature for sufficient duration to destroy all organisms which might adversely affect consumer health, as well as other more resistant organisms which could cause spoilage under normal storage conditions, and (2) retorting serves to cook a product so it can be eaten directly as it comes from the can.

A retort is a steel tank in which metal crates or baskets containing the cans are placed for cooking and subsequent cooling. It is fitted with a cover or door which can be closed to provide a seal to hold the cooking or cooling pressure. Three types of retorts are used in the food industry: (1) nonagitating, (2) continuous agitating, and (3) hydrostatic.

Nonagitating

Most canned meat products manufactured in this country are cooked in nonagitating retorts. The term still or stationary is sometimes used to characterize the nonagitating retort. These retorts are closed-pressure vessels that operate in excess of atmospheric pressure and use pure steam or superheated water as the heating medium for cooking. The steam comes from an outside source, such as a steam boiler or generator. The first retorts using steam from an outside source were developed about 1875. Since that time, they have received universal acceptance. Nonagitating retorts function on a batch basis; that is, the retort must be loaded, then closed, and the entire batch cooked before a second batch of product can be put in. Nonagitating retorts can be vertical or horizontal. Figure 11.2 shows a vertical and

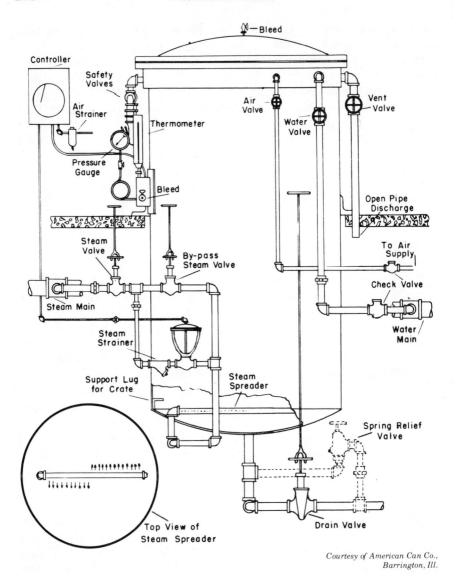

Bleed

Controller

Safety
Valves

Air
Strainer

Thermometer

Air
Valve

Vent
Valve

Water
Valve

Pressure
Gauge

Bleed

Open Pipe
Discharge

Steam
Valve

By-pass
Steam Valve

To Air
Supply

Check Valve

Steam Main

Water
Main

Steam
Strainer

Support Lug
for Crate

Steam
Spreader

Spring Relief
Valve

Top View of
Steam Spreader

Drain Valve

Courtesy of American Can Co.,
Barrington, Ill.

FIG. 11.2. VERTICAL RETORT WITH BOTTOM STEAM INLET AND AIR PRESSURE FOR COOLING

Fig. 11.3 a horizontal retort. They are constructed for various maximum pressures, but standard construction used in the meat industry is 15 psi maximum operating pressure.

Vertical retorts are more efficient than horizontal with respect to the number of cans they will hold per unit of retort volume. Vertical retorts also occupy less floor space for a given capacity, but more

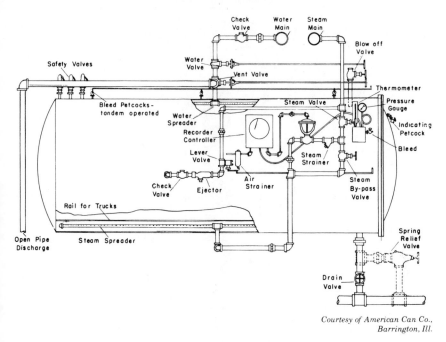

Courtesy of American Can Co.,
Barrington, Ill.

FIG. 11.3. HORIZONTAL RETORT WITH STEAM INJECTED AIR FOR COOLING

mechanical handling of the baskets or crates is required. Horizontal retorts vary greatly in size and shape; some are round and others square with doors at one or both ends. They can be made larger than vertical retorts, so that carts or trucks can be moved in and out direct from the canning floor. Confusion can be minimized and efficiency increased by having doors at both ends, thereby allowing uncooked products to enter at one point and cooked products to be discharged at another.

Continuous Agitating

As the name implies, the cans are agitated while in the retort. This results in a shorter processing schedule, made possible by a faster rate of heat penetration into the meat. Continuous retorts are used to some extent for Vienna sausage and potted meats.

Hydrostatic

Hydrostatic sterilization is so named because steam pressure is maintained by water pressure. These retorts or cookers, as they are commonly called, are made up of water and steam chambers referred to as legs. Figure 11.4 shows a hydrostatic cooker. The temperature of

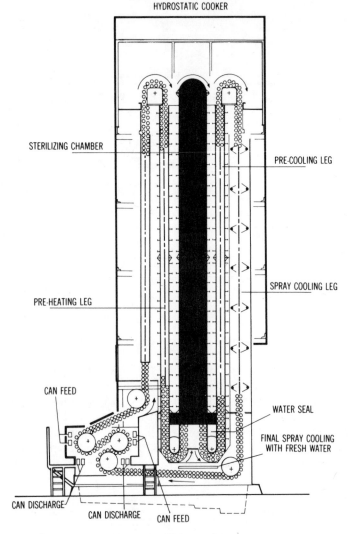

FIG. 11.4. HYDROSTATIC COOKER

the water in the water chamber varies from 60 to 260°F; that of steam in the steam chamber is controlled by pressure produced by the water chamber. Steam temperatures between 240 and 265°F are generally used. Operation of the hydrostatic cooker is basically as follows: cans are conveyed through the machine by means of carriers connected to chains. The cans enter a water chamber where the temperature is about 180°F. This is the down-traveling water chamber where the product temperature begins to increase. As the cans move down through this chamber, they encounter hotter water. In the lower part of the chamber, the water temperature reaches 225 to 245°F. Then, near the water seal area next to the steam chamber, the water temperature increasingly approaches that of steam. In the steam chamber, the cans are exposed to a temperature between 240 and 265°F. The temperature used depends on the product being cooked. Several models of these cookers are manufactured. In some, cans make two passes, one up and one down the steam chamber.

Hydrostatic retorts have several advantages over nonagitating retorts: (1) saving in floor space; (2) a great reduction in operating cost because steam and water costs are lower due to regenerative heating and cooling; and (3) greater capacity for high-volume operation. The main disadvantage of a hydrostatic retort is the large initial capital investment required. Also, there is the disadvantage of limitation on sizes that can be cooked in any given unit.

Establishment of Retort Schedule

To establish a retort schedule for a sterile canned meat product, it is necessary to determine the rate of heat penetration at the slowest heating point in the can, this being the geometric center of the product. Determination of heat penetration is done by fitting cans with needle-type thermocouples placed in the product. From temperatures recorded on a self-recording potentiometer, a temperature graph is obtained. With this information the lethal effect of a particular process can be integrated with respect to the thermal death time of a specific microorganism. The usual practice is to calculate this in terms of the destructive effect on *Clostridium botulinum* of an equivalent number of minutes at 250°F. This is expressed as the F_0 value. To better clarify F_0 consider the following example: if a heat penetration graph plotted for a process of 60 min at 240°F was converted into a graph based on the lethal rates compared to the effect on *Clostridium botulinum* of 1 min at 250°F and then integrated, a total value of about 7 could result. This would mean the process has an F_0 value of 7 or is equal in destructive effect on *Clostridium botulinum* to 7 min at 250°F, assuming instantaneous heating and cooling. Expressing a process by an F_0 value is really quite arbitrary. However, it is a useful way of expressing a process schedule in simple numerical form and also serves for purposes of comparison. As a general rule, the one basic criterion is that all canned foods having a pH of 4.5 or above must be given a minimum safe cook, sometimes referred to as a botulinum cook. For practical purposes, a botulinum safe cook is generally considered to be one having an F_0 of 2.78. However, this process does not necessarily ensure freedom from spoilage by organisms that are more heat-resistant than *Clostridium botulinum*.

PASTEURIZED CANNED PRODUCTS

Pasteurized canned hams and picnics are the two principal pasteurized canned meat products. Of these, canned hams are by far the more popular. Federal inspection regulations state that the word ham, without any prefix, may be used on labels only in connection with pork hams. The regulations further specify that preparation of hams for canning must not result in an increase of more than 8% in weight over the weight of fresh, bone-in, uncured hams. Compliance, as explained in Chapter 6, is determined by calculation from the results of chemical analyses. The protein constant or k factor for canned hams is 3.83. Federal regulations place the following additional restrictions on pasteurized products: (1) all products must be cured; (2) net weight of each canned product must be 12 oz or greater; (3) products must be cooked in cans to a center temperature of at least 150°F; (4) canned products must be labeled "Perishable—Keep Under Refrigeration"; and (5) canned products must be stored and distributed under refrigeration.

Hams and picnics to be canned are cured exactly as hams or picnics cured for other purposes. However, since canned hams and picnics do not experience a loss in yield during the cooking process, as do uncanned products, the amount of pump pickle must be restricted so that finished products will meet Federal inspection regulations on increase in weight over fresh, bone-in, uncured products.

Weights of hams used for canning vary from 12 to 25 lb. On occasion, even heavier hams are used. The size of ham used depends to a large extent on the quality of the canned product desired. Both whole hams and sections are canned. When sectioned for canning, a ham is usually divided into either two sections (1) cushion and (2) knuckle, or into three sections (1) knuckle, (2) top, and (3) bottom. Shank meat is frequently placed in a ham to fill the cavity resulting from removal of the femur or leg bone. Here again, the inclusion of shanks depends on the desired quality of the finished product. If frozen hams are used, they must be thawed prior to pumping. This can be done by placing the hams in a refrigerated room long enough to thaw, or by placing them in a warm brine solution. A 15° salometer brine heated to about 100° is generally used. It takes about 12 hrs. to thaw a frozen ham in brine. However, thawing time depends on (1) size of the ham, (2) temperature of the ham at the start of thawing, and (3) capacity of the equipment.

CLOSING

Before closing the cans, large cuts of meat such as hams and picnics are pressed to ensure correct can fit and to eliminate air pockets. Pasteurized canned meats are closed on a vacuum closing machine with 18 to 25 in. of machine vacuum; but because of entrapped air within the can, final can vacuum will seldom exceed 2 to 5 in. All canned meat products, whether pasteurized or shelf-stable, should be cooked as quickly as possible after they are closed to assure that maximum quality is maintained.

PASTEURIZING COOK

Pasteurized canned meat products are cooked in 155 to 170°F water in open cook tanks to an internal temperature of 150 to 155°F. Table 11.4 shows retort schedules for several representative size pasteurized canned meat products.

COOLING

After the heat process has been completed, all canned meat products should be cooled as quickly as possible to a level at which cooking and quality deterioration stop, and below the range at which any surviving thermophilic bacteria can grow. After final cooling, temperature

Table 11.4

COOK SCHEDULES FOR PASTEURIZED CANNED MEATS*

Product	Can Size	Cook Time Min	Water Temp. °F	Initial Meat Temp. °F
3-lb ham	1 base—300 high	120	165	35
4-lb ham	1 base—400 high	165	165	35
5-lb ham	2 base—308 high	165	165	35
8-lb ham	4 base—400 high	220	165	35
9-lb ham	4 base—404 high	255	165	35
10-lb ham	4 base—412 high	290	165	35
11-lb ham	4 base—500 high	330	165	35
12-lb ham	4 base—508 high	365	165	35
13-lb ham	4 base—600 high	400	165	35
8½ to 11-lb pullman	410x414x1200—1400	275	165	35
3-lb oblong luncheon meat	400 x 400 x 602	160	165	30
6-lb. oblong luncheon meat	400 x 500 x 1110	210	165	30

* Schedules based upon reaching can center temperature of 150°F as required by Federal Meat inspection regulations.

in the product center should not exceed 100°F, and temperatures of 70 to 80°F are more ideal. However, because the cans are wet, it is best to permit some heat to remain in them to accelerate evaporation of water. If water does not evaporate, rusting can occur which can affect can line sanitation and labeling efficiency. When cans are being cooled, they contract and are subjected to internal pressure changes. Under such conditions, even well-made seams may permit slight inward leakage. Thus it is necessary for the water used for cooling to be as near sterile as possible. To achieve the necessary microbiological quality, canning cooling water is chlorinated. For large-diameter cans and all products cooked in hydrostatic cookers, cooling must be done under pressure to prevent buckling of the can ends. Buckling is permanent deformation of can ends which can occur if the retort pressure is released suddenly after the cooking period. With pressure cooling, steam pressure is replaced by compressed air.

Sodium nitrite is frequently added to either the retort or cooling water to serve as a corrosion inhibitor. Sodium bisulfate is also permitted by Federal inspection regulations. Nitrite and bisulfate retard the formation of rust on meat containers not only during processing but also during subsequent storage. The exact mechanism by which nitrite and bisulfate function as inhibitors is not known, but it is thought they contribute to the development of a protective film. Although the concentration of nitrite or bisulfate necessary for effective inhibition varies depending on certain processing conditions, 600 ppm nitrite and 0.001% bisulfate in the process water will prevent external corrosion under the most severe processing conditions. To prevent accidental misuse of nitrite as table salt, Federal inspection regulations direct that sodium nitrite be decharacterized with charcoal. Generally, 0.05% finely ground charcoal is used to change the color of nitrite from white to gray.

STORAGE AND SHELF-LIFE

Sterile canned meats products should be stored in a cool, dry place. The storage place must be dry to prevent rusting of the cans and weakening of the fiber cases in which the cans are packed. Storage temperatures of sterile canned meat products markedly affect shelf-life and should not be above 70°F. In general, meat products stored at 70°F retain acceptable palatability characteristics for 4 to 5 years. If held at 40°F or below, even longer shelf-life will result.

Pasteurized canned products should be stored in a dry, refrigerated room at a temperature not exceeding 40°F. Properly handled pasteurized canned meat products packed in metal cans stored at 40°F or below will not show adverse quality effects for 2 years or more. However, for hams processed in plastic cans, shelf-life will generally not exceed 12 to 18 months before adverse oxidative changes involving surface color and flavor are noted.

ASEPTIC CANNING

In the normal retort canning process, meat products are cooked at temperatures well in excess of those consistent with maximum product quality. Aseptic canning was developed in an attempt to improve finished product quality. Aseptic canning refers to a method of sterilizing containers and products separately and then assembling them in an aseptic atmosphere to achieve a sterile package that can be stored at room temperature. The product to be canned is heated, while flowing continuously, to a temperature around 300°F. At this temperature, sterility is achieved in a very short time. In essence, aseptic canning involves (1) continuous, completely enclosed heat processing, (2) cooling of the product, and (3) filling and closing in a sterile container within a sterile atmosphere. Figure 11.5 shows a complete aseptic canning line. This processing out-of-the-can procedure permits subjecting all portions of a product to optimum conditions of time and temperature and in so doing avoids overcooking and the associated degradation of flavor, texture, and color. To this time, conventional aseptic canning procedures have not been readily accepted by meat canners. The main reason is that aseptically canned products must be homogeneous and be able to flow readily, and meat products do not usually meet these requirements.

An alternative method for avoiding overcooking which has proved commercially feasible is the "Flash 18" process. The principal characteristics of the "Flash 18" process are filling of cans in a pressurized room under 18 lb air pressure at a temperature of 255°F and holding at this temperature for sufficient time to achieve sterilization. The cans are closed under the same conditions, thus eliminating retorting. The rapid cooking method used, under 18 lb pressure, gives the process its name, "Flash 18". Under normal atmospheric conditions it is not possible to fill foods at a temperature above 212°F. By raising air pressure in the filling and can-sealing room the boiling-point temperature is raised, so it is possible to fill cans at much higher temperatures. When cans are closed with the product heated to around 255°F, sterility is achieved by retaining this temperature for a few minutes, whereupon the cans are cooled rapidly. Workers in the pressurized room must spend a short period of time in a pressure-adjusting airlock before entering and leaving the room.

256

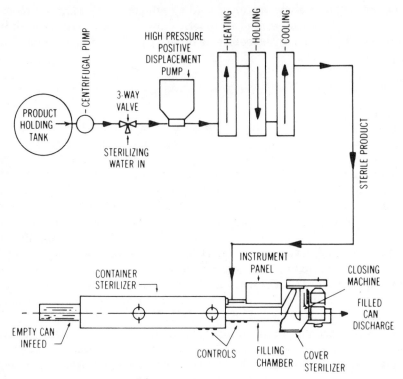

FIG. 11.5. ASEPTIC CANNING LINE

ANON. 1965A. Meat and poultry containers—rigid. American Can Co., Maywood, Ill.

ANON. 1965B. Meat can improvements. American Can Co., Maywood, Ill.

ANON. 1962. Time and temperature vs. storage life in canned meats. Natl. Provisioner *147*, 12.

ANON. The canning of ham. Continental Can Co., Chicago, Ill.

BOCK, J. H. Retorts for canning. Continental Can Co., Chicago, Ill.

HERSOM, A. C., and HULLAND, E. D. 1964. Canned Foods, 5th Edition. Chemical Publishing Co., New York.

JENSEN, L. B. 1954. Microbiology of Meats, 3rd Edition. Garrard Press, Champaign, Ill.

LECHOWITCH, R. V. 1971. Microbiology of Meat. *In* The Science of Meat and Meat Products, J. F. Price, and B. S. Schweigert (Editors). W. H. Freeman and Co., San Francisco, Calif.

LOCK, A. 1969. Practical Canning, 3rd Edition. Food Trade Press, Ltd., London.

LOPEZ, A. 1969. A Complete Course in Canning, 9th Edition. The Canning Trade, Baltimore, Md.

MacKENZIE, D. S. 1966. Prepared Meat Product Manufacturing, 2nd Edition. American Meat Institute, Chicago, Ill.

McKIRAHAN, R. D., and LUDWIGSEN, R. J. 1968. Coatings for cans: selection and performance. Mater. Protect. *7*, 29.

ROGERS, J. L. 1966. A "Course" in Canning, 4th Edition. Food Trade Press, Ltd., London.

U.S. Dept. of Agr. 1970. Meat inspection regulations. Federal Register, Part II, *35*, No. 193.

CHAPTER 12

Canned Meat Formulations

In the meat-processing industry, the manufacture and marketing of canned meats and meat products is sometimes separated into two areas, (1) pasteurized and (2) shelf-stable products. Canning of pasteurized canned-meat products is generally closely associated with the manufacture of other pasteurized processed meat products. However, shelf-stable canned meats and canned-meat products usually fall under the heading of grocery products, and in the largest meat-processing companies are commonly the marketing responsibility of a grocery products department. Invariably, all products handled by this department of a meat-processing company are shelf-stable.

This chapter provides formulations and processing directions for the manufacture of some of the best-known shelf-stable and pasteurized canned-meat products. With the exception of canned hams, the formulations are all expressed on the basis of a 100-lb meat block. Formulations shown in this chapter are meant to be representative of a wide variation in terms of meat as well as seasoning ingredients.

A word of caution is advised. The manufacturer of shelf-stable canned meats must constantly bear in mind that his products will not be stored under refrigerated conditions and may be held for many months, and perhaps years, before being consumed. Therefore, it is necessary that each product be retorted properly, and that, as a general rule, good manufacturing practices be followed to avoid the danger of botulism.

CORNED BEEF HASH

Federal Meat Inspection Regulations

Corned beef hash is the semisolid meat food product in the form of a compact mass which is prepared with beef, potatoes, curing agents, seasoning, and other optional ingredients. The finished product may not contain less than 35% cooked and trimmed beef, and the weight of the cooked meat used in this calculation may not exceed 70% of the weight of the uncooked fresh meat. The finished product may not contain more than 15% fat nor more than 72% moisture.

Formulation

Ingredients	Amount	
	lb	oz
cooked beef*	100	
potatoes, dehydrated	130	

Ingredients	Amount	
	lb	oz
beef broth	40	
onions, raw	9	
salt	4	
ground white pepper		4
sodium nitrite		0.25

* Cutter and canner grade. The beef should be cooked until it has lost 30% in weight.

Preparation for Canning

Meat.—The chilled meat should be cut into strips approximately 2 in. wide by hand or with a rotary cutter. Grinding the meat through a 2 in. plate is an alternate method. Then the meat is placed in wire baskets or perforated crates for cooking in 180°F water for about 10 to 20 min. About 5 gal water are used for every 100 lb meat. Stainless metal, aluminum, or black-iron steam-jacketed kettles can be used, but copper equipment cannot. Since 30% shrink is required during cooking (as noted in the formulation), it will be necessary to check the weights frequently during cooking to establish the proper time.

After the meat is cooked, cool and either grind through a 3/16-in. plate or chop to achieve the typical texture for hash. Save the broth.

Potatoes.—The potatoes should be soaked in hot water until they are rehydrated. This is usually about 15 to 20 min. About 1 part potato will combine with 4 parts water.

Onions.—The onions should be washed with cold water with a high-pressure spray. Blanch the onions in steam for 2 or 3 min to facilitate peeling and then pass them through a ⅜-in. plate. An equivalent amount of onion powder or onion flakes can be substituted for fresh onions.

Mixing and Heating

The ground precooked meat is weighed and placed in a meat mixer. Sodium nitrite is dissolved in a little water and added slowly while mixing. The other ingredients are added and the mixing continued for about 3 min. If the hash is to be filled hot, the meat and broth should be as hot as possible with additional heat supplied by a steam jacket on the mixer, a steam jacketed preheater-conveyor, or similar means.

Canning

The hash should be filled at a minimum temperature of 120°F and well packed into the can to provide at least 5/16 in. head-space for "steam-vac" closure.

The cans should be closed using a machine vacuum of 15 in. or higher and either mechanical vacuum or "steam-vac" closures.

After the cans are closed, pass them through a detergent spray washer to remove grease and other materials. The washing should consist of a hot-water pre-rinse, spray wash, followed by a fresh, warm-water rinse. The cans must be processed immediately after closing. Following is a list of general can sizes, approximate net weights, and suggested processes for corned beef hash; however, the process conditions used must be based on the specific packing operation to ensure that an adequate process is used:

				Processing Time if cooked at	
			Initial Temp.	240°F	250°F
Can Size	Net Weight of Can		of Hash		
	lb	oz		min	min
211 × 300		7.5	100	75	55
			140	65	50
300 × 407		15.5	50	100	80
			100	95	75
			140	90	65
307 × 409	1	4.0	100	115	95
			140	110	90

Immediately after processing, the cans should be cooled in water until the average temperature of the contents reaches 95 to 105°F to avoid thermophilic spoilage or can rusting.

Pressure-cooling is required for cans of greater than 307 diameter to prevent straining or buckling of the ends.

BEEF STEW

Federal Meat Inspection Regulations

Product labeled as meat stews shall contain not less than 25% meat computed on the weight of the fresh meat.

Formulation

Ingredients	Amount lb	oz
cooked beef*	100	
diced potatoes, rehydrated dehydrated	80	
water	75	
gravy	70	
diced carrots	52	
chopped onions	14	
flour (wheat or rice)	4	
salt	2	
ground black pepper		2

* The beef should be canner and cutter grade from cows, steers, or heifers, free from cartilage and tendons, and trimmed of excessive fat. The beef must be cooked so that 30% shrink occurs.

Preparation for Canning

Meat.—The meat should be cut into 3-in. chunks and placed in wire baskets for cooking. Simmer the meat for approximately 15 min to produce the required 30% shrinkage (as noted in the formulation). The time required to cook the meat to achieve this shrinkage should be established by trial.

Stir the meat during cooking to obtain uniformly cooked pieces. After the meat has been cooked, dice the cooked strips into ¾-in. cubes. The broth should be saved to make the gravy.

Potatoes.—The potatoes should be soaked in hot water until they are rehydrated and ready for use. They will yield approximately 300%.

Carrots.—The carrots should be washed in cold water. When carrots are peeled by an abrasive method or hand-scraped, it will be necessary to give them a short blanch before peeling. About 2 to 4 min in boiling water is an adequate blanch. After blanching and peeling, trim away any damaged portions or blemishes and slice the carrots into ½-in. pieces.

Onions.—The onions should be washed with cold water using a high-pressure spray. Blanch the onions in live steam for 2 to 3 min to facilitate peeling. Grind through a ⅜-in. plate and add them to the gravy.

Gravy

Ingredients	Amount lb	oz
broth from cooked meat	75	
processed flour	5	

Ingredients	Amount	
	lb	oz
salt	2	4
ground black pepper		1

Begin preparation of the gravy by mixing the flour with some cold water to make a smooth paste. Then dilute the paste by gradually adding the broth obtained when the meat is cooked. Add chopped onions, salt, and ground black pepper together while stirring constantly. Heat the gravy slowly to 180°F. If the color of the gravy is too light, it can be intensified by adding caramel coloring.

Canning

Fully enameled cans should be used. Before filling, the cans should be spray-washed with 180°F water according to meat inspection regulations.

Fill the cans with the meat and vegetables and then weigh. Add enough gravy to complete the can filling. At this point, the gravy temperature should not be lower than 160°F.

Vacuum in the cans is usually obtained by filling the product at a minimum temperature of 160°F using atmospheric pressure. However, the vacuum may also be obtained by machine vacuum, by "steam-vac" closure, or by thermal exhausting. A minimum machine vacuum of 15 in. is recommended. Steam-vac closures require that the beef stew be closed at a minimum temperature of 120°F and well packed in the can. When thermal exhausting is used, fill the cans at 160°F and exhaust for 7 to 10 min. The exhaust temperature should be 200°F.

After the cans are sealed, invert them in the retort cases to get a better mixture of the ingredients. A detergent spray washer should be used to wash the cans after they are closed.

The cans must be processed immediately after closing. Following is a list of general can sizes, approximate net weights, and suggested processes for canned stew; however, the process conditions used must be based on the specific packing operation to ensure that an adequate process is used:

Can Size	Net Weight of Can		Initial Temp.	Processing Time if cooked at:	
	lb	oz	of Stew	240°F	250°F
			°F	min	min
211 × 300		7.5	120	85	65
211 × 400		10.5	140	80	60
			160	75	55

Can Size	Net Weight of Can		Initial Temp. of Stew °F	Processing Time if cooked at:	
	lb	oz		240°F min	250°F min
300 × 409	1		120	100	75
			140	95	70
			160	90	65
303 × 402	1		120	105	85
			140	100	75
			160	95	70
307 × 409	1	4	120	115	85
			140	110	80
			160	105	75
404 × 309	1	8	120	130	100
			140	125	95
			160	120	90
401 × 411	1	14	120	140	110
404 × 404	"	"	140	135	105
			160	125	95

After processing, the cans should be cooled immediately in potable and noncorrosive water until the temperature of the contents reaches 95 to 105°F.

CHILI CON CARNE

Federal Meat Inspection Regulations

There is no Federal standard of identity for canned chili con carne. Among the requirements of Federal inspection regulations are the following: (a) chili con carne shall contain not less than 40% meat computed on the weight of the fresh meat; (b) chili con carne with beans shall contain not less than 25% meat; (c) head meat, cheek meat, and heart meat, exclusive of the heart cap, may be used to the extent of 25% of the meat ingredient under specific declaration on the label; (d) the mixture may not contain more than 8% individually or collectively of cereal, soya flour, vegetable starch, starchy vegetable flour, dried milk, or dried skimmilk.

Formulation

Ingredients	Amounts	
	lb	oz
beef and beef by-products	100	
beef broth or water	90	

Ingredients	Amount	
	lb	oz
wheat flour	8	
ground chili pepper	3	
salt	1	
ground domestic paprika		12
ground cumin		9
tomato paste		8
ground oregano		4
onion powder		4
garlic powder		2

This formulation contains about 49% meat. Chili con carne with beans is made by adding 82 lb soaked and blanched red kidney beans (equal to about 40 lb dry beans) and 1 lb salt. This reduces the meat to about 32%. The beans should be blanched in boiling water for 5 min.

Preparation for Canning

The meat should be ground through a ⅜-in. plate and then braised in a steam-jacket kettle for 25 min at 220°F. Stir the meat to achieve uniform cooking. Add the flour, salt, spices, and water to the ground braised meat and cook all the ingredients together. A smooth paste should be made with the flour and water before the flour is added to the meat.

Fill the cans with the cooked chili and weigh. Close the cans by using the procedures described for beef stew. After the cans are filled and closed, they should be washed with a hot water and detergent spray.

Canning

Chili con carne varies in consistency and formulation. Thus, it is very important to note that any change that affects consistency will change the processing time.

Can Size	Net Weight of Can	Initial Temp.	Processing Time if cooked at:	
	oz	of Chili °F	240°F min	250°F min
211 x 400	10.5	120	90	70
		140	85	65

Can Size	Net Weight of Can oz	Initial Temp. of Chili °F	Processing Time if cooked at: 240°F min	250°F min
		160	80	60
		180	75	55
300 x 409	16	140	100	75
		160	95	70
		180	90	65
303 x 402	16	120	120	90
		140	110	85
		160	105	80
		180	95	70

After processing, the cans should be cooled immediately in potable and noncorrosive water until the temperature of the contents reaches 95 to 105°F.

VIENNA SAUSAGES

Federal Meat Inspection Regulations

There is no Federal standard of identity for canned Vienna sausages. When shipped interstate, the product must be made in a Federally inspected establishment and is subject to Federal inspection regulations. Among these are the following: (a) there can be only 10% added moisture in the final product; (b) a statement regarding the packing medium, such as water or brine, must appear on the label; (c) the weight stated on the label is the drained weight; (d) cereal or milk powder, when used, must be limited to 3.5% and the label must state "Vienna Sausage, cereal added." If more than 3.5% cereal is used, the product must be labeled "Imitation."

Formulation

Ingredients	Amount lb	oz
bull meat	50	
beef trimmings	20	
regular pork trimmings	20	
beef hearts	10	
crushed ice or cold water	15	
salt	3	
sugar		6

| Ingredients | Amount |
	lb oz
ground pepper	6
ground mustard	4
sodium nitrite	0.25

Preparation for Canning

Even though Vienna sausages are canned, prepare the Vienna sausage emulsion following the procedures used to manufacture frankfurters. After stuffing into casings, Vienna sausages are either linked or simply looped over smoke sticks. After cooking, the sausages are cut into the lengths required for canning.

Canning

For Vienna sausages, key-opening cans are sometimes used. In this case, cans made from plain hot-dipped or electrotin plate bodies and enameled electrotin plate ends are recommended. For non-key opening cans, enameled electrotin plate may be used for both bodies and ends. Aluminum pull-top cans are frequently used for canned Viennas today. Before filling, spray wash the empty cans with 180°F water in accordance with Federal meat inspection regulations.

Fill the cans with the required number of sausages. Then fill the remaining space with boiling water. The sausage strands are usually cut so 7 pieces will weigh 4 to 4⅛ oz. The links lose approximately 0.25 oz. during retorting, but regain most of this weight after 72 hr. The all-meat sausage continues to gain slowly for several weeks but rarely gains more than 0.25 oz. Viennas formulated with cereal may pick up 0.5 oz. or more over a period of several weeks.

208 x 208 cans are usually prepared by filling completely with 190 to 200°F water and closing atmospherically. Larger cans are filled with cold water and closed under as high a mechanical vacuum as possible, with excess water removed. After the cans are filled and closed, wash and then rinse in warm water. The filled cans should be retorted immediately. Following is a list of general can sizes, approximate net weights, and suggested processes for canned Vienna sausages:

| Can Size | Net Weight of Can oz | Initial Temp. of Fill °F | Processing Time if cooked at | | |
			225°F min	230°F min	240°F min
208 x 208	4	70	65	45	30
211 x 400	9	70	80	60	40

Can Size	Net Weight of Can oz	Initial Temp. of Fill °F	Processing Time if cooked at		
			225°F min	230°F min	240°F min
401 x 411	24	70	180	135	90
404 x 404	24	70	180	135	90

After processing, cool the cans immediately in potable and noncorrosive water until the temperature of the contents reaches 95 to 105°F.

MEAT BALLS WITH GRAVY

Federal Meat Inspection Regulations

Meat balls with gravy consists of ground meat which has been mixed with bread crumbs, onion, and spices, formed into spheres and placed in a gravy. There is no Federal standard of identity for canned meat balls with gravy. A regulation of the Federal Meat Inspection Service states that beef with gravy cannot be made with beef which, in the aggregate for each lot, contains more than 30% trimmable fat.

Formulation

Ingredients	Amount		
	lb	oz	gal
Meat Balls			
cow meat	100		
bread crumbs	5	8	
salt	1		
onion powder		12	
pepper		4	
Gravy			
beef stock			10
flour	5		
beef fat	2		
salt	1	4	
beef extract	1	2	
onion powder		12	
caramel coloring	6		
celery salt	8		
pepper	6		

Preparation for Canning

Meat balls.—The beef is ground through a ¾-in. plate. Then the other ingredients are added and the mixture is reground through an ⅛-in. plate. The meat balls may be formed by molding by: (1) hand, (2) mechanically, or (3) a sausage stuffer. When a stuffer is used, the meat is put through a 1½ in. diameter horn onto trays. It is then cut into the desired lengths and formed by hand or mechanically. Raw meat balls should be about 1¼ in. in diameter and weigh about 1 oz, and should be floured lightly before being precooked. Excess flour should be removed by passing the meat balls over a shaker screen.

The meat balls may be canned either precooked or raw. For precooking, pass them through hot vegetable fat at a temperature of 375°F or through a gas flame or electrically heated oven. The time required to deep-fat fry is approximately 1 min; oven-cooking requires 10 min. This results in a weight loss of approximately 15%.

Gravy.—Beef stock prepared by cooking 20 gal cold water and 100 lb. raw bone may be used instead of water. The bone should be split to expose the bone marrow, as this enriches the flavor of the stock. The bones should be simmered for approximately 4 hr.

The flour should be mixed with a portion of cold water to make a smooth paste. Then beef fat is added to the paste. The paste is gradually diluted by adding the filtered beef stock. All the other ingredients are added with constant stirring until blended thoroughly. Bring the gravy to a simmering temperature with constant agitation. Continue agitation during filling.

Canning

Fully enameled cans should be used. Prior to filling, they should be spray-washed with 180°F water. Ten precooked meat balls weighing about 8⅛ oz are placed in a 300 x 407 can and the fill is completed with about 7½ oz gravy. The gravy should be maintained at a temperature of at least 160°F. The weight of the meat balls should be about 40% of the net weight of the container after processing. Hot gravy may be filled by means of a pulp or plunger-type filler, depending on consistency.

Vacuum in the cans may be obtained by filling at a minimum product temperature of 160°F using atmospheric closure. Steam-vac closure may be used provided that the product is closed at a minimum temperature of 120°F and is well packed in the can with a minimum head space of 5/16 in.

Pass the cans through a detergent spray washer after closure to remove grease and other materials adhering to the outside of the cans.

The cans should be stacked in a crate in a way to permit free circulation of steam throughout the retort load. Following is a list of can sizes and approximate net weights and suggested processing schedules:

Can Size	Net Weight lb oz	Initial Temp. of Contents °F	Processing Time if cooked at 240°F min	250°F min
211 x 304	8	120	80	60
		140	75	55
		160	70	50
211 x 400	10.5	120	80	60
		140	75	55
		160	70	50
300 x 409	1	120	95	70
		140	90	65
		160	85	60
401 x 211	1	120	100	75
		140	95	70
		160	90	65
307 x 409	1 4	120	110	85
		140	105	80
		160	100	75

Immediately after processing, the cans should be cooled in water until the average temperature of the contents reaches 95 to 105°F.

SLICED DRIED BEEF

Federal Meat Inspection Regulations

Canned, sliced, dried beef is prepared from dried, cured, smoked beef rounds. There is no Federal definition or standard of identity for sliced dried beef.

Formulation

Ingredients	Amount lb oz
Meat beef round sections (insides, outsides, knuckles)	100

Ingredients	Amount	
	lb	oz
Cure		
water	42	
salt	12	
sugar	5	
sodium nitrate		1.5

Preparation for Canning

Meat.—Either fresh or frozen beef rounds can be used. Fresh beef should be chilled to an internal temperature of 38°F before curing. Frozen beef should be thawed. The best weight per piece is approximately 12 lb.

Curing.—Beef rounds are sprinkled lightly with fine salt and packed in vats or tierces and covered with pickle. About 5 gal pickle are used for 100 lb beef. The beef is cured for 7 days per lb at 38°F. A 12-lb piece should be cured for approximately 84 days. The meat should be overhauled at 10, 25, and 40 days during the curing period. After the beef has been cured, it is soaked in water at approximately 60°F for 24 hr to prevent salt stains from appearing during the smoking and drying operation. The water should be changed at 6-hr intervals to ensure uniform soaking. After soaking, the meat is air-dried thoroughly and placed in a smokehouse.

Drying and Smoking.—The smokehouse should be heated to approximately 110°F and the meat held at this temperature for 12 hr. The temperature is increased gradually to 132°F at the end of 40 hr. During the first 24 hr of smoking, drying must be controlled so that moisture is removed from the surface by evaporation as rapidly as it appears, but avoiding formation of a dry crust. On about the second or third day, smoke is introduced into the smokehouse and the meat is subjected to a light smoke for 3 to 5 hr. By the end of the drying and smoking period, an internal meat temperature of 120 to 125°F should be reached. Drying and smoking time should average 4 to 6 days. At the end of this period, the beef is cooled in a hanging room. Product weight loss during drying and smoking should be about 35%. Finished dried beef should contain approximately 50% moisture and 10% salt.

Slicing.—The cured dried beef, after being well chilled, is sliced to a thickness of 1/32 to 1/64 in.

Filling.—Filling of the cans is a hand operation. Vacuum in the cans is obtained by closure in a vacuum seamer. A minimum machine vacuum of 25 in. is suggested for smaller cans. A machine vacuum of 20 in. is suggested for 603 × 700 cans. To facilitate slice separation, the cans may be sealed in a carbon dioxide or nitrogen atmosphere.

The following table shows typical cans used to pack dried beef and the product weight they contain.

Can Size	Net Weight	
	lb	oz
202 × 214		2
211 × 400		7
404 × 200		9
404 × 402	1	8
603 × 700	6	

It is important that the cans be completely dry. It is not usually necessary to wash the filled cans.

No retorting of the filled and sealed cans is required if the beef is dried sufficiently. The beef should have a moisture content of approximately 50% and a salt content of 10%.

LUNCHEON MEAT

Federal Meat Inspection Regulations

Canned luncheon meat is a ready-to-eat finely ground or chopped product. It is generally made from pork, although beef, veal, and lamb may be used. There is no Federal standard of identity for luncheon meat. Federal inspection regulations state that to facilitate chopping and to dissolve the curing agents, water or ice may be used during preparation; but the total amount of water cannot exceed 3% of the ingredients, and its presence must be declared.

Formulation

Ingredients	Amount	
	lb	oz
picnics	70	
butts	15	
shanks	15	
salt	3	8
sugar	2	
sodium nitrite		0.25

The fat content of the meat block should not exceed 30% of the product. For pasteurized products, sugar (sucrose) can be replaced by corn syrup solids and dextrose to improve yields. The quantity of corn syrup solids is limited to 2% of the total ingredients. Therefore, dextrose is usually added in addition to the corn syrup solids to provide the original sweetness level obtained by sucrose. Sugar is important, since it masks the salt flavor. The salt content must be maintained at a sufficiently high level because of the low sterilizing value of the cooking process. A 6% salt-to-moisture ratio in the product is suggested. Although Federal regulations allow the addition of 3% water, the amount of added water is calculated by analysis and is dependent on the moisture-protein ratio of the meat ingredients.

Preparation for Canning

Grinding and Mixing.—Grind the meats through a ⅜-in. plate and then mix meat, salt, sugar, and nitrite in a vacuum mixer for 5 to 8 min under 26 to 28 in. of vacuum. The nitrite should be dissolved in a small amount of water to aid proper distribution. To minimize purge in the can, the mix should be maintained at 28 to 30°F. Frozen meats or dry ice can be utilized to help achieve this temperature.

Canning

Cans.—Enameled cans should be used for sterile luncheon meat. The enamel contains a release agent to facilitate removal of the loaf. Cans made with either plain or enameled bodies and enameled ends are recommended for pasteurized luncheon meat. All enameled cans for pasteurized products are fitted with an aluminum anode to lessen corrosion and subsequent discoloration. Before filling, the cans are washed with a spray of 180°F water.

Filling.—Filling of larger cans (3 to 8 lb) can be done with a sausage stuffer having a special attachment to deliver definite volumes. The cans should be pressed firmly onto the filling attachments to avoid air pockets. Small cans (12 oz) are filled with automatic fillers attached to sausage stuffers.

Closing.—Vacuum in the cans is obtained by mechanical vacuum closure. A machine vacuum of 25 in. is suggested. High mechanical vacuum closure depends on proper vacuum mixing and filling to prevent the product from being drawn out of the can. Avoid spreading the meat over the entire area and closing any passages for removal of air. The two wide sides of the closed rectangular can should show distinct concavity. After closure, the cans should be passed through a detergent spray washer to remove grease and bits of product adhering to the exterior of the cans. The washing operation should consist of a hot-water pre-rinse and a detergent spray, followed by a warm fresh-water rinse. There should be no delay in placing the closed cans in the retorts and starting the process.

Processing

Sterile.—A 12-oz oblong can is used for all domestic packs of commercially sterile meat products that are stored without refrigeration. Any size can may be given a commercially sterile process, although this type of process is usually limited to 12-oz cans because of the severe heat treatment required for larger cans. Following is a list of can sizes and suggested processing conditions for sterile luncheon meat:

Can Size	Net Weight oz	Initial Temp. of Contents °F	Processing Time if cooked at 225°F min	230°F min	240°F min
300 × 308	12	45	90	80	70
115 × 312 × 310	"	"	"	"	"
202 × 314 × 304	"	"	"	"	"

Pasteurized.—Pasteurized luncheon meat is normally packed in the larger 3- and 6-lb oblong cans or in square-base 4 × 4 containers made in heights to hold 3, 6, or 6½ lb of product. Pasteurized luncheon meat must be stored under refrigeration. The label must state "PERISHABLE—KEEP UNDER REFRIGERATION." Pasteurized canned products should be cooked in water to an internal temperature of 160°F. Following is a list of can sizes and suggested processing conditions for pasteurized luncheon meat:

Can Size	Net Weight lb	oz	Initial Temp. of Contents °F	Processing Time if cooked at 165°F min	170°F min
310 × 402 × 608 (oblong)	3		30	220	180
310 × 402 × 1208 (oblong)	6		30	250	205
400 × 400 × 1110 (4 × 4)	6		30	300	245
400 × 400 × 1208	6	8	30	300	245

Immediately after processing, the cans should be cooled in water until the contents reach 100°F. Pressure cooling is required for the round or rectangular cans larger than 307 diameter to prevent straining or buckling of the ends. Pasteurized luncheon meats should be chilled further by holding at 38°F or below.

POTTED MEAT

Federal Meat Inspection Regulations
No Federal standard of identity exists for potted meat; however, inspection regulations do not allow the use of extenders unless their presence is made part of the product name. As an example, product containing up to 5% cereal must be labeled POTTED MEAT, CEREAL ADDED. The amount of water added to potted meat must be limited to that necessary to replace the moisture lost during processing.

Formulation

Potted meat products may be prepared from a variety of materials. The formulations are varied and quite elastic. Products usually contain fresh or cured beef or pork together with meat by-products. A typical potted meat formulation follows:

Ingredients	Amount lb oz	
cow meat	30	
regular pork trimmings	20	
pork tongue trimmings	25	
beef hearts	15	
beef tripe	10	
salt	1	8
white pepper, ground		6
mustard		0.8
paprika		0.8
nutmeg, ground		0.4
sodium nitrite		0.12

Precooking.—The tongue trimmings, heart, and tripe should be parboiled until tender. To do this, these by-products should be placed in sufficient water to cover them and simmered for approximately 1 hr at 185°F. The time will depend on the size of the pieces of meat. During parboiling, the meat may be held in wire baskets or crates.

Grinding and Chopping.—After being cooked, the meat should be ground through a ¾-in. plate. Place all the meats together with all the other ingredients in a chopper and chop to a smooth paste. Broth from cooking the by-products or water is added during the chopping operation to give the product the desired consistency. The amount of water or broth to be added cannot be standardized, since the meat ingredients used vary in their binding power. The formulas are generally flexible enough to utilize whatever meat ingredients are available. Judgment of the quantity of water to be added to maintain a uniform consistency is a matter of experience.

To prevent possible black iron sulfide formation, tripe should be placed in 50-grain vinegar for 10 min. This will neutralize any alkali which may remain from the tripe washing operation.

Canning

Heating and Filling.—Cans can be filled with the meat paste by either of the following methods: (1) heat the meat paste in a steam-jacketed kettle to 160°F and pump the heated product to the filler; or (2) heat to 160°F while the product is moved through a mixer-preheater or conveyor equipped with a steam jacket. Mechanical fillers can be used because of the consistency of the product. Minimum headspace and maximum can vacuum are desirable to prevent air discoloration on the surface of the product.

Closing.—Vacuum or steam-vac closure should not be used for potted meat because the cans are usually filled completely. Instead, the proper vacuum is obtained by filling the cans with the meat paste at a minimum closing temperature of 160°F. After the cans are closed, they are passed through sprays of hot water to remove grease and other extraneous materials from the outsides of the cans.

Retorting.—As soon as the cans are closed, they should be placed in a retort and cooked. The following is a list of cans frequently used and suggested processing schedules:

Can Size	Net Weight oz	Initial Temp. of Contents * °F	Processing Time if cooked at 240°F min	250°F min
202 x 115	3	120	65	40
		160	60	35
208 x 109	3¼	120	65	40
		160	60	35
208 x 208	5½	120	80	50
		160	75	45
300 x 102	3	120	60	35
		160	55	30

*Initial temperature is the average temperature of the can contents at the time the steam is turned on for the process.

Cooling.—Immediately after the cans are retorted, they should be cooled in cold water until the average temperature of the contents reaches 95 to 105°F. Cans of greater than 307 diameter should be pressure cooled to prevent straining or buckling of the ends.

CANNED HAMS, PASTEURIZED AND STERILE

Federal Meat Inspection Regulations

Federal meat inspection regulations allow canned hams a maximum weight increase of 8% over the weight of the fresh uncured ham. To help reduce liquid purge during cooking, regulations allow the use of an approved phosphate. Finished hams may contain no more than 0.5% added phosphate.

Hams

Only boneless hams, either whole or sectioned, are canned. Since canning does not improve the quality of the ham going into the can, hams selected for canning should be representative of the quality product desired.

Curing

Artery- or multiple needle-injection methods are used to pump hams with pickle. For maximum quality in the finished product, the pumped hams should be placed in cover pickle and allowed to cure for a minimum of 3 days prior to being canned. Gain in weight due to the cure ingredients must not exceed 8%. The following curing formula can be used to pump hams for canning:

Ingredients	Amount		
	lb	oz	gal
salt	150		
phosphate	50		
sucrose	37	8	
sodium nitrite	2		
water			100

Smoking

Most canned hams are not smoked. However, if smoke flavor is desired, the hams can be placed in a 130 to 140°F smokehouse and subjected to smoke for 1 to 3 hr. An alternative to natural smoke is liquid smoke, either in the pump pickle or applied as a dip or spray. With exception of the cooking to which the hams are subjected if they are smoked, hams to be canned are not cooked prior to canning.

Cans

There are two styles of cans used for canning hams: (1) pear-shaped and (2) pullman base.

Pear Shaped.—Pear-shaped cans come in 4 bases, as follows:

Miniature Base.—1½-lb ham sections are packed in this can. Hams packed in these cans are generally given a sterile cook to make them shelf-stable.

No. 1 Base.—Available in various heights; this base can is usually used for sectioned hams. Most hams in this size can are given a pasteurizing cook for refrigerated storage.

No. 2 Base.—Available in various heights; both split and small whole hams are packed in this base can for the consumer trade. These hams are given a pasteurized cook.

No. 4 Base.—Available in various heights; whole hams are packed in these cans and given a pasteurizing cook. This size is furnished for both the consumer and slicing trade.

Following is a list of approximate fill weights for pear-shaped cans:

	Can Height in.	Approximate Fill-in Weight				
		lb	oz		lb	oz
Miniature Base Can (5¾ x 4″)	2 11/16	1	8			
#1 Base Can (7⅝ x 5⅜″)	3	3				
	3¾	4				
	3⅞	4				
	4	4				
#2 Base Can (9¼ x 6⅜″)	3¼	4	12	and	5	
	3½	5				
	4	6				
	4½	6	12			
#4 Base Can (10 11/16 x 7 9/16″)	3¾	7	11	to	8	3
	4	8	4	to	8	12
	4¼	8	13	to	9	5
	4½	9	6	to	9	14

Can Height in.	Approximate Fill-in Weight				
	lb	oz		lb	oz
4¾	9	15	to	10	7
5	10	8	to	11	0
5¼	11	1	to	11	9
5½	11	10	to	12	2
5¾	12	3	to	12	11
6	12	12	to	13	4
6¼	13	5	to	13	13

Pullman Base.—Pullman-base cans are available in 1 oblong base and a number of heights. This style is used primarily for canning hams for slicing, where slices of sandwich dimensions are desired by either the consumer or institutional trade. The ham receives a pasteurizing cook. Fill weights for 4⅞ x 4⅝-in. base pullman cans are as follows:

Can Height in.	Range of Fill-in Weights				
	lb	oz		lb	oz
10½	7	8	to	7	14
11	7	15	to	8	5
11½	8	6	to	8	12
12	8	13	to	9	3
12½	9	4	to	9	10
13	9	11	to	10	1
13½	10	2	to	10	8
14	10	9	to	11	0

To prevent product discoloration, ham cans are normally anodized and have an inside enamel coating on bodies and ends. Anodized cans have an aluminum square welded to the inside of the bottom end.

Filling and Pressing

Cans should be washed in 180°F water before being filled. Hams or ham pieces are weighed after final trimming and the cans filled by hand to the desired weight. The cured hams are pressed to the can shape with a ham press. Hams should be cold when pressed to maintain shape better and to avoid problems during vacuum closure. Proper pressing is necessary to achieve the needed vacuum in the cans to avoid double seaming. Automatic can vacuum presses operated at 25 in. should be used.

Place a small amount of dry granular high-bloom gelatin in the can after the can is filled. This should be done only for hams to be given a pasteurizing process for the purpose of partially solidifying cooking purge. Cook-out or purge in sterile processed hams is so great that it is not practical or appealing to solidify the liquid portion with gelatin. The amount of gelatin to use in a can will vary with the size of the ham; generally no more than 1 oz is needed for the larger hams. The gelatin should be placed over the top of the ham after pressing. A small portion should also be placed in the aitch bone cavity to bind the meat in this area.

Closing

Wipe the flange area of each can body to remove any extraneous matter before the lid is seamed. Close the cans under vacuum in a vacuum closing machine. Chamber vacuums of 25 in. or more should be used during the seaming operation to maintain maximum vacuum in the cans and to avoid "loose tin," which Federal meat inspection regulations prohibit. "Loose tin" refers to tinplate body panels not pulled in tight against the meat. Pullman hams require ½ to ¾-in. head space for proper vacuum closure.

Processing

Two methods of heat processing are employed for the canning of hams: (1) a low-temperature pasteurizing process for perishable products to be held under refrigeration, and (2) a high-temperature sterilizing process for products to be stored at room temperature. Hams weighing 3 lb and over are generally given a pasteurizing process because the severity of the cook required to produce commercial sterility causes excessive moisture cook-out and shrinkage of the ham. Hams under 3 lb are generally given a sterile cook. However, there is no hard-and-fast rule regarding this matter, and there is some overlapping at the 3-lb dividing line in both directions.

Pasteurized.—Pasteurized canned hams are cooked in agitated water at 160 to 170°F until the can center reaches a minimum of 150°F, preferably 160°F. To prevent overcooking, different size cans should be cooked in different cook tanks. Following is a list of processes for pasteurized canned hams:

Can Base	Initial Ham Temp. °F	Cook Water Temp. °F	Approx. Cook Time to Reach 150°F Internal Temperature (min. per lb of meat)
No. 1	50	160	47
(7⅝ x 5⅜")	50	165	41
	50	170	37
No. 2	50	160	39
(9¼ x 6⅜")	50	165	35
	50	170	32
No. 4	50	160	33
(10 11/16 x 7 9/16")	50	165	29
	50	170	26

Following cooking, the cans should be chilled rapidly in cold water to an internal temperature of 100°F. Cans should then be placed in a cooler at 38 to 40°F for further cooling and storage. Canned pasteurized hams must be labeled PERISHABLE—KEEP UNDER REFRIGERATION.

Sterile.—Canned hams to be sterilized so they can be stored without refrigeration are cooked in a conventional retort with steam. The following schedule can be used to process sterile canned hams:

Can Base	Initial Temp. °F	Retort Temp. °F	Processing Time min.
Miniature	40	230	160
(5¾ x 4")	40	240	110

Following retorting, the cans should be pressure-cooled in water until the temperature of the contents is 95 to 105°F.

CHAPTER 13

Analytical Methodology

Most of the analytical procedures detailed in this chapter have been used by one of the authors for a number of years. They have given excellent results in the hands of technicians under general supervision. Some of the methods are modifications of those of the Association of Official Agricultural Chemists. They are especially suited where accurate, reliable methods for analyzing raw materials, emulsions, and finished products are needed.

The proximate analysis utilizes one 30-g sample. This single sample is used to analyze for moisture, protein, fat, and ash. With this method, the variation in composition of single frankfurters can be determined. The sample is dried by heat for moisture, and the dried residue is extracted with a fat solvent for fat content. The solvent is removed by heating and the fat residue is weighed. The fat-free residue is also weighed, and this acts as a check on the fat content by difference. The fat-free residue is split into aliquots for protein analysis by the Kjeldahl method. An aliquot sample is used for ash by incinerating and weighing the ash residue. The ash-plus-protein in all-meat product is equal to the fat-free residue (f.f.r.) weight. When the fat-free residue is in excess of the ash-plus-protein, this indicates the presence of carbohydrate materials and is suggestive of non-meat additives such as milk products or vegetable residues.

Rapid methods which sacrifice some accuracy are commonly used today in processed-meat operations for control of the fat, moisture, and protein content of raw materials at various stages of processing and in the finished products. Knowledge of the content provides a reasonable means of control and many methods for rapid fat analysis have been devised. These methods utilize one of the following: rendering and weighing, volumetric measurement, specific gravity, x-ray, dielectric measurements, or ultrasonic waves.

MOISTURE

Theory

Determination of moisture is made by drying the sample at elevated temperatures. Percent moisture is derived from the difference in weight of the sample before and after drying.

Apparatus

(1) analytical balance
(2) drying oven
(3) aluminum cans with covers, 2½ in. diameter, 3¾ in. deep
(4) desiccator
(5) laboratory grinder, chopper, or blender

Procedure

Select a representative product sample. If not already finely comminuted, grind, chop, or comminute in a blender until finely divided and uniform in composition. Weigh exactly 30.0 g of the chopped sample into a previously weighed aluminum can. Dry in an oven at 212°F to a constant weight (about 12 to 16 hr). Cover the can and allow to cool in a desiccator before weighing.

Calculation of Results

weight of solids = weight of dried sample and container
− weight of container

$$\% \text{ solids} = \frac{\text{weight of solids}}{\text{weight of original sample (30.0 g)}} \times 100$$

% moisture = 100.00 − % solids

Test Limitation

The method is dependent on the volatilization and subsequent evaporation of water from the sample. The meat sample may contain substances other than water that are volatile at 212°F.

FAT

Theory

Determination of the fat content of the moisture-free sample is done by extracting the fat with a suitable solvent.

Apparatus

(1) spatula
(2) Soxhlet apparatus with heat-controlled unit
(3) drying oven
(4) glass funnel
(5) analytical balance

Chemicals

250 ml Skellysolve F (technical grade solvent, chiefly hexane or petroleum ether, obtainable from Skelly Petroleum Products Co.).

Procedure

Carefully transfer the moisture-free sample to an extraction thimble. Small particles of solids and separated fat in the aluminum can are removed by repeated washing with the solvent. Place extraction thimble in the extractor with an attached receiving flask and pour the solvent washings into the thimble through a glass funnel. Connect the extractor and receiving flask to the Soxhlet condenser. Adjust the electrical heating unit so the solvent syphons over 5 to 6 times per hr and extract the fat on the Soxhlet apparatus for 16 to 20 hr. Remove the extraction thimble and place it in the original aluminum can. Evaporate the remaining trace solvent from the fat-free residue by drying in the 212°F oven (about 2 hr). With the aid of a spatula, carefully transfer all residue from the thimble to the aluminum can. Weigh the can containing the fat-free residue.

Calculation of Results

weight of fat-free residue = weight of fat-free residue and container − weight of container

$$\% \text{ fat-free residue} = \frac{\text{weight of fat-free residue}}{\text{weight of original sample (30.0 g)}} \times 100$$

weight of fat = weight of moisture-free solids and container − weight of fat-free residue and container

$$\% \text{ fat} = \frac{\text{weight of fat}}{\text{weight of original sample (30.0 g)}} \times 100$$

Test Limitation

Skellysolve F (hexane), in addition to the fat, may, on rare occasions, extract other materials present in the sample.

Safety Precaution

Skellysolve F (hexane) is flammable. Use adequate ventilation and avoid open flames.

PROTEIN

Theory

Determination of protein in a meat sample is done by measuring total nitrogen in the sample by the standard Kjeldahl method and converting this value to percent protein.

Apparatus

(1) Kjeldahl digesting apparatus
(2) Kjeldahl distilling apparatus
(3) 2 800-cc Kjeldahl flasks
(4) 1 100-cc graduate cylinder
(5) 2 500-cc Erlenmeyer flasks
(6) 1 50-cc burette
(7) analytical balance
(8) 2 pieces of tared nitrogen-free filter paper
(9) 4 glass beads

Chemicals

copper wire (#18 gauge, 3 in. length)
35 cc sulfuric acid
15 g potassium sulfate (granulated analytical reagent
  ACS Standard)
400 ml distilled water
60 ml 50% sodium hydroxide
50 ml 2% boric acid
5 parts 0.1% Bromcresol green⎫
1 part 0.1% Methyl red ⎬ in alcohol
4 g mossy zinc (C.P., ACS Standard)
0.5N hydrochloric acid

Procedure

Prepare the sample by grinding the fat-free residue (see analysis of fat). Weigh an aliquot of sample on a piece of tared nitrogen-free filter paper. Carefully fold the filter paper containing the sample and transfer to a Kjeldahl flask. Add a piece of copper wire, 35 ml sulfuric acid, 2 glass beads, and 15 g potassium sulfate. Heat the mixture gently on the digestion apparatus until frothing ceases. Boil briskly, and continue the digestion for a time after the mixture is colorless (about 2 hr). Cool the flask. Slowly add 400 ml distilled water and 60 ml

50% sodium hydroxide. Pour the sodium hydroxide solution down the side of the flask so that it does not mix at once with the digest. Add a chunk of the mossy zinc to the flask. Transfer the Kjeldahl flask to the distilling apparatus and connect it to the condenser by means of the Kjeldahl connecting bulb. Place the condenser tip in a 500-ml Erlenmeyer receiving flask containing 50 ml 2.0% boric acid solution. Mix the contents by shaking; heat gently, and distil 150 to 200 ml of distillate into the receiving flask. Break contact of the condenser tip with the distillate and continue distillation 2 to 5 min to steam out the condenser.

Titrate the distillate with standardized 0.5N hydrochloric acid. The end point is reached when the distillate color changes from blue-green to colorless.

Calculation of Results

$$\% \text{ protein} = \frac{\text{ml hydrochloric acid} \times \text{normality} \times .014 \times 6.25 \times 100}{\text{weight of aliquot sample}}$$

If numerous Kjeldahl determinations are to be made, a practical modification is an adjustment of the normality of the standardized hydrochloric acid to $0.57143N$. The protein factor (normality $\times$ .014 $\times$ 6.25) is then 0.0500. If the weight of the sample aliquot is calculated at 1/10 of the percent of fat-free residue, percent protein is calculated as follows:

$$\frac{\text{ml of titer}}{2}$$

Test Limitation

It is assumed that all the nitrogen is found in the proteins and that the nitrogen content of the protein is 16%. Therefore, a factor of 6.25 is used.

Safety Precautions

Kjeldahl digestion should be carried on under a fumeless hood. Exercise care when handling strong acids. Wear safety glasses.

ASH

Theory

Removal of organic material is done by heating and the remaining inorganic salts are determined gravimetrically.

Apparatus

(1) muffle furnace
(2) analytical balance
(3) 2 tared porcelain crucibles (30-cc)
(4) pair crucible tongs
(5) spatula

Procedure

Weigh an aliquot of fat-free residue into a porcelain crucible. Place the crucible in a muffle furnace not exceeding 500°C for 12 hrs. Cool in a desiccator. Then weigh ash and crucible.

Calculation of Results

weight of ash = weight of ash and crucible − weight of crucible

$$\% \text{ ash} = \frac{\text{weight of ash}}{\text{weight of sample}} \times 100$$

Test Limitation

Ash content is dependent to a degree on the nature of the ash. Certain constituents (chlorides) may be volatilized, reduced (sulfates), or distilled as complexes during the early stages of ashing.

NITRITE

Theory

Determination of nitrite in cured meat depends upon formation of a red azo-color by interaction of nitrites with Griess Reagent (sulfanilic acid plus alpha-naphthylamine).

The salts of nitrite are first extracted from meat samples with hot water and the soluble proteins of the meat coagulated by a mercuric chloride solution.

After cooling, the solution is made up to 500 ml volume and a small aliquot of 1 to 10 ml is then taken for the color development with Griess Reagent, the intensity of which is measured spectrophotometrically.

Apparatus

(1) 2 500-ml Erlenmeyer flasks
(2) spectrophotometer

(3) 2 50-ml volumetric flasks
(4) pipette
(5) blender
(6) oven

Chemicals

hot alkaline water: take approximately 300 ml distilled water in a 400-ml beaker. Make it just alkaline to litmus paper using 0.1N sodium hydroxide. Heat it close to boiling before using.

sulfanilic acid solution: dissolve 0.3334 g of the reagent in 15 ml glacial acetic acid. Make up to 100-ml volume with water. This reagent is very stable.

alpha-naphthylamine: dissolve 0.1 g of the reagent in 15 ml glacial acetic acid and make up to 100-ml volume with water. This reagent is stable for 2 to 3 weeks. Keep in a brown bottle.

glacial acetic acid

saturated mercuric chloride solution

Procedure

Weigh 20.0 g of a meat sample and place it in a blender. Mix it thoroughly, using a small amount of hot alkaline water. Transfer the contents to a 500-ml Erlenmeyer flask. Wash the container and cover with several portions of the hot water, adding all washings to the flask.

Add enough hot alkaline water to bring the volume to approximately 300 ml. Place the flask with a stopper in an oven at 80°C for 2 hrs, shaking occasionally.

Add 5 ml of a saturated mercuric chloride solution; mix and cool to room temperature.

Transfer the entire contents to a 500-ml volumetric flask; bring to volume with water and shake well.

Filter a portion through No. 42 Whatman filter paper into a test tube. Pipette 2 ml aliquot of the filtered solution into a 50-ml volumetric flask in which 1 ml of sulfanilic acid and 1 ml of alpha-naphthylamine reagents are already present. Fill the flask to the 50-ml volume mark with water, mix well, and let it stand for 1 hr to develop the red color. Prepare a blank containing the reagents only and water.

Transfer a portion of solution to a photometer cell and determine the absorbance at 520 mμ, setting instrument to zero absorbance with the blank.

Take the reading and find the percent nitrogen directly from a prepared chart or calibration curve.

The chart should be calibrated on the basis of a 20-g sample, 2 ml aliquot (out of 500-ml volume) and 50-ml volumetric flask where the color is developed.

Any deviations from the above constant weights and volumes would involve necessary corrections.

To convert % nitrogen into % nitrite ion, multiply the % nitrogen by 3.284. To convert into % sodium nitrite, multiply by 4.921.

MEAT PIGMENTS IN CURED MEAT PRODUCTS

Theory

This procedure is based on the extraction of hematin from cured meat products in a water-acetone solvent. The moisture content of the meat sample is normally taken into account such that a calculated 80% acetone/water extraction results. Procedure and calculations have been worked out by H. C. Hornsey in which nitroso-hemoglobin versus total acid-hematin are quantitatively determined as parts per million for a given meat sample size and a given acetone/water ratio. The degree of meat curing (nitroso pigment/total pigment × 100) is expressed directly as percentage.

Good or acceptable pigment conversion generally falls in an area between 80 and 90% of the pigment as nitrosohemochromagen.

Levels of about 100 ppm are considered a fair minimum for total pigments available for conversion. Generally, levels above 140 ppm for all meat products and higher for all beef products are very good. Pigment levels depend a great deal on the type of materials used in the sausage products.

Apparatus

(1) 2 45-ml polypropylene centrifuge tubes with cover
(2) 1 glass stirring rod with tapered end to fit tip of the centrifuge tube
(3) 2 Pyrex test tubes, 15 × 90 mm
(4) spectrophotometer with 1-cm cells
(5) 2 glass funnels, 50-mm diameter
(6) 2 watch glasses, 2-in. diameter

Chemicals

acetone (a): 18.0 ml distilled water in a 200-ml volumetric flask; add C.P. acetone, mix and bring to volume.

acetone (b): To 4.0 ml concentrated hydrochloric acid, add distilled water, mix and bring to 20-ml volume. Transfer the diluted hydrochloric acid to a 200-ml volumetric flask, add C.P. acetone, mix and bring to volume with additional C.P. acetone.

Procedure

Procure meat sample by means of a #6 cork borer. Weigh out exactly 2.0 gm sample and transfer to the polypropylene centrifuge tube. Add 9.0 ml acetone (a) to the centrifuge tube by means of a pipette. Macerate the meat mass thoroughly with the glass stirring rod (2 to 3 min required). Stopper the tube with centrifuge tube cover and mix by gentle swirling. Allow to stand 10 min, then filter through 2 #42 Whatman papers (9.0-cm dia.) into a test tube. The above operations should be carried out in very subdued light to lessen fading of pigment extraction.

Transfer filtrate into a 1-cm Beckman cell and read optical density within 1 hr at 540 mμ and calculate as nitroso pigment.

Another 2.0-g sample is now prepared as above and transferred to another polypropylene centrifuge tube. Add 9.0 ml acetone (b) by means of a pipette. The meat sample is thoroughly macerated with the stirring rod and allowed to stand 1 hr before filtering. Filter the extract into another test tube and read the optical density at 640 mμ. Calculate as total pigment.

Calculation of Results

ppm nitroso pigment = optical density (at 540 mμ) × 290

ppm total pigment = optical density (at 640 mμ) × 680

$$\% \text{ conversion} = \frac{\text{ppm nitroso pigment}}{\text{ppm total pigment}} \times 100$$

Test Limitation

The procedure has been scaled down to a smaller sample size; therefore, the meat sample should be as homogeneous as possible. The sampling is taken by means of a cork borer using the center portion of a meat product, such as a frankfurter, to eliminate other coloring substances as food dye, ordinarily found at the peripheral surface. Filtrate must be crystal clear, which is easily accomplished where two combined fine filter papers are used. Percent conversion is calculated on a theoretically possible 100% if all hematin can actually be converted to nitroso pigment.

Other Additives

The methods of determining some of the most prominent intentional additives—phosphate, salt, cereal, soybean flour and soy protein concentrate, lactose, and corn syrup solids—are used by the meat and poultry inspection laboratories of the United States Department of Agriculture. They have been used for a number of years and have a high degree of reliability when used within the intended reference framework.

PHOSPHATE

In this procedure a partially dried sample is ashed and the phosphates hydrolyzed to the ortho form and separated as quinolinium phosphomolybdate.

Theory

Phosphomolybdic acid is formed first (in the presence of citrate), which then forms quinolinium phosphomolybdate (QPM), with the base, quinoline. The citrate in the reagent complexes any ammonium ion, thereby preventing the precipitation of ammonium phosphomolybdate.

The original version of this procedure required two separate solutions in order to form the QPM precipitate: a citric-molybdic acid solution and quinoline solution. The inclusion of acetone permitted these two solutions to be combined, such that a single reagent could be employed as the precipitant. This reagent is known as the quimociac reagent, and derives its name from the *QUI*noline, *MO*lybdate, *CI*trate and *AC*etone constituents of the mixture.

Apparatus

(1) Gooch crucible (Coors No. 4)
(2) glass fiber filter paper (2.4-cm circles)

Place the Gooch crucible containing a glass fiber filter disk in the suction apparatus. Center paper and wash with approximately 50 ml water. Dry the crucible at 250°C for 30 min in a forced-draft oven, cool in desiccator and weigh.

Chemicals

dilute nitric acid: 1 volume concentrated nitric acid plus 4 volumes water

quimociac reagent: Dissolve 70 g sodium molybdate dihydrate ($Na_2 MoO_4 .2H_2O$) in 150 ml water. Dissolve 60 g citric acid in a mixture of 85 ml nitric acid and 150 ml water, and cool. Gradually add the molybdate solution to the citric-nitric acid solution while stirring. Dissolve 5 ml synthetic quinoline, with stirring, in a mixture of 35 ml concentrated nitric acid and 100 ml water. Gradually add this solution to the molybdic-nitric acid solution, mix well, and let stand for 24 hr. Filter, add 280 ml acetone, dilute to 1 liter with water, and mix. Store in either a noncolored polyethylene bottle or a dark brown glass bottle.

Procedure

Weigh accurately about 2.5 g (no more than 25 mg P_2O_5) of sample into an ashing dish and dry for 30 min at 125°C in a forced-draft oven. Ash at 550°C until white or nearly white ash is obtained.

Cool; add 25 ml dilute nitric acid and heat on a steam bath for 30 min. Filter into a 400-ml beaker. Wash dish and paper with distilled water such that total volume in beaker is approximately 100 ml.

At this point, run a reagent blank in parallel, using 25 ml dilute nitric acid and 75 ml distilled water. Add 50 ml quimociac reagent, cover with a watch glass, and boil for 1 min. (Do not use an open flame.) Cool to room temperature while swirling carefully; transfer the precipitate to the prepared crucible and wash 5 times with 25-ml portions of distilled water, allowing each portion to drain thoroughly (use suction) before adding the next portion. Dry the crucible and contents for 30 min at 250°C; cool in a desiccator and weigh.

Calculations

$$\text{phosphorus content} = \frac{(100)\,(A\text{-}B)\,(0.014)}{C} - (0.0106)\,(\%\text{ meat protein})$$

A = weight of precipitate
B = weight of blank
C = sample weight
0.014 = gravimetric factor derived from:

atomic weight of phosphorus = 30.97
molecular weight of (QPM) = 2212.71 = $(C_9H_7N)_3H_3PO_4 12MoO_3$

$$\frac{\text{Phosphomolybdic}}{\text{Quinolinium Phosphomolybdate}} = 0.014$$

0.0106 = factor to correct for the phosphorus content of meat protein
phosphate content = (phosphorus content) (F)

$$F = \frac{\text{anhydrous molecular weight of desired phosphate}}{(X)\,(\text{atomic weight of phosphorus})}$$

X = no. of atoms of phosphorus in 1 molecule of the phosphate.

The following table lists phosphates and their corresponding factors:

Name and Formula		Factor
disodium phosphate	Na_2HPO_4	4.58
sodium hexametaphosphate	$(NaPO_3)_6$	3.29
sodium tripolyphosphate	$Na_5P_3O_{10}$	3.96
tetrasodium pyrophosphate	$Na_4P_2O_7$	4.29
sodium dihydrogen phosphate	NaH_2PO_4	3.87
sodium acid pyrophosphate	$Na_2H_2P_2O_7$	3.58

SALT

In this procedure, the sodium chloride content is determined by the well-known Volhard method, first described in 1874. The sample is treated with silver nitrate and nitric acid and then wet-ashed, followed by back-titration of the excess silver nitrate with potassium thiocyanate.

Theory

From the outset, the order in which silver nitrate and nitric acid are added to the flask is quite critical. The silver nitrate solution must be added first, followed by the concentrated nitric acid. This order of addition ensures complete precipitation of the chlorides. If nitric acid is added first, loss of chloride by volatilization as hydrochloric acid could occur, since hydrochloric acid has a far greater vapor pressure than nitric acid.

The volume of silver nitrate solution added must be in excess of that required to react with the chloride content of the sample. The concentrated solution of potassium permanganate is added to oxidize any organic matter not disposed of by the nitric acid. Should too much potassium permanganate be accidentally added, color removal can be effected by the addition of small quantities of sugar.

Following boiling, cooling, and dilution, add nitrobenzene or diethyl ether and back-titrate the excess silver nitrate with potassium thiocyanate solution, employing ferric ammonium sulfate solution as an indicator.

After all the silver has been back-titrated, an excess of thiocyanate may react with the precipitated silver chloride, since the solubility product of silver thiocyanate is 1/100 that of silver chloride.

$$SAgCNS = 1.0 \times 10^{-12}$$
$$SAgCl = 1.1 \times 10^{-10}$$

The addition of nitrobenzene or diethyl ether overcomes this difficulty by coating the precipitated silver chloride, thereby withdrawing it from the action of the thiocyanate solution.

The $FeNH_4(SO_4)_2$ reacts with an excess of thiocyanate, forming the red-colored complex, ferric thiocyanate, $(FeCNS)^{++}$, indicating the end point has been reached.

Chemicals

ferric alum indicator: saturated aqueous solution of reagent grade $FeNH_4(SO_4)_2 \cdot 12H_2O$.

silver nitrate, 0.100N: Dissolve 17.04 g silver nitrate, previously dried at 110°C, in distilled water, and dilute to 1 liter. Standardize, using excess silver nitrate against 0.100N sodium chloride (5.845 g per liter), according to the Volhard method.

potassium thiocyanate, 0.100N: Dissolve 9.72 g reagent-grade potassium thiocyanate in distilled water, and dilute to 1 liter. Verify the strength of this solution as follows: Pipette 25 ml standard silver nitrate solution into a 300-ml Erlenmeyer flask; add 80 ml distilled water, 5 ml of 1 + 1 nitric acid, and 2 ml of the ferric alum indicator. Titrate with potassium thiocyanate solution to a permanent light-brown end point. The ratio of the volume of potassium thiocyanate to the volume of silver nitrate should be 1 : 1.

potassium permanganate, 5% aqueous solution.

Procedure

Weigh 3 ± 0.05 g of finely comminuted and thoroughly mixed sample into a 300-ml Erlenmeyer flask. Add 25.0 ml of 0.100N silver nitrate solution; swirl flask until the sample and solution are in intimate contact and then add 15 ml concentrated nitric acid. Boil until meat dissolves and add potassium permanganate until color disappears and solution becomes almost colorless. Add 25 ml water; boil for 5 min; cool and dilute to 150 ml with water.

Add 1 ml nitrobenzene or 25 ml diethyl ether, 2 ml of the ferric alum indicator and shake vigorously to coagulate the precipitated silver chloride. Titrate the excess silver nitrate with potassium thiocyanate solution to a permanent light-brown end point.

Calculations

$$\% \text{ salt} = \frac{(25.0 \text{ ml} - \text{ml KCNS}) (0.1N) (5.85)}{\text{sample weight}}$$

CEREAL

Cereal is added to meat food products as a binder. In this procedure, the cereal starch is dissolved in 1+1 hydrochloric acid, re-precipitated, and determined gravimetrically. A rapid, semiquantitative method is also described.

Theory

As in the soybean flour and soy protein concentrate determinations, the meat is rendered soluble by treatment with an alcoholic solution of caustic potash; spices and cereal starch remain as a sediment. If a semiquantitative estimation of the cereal content is desired, this residue volume is read and a deduction allowed for spices.

A more accurate quantitation is obtained if the cereal starch is dissolved in 1+1 hydrochloric acid, re-precipitated with 95% ethanol, dried and weighed.

Apparatus

(1) centrifuge
(2) centrifuge tubes, Goetz, 100-ml Arthur H. Thomas, Catalog #3011-K35, or equivalent
(3) Gooch crucible

Chemicals

95% ethanol
alcoholic caustic potash solution, 8%: Dissolve 50 g potassium hydroxide in 300 ml 95% ethanol, and dilute to 500 ml with 95% ethanol.
dilute hydrochloric acid, 1 + 1: Mix 1 volume concentrated hydrochloric acid with 1 volume distilled water.

Semiquantitative Procedure

This procedure is applicable only in the absence of soybean flour and soy protein concentrate.

Weigh 10.0 g of sample into a 100-ml Goetz tube. If corn syrup, corn syrup solids, nonfat dry milk, and/or calcium-reduced dried skimmilk are present, extract with 2 successive 50-ml portions of warm distilled water; shake, centrifuge, decant and discard the supernatant liquid after each extraction. (If corn syrup, corn syrup solids, nonfat dry milk, or calcium-reduced dried skimmilk are absent, this extraction should be omitted.)

Add 50 ml 8% alcoholic potassium hydroxide solution and digest on a steam bath for 20 min with occasional stirring. Dilute to 100 ml with 95% ethanol. Allow to stand for 1 hr and read volume of sediment in tube.

Calculations:

% cereal = volume of sediment in tube − 0.5% for spices, if present.

Gravimetric Procedure

Centrifuge the 100-ml suspension for 5 min. Decant and discard the supernatant liquid. Wash the residue with 25 ml 95% ethanol, stirring the sediment thoroughly. Centrifuge, decant and discard the supernatant liquid.

Add 50 ml of 1+1 hydrochloric acid, mix thoroughly, stopper and shake for 1 min. Centrifuge at 2000 rpm for 4 min. If supernatant liquid is not clear, filter it through a double-thickness 541 Whatman paper, or equivalent.

Transfer 25 ml of clear supernatant liquid to a 150-ml beaker containing 75 ml 95% ethanol; mix well, and let stand for 1 hr. Filter through a tared Gooch crucible, wash with 2 25-ml portions of 95% ethanol, dry for 30 min at 75°C, and weigh.

Calculations

$$\% \text{ cereal} = \frac{(A - B)\,(1.45)\,(100)}{\dfrac{C}{2}}$$

A = weight of Gooch crucible plus starch
B = weight of Gooch crucible
C = sample weight
1.45 = factor for converting from starch to cereal, assuming that cereals contain an average starch content of 69%.

SOYBEAN FLOUR AND SOY PROTEIN CONCENTRATE

With this method, advantage is taken of the fact that dilute acid will dissolve the hemicelluloses of soybean flour and soy protein concentrate, but will not affect cereal flour starch. Therefore, it is possible to determine soybean flour or soy protein concentrate in the presence of cereal flour.

Theory

If a meat food product is heated in an alcoholic solution of caustic potash, the fat is saponified and the protein hydrolyzed. This treatment renders the major solid components of meat (fat and protein) soluble in the medium. Spices, cellulose, and starch (from cereal, if present) remain as a sediment.

Dilute acid is then employed to dissolve the soybean flour hemicelluloses, which are subsequently re-precipitated with 95% ethanol and quantitated following a carefully controlled centrifugation. Quantitation is done by employing empirical factors—6.0 for soybean flour and 2.5 for soy protein concentrate.

Because of the empirical nature of this determination, it is imperative that the time and speed of centrifugation be closely adhered to.

Apparatus

(1) centrifuge
(2) centrifuge tubes, Goetz, 100-ml, Arthur H. Thomas, Catalog #3011-K35, or equivalent

Chemicals

95% ethanol
alcoholic caustic potash solution (8%): Dissolve 40 g potassium hydroxide in 300 ml 95% ethanol, and dilute to 500 ml with 95% ethanol.
dilute hydrochloric acid (1 + 3): Mix 1 volume concentrated hydrochloric acid with 3 volumes distilled water.

Procedure

Weigh 10.0 g of sample into a 100-ml Goetz tube. Add 50 ml 8% alcoholic potassium hydroxide solution and digest on a steam bath for 30 min with occasional stirring. Shake well and centrifuge for 4 mins. Decant and discard the supernatant solution. Wash residue with 25 ml 95% ethanol, stirring sediment thoroughly. Centrifuge and decant. Discard the alcoholic solution.

Add 50 ml dilute hydrochloric acid, mix thoroughly, stopper, and shake for 1 min. Centrifuge at 2000 rpm for 4 min. (Retain residue for cereal determination.)

If supernatant is not clear, filter it through a double-thickness 541 Whatman paper or equivalent. Transfer 25 ml of clear supernatant to a second Goetz tube containing 75 ml 95% ethanol, shake well, and allow to stand for 1 hr.

Accelerate from 0 to 1,500 rpm for 1 min, and centrifuge at 1,500 rpm for exactly 2 min. Read volume of sediment in tube.

Calculations

% soybean flour = volume of sediment × 6
% soy protein concentrate = volume of sediment × 2.5

NOTE: The sediment remaining from the dilute hydrochloric acid leaching may be used to determine cereal content, if present. Decant the hydrochloric acid. Mix the residue with 50 ml of 1:1 hydrochloric acid, and proceed as under gravimetric section of Cereal Determination.

LACTOSE

Nonfat dry milk and calcium-reduced dry skim-milk, each consisting of 50% lactose, is added to meat food products as an extender. With this method, the amount of nonfat dry milk or calcium-reduced dry skim-milk which has been added is determined by analyzing the product for its lactose content.

Theory

This procedure requires that much attention be paid to minute details. Bakers' yeast (Saccharomyces cerevisiae) is washed to ferment all reducing sugars other than lactose and maltose. If corn syrup or corn syrup solids, in addition to nonfat dry milk or calcium-reduced dry skim-milk has been added to the product, a maltose-acclimated yeast must be prepared to ferment the maltose. If active dry yeast is used in place of bakers' yeast, care must be exercised when the yeast is washed that the yeast be added to the water, for if the reverse procedure is employed (water added to the dry yeast), approximately 50% of the yeast population will be destroyed. If it is remembered that yeast consists of living unicellular plant organisms and that the dry variety must be wet thoroughly prior to stirring, one may proceed with reasonable confidence that the yeast is viable.

The acclimation procedure is rather straightforward, but care should be taken that the temperature during incubation does not exceed 30°C. This could occur if a mechanical stirrer is used, because the stirrer motor may supply additional heat to the incubation oven. This procedure is based upon the analysis of a labile component of nonfat dry milk or calcium-reduced dry skim-milk—a fact that should be kept constantly in mind. Lactose can be readily fermented to lactic acid by certain microorganisms, especially Streptococcus lactis, which is generally present in muscle tissue. Lactose can also be quickly hydrolyzed to glucose and galactose by the action of hot, dilute acids. If these reactions occur, the analytical results will be low, since nonfat dry milk or calcium-reduced dry skim-milk is calculated on the basis of amount of lactose found. This analysis should be initiated as soon as the sample is ground, and, if possible, completed on the same day.

The small amount of water initially added to the 20-g sample should be at room temperature when added to the sugar flask. If it is hot, coagulation of the meat and milk protein may occur, making it difficult to macerate the sample and leach out the lactose. If, following the 30-min heating time on the steam bath, the flask and contents are not cooled to room temperature before adding the hydrochloric acid, loss of lactose may take place by hydrolysis.

The viability and potency of the acclimated yeast suspension can be determined as follows: Weigh 500 mg maltose and 800 mg dextrose and transfer to a 100-ml volumetric flask. Dilute to volume with distilled water. Stopper and mix well. Pipette a 10-ml aliquot into a 50-ml volumetric flask and proceed through the incubation procedure. Boil 10 ml of this solution (following centrifugation), with 20 ml of Benedict's solution for exactly 3 min. This should yield no precipitate or suspension of cuprous oxide, indicating that the yeast did, in fact, ferment the sugars as desired. If a precipitate or suspension is obtained, the yeast should be discarded. This is the only procedure which will definitely assure that the yeast is "working" properly. *NOTE:* If washed yeast is used, weigh only 800 mg dextrose. Do not use any maltose.

The reduction portion of this method is extremely critical because it involves an empirical procedure. The 3-min boiling time must be strictly adhered to, and the flask should be cooled rapidly after boiling. This may be accomplished by inverting a beaker over the neck of the flask and allowing a stream of cold tap water to flow over the flask.

Titration should be performed immediately after addition of the phosphoric acid to avoid any possible loss of iodine. Use of iodine flasks, although they are considerably more expensive than Erlenmeyer flasks, will also serve to avoid loss of iodine.

Chemicals

(A) washed yeast suspension: Mix four cakes of bakers' yeast (or 30 g active dry yeast) to a smooth suspension with 300 ml distilled water. If active dry yeast is used, the yeast must be added to the water. Centrifuge for 5 min and discard the aqueous layer. Repeat 4 more times, or until the supernatant is clear following centrifugation. Finally re-suspend the yeast in distilled water, dilute to 200 ml with distilled water, and refrigerate at about 4°C.

(B) acclimated yeast suspension: Prepare acclimating medium by dissolving each of the following ingredients in a small amount of distilled water and adding, in the order given, to 1,000 ml distilled water the following: 2.0 g anhydrous magnesium sulfate, 4.0 g ammonium chloride, 2.0 g anhydrous dipotassium hydrogen phosphate, 1.0 g potassium chloride, 0.04 g $FeSO_4.7H_2O$, 1.4 g peptone, and 40.0 g technical maltose. Dilute to 2 liters, warm, and filter. Bring filtrate to a rolling boil and allow it to cool to room temperature. Shake well the washed yeast suspension obtained in (A), remove 100 ml, and centrifuge. Discard the aqueous layer, add the washed yeast to 1 liter of the acclimating medium and incubate for approximately 24 hr at 30°C, stirring frequently the first few hours. Separate yeast by decanting and centrifuging. Wash twice with distilled water and repeat incubation with the remaining 1 liter of acclimating medium. Separate yeast again, wash 4 or 5 times with distilled water. Suspend the yeast in distilled water, dilute to 100 ml with distilled water and refrigerate at about 4°C.

(C) dilute hydrochloric acid: 1 volume conc. hydrochloric acid + 4 volumes distilled water.

(D) phosphotungstic acid, 20% W/V

(E) chlorophenol red indicator: Dissolve 0.1 g chlorophenol red in 2.4 ml $0.1N$ sodium hydroxide and dilute to 250 ml with distilled water.

(F) bromthymol blue indicator: Dissolve 0.1 g bromthymol blue in 1.6 ml $0.1N$ sodium hydroxide and dilute to 250 ml with distilled water.

(G) buffer solution pH 4.8: Prepare $0.1M$ citric acid (19.21 g/liter) and $0.2M$ disodium hydrogen phosphate (28.4 g anhydrous/liter). Mix solutions in proportions of 10.14 ml citric acid to 9.86 ml disodium hydrogen phosphate and adjust to pH 4.8, using a pH meter. Store in refrigerator and discard if solution becomes turbid.

(H) Benedict solution: Dissolve 16 g $CuSO_4 \cdot 5H_2O$ in 150 ml distilled water. Dissolve 150 g sodium citrate, 130 g anhydrous sodium carbonate, and 10 g sodium bicarbonate in 650 ml distilled water. Combine the two solutions. Then cool and dilute to 1 liter with distilled water and then filter.

(I) dilute acetic acid: Dilute 240 ml glacial acetic acid to 1 liter with distilled water.

(J) dilute phosphoric acid: Dilute 240 ml phosphoric acid to 1 liter with distilled water.

(K) iodine standard solution: Dissolve 10.2 g potassium iodide in a minimum quantity of distilled water and use this solution as a solvent for 5.08 g iodine. Filter, if necessary, through glass fiber filter paper and dilute to 1 liter with distilled water.

(L) sodium thiosulfate standard solution: Dissolve 9.92 g $Na_2S_2O_3 \cdot$

$5H_2O$ in recently boiled, cooled distilled water. Add 0.1 g sodium carbonate and dilute to 1 liter with distilled water.

(M) starch indicator solution: Triturate 2 g soluble starch and 10 mg mercuric iodine with a small amount of distilled water. Add the suspension slowly to 500 ml boiling distilled water, and boil until clear.

(N) lactose standard solution: Dissolve 1.5789 g lactose monohydrate in distilled water and dilute to 1 liter with distilled water (10 ml = 15 mg anhydrous lactose).

Procedure

Weigh a 20.0 g sample into a 200-ml volumetric sugar flask. Add 50 ml distilled water, stir or shake to break up any lumps and heat on a steam bath for 30 min. Cool to room temperature. Add 20 ml dilute hydrochloric acid and dilute to volume using bottom of the fat layer as a meniscus. Add 10 ml 20% phosphotungstic acid solution. Mix and let stand for a few minutes and then filter through moistened filter paper. Pipette 40 ml filtrate into a 50-ml volumetric flask. If corn syrup or corn syrup solids are absent, neutralize just to the acid side of bromthymol blue indicator. Dilute to volume with distilled water and mix. If corn syrup or corn syrup solids are present, neutralize just to the acid side of chlorophenol red indicator. Add 5 ml of the buffer solution and dilute to volume with distilled water, and then mix.

Transfer about 40 ml of this solution to a centrifuge tube to which 5 ml of yeast suspension (washed yeast if corn syrup or corn syrup solids are absent, acclimated yeast if either one is present) has been added, and from which the water has been separated. Mix yeast and sample well, and incubate washed yeast for 1 hr at 30°C, or acclimated yeast for 3 hr at 30°C. Stir frequently. Centrifuge and determine reducing sugars. Pipette 10 ml of clear supernatant into a 300-ml Erlenmeyer flask. Add 20 ml Benedict solution. Bring to boil in 3 to 5 min and boil for exactly 3 min. Remove from heat, cool rapidly, add 100 ml distilled water and 10 ml dilute acetic acid slowly while swirling. Add a definite volume of standard iodine solution (15 ml for about 1.5% lactose, or 30% excess), and agitate to dissolve the cupric oxide. Allow flask to stand at least 5 min. Add 20 ml of the dilute phosphoric acid solution and titrate excess iodine with standard sodium thiosulfate solution using the starch solution as indicator.

Determine iodine/sodium thiosulfate ratio by using 10 ml distilled water, and carrying through determination as above, beginning ". . . Add 20 ml Benedict solution. . . ".

Express ratio as : $\dfrac{\text{Volume iodine (in ml)}}{\text{1.0 ml sodium thiosulfate}} = A$

Determine lactose/iodine ratio by using 10 ml of standard lactose solution, and carrying through determination as above, beginning ". . . add 20 ml Benedict solution. . .".

Express ratio as : $\dfrac{\text{mg lactose}}{\text{1.0 ml iodine}} = B$

Calculations

% lactose = $\dfrac{100\,[\text{ml iodine added to flask} - (A)\,(\text{ml sodium thiosulfate required for back titration})]\,[B]}{C}$

A & B = ratios defined above

C = milligrams of sample in aliquot (consider the volume of the original sample solution as 200 ml, rather than 210 ml, to take into account the volume occupied by the sample).

% nonfat dry milk or % calcium-reduced dry skim-milk =
(% lactose × 2) − correction

Correction: 0.4% in the absence of corn syrup or corn syrup solids, and 0.8% in the presence of corn syrup or corn syrup solids.

CORN SYRUP SOLIDS

Corn syrup solids is added to meat food products as a flavoring agent. In this procedure, the amount of corn syrup solids which has been added is determined by analyzing the product for its maltose content.

Theory

Because recent studies have indicated that the maltose content of corn syrup solids is quite variable, it is imperative that different lots of corn syrup solids be analyzed for this constituent; this value is then used in calculating the corn syrup solids content of the product.

If corn syrup is used, a sample should be analyzed for moisture content, and only those samples which assay 20% or less should be permitted to be added to the product.

Products to which corn syrup solids or corn syrup and nonfat dry skim-milk or calcium-reduced dried skim-milk have been added are analyzed for corn syrup solids content by determining the difference between the reducing sugars remaining in the samples after the samples have been subjected to two fermentations by (1) washed yeast (which leaves lactose and maltose), and (2) yeast acclimated to maltose (which leaves lactose).

Products to which corn syrup solids or corn syrup, but neither nonfat dry milk nor calcium-reduced dried skim-milk, have been added are analyzed for corn syrup solids content by determining the amount of maltose present following a washed yeast fermentation.

Chemicals

(A) washed yeast suspension: Mix 4 cakes of bakers' yeast (or 30 g active dry yeast) to a smooth suspension with 300 ml distilled water; if active dry yeast is used, the yeast must be added to the water. Centrifuge for 5 min and discard the aqueous layer. Repeat 4 more times, or until the supernatant is clear, following centrifugation. Finally re-suspend the yeast in distilled water, dilute to 200 ml with distilled water, and refrigerate at about 4°C.

(B) acclimated yeast suspension: Prepare acclimating medium by dissolving each of the following ingredients in a small amount of distilled water and adding, in the order given, to 1,000 ml distilled water: 2.0 g anhydrous magnesium sulfate, 4.0 g ammonium chloride, 2.0 g anhydrous dipotassium hydrogen phosphate, 1.0 g potassium chloride, 0.04 g $FeSO_4 \cdot 7H_2O$, 1.4 g peptone, and 40.0 g technical maltose. Dilute to 2 liters, warm, and filter. Bring filtrate to a rolling boil and allow it to cool to room temperature. Shake the washed yeast suspension obtained in (A) well; remove 100 ml and centrifuge. Discard the aqueous layer; add the washed yeast to 1 liter of the acclimating medium and incubate for approximately 24 hr at 30°C, stirring frequently the first few hours. Separate yeast by decanting and centrifuging. Wash twice with distilled water, and repeat incubation with the remaining 1 liter of acclimating medium. Separate yeast again, wash 4 or 5 times with distilled water. Suspend the yeast in distilled water, dilute to 100 ml with distilled water and refrigerate at about 4°C.

(C) dilute hydrochloric acid: 1 volume conc. hydrochloric acid + 4 volumes distilled water.

(D) phosphotungstic acid, 20% W/V.

(E) chlorophenol red indicator: Dissolve 0.1 g chlorophenol red in 2.4 ml 0.1N sodium hydroxide and dilute to 250 ml with distilled water.

(F) bromthymol blue indicator: Dissolve 0.1 g bromthymol blue in 1.6 ml 0.1N sodium hydroxide and dilute to 250 ml with distilled water.

(G) buffer solution, pH 4.8: Prepare 0.1M citric acid (19.21 g/liter) and 0.2M disodium hydrogen phosphate (28.4 g anhydrous/liter) solutions. Mix solutions in proportions of 10.14 ml citric acid to 9.86 ml disodium hydrogen phosphate and adjust to pH 4.8. Store under refrigeration and discard if solution becomes turbid.

(H) Benedict solution: Dissolve 16 g $CuSO_4 \cdot 5H_2O$ in 150 ml distilled water. Dissolve 150 g sodium citrate, 130 g anhydrous sodium carbonate, and 10 g sodium bicarbonate in 650 ml distilled water. Combine the two solutions. Then cool and dilute to 1 liter with distilled water and filter.

(I) dilute acetic acid: Dilute 240 ml glacial acetic acid to 1 liter with distilled water.

(J) dilute phosphoric acid: Dilute 240 ml phosphoric acid to 1 liter with distilled water.

(K) iodine standard solution: Dissolve 10.2 g potassium iodide in a minimum quantity of distilled water and use this solution as a solvent for 5.08 g iodine. Filter, if necessary, through glass fiber filter paper and dilute to 1 liter with distilled water.

(L) sodium thiosulfate standard solution: Dissolve 9.92 g $Na_2S_2O_3 \cdot 5H_2O$ in recently boiled, cooled, distilled water. Add 0.1 g sodium carbonate and dilute to 1 liter with distilled water.

(M) starch indicator solution: Triturate 2 g soluble starch and 10 mg mercuric iodide with a small amount of distilled water. Add the suspension slowly to 500 ml boiling distilled water, and boil until clear.

(N) maltose standard solution: Dissolve 1.5789 g maltose monohydrate in distilled water and dilute to 1 liter with distilled water (10 ml = 15 mg anhydrous maltose).

Procedure

For samples containing both corn syrup solids or corn syrup and nonfat dry milk or calcium-reduced dried skim-milk, proceed as under Lactose "Procedure" section, pipetting 2 40-ml aliquots of protein-free filtrate into 50-ml volumetric flasks. Neutralize one just to the acid side of bromthymol blue indicator, dilute to volume with distilled water, and mix. Neutralize the other just to the acid side of chlorophenol red indicator, add 5 ml buffer solution, dilute to volume with distilled water, and mix. To a centrifuge tube add 5 ml washed yeast suspension; to another centrifuge tube add 5 ml acclimated yeast suspension. Separate the water by centrifuging and decanting. Transfer about 40 ml of the unbuffered solution to the centrifuge tube containing the washed yeast. Transfer about 40 ml of the buffered solution to the centrifuge tube containing the acclimated yeast. Mix yeast and sample well. Incubate washed yeast for 1 hr at 30°C and acclimated yeast for 3 hr at 30°C, stirring frequently. Continue as under lactose "Procedure" section, except that, in lieu of a lactose:iodine ratio, determine a maltose:iodine ratio using 10 ml of standard maltose solution. Express ratio as:

$$\frac{\text{mg maltose}}{1.0 \text{ ml iodine}} = B$$

For samples containing either corn syrup solids or corn syrup, but neither nonfat dry milk nor calcium-reduced dried skim-milk, pipette a single 40-ml aliquot of protein-free filtrate into a 50-ml volumetric flask. Neutralize just to the acid side of bromthymol blue indicator, then dilute to volume with distilled water and mix. Transfer about 40 ml of this solution to a centrifuge tube to which 5 ml washed yeast suspension has been added and from which the water has been separated. Mix yeast and sample well and incubate for 1 hr at 30°C. Proceed as under lactose "Procedure" section, using a maltose:iodine ratio rather than a lactose:iodine ratio.

Calculations

For product containing corn syrup solids or corn syrup and nonfat dry milk or calcium-reduced dried skim-milk:

$$\% \text{ maltose} = \frac{100\,[(D - AE) - (F - AG)]\,[B]}{C}$$

For product containing corn syrup solids or corn syrup but neither nonfat dry milk nor calcium reduced dry skim-milk:

$$\% \text{ maltose} = \frac{100\,[D - AE]\,[B]}{C}$$

A = iodine:sodium thiosulfate ratio
B = maltose:iodine ratio
C = milligrams of sample in aliquot (consider the volume of the original sample solution as 200 ml, rather than 210 ml, to take into account the volume occupied by the sample)
D = ml iodine added to flask (washed yeast)
E = ml sodium thiosulfate required for back titration (washed yeast)
F = ml iodine added to flask (acclimated yeast)
G = ml sodium thiosulfate required for back titration (acclimated yeast)

$$\% \text{ corn syrup solids} = (100)\,\frac{\% \text{ maltose}}{\% \text{ maltose in corn syrup solids}} - H$$

H = Correction factor to be applied when nonfat dry milk or calcium-reduced dried skim-milk is absent = 0.4%

No correction factor should be applied when nonfat dry milk or calcium-reduced dried skim-milk is present.

RAPID FAT AND MOISTURE DETERMINATIONS

A rapid method for determining the fat content of sausage raw materials, sausage emulsions, and finished products is of great practical and economic significance today. A relatively large number of fast methods have been developed. However, it is quite necessary that proper selection of a fat method be made for the particular item to be tested. The time for completing the analysis is very important in some plants, while in others, the sampling technique or the accuracy becomes a limiting factor. Each plant must establish the method best suited for its routine needs.

The sampling for analysis is critical with all the methods. Handling of the material prior to sampling, obtaining a proper size sample, and the handling of the sample must be done in a precise manner.

RAPID FAT

Rapid fat analyses are usually run on raw materials such as beef and pork trimmings. The methods are usually of two general types: (1) direct, where the fat is separated and weighed or measured, and (2) indirect, where the meat is measured for a characteristic that reflects the fat content. Direct methods are solvent extraction and modified Babcock procedure.

Solvent Methods

Solvent extraction methods involve a small test sample and rapid refluxing with ether, chloroform, or some special solvent system, followed by evaporation of the solvent and weighing or measuring the fat residue.

Babcock Method (Paley)

Modified Babcock methods may vary as to sample size and the type of acid digestion used for releasing the fat. A 9- or 30-g sample is most commonly used with a Paley bottle. The Paley bottle has a graduated stem in which the fat can be measured and related to percent fat in the sample. The following modification of this method has been used in the laboratory of one of the authors for several years. It can be used to determine the fat content of raw materials, emulsions, and finished products. Hydrochloric acid is preferred to sulfuric since it causes less charring, especially when some sugar is present in the sample.

Theory.—When analyzing for fat in raw or finished products, the proteins must be broken down to allow the encapsulated fat to separate. Concentrated hydrochloric acid and heat are used to accomplish this. The hydrolysis of proteins should be controlled and carried only so far as to solubilize them. If the "breaking down" is carried too far, it may result in charring of the meat sample. The charred particles then have a tendency to enter into the fat column and interfere with fat determination by blurring the readings. The proper time to interrupt the further rapid destruction of proteins is soon after foaming subsides. This is done by adding water to the bottle at that time.

Apparatus.—
 (1) blender
 (2) magnetic stirrer
 (3) large Paley fat bottle
 (4) water bath
 (5) analytical balance

Chemicals.—
 concentrated hydrochloric acid
 dimethyl sulfoxide

Procedure.—The meat sample (3 to 6 oz) is placed in a blender and chopped at low speed for 15 to 30 sec. (This treatment results in good mixing without excessive emulsifying.)

A 1-oz* sample is weighed out in a tared fat bottle. The large Paley bottle uses a 28.4-g (1-oz) sample.

Tighten the glass stopper, add a magnetic stirring bar and approximately 60 ml conc. hydrochloric acid.

Shake the bottle by hand or place it over a magnetic stirrer for 1 to 3 min until the meat is finely dispersed. Raw meat samples require longer and more vigorous stirring. (A fine dispersion of meat in cold acid is a very important step in this procedure.)

Place the bottle in a near-to-boiling water bath, shaking occasionally.

When the foaming subsides or ceases, add 15 to 25 ml dimethyl sulfoxide and mix. Remove the beaker from the source of heat and leave the bottle in the hot bath for an additional 6 min.

* When testing raw meats or if the sample is expected to contain more than 35% fat, take only a ½-oz sample and multiply the reading by 2 to obtain percent fat.

Add conc. hydrochloric acid to bring the separated fat into the calibrated neck of the bottle in such a manner that the cold acid does not mix with the hot acid layer. If the fat layer is not well-defined, add additional dimethyl sulfoxide dropwise to separate the fat from the acid layer.

Read percentage of fat directly from the calibrated stem.

The use of a magnetic stirrer is preferable to a centrifuge for separation of the fat from the acid solution, since the breaking of a flask in the centrifuge is time-consuming in cleanup, and an element of danger may exist.

Agreement between the Babcock method and the official method is good. Usually a ±1% variation is observed; the Babcock runs on the high side of the official method for finished sausages and on the low side for raw meat materials. Approximately 30 min is required to complete the test from sampling through reading the fat level in the graduated tube of the Paley bottle.

Test Limitation.—The procedure as described should not be applied to the determination of fat in liver or liver sausage. It also does not give satisfactory results with meat products containing milk powder.

This method requires some chemical training but the equipment used is of relatively low cost. Accuracy is good but some care is necessary with sampling and handling.

Indirect methods include x-ray and specific gravity procedures. These two methods have received a most favorable reaction from meat processors.

X-Ray Method

The Anyl-Ray equipment has considerable acceptance by the trade. A large sample is used for a test measurement but the sample can be returned to the production line. While the readings can be made in a few seconds, the time for filling the sample cup and handling may require 10 min. The machine functionally operates by the difference in absorption of x-rays. The transmitted energy activates a meter that is calibrated for percent fat. A 13-lb sample is used and nontechnical personnel can be trained to run the test. This is quite suitable for raw materials such as pork or beef trimmings. Sausage emulsions or finished products with added salt require various corrective factors and do not give satisfactory readings. A 1% accuracy compared to official laboratory methods is claimed by the manufacturer of the equipment.

Specific Gravity Method

The Honeywell digital fat controller measures the fat content of meat samples by compacting the ground meat sample, weighing the compacted mass and then calculating the specific gravity. A 750-g sample ± 25 g is preferred. The specific gravity of lean meat is reported as 1.068, while fat is 0.947. Temperature control and a minimal amount of voids are necessary for good precision. The method is promising, but may need some additional testing before acceptance by the trade is obtained in any measure.

Steinlite Method

The Steinlite method for determining fat is essentially a solvent-extraction procedure in which the solvent and fat are placed in a special cell and a dielectric measurement is made. The fat content is read from a reference chart. High fat levels in a sample require some dilution or adjustment of sample size in order to obtain reliable values. As the solvent odor (*ortho*-dichlorobenzene) is objectionable to some analysts, a ventilation hood is needed for proper utilization of this method.

All the rapid fat methods have some advantages and disadvantages. Each operation should determine the method or methods best suited for its need. The modified Babcock and the Anyl-Ray have reasonably good acceptance by the trade; the Anyl-Ray by its rapidity of obtaining results without skilled technicians, and the Babcock by its versatility, rapidity, and degree of accuracy are most likely to continue in acceptance.

RAPID MOISTURE

The determination of moisture by vacuum drying or other means described by the Association of Official Agricultural Chemists are quite lengthy procedures requiring 12 to 16 hr.

Several rapid methods for meat products are useful if the accuracy required can be achieved. Two of the most commonly used methods will be described in this chapter.

Infrared Moisture Balance

The infrared moisture balance is a unique instrument on which the prepared sample can be weighed directly, dried, and percent moisture read on a rotating scale. The instrument is equipped with a torsion wire to weigh a 5-g sample. Drying of the sample is accomplished in approximately ½ hr by means of an infrared lamp. Reproducibility is good with reasonable accuracy as compared with official moisture determination methods. This method is by far the most rapid.

Sample Preparation.—The manner in which meat samples are prepared is of paramount importance. A good homogeneous sample may be difficult to prepare, particularly in the case of raw meat materials. In the case of finely chopped cooked and processed meats, a blender may be quite satisfactory to comminute 50 to 100 g of meat product. A variable transformer is usually essential to control the speed of the blender cutting blades. Good chopping and mixing are thus attained without undue maceration of the meat product. Excessive chopping at high speeds tends to cause fat separation as the meat sample warms up. Also, with the centrifugal forces involved, good mixing is lost. Another problem which arises when raw materials are being prepared with a blender is that the connective tissues are not well comminuted.

Procedure.—A 5-g sample is placed on the disposable aluminum pan designed for use with this moisture balance. The instrument is first set at exactly 100%. The meat sample is distributed over the bottom of the pan in such a manner as to balance the pan suspended on a pointed needle wire. The instrument is equipped with a variable transformer with calibration from 0 to 120 volts. A 250-watt infrared lamp is used. The transformer should be set at 90 volts. This setting appears to be the optimum because decomposition in the form of charring of the sample during the drying operation does not occur, yet the sample does dry to a constant weight after 30 min. Percent moisture in the sample is read directly from the scale.

Azeotropic Distillation

This method for determining moisture requires special apparatus and a suitable azeotrope for measuring the moisture content of meat products. The time required is usually from 2 to 2½ hr. A large sample can be used, especially for low moisture content products. Toluene is a common solvent that forms an azeotrope with water. The procedure involves distillation of water from the sample to a collecting tube where the water separates on cooling the azeotrope. The percent moisture can be read from the graduated collecting tube. Excellent results can be achieved with this method; however, the time involved is considerably greater than that required to determine moisture with the infrared moisture balance.

Methods of the Association of Official Agricultural Chemists and the rapid methods have a particular sample size and type of product for which they work best. A.O.A.C. methods are generally more accurate and reliable. They carry a mark of authenticity where legal or technical judgments may be needed. The rapid methods most suitable for a particular situation can be selected by a technologist so the overall needs of a plant operation can be met.

ROUTINE ANALYTICAL LABORATORY
FOR MEAT PRODUCTS

The laboratory requires a 10 × 15 ft area for conducting the analytical procedures. This space should have suitable work benches and

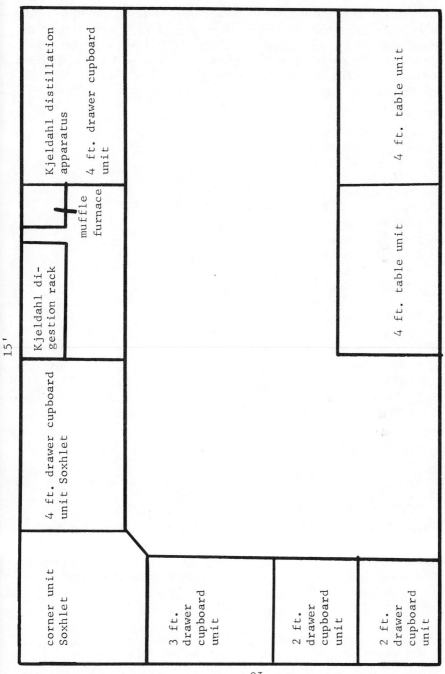

FIG 13.1 ANALYTICAL LABORATORY LAYOUT

facilities such as a fume hood, water, gas, electricity, compresser, air, a vacuum line, good drains or sewers, and possibly some type of air conditioning unit. An office space of 10×10 ft is desirable and should adjoin the laboratory. The laboratory space may cost $50 to $60 per sq ft but the office should be considerably less. The laboratory furnishing should include:

2 4-ft drawer cupboards
1 corner unit cupboard
1 3-ft drawer cupboard
1 2-ft drawer cupboard
1 2-ft sink unit
2 table units
1 fume hood unit
1 Kjeldahl digestion rack and fume duct
1 muffle furnace
2 Soxhlet extraction (6 unit size) apparatus
2 6-unit electric heaters for Soxhlets
1 Kjeldahl distillation apparatus
1 vacuum oven and water aspirator
1 electric meat grinder
1 torsion balance (2-mg sensitivity)
1 pH (hydrogen ion) meter
1 colorimeter
1 hot plate
1 analytical balance
1 spectrophotometer
18 800-ml Kjeldahl flasks
12 500-ml Erlenmeyer flasks
12 250-ml Erlenmeyer flasks
100 assorted beakers and test tubes
3 burettes (50 ml)
24 porcelain crucibles

The reagents required will cost approximately $1,000. The furnishings, equipment, and glassware will cost approximately $10,000. A layout for the laboratory is shown in Fig. 13.1. In general, the laboratory should be close to quality control or production control areas.

BIBLIOGRAPHY

Association of Official Agricultural Chemists. 1960. Official Methods of Analysis, 9th Edition. Association of Official Agricultural Chemists, Washington, D.C.
HORNSEY, H. C. 1956. The color of cooked cured pork. I. Estimation of the nitric oxide-haem pigments. J. Sci. Food Agr. 7, 534.

U.S. Dept. of Agr. 1971. Chemistry Laboratory Guidebook. U.S. Department of Agriculture, Technical Services Division, Washington, D.C.
WHITEHEAD, R. C. 1966. Rapid fat determination. *In* Proceedings of the Meat Industry Research Conference. American Meat Institute Foundation, Chicago, Ill.

CHAPTER 14

Other Methods of Processing

Although canning, curing, and sausage production comprise the major processing procedures utilized for meat, several other methods are being used by the meat industry. Obviously, some of the processing procedures are used primarily for fresh meat, but are considered in this text because they are closely interrelated. Many of those mentioned are still in the developmental stages and could well become important within the next few years. New methods of processing and new-product development are often inseparable and will be discussed together.

Industry, universities, and governmental agencies are all concerned with development of new processes and new products. The entire area is most important to the potential growth and viability of the meat industry. Therefore, processing methods must be constantly reviewed and updated by research and development groups. But even more important, these groups also must consider other promising ways of more effectively and efficiently processing meats. Procedures necessary in developing and gaining approval of new processing methods, however, are involved and generally require approval of either the Food and Drug Administration or Animal and Plant Health Inspection Service before adoption by the industry. Even minor changes in processing procedures must be carefully considered because of implications to human health and nutrition. Thus, development of new techniques for processing requires careful experimentation and accumulation of data before they can be instituted at the plant level.

PURPOSE OF DEVELOPING NEW METHODS

There are a great many reasons for development of new processing methods, among which are the following: speeding up production, economy, decreasing spoilage, increasing the variety of products, providing a greater amount of convenience, reducing labor costs, and increasing utilization of by-products. Many of these purposes overlap and are closely related, but each is also important itself.

Speed of Processing

This results in a reduction of inventory and permits a greater turnover of investment in raw materials. Generally, volume is indicative of profit, although this is not always true; in fact, a greater volume of product can also result in a larger loss if margins are negative. Thus, speed of processing is important only if the final product is profitable. There are many examples where speeding up processing has played an important role, such as changing from dry-cured to stitch-pumped bacon, or from batch to continuous processing of frankfurters. Although rapid processing results in greater turnover of capital outlay and investment of less funds in the same amount of product, these advantages must be balanced against disadvantages, which are often associated with a decrease in quality. For example, stitch-pumped bacon can be produced much faster, but dry-cured bacon brings a higher price. Consequently, many small operators have been able to profit by production of quality products.

Speeding up processing has distinct advantages in reducing inventories and hence capital outlay, but should be considered in all its ramifications before any new processing procedure is adopted. Furthermore, the importance of maintaining quality while altering processing procedures should not be overlooked. Reduction in quality, which often results from increasing output, is very difficult to compensate for by increasing speed of production.

Economy

Economy is usually achieved by a variety of procedures and must be carefully considered at all phases of production. The success of any process will ultimately depend on its being economically feasible. Nevertheless, one should not lose sight of the fact that even economical processes are not always self-supporting. New developments almost always require some subsidization during their early phases and are seldom profitable immediately. However, research and development personnel must be able to visualize profitable production and project the costs of production and ultimate profits from any new process or product.

Reduction in Losses from Spoilage

This can lead to more profitable production, providing, of course, that it can be achieved economically. The great awareness of food spoilage and placing the responsibility of policing their own operations upon the meat industry itself has emphasized the importance of this area. Knowledge of the causes of spoilage and their control is not only important to existing operations but also to development of new products and processes. The industry must never lose sight of the fact that it has a great responsibility for prevention of spoilage. Probably even more important is its responsibility for food safety and freedom from food poisoning.

New Product Development

Product development is of utmost importance to the meat industry. Although development of new products or even changes in old products are often expensive, they pump new life into the industry and are necessary to keep it competitive with other foods. New product development requires both foresight and imagination, which are obviously key elements to profit. On final analysis, however, new product development is only a beginning; many new products never reach production, and even fewer are successful. Nevertheless, new products provide diversity and are essential to success.

Convenience

This is a most important element in new-product development. The consumer has become increasingly aware of convenience foods, which are fully or partially prepared. Convenience has become even more important as more and more housewives have begun to work outside the home. Speed and ease of preparation have become particularly important and have demanded more processing. Thus a greater amount of technology and labor can be marketed by production of convenience foods. Producers of convenience items must always exercise very careful control of processing techniques to maintain quality of the final product.

Reduction of Labor Costs

Lower labor costs are often an important consideration in production of new products or in altering existing processing procedures. Trends have led toward mechanization wherever feasible.Continuous processing of frankfurters was developed to make more effective use of labor and to streamline the manufacturing process by mechanization. Replacement of batch processing by an on-the-line method has distinct advantages in labor costs, even though the initial outlay may be high. Streamlining and mechanization of meat processing will no doubt continue. Decisions should be arrived at first by considering the alternatives, including quality of the finished product, and then the economics involved. Obviously, any process alteration that will reduce labor costs has distinct advantages, other things being equal, because labor costs usually comprise the major portion of the cost of processing.

Reduction of labor costs should not, however, be the sole criterion for deciding on an alteration in processing procedures or development of a new product. Many new products have failed, although labor costs were lower, because quality was sacrificed. Maintenance of quality should always be considered. In fact, sacrificing quality for reduction in costs is usually a signal of future economic problems. Nevertheless, reduction of labor costs is a most important step as long as quality can be satisfactorily maintained.

Increased Utilization

Finding new uses for by-products has long played a most important role in meat processing. In fact, sausage originated as a consequence of attempts to more effectively utilize by-products of slaughtering and cutting. Forward-looking research and development groups are not satisfied with mere disposal of by-products, but are constantly seeking better utilization of them.

Utilization requires imagination and foresight. One cannot be satisfied with traditional uses of by-products, but must constantly consider new uses and new approaches. The meat-packing industry today faces the problems of water and air pollution. Although dumping of plant effluent into streams and burning of waste products seemed simple solutions to disposal of packing house wastes, today meat-packing companies have either installed their own waste-treatment facilities or utilize those of the community in which the plant is located.

OTHER METHODS OF PROCESSING

The methods reviewed herein are not the only promising developments in meat processing. However, they do include the more recent methods in use, including some which are being used commercially. Other procedures discussed are not in use, but are being investigated commercially and show some promise.

Freeze-Drying of Meat

Although dehydration can be achieved by either freeze-drying or heat dehydration, the latter method is not being used for meat, and thus will not be discussed. Freeze-dehydrated meat is, however, being manufactured and marketed commercially. The largest portion of dehydrated meat now being manufactured is found in dehydrated soup mixes, where meat is only one, although a most important, ingredient. Dehydrated meat is also available for campers or hikers where light weight and stability are essential. Even though the total volume of dehydrated meat is small, its advantages will probably continue to create a growing demand for these products in special markets.

The exploratory work on development of dehydrated meats has largely been under the auspices of the Armed Forces. Light weight and the lack of a need for refrigeration are major advantages of dehydrated meats for military personnel. These same factors have also contributed to the demand for freeze-dried products by the civilian population.

The method of freezing meat to be dehydrated was originally thought to be unimportant, but recently, it has been shown that the freezing procedure is just as important as the drying method. It has been established that slowly frozen meat produces a better-textured freeze-dried product than that frozen rapidly. Thus, meat to be freeze-dried should be frozen slowly, preferably at about 15 to 25°F. Rapidly frozen meat rehydrates more slowly and is tougher and poorer in texture. Since poor texture and slow rehydration are major problems in all freeze-dried foods, the use of slow freezing in preparing meat for dehydration is most important.

The dehydration process is accomplished by sublimation, or the transfer of ice from the product to the atmosphere in the form of vapor. Since each pound of ice sublimed requires 1200 BTU's, heat or energy must be supplied to remove the moisture. During dehydration, heat transfer occurs both within the product and outside or away from the product. Transfer of heat within the product during freeze-drying occurs in three ways: (1) by sublimation of the ice layer, (2) by evaporation or desorption of the adsorbed water in the ice-free layer, and (3) by elevation of the dry layer temperature. Heat transfer at the food surface occurs by a combination of radiation and convection which accounts for removal of moisture from the surface of the product.

In addition to application of heat or energy to facilitate moisture removal during freeze-drying, establishment of a vacuum also plays an important role in moisture transfer. Although the vacuum greatly speeds up drying, too low a pressure is expensive to produce and may even slow down the drying rate.

There are a number of different types of freeze-dryers available. Earlier types usually contain fixed plates, although they come in a number of designs; but more recent types are arranged so the freeze-drying plates can be adjusted relative to each other, and are used almost exclusively for pressure-contact freeze-drying. This method is usually called vacuum contact drying (VCD) or accelerated freeze-drying (AFD). Basically, the method increases heat transfer by bringing the plates into close contact with the food. An expanded metal grid is placed between the plates and the food to allow the vapor to escape and to increase penetration of heat into the food during contact drying. This design makes it possible to speed up the drying rate or else to lower temperatures, while still achieving the same rate of moisture removal.

Optimum residual moisture content varies with the food. Meat, fish, and poultry are shelf-stable at a level of about 3.5% moisture at 72°F. There appears to be little advantage in going to levels lower than this, although 2% moisture is often advocated. The latter value is a hold-over from freeze-drying of pharmaceuticals and biological materials and does not apply to foods.

Organoleptic acceptability of freeze-dried meat is most often limited because of toughness and lack of juiciness, which is apparently due to denaturation of actomyosin. Another serious problem is development of browning and loss of natural meat color. This appears to be due to both carbonyl-amino browning and oxidative browning of the meat pigments. The end result is not only poor color but also undesirable bitter flavors that make the meat unacceptable. However, many of these changes can be prevented by proper storage, as will be discussed later. Poor acceptability can also result from the enzymatic activity of residual enzymes in the tissues. Although residual enzymatic activity is not commonly a problem in dehydrated meat, poultry, or fish, it can cause some oxidative changes in the pigments. It can usually be prevented by heat-inactivating the enzymes by precooking before freeze-drying.

Storage of freeze-dried meat is an important consideration. Since it becomes rancid rapidly in the presence of oxygen, it must be packaged in a vacuum or under an inert gas to avoid oxidative deterioration. Freeze-dried meat is normally packaged in nitrogen, using a high-grade packaging material. If properly processed and packaged in an inert atmosphere, dehydrated meat is shelf-stable and can be held for long periods without deterioration.

Costs of distribution of dehydrated meat are less than those of frozen meat. In fact, they appear to be about the same as the costs of distributing canned foods.

Dehydrated meat shows considerable promise as a shelf-stable food item. Although spectacular growth of the market for dehydrated meat is not likely, it shows some promise and will probably continue to meet a specialized demand with slow but continuous growth.

Intermediate-moisture Meats

The term "intermediate-moisture" has been used to identify a heterogeneous group of foods, which resemble dry foods in that they are resistant to bacterial spoilage but contain too much moisture to be considered as dry foods. Generally, their moisture content is of the order of 20 to 30%, yet they can be held without refrigeration. Among the traditional intermediate-moisture foods are air-dried figs and dates, prunes, marshmallows, soft candies, jams, jellies, fruit cakes, and a variety of meat products, such as Country cured ham, jerky, pepperoni, and other dry sausages.

Although the principles underlying the preparation of intermediate-moisture foods are well known, recent interest in development has been stimulated by practical application in producing intermediate-moisture pet foods. Several recent patents have been granted in this area and intermediate-moisture pet foods are now available in a variety of forms.

Stability of Intermediate-moisture Products.—Although intermediate-moisture foods are relatively soft, easily masticated, and have a moist feeling in the mouth, they are microbiologically stable. The more recent developments in this area have been made possible by commercial availability of antimycotics, which suppress the growth of yeasts and molds.

Even though intermediate-moisture food products are microbiologically stable, they are more susceptible to the browning reaction than dry foods. They are, however, less susceptible to oxidative deterioration. Unless suitable precautions are taken to inactivate the indigenous enzymes, they are also liable to a variety of enzymatic alterations.

The basic principle underlying microbiological stability of intermediate-moisture products is the reduction in water activity (a_w), which prevents spore germination and microbial growth. For the purposes of this discussion, water activity may be defined as the ratio of the vapor pressure of water in the food (P) to the vapor pressure of pure water (P_o) at the same temperature. The formula for expressing this relationship is $a_w = P/P_o$. Temperature can be disregarded for normal mesophilic food spoilage organisms, since their a_w is practically independent of temperature.

Although safety from microbiological spoilage depends upon the food, its previous treatment, the organisms present, handling, storage, and a variety of other conditions, pet foods with an a_w of approximately 0.85 have an excellent record for stability under market conditions. Thus, meat items properly processed and packaged would normally require an a_w of 0.85. This assumes, of course, that antimycotic agents are used.

Production of Intermediate-moisture Foods.—Development of intermediate-moisture foods has been pioneered by researchers at the U.S. Army Natick Laboratories, who have developed several such products for military feeding. They have shown that several additives can be utilized for lowering the water activity of the products to produce intermediate-moisture foods (Brockmann 1970). The most common compounds used for this purpose are sugar, glycerol, and salt. All three of these compounds have certain disadvantages, so a combination is most commonly recommended for achieving the desired moisture level.

To produce the most acceptable meat items in the intermediate-moisture range, experience has shown that the desired a_w can best be achieved by equilibrating the food in an aqueous solution of glycerol, salt, and antimycotics. The food is immersed in a solution of the proper concentration to give the desired a_w and also the proper level of antimycotic. It is then cooked in a water bath at 203 to 212°F.

Table 14.1 shows a number of equilibrating solutions used in making different meat products. The equilibrating medium is variable, depending upon the composition of the original product and its water content. Similar equilibration procedures have been successfully applied not only to beef, pork, and sweet and sour pork, but also to lamb, ham, tuna, and chicken. It has also been used in producing a number of meat casserole items, including beef stew, creamed tuna and noodles, chicken a la King, and Hungarian goulash. The method also appears to be suitable for a variety of other meat products.

Except for a slight recognizable sweet taste, foods at an a_w of 0.80 to 0.85 have normal flavor, aroma, and texture. The flavor can be further improved by addition of soup or gravy bases to the immersion or equilibration medium.

The future appears favorable for intermediate-moisture foods, although to date their development is still in the experimental stages. Their stability appears excellent and the ease of storage and handling

Table 14.1

COMPOSITION OF EQUILIBRATION SOLUTION FOR INTERMEDIATE-MOISTURE MEAT PRODUCTS

Components	Products		
	Pork	Beef	Sweet & Sour Pork*
Glycerol	45.6	87.9	25.00
Water	43.2	—	15.00
Salt	10.5	10.1	2.59
Sucrose	—	—	11.84
Potassium sorbate	0.7	—	0.30
Sodium benzoate	—	2.0	—
Catsup	—	—	23.84
Vinegar	—	—	13.50
Starch hydrolyzate	—	—	4.22
Corn starch	—	—	2.30
Monosodium glutamate	—	—	1.15
Mustard powder	—	—	0.23
Onion powder	—	—	0.02
Garlic powder	—	—	0.01

* a_w= 0.85
Source: Brockmann 1970

should make intermediate-moisture meat products a valuable adjunct to present methods of meat preservation.

Preservation of Meat with Antibiotics

Soon after antibiotics became accepted by the medical profession as a means of controlling bacterial infections, their use in extending the shelf-life of fresh meat was suggested.

Selection of an Antibiotic.—Since a variety of spoilage organisms are normally present in meat products, it is best to select a broad-spectrum antibiotic. The two most common and cheapest of these are oxytetracycline and chlorotetracycline, both of which have been utilized on meat. However, other broad-spectrum antibiotics may also be equally effective in controlling microbial growth. Other special antibiotics with a narrow spectrum may also be used to control food spoilage that is primarily due to a specific microorganism. A combination of antibiotics may prove to be the most effective under normal conditions.

The second factor to be considered is the matter of cost, assuming the antibiotics available are of equal value for controlling bacterial growth. Since cost is easy to assess, further discussion is not necessary.

Application of Antibiotics.—Antibiotics can be applied to meat readily by using sprays and dips. Generally, the greatest level of contamination is on the surface, so that spraying and dipping are effective.

Where deep tissue spoilage occurs, spraying and dipping are not effective, and infusion through the arterial system, as is done in pumping hams, is preferable. The latter system can be applied to cuts in which the arterial system is intact, such as beef rounds or pork hams, but cannot be used on many other cuts. The entire carcass can also be infused with antibiotics. This technique has been used effectively by Weiser et al. (1954). These investigators normally used the carotid artery for injection of the antibiotic solution.

Still another method of using antibiotics is that of injecting the animal prior to slaughter. Antemortem intramuscular injection 30 min before slaughter gave just as good results as spraying or dipping of the cuts from the carcass.

Levels of Antibiotics.—Results with oxytetracycline have shown that adequate control of spoilage can be achieved by spraying or dipping with 20 ppm. Antemortem injection at a level of 0.8 mg per lb of live weight gave good control of spoilage. Infusion of chlorotetracycline into either intact beef rounds or the entire carcass was effective at a level of 55 ppm.

If antibiotic treatment is used, exact levels should be determined in cooperation with the manufacturers. Nevertheless, the level is quite low.

Present Applications.—Although antibiotics were widely used on cut-up poultry a few years ago, this was often a substitute for cleanliness and good sanitation. As a result, it has been abandoned, and proper processing techniques have achieved essentially the same shelf-life. Thus, it is emphasized that antibiotics should not be looked upon as a substitute for good sanitary practices but only as a means of extending the shelf-life of a relatively good product.

Antibiotics have also been used on red meats. Attempts were made to use them on carcasses shipped from New Zealand and Australia to England. However, the uncertainty of ship movements and delays in loading suggested that the use of antibiotics was not feasible under current management practices. However, better scheduling and more reliable shipping could overcome many of these problems and make antibiotics applicable to the meat industry. Currently, antibiotics are not approved by Federal meat inspection regulations for use in meats in the United States.

Other Problems with Antibiotics.—The most serious problem with antibiotic preservation of foods is the matter of cross-resistance transmitted from one bacterial species to another. This means not only that bacteria may become resistant to antibiotics, but (even more important) that a group of bacteria with increased resistance may develop. Although some research is contrary to the theory of cross-resistance, it is not likely that any additional usage of antibiotics will be permitted until the entire story becomes clear. Thus increased use of antibiotics for preservation of meat is questionable.

Preservation of Meat by Irradiation

Irradiation of foods is not a new process, as it has been used in production of vitamin D-enriched milk for many years, as well as in controlling microbial growth during the aging of beef to permit high temperatures, and thus more rapid tenderization. The latter process makes use of ultraviolet radiation. When the carcasses and the radiation sources are arranged properly to permit all surfaces to be exposed, microbial growth is inhibited and the aging room temperature can be increased to about 65 to 68°F for a period of approximately 48 hr. This results in rapid tenderization. The process is patented and beef produced by this method is trade-marked "Tender Ray".

Shortly after the conclusion of World War II, the U.S. Atomic Energy Commission became interested in exploiting peaceful uses for atomic radiation. The use of irradiation as a means of preserving foods, and especially meat, was one of those applications. Although both β- and γ-rays were applicable to destruction of food-spoilage organisms, β-rays possessed only a limited ability to penetrate and were suitable for only thin cuts of meat or surface radiation. Consequently, γ-rays have been used mainly for irradiation of meat products. Irradiation can produce either a pasteurized product or a commercially sterile product.

Levels of Irradiation.—The basic unit of measuring irradiation is the rad. Commercially sterilized meat has been calculated to require about 3.2 million rads. Pasteurization, of course, is achieved at much lower levels. Meat will require from 50,000 to 250,000 rads. The exact level for pasteurization will depend upon how long the storage life is to be extended and also upon the level of flavor changes that will be tolerated. However, in actual practice about 75,000 to 150,000 rads are used to pasteurize meat products.

Commercially Sterile Meat Products.—Generally, irradiation is with cobalt-60 or spent fuel rods, although there also are other suitable methods. Two major problems have been encountered with irradiated meat: (1) immediate flavor changes due to irradiation *per se,* and (2) flavor and textural changes during subsequent storage.

Irradiated meat has been described as having a wet-dog or chicken-feather aroma. This flavor is extremely objectionable and has made irradiated meat undesirable. It has been shown that the objectionable aroma and flavor are closely related to the level of irradiation. Recently, some progress has been made in solving this problem by low-temperature irradiation. If meat is irradiated at temperatures of −50°F or below, there is decided improvement in flavor and odor. This suggests that some of the chemical changes are temperature-related and can be prevented by low temperatures. Studies at the U.S. Army Natick Laboratories have shown that low-temperature irradiation has real promise for production of commercially sterile meat products.

The flavor and textural changes that occur during storage of commercially sterile meat have been shown to be due to enzymatic activity. These can largely be prevented by destruction of the enzymes either before or after irradiation. Heating to inactivate the enzymes appears to be the most effective method for preventing enzymatic changes. An internal temperature of 150 to 155°F is necessary for enzyme inactivation.

Shelf-stable meats can be produced by sterilization but appear likely to find their greatest use for military feeding. With improved flavor and texture, it is also possible that irradiated meat may become available to other consumers.

Pasteurization of Meat by Irradiation.—Although flavor problems are also encountered in irradiation-pasteurized meat, the extent is much less than for the sterile product. Thus, one selects a level that will extend the shelf-life but minimize flavor deterioration due to radiation.

Since pasteurized irradiated meat products are suitable for extension of shelf-life and could be used in centralized packaging of fresh meat, the problem of color is of primary importance. Some work has indicated that color and even flavor can be improved by using polyphosphates. The meat should be packaged in vacuum, which would reduce the oxymyoglobin to myoglobin. In the presence of polyphosphate and upon exposure to air at the retail level, the myoglobin takes up oxygen readily and forms the light red pigment, oxymyoglobin.

The use of irradiation pasteurization of meat has been permitted on an experimental basis to determine its feasibility in centralized packaging. Since the storage life of fresh meat can be easily extended to 18 to 21 days by this process, it is potentially an important development.

Both commercially sterile and pasteurized irradiated meat products are still in the experimental stages. However, it seems probable that one or both of these methods will be used in the future.

Microwave Processing

Microwave heating of foods is not new, but most of the work in this area has occurred since World War II. The method is based upon the fact that foods are composed of both positively and negatively charged particles, but as a result of the balance between the two, are electrically neutral. Thus, a food is nonconducting or dielectric. When it is placed in an electromagnetic field, the charged asymmetric molecules of the dielectric food are driven first in one direction and then in another in an attempt to align themselves with the positive and negative poles. The movement back and forth creates intermolecular friction, which produces heat within the food.

Of the frequencies, which have been allocated for industrial, scientific, and medical uses, 915 and 2450 megacycles have been utilized most often. Several devices have been developed for use on foods, which include both batch-type and continuous equipment.

Microwave processing of food is still in its infancy, but has the following three advantages for food processing: (1) it rapidly provides uniform energy throughout the product without the limitations of normal heating, such as losses by conduction and convection and surface crust formation; (2) microwaves have only one effect upon a food, that is the effect of heating; and (3) during microwave processing, the amount of heat absorbed is strictly a function of frequency and of the dielectric loss characteristics of the food.

Microwave heating has been used for thawing of frozen pre-cooked meals for institutional use and for thawing other frozen foods. It appears to have special possibilities for destruction of foot-and-mouth disease viruses in meat, but at the same time avoiding development of a cooked meat flavor. Microwaves also appear to have definite possibilities for supplying the energy needed for sublimation of ice in production of freeze-dried meats.

Microwaves are not only useful for cooking but also have been shown to be effective in sterilization of different foods. Although much remains to be done in application of microwave energy to foods, it is a promising field and seems to have application in meat processing.

Freezing as a Means of Preserving Meat

The present discussion is not intended to be a complete discussion of freezing, but merely an introduction. Those wishing additional information on freezing and its application to meat processing should refer to the bibliography.

Freezing is an excellent method of preserving meat and causes little adverse change if done properly. Fresh meat and frozen meat after thawing are extremely difficult, if not impossible, to tell apart. Nevertheless, frozen meat is often inferior because proper precautions in preparation, freezing, and storage are not taken into account.

Preparation for Freezing.—Freezing of meat is often practical as a means of storing surplus meat for later use. It is a common practice for slaughterers and processors to freeze meat during peak slaughtering or production to either sell or process later. Freezing also provides a means of reaching distant markets, where an otherwise perishable product would not be available. It has become particularly important in Australia, Argentina, Uruguay, New Zealand, and other meat-exporting countries.

Preparation for freezing is most important, as the frozen product does not improve upon the raw product. The best one can hope is that the meat will be nearly as good when it comes out of the freezer as when it went in. Thus one should take every precaution to see that any product to be frozen is in very good condition at the time of freezing. Generally, this means the meat should have passed through rigor mortis and be aged to reach its optimum tenderness without any loss in quality. For best results, meat should not be frozen until at least 48 hr after slaughter, and preferably only after 5 to 7 days.

In general, excessive amounts of bone and fat should be removed prior to freezing. Any contaminated or dirty areas should also be removed. Some research has suggested that meat to be used for making sausage will have a greater emulsifying capacity if it is chopped and the salt added before the onset of rigor mortis.

Packaging is probably the most important single step in preparing a good quality frozen product. Only high-grade packaging material should be used, and it should be carefully applied in order to protect the frozen product. Improperly wrapped meat will deteriorate rapidly due to freezer-burn and fat oxidation. Poor packaging is probably the biggest single problem affecting frozen meat, although improper storage conditions may rival it and confound the picture. Not only should the package be impermeable to air and moisture, but it should fit closely the contour of the meat. Dead spaces within the wrapper can result in freezer burns just as serious as those arising from torn or poorly applied wrappers.

Freezing Process.—The freezing process should be fast enough to prevent deterioration. If freezing is too slow, bacterial growth will continue and quality will decline. Some controversy exists as to the importance of rapid freezing, but all agree it should be fast enough to prevent any deterioration in quality. Temperature alone does not necessarily govern the rate of freezing, but the rate of air movement or contact with the refrigerating medium will have an even greater effect upon the speed of freezing.

There do not appear to be any disadvantages associated with rapid freezing aside from costs. Therefore, freezing at a rapid rate seems best. A temperature of 0 to -20%F is quite satisfactory, if the heat can be removed from the product at a reasonably rapid rate. If the temperature remains too high for extended periods of time, spoilage can occur. This would require several days at temperatures well above freezing in the interior of the product.

Freezer Storage Conditions.—Frozen storage conditions have a profound influence on the quality of the final product. Next to the quality of the original product and method of packaging, freezer storage conditions have the greatest effects on the quality of the frozen meat. Fluctuations in temperature accelerate freezer-burn and cavity ice formation, both of which have the same final effects. Losses of weight during freezing are caused by variations in temperature as well as by poor packaging. High temperatures and particularly fluctuating temperatures result in deterioration of flavor and increased thawing losses. Freezer storage temperatures of 0 to $-10°$F are probably low enough if properly controlled to give a uniform environment with a minimum of variation.

Distribution.—Breakdown in the distribution system or in its efficiency can also result in serious problems with the quality of frozen meat. As is the case with storage temperatures, fluctuations in temperature during distribution also severly impair quality. The problems created are even more acute, since the distribution system is frequently in the hands of a retailer or distributor over which the processor has no control. Many attempts to market frozen meat appear to have failed largely because of problems in distribution.

Color of Frozen Meat.—The color of frozen meat can be a serious problem. Freezing accelerates metmyoglobin formation, thus creating problems in marketing. This is particularly noticeable in storage under display lighting. Blind packages and storage in the dark minimize metmyoglobin formation in frozen meat. Rapidly frozen meat is lighter in color than slowly frozen, but the relative desirability of the different products has not yet been determined by consumer panels.

Precooked Frozen Meat Products.—Precooked frozen meat products have increased rapidly in recent years. These products often are complete meals, such as T.V. dinners, of which meat is the major component. The same problems that apply to frozen meats also apply to the precooked frozen items.

Selection of good raw products and proper cooking methods are necessary to obtain good precooked frozen products. Selection of the other foods that are often used with these products becomes more complicated, as every item must be of adequate quality. Since precooked products are cooked, rapid cooling is also necessary to prevent deterioration prior to freezing. Packaging is quite as important as for fresh-frozen meat.

The addition of other foods to the complete meal may have its advantages, as one can use spices and sauces to aid in preventing oxidative rancidity. Many of the vegetables contain natural antioxidants and can protect precooked meats from oxidative rancidity during freezing and storage.

Precooking methods must also be carefully considered, to obtain the best products, since different methods of cooking have a major influence upon flavor and acceptability. Partial cooking of the meat is often practiced before adding the other ingredients.

The problems encountered in distribution of fresh-frozen meat are not unique, but are also associated with precooked frozen meats. Satisfactory results require close work with distributors and constant stressing of the importance of proper temperature control. Quality control becomes a problem that extends from the raw product to the dinner table and the solution can come only through joint responsibility and effort.

Enzyme Treatment

Enzyme treatment of meat has been confined to tenderization. Large quantities of meat are being tenderized commercially, and in addition, tenderizers are also being purchased and used in the home. A new segment of the meat business has developed around enzyme tenderization of meat. Enzyme tenderization of low-grade beef cuts has made beef competitive with chicken and fish. Fast service and low prices with a rapid turn-over in volume have also been an outgrowth of enzyme tenderization.

Theory of Enzymatic Treatment.—Enzymes are capable of breaking down the connective tissues and contractile proteins, and thus increase tenderness. Although different enzymes differ in their specific action, most of those used as tenderizers attack collagen, ground substance, and actomyosin. Some are also effective against elastin.

Most of the action, however, is on the surface of the meat. It has been shown that tenderization can be more easily and rapidly achieved by adding tenderizing agents to the water used in the rehydration of freeze-dried meat. Nevertheless, an appreciable amount of tenderization can be obtained by treating individual steaks with tenderizer. This is the way most meat is currently being tenderized.

Source of Enzymes.—A variety of proteolytic enzymes are being utilized for tenderization of meat. They include not only animal and plant enzymes, but also those of fungal or bacterial origin. Of the animal enzymes, trypsin and VioKase from the pancreas are both effective, but pepsin has little or no influence on tenderness. The plant enzymes most commonly used in meat tenderizers include papain from the papaya, ficin from the fig, and bromelin from the pineapple. Although bromelin is not effective in breaking down the sarcolemma, the membrane surrounding the muscle fiber, the plant enzymes are all quite active on the components of muscle, and are widely used as tenderizers.

Bacterial proteases are available as tenderizers under various trade names and are effective meat tenderizers. They are largely derived from selected cultures of *Bacillus subtilis*. However, other organisms that produce proteolytic enzymes can be used for tenderization. *Aspergillus oryzae* and *Aspergillus flavus* are widely used for producing fungal proteases, which are also being utilized for enzymatic tenderization of meat.

Some researchers have suggested that different proteases can be used to complement each other and act upon specific components, whereas others will break down other meat components. However, mixtures are not always effective, as some enzymes interact and destroy each other's specific activity. Generally, most commercial operators of tenderizing operations find it advisable to buy enzyme preparations from reputable manufacturers, who can advise them on levels and methods of application.

Enzymatic tenderizers commonly contain other ingredients for seasoning or even to enhance tenderness. It is well known that sodium chloride alone will improve tenderness, so it is usually an ingredient of most tenderizers. Polyphosphates are also common ingredients of tenderizers, not only because of an effect on tenderness but because they reduce losses during processing and cooking. Tenderizers also commonly contain other enzymes as impurities, which may or may not improve the final product.

Method of Application.—Tenderizers are most frequently applied as dips or sprays, although some are added in dry form. Dipping and spraying are the common methods of commercial application. The meat is usually frozen afterwards, which gives better control of the process in large-scale operations. Powdered dry tenderizers are available from grocery stores and are utilized most commonly in the home. However, some may be used by small restaurants.

Application should be according to the manufacturer's direction or the result of experimentation by the user. It should be remembered that too much tenderizer will make the steaks mushy. The level of application depends on the strength of the preparation and method of applying. Since different enzymes and combinations of enzymes behave differently, their properties must be considered in arriving at the best method of application. For example, papain demonstrates most of its tenderizing action during cooking, so uniform cooking of the treated product must be considered.

Antemortem Injection.—Swift and Company Research Laboratories have patented antemortem injection of a proteolytic enzyme solution to obtain uniform distribution throughout the carcass (Goeser 1961). In this system, the vascular system distributes the enzyme solution throughout the tissues, the heart of the live animal serving as the pump. Beef produced by this procedure is sold under the trade name ProTen.

The enzyme utilized is fractionated papain and is active at cooking temperatures of 140 to 160°F. It has been shown to cause significant improvement in tenderness. However, it has several disadvantages, one being the fact that each animal must be individually injected. Furthermore, the meat produced would not appear to be suitable for use where the temperature is kept high for long periods, as occurs in institutional use or restaurants. Under these conditions, the high temperatures maintained for long periods of time continue to keep the enzyme active and thus cause tissue breakdown. Overtenderization of the soft tissues such as the brains, liver, and kidneys also seems likely.

Antemortem tenderization of meat is a most interesting application that illustrates how scientific principles can be applied to achieve a practical solution to meat tenderness. Significant improvement in tenderness can be obtained by this procedure. The process can be used by other processors through a licensing arrangement.

Other Possibilities for Enzymatic Tenderization.—Although all the methods mentioned earlier involve use of added enzymes, it is well accepted that natural enzymes in meat play a role in development of tenderness during natural aging of meat. It should be possible to effectively activate these enzymes in meat and thereby achieve tenderization. Although a considerable amount of work has been done, results to date have not been promising.

Chemical Additives

Chemical additives have long been added to foods to preserve them or to enhance their physical properties. Salt is added not only as a seasoning but also as a curing agent. Phosphates are added to increase water binding. Ascorbates are added to stabilize color and to serve as antioxidants. These are all examples of chemical additives that are commonly accepted by both the consumer and industry. Although new additives must be approved by the FDA, other additives are certain to play important roles in the preservation and processing of meat.

BIBLIOGRAPHY

BALLS, A. K. 1960. Catheptic enzymes in muscle. *In* Proceedings of the 12th Meat Industry Research Conference. American Meat Institute Foundation, Chicago, Ill.

BAVISOTTO, V. S. 1958. Meat tenderizing by enzymes. *In* Proceedings of the 10th Meat Industry Research Conference. American Meat Institute Foundation, Chicago, Ill.

BROCKMANN, M. C. 1970. Development of intermediate moisture foods for military use. Food Technol. *24*, 896.

BURKE, R. F., and DECAREAU, R. V. 1964. Recent advances in the freeze drying of food products. Advan. Food Res. *13*,1.

DESROSIER, N. W., and ROSENSTOCK, H. M. 1960. Radiation Technology in Food, Agriculture and Biology. Avi Publishing Co., Westport, Conn.

GOESER, P. A. 1961. Tendered meat through antemortem vascular injection of proteolytic enzymes. *In* Proceedings of the 13th Meat Industry Research Conference. American Meat Institute Foundation, Chicago, Ill.

GOLDBLITH, S. A. 1966. Basic principles of microwaves and recent developments. Advan. Food Res. *15*, 277.

GOODING, E. G. B. 1962. The storage behavior of dehydrated foods. *In* Recent Advances in Food Science, J. Hawthorn, and J. M. Leitch (Editors). Butterworths, London.

HARPER, J. C., and TAPPEL, A. L. 1957. Freeze-drying of food products. Advan. Food Res. *7*, 172.

KAPLOW, M. 1970. Commercial development of intermediate moisture foods. Food Technol. *24*, 889.

MIYADA, D. S., and TAPPEL, A. L. 1956. The hydrolysis of beef proteins by various proteolytic enzymes. Food Res. *21*, 217.

SLEETH, R. B., and NAUMANN, H. D. 1960. Efficiency of oxytetracycline for aging beef. Food Technol. *14*, 98.

SLEETH, R. B., ARMSTRONG, J. C., GOLDBERG, H. S., and NAUMANN, H. D. 1960. Antibiotic preservation of beef with subsequent feeding to experimental animals. Food Technol. *14*, 505.

TRESSLER, D. K., and EVERS, C. F. 1957. The Freezing Preservation of Foods, Vol. I—Freezing of Fresh Foods. Avi Publishing Co., Westport, Conn.

WANG, H., WEIR, C. E., BIRKNER, M., and GINGER, B. 1957. The influence of enzyme tenderizers on the structure and tenderness of beef. *In* Proceedings of the 9th Meat Industry Research Conference. American Meat Institute Foundation, Chicago, Ill.

WEISER, H. H. *et al.* 1953. Observations on fresh meat processed by infusion of antibiotics. Food Technol. *7*, 495.

WEISER, H. H., KUNKLE, L. E., and DEATHERAGE, F. E. 1954. The use of antibiotics in meat processing. Appl. Microbiol. *2*, 88.

WIERBICKI, E., and HEILIGMAN, F. 1964. Present status and future outlook of radiation sterilization processing of meats. *In* Proceedings of the Meat Industry Research Conference. American Meat Institute Foundation, Chicago, Ill.

essed Meat Deterioration

essed meat products contend with two types
–(1) flavor and (2) appearance. Each of these
referred to at both the processor and retail
ct spoilage can be obvious to the eye, as in
ning, or obvious only to the nose or palate,
ite possible to have both types of deterioration
it products to a significant extent at the same
ays the case.
is a continuing phenomenon, beginning at
e addition of curing agents, spices, and antioxi-
ial processing and smoking, contribute to slow-
process. All meat used for manufacture of
processed meat products should be free of significant deteriorative
flavor changes because it is impossible to reverse such changes. While
the use of curing agents and thermal processing can greatly slow the
onset of visible deterioration caused by microorganisms, flavor deterioration of meat prior to processing will carry through to the finished
product. Seasonings, curing agents, and smoke tend to mask a limited
amount of pre-processing deterioration, but significant raw material
deterioration carries through and can usually be detected in processed
meat products immediately after manufacture.

Meat processors strive to prevent deterioration for a reasonable
length of time to allow for marketing of their products. The period
of time during which products remain saleable is commonly referred
to as shelf-life.

FLAVOR

Deterioration of processed meat flavor results when rancid, putrefactive, or sour flavors develop.

Rancidity

Rancidity develops by (1) action of bacterial enzymes and (2) oxidation
of unsaturated fatty acids. Enzymes cause rancidity either by hydrolysis
induced by lipases or by oxidation of fatty acids by oxidases. Either
source gives rise to the odors and flavors that are associated with
the development of rancidity.

Most rancidity problems encountered in meat products are not of
microbial origin but result from the reaction of oxygen with unsaturated

331

fats. Oxidation of fats is influenced by quantity of oxygen present, temperature, light, and pro-oxidant catalysts. Salt is the best example of such catalysts. In addition, various chemicals, such as ozone, hydrogen peroxide, and other strong oxidizing agents markedly influence the development of rancidity. One of the main reasons microorganisms are not a significant factor contributing to the development of rancidity in meats is because the free fatty acids liberated by hydrolytic cleavage of fats inhibit the growth of many types of microorganisms. In addition, the peroxides formed during oxidation of unsaturated fatty acids are quite toxic to many microorganisms.

Putrefaction

Certain bacteria, referred to as proteolytic, metabolize meat proteins through production of enzymes. Some cannot attack proteins but can metabolize peptides or free amino acids. Many of the degradation products resulting from bacterial metabolism of meat proteins have foul odors. The term putrefaction is generally used to describe this type of spoilage.

Souring and Gassing

Anaerobic metabolism of carbohydrates in meat products by bacteria results in various fermentation products, primarily organic acids. The principal acid formed is lactic acid; its presence brings about lowering of the meat pH and development of a sour flavor. Anaerobic bacteria can grow in the interior of large sausage products, and if a gas-producing variety is present, the gases evolved cause the sausage to become distended. This, however, is rare in the meat-processing industry. A much more common situation is the gassy vacuum package, in which gas-producing organisms on the surface of the sausage evolve a gas which in turn causes the package to become distended. The gas is carbon dioxide, which is colorless, odorless, and tasteless. Aerobic bacteria, yeasts, or molds are never implicated in this problem, but only anaerobic or facultative bacteria. The carbon dioxide results from a fermentation process induced by the anaerobic bacteria. Usually, but not always, when gas is produced, acid is also present, as the bacteria that cause gas formation usually form acid as well.

APPEARANCE

Subtle deterioration of processed meat flavor can be detected by the nose and mouth, but not by the eye. As has been pointed out, flavor deterioration is not always microbiologically induced. Such is the case with deterioration caused by changes in product appearance. Spoilage associated with appearance of noncanned meat products is of three types: (1) microbial discoloration, (2) macroscopic microbial growth, and (3) nonmicrobial discoloration.

Microbial Discoloration

Microbial discoloration can be exhibited as green cores, green rings, surface greening, and color fading.

Green Cores.—This condition is usually associated with large sausages such as bologna. It occurs when greening bacteria are introduced into sausage emulsions and are not destroyed during cooking. The bacteria survive in the interior of the sausages, but greening of the meat pigments does not occur until the sausages are cut and exposed to air. Greening bacteria, principally *Lactobacillus viridescens,* produce hydrogen peroxide, a strong oxidizing agent which degrades the meat pigment. Greening may occur within minutes, or it may be hours before the cut meat surfaces begin to turn green. Color changes begin in small areas, usually in the center of the meats, and extend from there to the periphery. Spreading of the green area is one of the characteristics which distinguishes microbiological greening from that caused by chemical or metallic sources. Cooking processed meat products to temperatures of 152 to 155°F destroys greening organisms. However, on rare occasions, when the contaminating level is quite high, it is necessary to cook to an internal temperature of 160°F.

Green Rings.—The appearance of green rings in sausages is a very rare occurrence. Although this problem has never adequately been explained, it appears that a combination of factors must be present. Green rings appear at varying depths beneath the sausage surface. They usually develop within 1 to 2 days after the sausages are processed, and are noticeable as soon as the sausages are cut into, even though they have been held under adequate refrigeration. Although greening bacteria are present throughout the sausages, the discoloration develops in the form of rings probably because it is in this zone that the oxygen tension is conducive to pigment oxidation. At least this is the most frequently accepted theory for the occurrence of green rings. As with green cores, the condition is associated with the presence of large numbers of greening bacteria in the emulsion and subsequent undercooking of the sausages.

Surface Greening.—One of the most common types of discoloration associated with sausages and smoked meats is surface greening. Unlike metallic or chemically induced greening, greening caused by bacteria does not show up within a matter of hours after processing. The time of onset varies with the concentration of greening bacteria and conditions for their growth; but usually surface greening is not noticeable for at least 5 days after processing and often a couple of weeks. The bacteria that cause surface greening are the same as those which cause green rings and green cores. These bacteria are common contaminants of meat-processing operations. Therefore, given enough time and the proper environment for growth of greening bacteria, many nonvacuum-packaged meat products will eventually show evidence of surface greening. Because these bacteria are aerobic, surface greening will not occur on products that have been vacuum-packaged.

Macroscopic Microbial Growth

Slime.—When meat is heavily contaminated with bacteria or yeasts or both, a white or on occasion yellow slime will appear on the surface. This microbiological slime is not a metabolic substance produced by bacteria or yeasts but is, in fact, an accumulation of their cells. Since neither bacteria nor yeasts can be seen with the naked eye, it is apparent that slime appears only when a product is contaminated with large numbers of cells. Seldom is slime noted on the surfaces of vacuum-packaged products, because there are fewer anaerobic than aerobic bacteria in nature and therefore they are less likely to contaminate meat products. Then, too, anaerobic bacteria usually produce enough acid to inhibit extensive aerobic growth. However, after a period of time, even in vacuum packages, contaminants multiply to the extent the organisms can be seen with the naked eye. This is usually noted as a whitish liquid. Ordinarily, the free liquid associated with vacuum-packaged products is clear or straw-colored. When product contamination becomes severe, this liquid becomes milky in appearance. On nonvacuum-packaged products slime appears in the form of characteristic beads, sticky to the touch, and having an off-odor sometimes described as yeast-like.

Molds.—Molds are common contaminants of many processed meat products. To a much greater extent then bacteria or yeasts, molds are air-borne contaminants. Bacteria and yeast contamination of processed meat products results primarily from direct surface contact. Molds require less moisture than either bacteria or yeasts to survive. However, like aerobic bacteria and yeasts, molds need oxygen. In addition, they need head space to allow for growth of their stalks. Because they require both oxygen and head space, molds do not grow on meat products that have been vacuum-packaged. They are commonly found on bulk-packed processed meat products, and in particular those requiring extended ripening periods, such as dry sausages and Country cured hams. Molds are largely destroyed by the heat employed during thermal processing. Therefore, they normally occur on cooked products as the result of post-processing contamination.

Nonmicrobial Discoloration

Among the benefits achieved in curing meats is the conversion of oxygen-sensitive fresh meat pigments to more stable cured meat pigments. Nevertheless, the main cause of nonmicrobial discoloration, usually observed as color fading, is oxygen. Factors affecting the rate and extent of nomicrobial discoloration are: (1) amount of pigment actually converted to nitrosomyoglobin, (2) quantity of oxygen available for reaction with pigments, (3) storage temperatures, and (4) intensity of lighting.

The greater the efficiency of the curing process, the more resistant cured meats are to color degradation. At least 70% of the meat pigment available for curing should be cured. If curing efficiencies fall much below this, meats are undercured. The interior color of undercured meat products may range from faded pink through gray to a light green. Cured meat surfaces are typically more efficiently cured than interiors because they are subject to conditions favoring pigment conversion, such as higher temperatures for longer periods and the acid components of smoke.

Fading is an oxidative process accelerated by light and influenced by storage temperatures. Vacuum packaging has contributed greatly to lengthening the shelf-life of cured meat. The low levels of oxygen in vacuum packages result in protecting processed meats from rapid onset of microbial spoilage, rancidity, and color fading.

For maximum prevention of deterioration, both microbial and nonmicrobial, meat products should be stored as close to 28°F as possible. However, in practice, cured meats are generally stored between 38 and 45°F. Light, especially display-case illumination, catalyzes the oxidation of cured meat pigments and can accelerate the fading rate. For this reason, it is best not to expose cured meats to strong lights.

CANNED MEAT SPOILAGE

Canned food products are spoiled when: (1) the contents have undergone deleterious changes, or (2) cans are damaged. Damage to cans does not necessarily indicate spoilage of the contents. However, can damage makes spoilage of the contents possible.

The ends of normal cans with good vacuums are slightly concave or flat. Cans which have their ends distended because of positive internal pressure caused by the formation of gas within them are referred to as swells. The terms puffer or blower are sometimes used in place of swell. Swells vary from those that barely bulge the ends of cans to those that are strong enough to cause cans to burst. The term soft swell refers to cans whose ends can be moved by thumb pressure but cannot be forced back to their normal position. Hard swells are those in which both ends of the cans are firmly and permanently bulged. Flippers are normal-appearing cans whose end flips out when the cans are struck a hard blow; when light pressure is applied, the end snaps back to its original position. Springers are cans that have one end distended; when the end is forced back into its normal position, the opposite end bulges out. Swelled cans pass progressively through the flipper and springer stages. In the beginning, enough gas is produced to relieve the vacuum in the cans. At first, the cans may be flippers. As more gas is formed, the cans become springers and eventually swellers.

It is not always possible to tell the condition of the contents by appearance of the cans. Cans with spoiled contents may appear quite normal and show no signs of distortion. The causes of product spoilage or can defects are: (1) microbial, (2) chemical, and (3) physical.

Microbial

Microbial spoilage results from: (1) spoilage prior to retorting, (2) undercooking, (3) inadequate cooling, and (4) contamination resulting from leakage through can seams.

Spoilage Prior to Retorting.—This occurs when gross bacterial growth takes place during preparation. If filled cans are not retorted promptly and are allowed to remain at elevated temperatures, bacterial contaminants may produce sufficient gas to cause the cans to swell. When the cans are retorted, the bacteria are killed, but the gas remains. Upon microbiological examination of the can contents, no viable organisms are isolated. While cultures prepared from these cans are invariably sterile, upon microscopic examination numerous organisms can be observed.

Undercooking.—Canned meat products that have not been cooked thoroughly enough to destroy bacteria or stop their activity are subject to spoilage. These bacteria may produce gas, causing the cans to become swellers. In some cases, gas is not formed, but acid is. When bacteria grow without evolving gas, the affected cans appear normal. Spoilage can be detected only when the cans are opened. Unless cans have been grossly undercooked, spoilage is generally due to a single type of organism, usually a spore-former.

Inadequate Cooling.—Thermal processing to the extent necessary to destroy all microbial life usually results in severe deterioration of product quality. For this reason, retort schedules employed for cooking meat products are not so demanding and allow some thermophilic bacteria to survive the retorting process. Control of these bacteria depends primarily on rapid cooling of cans and their contents and storage at temperatures which do not allow thermophilic growth. Flat-sour thermophiles multiply rapidly between 120 and 160°F. Failure to cool cans immediately after retorting to below 120°F can lead to flat-sour spoilage.

Seam Leakage.—Leakage through can seams is responsible for more microbial product spoilage than any other one factor. The principal source of bacteria which enter through leaks is the can cooling water. Use of chlorine in the cooling water drastically cuts the incidence of spoiled cans due to seam leakage. The principal type of leaker spoilage is swelling. This indicates that the leaks somehow become sealed. However, not every case of leaker spoilage is a sweller. If leaks are so large that they permit gas to pass freely, the cans will not swell. Sometimes the bacteria which contaminate the contents are not gas producers, and the cans remain normal in appearance.

Chemical

Spoilage that can be described as chemical results in formation of a swell referred to as a hydrogen swell. This type of spoilage applies to cans that are distended as the result of evolution of hydrogen gas during internal corrosion of the cans. Chemical spoilage is associated primarily with the can and not the contents.

Internal corrosion occurs most frequently in cans with foods containing organic acids such as fruits or, in the case of meat products, those containing curing salts. Use of properly enameled cans minimizes the chances for reaction of product with the tin plate.

Physical

Physical spoilage does not refer to the spoilage of contents but essentially to the appearance of cans. Often cans are distorted, leaving evidence of swells. However, the causes of this swell are not of bacterial or chemical orgin but are the result of the processing techniques. Physical spoilage may also refer to rusting and physical damaging of cans.

Faulty Retort Operation.—When steam pressure is reduced too quickly at the end of the retort process, high pressures develop inside cans. This may result in severe straining and distortion, so that when the cans are cooled they have the appearance of swells. Cans which are distorted in this manner have no positive internal pressure and the ends can be forced back more or less to their normal position. These cans are subject to a high incidence of leaker spoilage.

Cans not properly exhausted during the retort process may undergo severe strain due to excessive internal pressure built up by expansion of entrapped gases. If the amount of gas present is slight, underexhausted cans may show evidence only of slight flipping. On the other hand, if the amount is great, the cans may be greatly distended.

Over-filling.—Cans which are over-filled often become strained during retorting due to expansion of the contents. The absence of vacuum in an over-filled can results in flipping or, in more severe cases, springing of the ends.

Paneling.—This condition is primarily associated with larger size cans in which there is a very high vacuum. In this case, the can bodies are forced inward by atmospheric pressure. Paneling can also be observed in pressure-cooled cans which have been exposed to extremely high air pressure or in cans composed of thin tin plate. In severe cases paneling can result in seam leakage, particularly if the seam is already of marginal quality.

Rust.—Product spoilage does not usually accompany can rusting; however, there is always a danger that severe pitting may accompany rusting. Proper drying of cans after retorting followed by dry storage is necessary to prevent rusting. Cans should be allowed to retain sufficient heat after they have passed through the cooling bath to evaporate water remaining on them. An internal product temperature of 95°F is usually sufficient to ensure rapid can drying.

Damage.—Physical damage of cans caused by rough handling is cause for concern to the meat canner from the aesthetic viewpoint and because of the possibility such cans could become leakers. Unfortunately, physical damage usually puts severe strain on can seams.

Spoilage Bacteria

Canned meats and meat products are classified as low-acid, which means they have a pH of 5 or higher. Below pH 4.5, *Clostridium botulinum*, the most heat-resistant of the food-poisoning microorganisms, is inhibited. Therefore, for foods with a pH below 4.5, pressure-cooking is considered to be unnecessary. Canned cured meats such as ham, luncheon loaf, and bacon usually are subjected to a relatively low thermal process because the curing salts present in the meat, together with the heat treatment, exert an inhibitory affect on the growth of *Clostridium botulinum* and other putrefactive anaerobes. The principal microorganisms causing spoilage in shelf-stable canned meats can be classified into two groups: (1) aerobic spore-formers, and (2) anaerobic spore-formers.

Aerobic Spore-Formers.—Aerobic spore-formers responsible for spoilage of canned meat products are from the genus Bacillus. These bacteria are widely distributed in nature, originating in soil and water, and are frequently present in the raw materials used in canning. The optimum growth temperature for most members of this group lies between 82 and 104°F, but many are also thermophilic and can grow at 131°F. Some of these microorganisms are strict aerobes, but others are facultative anaerobes. Their growth in canned foods is not inhibited by vacuum and many of the thermophilic strains exhibit exceptional resistance to heat destruction. The principal form of spoilage caused by aerobic spore-formers is the flat-sour type. Flat-sour refers to bacteria which attack carbohydrates with production of acid but without gas formation. In meat products that develop flat-sour spoilage, there is no loss of can vacuum and the can ends remain flat or concave. However, there are some members of this group which can form gas and, in this case, the ends of the cans become distended.

Anaerobic Spore-Formers.—Anaerobic spore-formers are derived principally from soil and are quite widely distributed in food materials. Some species are present in animal intestines and are frequent contaminants of meat. As a result, spore-forming anaerobes are often associated with spoilage of canned meat products. Spore-forming anaerobes of the genus *Clostridium* can be grouped into two categories: (1) thermophilic and (2) mesophilic.

Thermophilic Anaerobes.—These organisms grow at temperatures well above 100°F. Since most shelf-stable canned meats are not stored at these high temperatures, members of this group are not responsible for appreciable losses. This is not true, however, for members of the mesophilic group.

Mesophilic Anaerobes.—A prominent member of this group is the pathogenic organism, *Clostridium botulinum*. Destruction of Clostridia spores is generally accepted as the minimum standard of processing for low-acid canned meat products. However, *botulinum* organisms are not as heat-resistant as some other spore-forming anaerobes. Mesophilic spore-forming anaerobes can be classed roughly into two groups based on the relative ability of various species to attack proteins and carbohydrates. Those which are of greatest significance to the canned meat industry are the proteolytic or putrefactive anaerobes. *Clostridium sporogenes* and related strains appear to be the principal putrefactive anaerobes associated with spoilage of canned meat products. Generally, spoilage caused by putrefactive anaerobes is of the gaseous type, and usually the contents are at least partially disintegrated. This results in formation of the characteristic foul odors associated with putrefactive spoilage.

Pasteurized Canned Meat

Pasteurized canned meats must be stored under refrigeration. Provided they are refrigerated properly, pasteurized canned meats have a shelf-life well in excess of one year. Pasteurized canned meats are cooked sufficiently to kill all vegetative bacteria, but depend upon adequate refrigeration and the cure ingredients, salt and nitrite, to prevent germination and growth of spores. If pasteurized meats are not cooked adequately, the most common spoilage microorganisms that survive are *Streptococcus faecium* and some lactic acid bacteria. They can cause souring and product discoloration. Still other bacteria that may survive produce gas, digest gelatin added to bind meat juices, or partially digest the meat. If pasteurized meats are adequately cooked but not refrigerated properly, both aerobic and anaerobic spore-formers may germinate and grow. Many of these can produce gas and may cause extensive putrefaction.

BIBLIOGRAPHY

ERTLE, N. L. 1969. Sausage shelf-life as affected by packaging. *In* Proceedings of the Meat Industry Research Conference. American Meat Institute Foundation, Chicago, Ill.

EVANS, J. B., and NIVEN, C. F., Jr. 1955. Slime and mold. Problems with prepackaged processed meat products. American Meat Institute Foundation Bull. *24*.

HERSOM, A. C., and HULLAND, E. D. 1964. Canned Foods, 5th Edition. Chemical Publishing Co., New York.

HORNSEY, H. C. 1956. The color of cooked cured pork. I. Estimation of nitric oxide—haem pigments. J. Sci. Food Agr. *1*, 534.

INGRAM, M. 1962. Microbiological principles in prepackaging meats. J. Appl. Bacteriol *25*, 259.

JENSEN, L. B. 1954. Microbiology of Meats, 3rd Edition. Garrard Press, Champaign, Ill.

KRAMLICH, W. E., ERTLE, N. L., and SIMON, S. 1965. Sausage—a $2 billion market. VIII. Sanitation. Meat *31*, 46.

LECHOWICH, R. V. 1971. Microbiology of meat. *In* The Science of Meat and Meat Products, J. F. Price, and B. S. Schweigert (Editors). W. H. Freeman and Co., San Francisco, Calif.

LOCK, A. 1969. Practical Canning, 3rd Edition. Food Trade Press, Ltd. London.

NIVEN, C. F., Jr., 1951. Sausage discolorations of bacterial origin. American Meat Institute Foundation Bull. *13*.

NIVEN, C. F., Jr., and EVANS, J. B. 1957. *Lactobacillus viridescens* Nov. Spec., a heterofermentative species that produces a green discoloration of cured meat pigments. J. Bact. *73*, 758.

NIVEN, C. F., Jr., BUETTNER, L. G., and EVANS, J. B. 1954. Thermal tolerance studies on the heterofermentative lactobacilli that cause greening of cured meat products. Appl. Microbiol. *2*, 26.

NIVEN, C. F., Jr., CASTELLANI, A. G., and ALLANSON, V. 1949. A study of the lactic acid bacteria that cause surface discolorations of sausages. J. Bact. *58*, 633.
ROGERS, J. L. 1966. A "Course" in Canning, 4th Edition. Food Trade Press, Ltd., London.
SILLIKER, J. H., GREENBERG, R. A., and SCHACK, W. R. 1958. Effect of individual curing ingredients on the shelf stability of canned comminuted meats. Food Technol. *12*, 551.
WARNECKE, N. O., OCKERMAN, H. W., WEISER, H. H., and CAHILL, V. R. 1966. Quality of processed comminuted meat as affected by microbial flora of the raw constituents. Food Technol. *20*, 118.

Index